COLLECTABLES
HANDBOOK

COLLECTABLES
HANDBOOK

Judith Miller
and Mark Hill

MILLER'S

Miller's Collectables Handbook

First published in Great Britain in 2010 by Miller's, a division of Mitchell Beazley,
imprints of Octopus Publishing Group Ltd, Endeavour House,
189 Shaftesbury Avenue, London, WC2H 8JG.
An Hachette Livre UK Company.
www.hachette.co.uk

Miller's is a registered trademark of Octopus Publishing Group Ltd.
www.millersonline.com

While every care has been exercised in the compilation of this guide,
neither the authors nor publishers accept any liability for any financial or
other loss incurred by reliance placed on the information contained in
Miller's Collectables Handbook.

ISBN 978 1 84533 514 4

A CIP catalogue record for this book is available from the British Library.

Set in Frutiger

Colour reproduction by United Graphics, Singapore
Printed and bound in China by Toppan Printing Company

Authors Judith Miller & Mark Hill

Publishing Manager Julie Brooke
Editors Davida Saunders, Carolyn Madden
Digital Asset Co-ordinator Katy Armstrong
Editorial Assistants Laura Hill, Danielle Shaw
Advertising Sales Christine Havers

Photography Graham Rae, Jeremy Martin, Robin Saker

Design Tim & Ali Scrivens, TJ Graphics
Indexer Diana LeCore
Production Lucy Carter
Jacket Design Pene Parker

Photographs of Judith Miller and Mark Hill by Simon Upton and Graham Rae

CONTENTS

LIST OF CONSULTANTS

AUTOMOBILIA
Geoffrey Weiner
carsofbrighton.co.uk

BEADS
Victor Caplin
Alfie's Antiques Market, London

BOOKS
Roddy Newlands
Bloomsbury Auctions, London

CERAMICS
Beth & Beverley Adams
Alfie's Antiques Market, London

Dr Graham Cooley
Private Collector

William Farmer
Fielding's Auctioneers, Stourbridge

Kevin Graham
potteryandglass.forumandco.com

Patrick & Petra Folkersma
outernational.info

FASHION & ACCESSORIES
Dawn Crawford
candysays.co.uk

Kerry Taylor
Kerry Taylor Auctions, London

Sparkle Moore & Cad van Swankster
thegirlcanthelpit.com

GLASS
Dr Graham Cooley
Private Collector

William Farmer
Fielding's Auctioneers, Stourbridge

Nic Wilson
zeitgeist-i.com

INUIT ART
Duncan McLean
Waddingtons, Toronto, Canada

PENS & WRITING EQUIPMENT
Simon Gray
penhome.co.uk

POSTERS
Patrick Bogue
onslows.co.uk

RADIOS
Steve Harris
vintageradio.co.uk

TOYS, TEDDY BEARS & DOLLS
Susan Brewer
britishdollshowcase.co.uk

Colin Lewis
The Magic Toybox, Hampshire

Leanda Harwood
leandaharwood.co.uk

SPORTING
Graham Budd
Graham Budd Auctions, London

We are also grateful to all our friends and experts who gave us so much help and support – Nigel Benson of 20thcentury-glass.com, Ian Broughton of Alfie's Antique Market, Mark Block, Simon Cooper of Rosebery's, David Encill, Julie D'Arcy Evans, Jeanette Hayhurst, Kevin Harris of undercurrents.biz, Michael Jeffrey of Woolley & Wallis, Mark Laino of Mark of Time, Peter Layton, Kathy Martin, Lesley McNamee of retropolitan.co.uk, Marcus Newhall of sklounion.com, Steven Moore of Anderson & Garland, Wesley Payne of Alfie's Antiques Market, Thomas Plant of Special Auction Services, Geoffrey Robinson of Alfie's Antiques Market, Alison Snelgrove of thestudioglassmerchant.co.uk, Ron & Ann Wheeler of artiusglass.co.uk, and Nigel Wiggin of The Old Hall Club.

HOW TO USE THIS BOOK

Subcategory heading Indicates the sub-category of the main heading.

Page tab This appears on every page and identifies the main category heading as identified in the Contents List on pages 5-6.

Caption The description of the item illustrated, including when relevant, the period, the maker or factory, medium, the year it was made, dimensions and condition. Many captions have **footnotes** which explain terminology or give identification or valuation information.

The price guide These price ranges give a ballpark figure for what you should pay for a similar item. The great joy of collectables is that there is not a recommended retail price. The price ranges in this book are based on actual prices, either what a dealer will take or the full auction price.

Quick reference Gives key facts about the factory, maker or style, along with stylistic identification points, value tips and advice on fakes.

Quick reference and **closer look** These are where we show identifying aspects of a factory or maker, point out rare colours or shapes, and explain why a particular piece is so desirable.

The object The collectables are shown in full colour. This is a vital aid to identification and valuation. With many objects, a slight colour variation can signify a large price differential.

Source code Every item has been specially photographed at an auction house, a dealer, an antiques market or a private collection. These are credited by code at the end of the caption, and can be checked against the Key to Illustrations on pages 408-410.

Welcome to the new edition of Miller's Collectables Handbook. As ever, you will find a selection of thousands of items from across the world, all illustrated in colour and accompanied by a descriptive caption and price guide. Additional information and insiders' tips are included in the 'Quick Reference' sections and footnotes, while our 'Closer Look' features help you to understand more. The result is the best full-colour, fully illustrated collectables price guide in the world.

This year is an important one for Miller's. As well as continuing to publish a range of exciting books, we are developing our new website at www.millersonline.com. We are delighted that many of you have already explored the site. For those of you who have not visited it yet, the site is packed with useful tips and information including what we believe is the most comprehensive fully illustrated A-Z of terms available. You can also search a catalogue containing tens of thousands of antiques and collectables, each with a description and price guide, and browse the innovative Dealers & Auctioneers listings. All of this is available at no cost. And we are not stopping there. Keep checking back, as there are plenty of exciting developments in store.

Of course, the past year has been a notable one. With the collapse of an international bank and the 'credit crunch' it's not surprising that the market for antiques and collectables has been dramatically affected. However, a couple of months after the recession began, an unexpected development occurred: rather than saving their money, many people began to buy antiques and collectables. Perhaps they saw it as a way to invest their cash in tangible goods that had the potential to hold their value. Attendance at fairs rocketed, and auctions reported strong sales, particularly for scarcer, finer pieces.

Although this has subsided, many dealers and auction houses continue to report strong sales. This follows the advice of an analyst at the firm of accountants, Deloitte, who reported that he believed the credit crunch had encouraged people 'to put their money into a range of assets' and that antiques 'generally avoid the big price swings seen in financial markets'. It's certainly true that vintage, retro and antique items hold more value than most

A Czechoslovakian Chlum u Trebone glassworks vase worth £100-150

of their contemporary counterparts. Not only that but you can cherish and enjoy them in your home – they are far more attractive than money or shares in a bank.

Another exciting development is the new initiative Antiques are Green, which aims to promote antiques as an alternative form of recycling and means of conserving natural resources. By encouraging new and existing antiques and collectables buyers to see their collections as the ultimate in recycled goods, it hopes to make a tangible difference and be part of an environmental conscience which will eventually permeate all areas of daily life.

A De La Rue 'Onoto The Pen' worth £120-180

While prices for low- and mid-range items have remained largely static, or have perhaps even fallen slightly, prices for the very best have risen. Fashion also plays an important role. Even though the 'Ikea-style' modern look is still popular, a strong trend for creating unique interiors filled with antique and vintage statement pieces is developing. If the style of an item appeals, it will be desirable. Although many traditional areas such as blue and white ceramics are still in the doldrums, it seems we are not the only ones who have noticed that low prices mean now is the time to buy, and a revival in these areas seems likely.

On more specific fronts, costume jewellery continues to be hotly soughtafter, particularly pieces by major designers and makers. Twentieth century glass, especially examples from Murano and Czechoslovakia, is also receiving the attention it deserves, at long last. As demand from an increasing number of collectors grows against a limited supply, prices have risen. Now that fountain pens dating from before WWII have become both valuable and scarce, models from the 1960-90s have risen in price. You will find comprehensive sections covering all these areas in this edition.

We have also included some new sections this year, including ceramics by Pablo Picasso, paperweights, and ceramics by Wade. You will also notice that we have included areas from other countries, such as the work of a few American potteries. This reflects the truly global nature of collecting today, and also gives you the edge over everyone else. Often ignored in this country, values can be high. We feel that our new, larger format combined with this variety and depth of information and coverage makes this edition the best yet. We hope you agree.

Judith Miller.

QUICK REFERENCE

- Vintage advertising is a good way to track changing styles, social trends and aspirations. Although 19thC advertising and packaging can be found, most items available today date from the early 20thC, when advertising began to diversify rapidly. Collectors typically focus on one subject area, such as tobacco, or one type of object (tins or signs are the most popular), or a brand. Items from popular brands, such as Kellogg's, attract the most collectors and therefore tend to fetch the highest prices. Items with cross-market interest, such as railway advertising, will appeal to a greater number of collectors.

- Tins holding biscuits, tobacco and sweets were common between 1860-1950. From the 1890s, the shapes of these became more inventive, as companies tried to outdo each other to appeal to customers. Many tins from this period were designed to be kept and used as storage containers or toys.

- Examples by major manufacturers, such as Huntley & Palmers, and those with moving parts, are often the most valuable.

- Do not ignore packaging that would have been thrown away. Even if many examples were produced, few may have survived. If both rare and desirable, the item's value can be surprisingly high. Vintage packaging in mint condition is particularly rare and consequently sought after. If the original contents are included this will not necessarily increase value, unless the package is also sealed.

- Look for visually appealing advertising in good condition, which represents the brand effectively, subject area or period. The colour, style of lettering and logo will help with dating. Art Nouveau, Art Deco and 1950s-style pieces will usually find favour with collectors, as will eye-catching, designs featuring bright colours, recognisable logos and popular characters.

A very rare W.K. Kellogg 'Drinket' tin, with dated paper label.

Kellogg' s sold two soft drinks, the coffee-like 'Drinket' from 1914-21 and 'Fizz-Aide' from 1956-58. The early date makes this one of the first tins of ' Drinket' produced.

1915.   *4.25in (10.5cm) high*

£40-60   BH

An American 'Postmaster Smokers' printed tinplate tobacco tin.

Although dented, the graphics and bright colour are appealing, and tobacco advertising and packaging is sought after.

5.5in (13.5cm) high

£15-20   BH

A 1960s Huntley & Palmers 'Butlinland' biscuit tin, with printed photographic decoration, and printer's code '61/2649'.

8.75in (22cm) wide

£5-8   SAS

A Co-operative Wholesale Society lithographed tinplate 'Crumpsall Cracker' travelling trunk biscuit tin, in good condition.

4.75in (12cm) wide

£20-30   SAS

A Wade Bell's Scotch Whisky commemorative advertising ceramic bell-shaped bottle, with applied gilt label with wording 'A MEMENTO OF YOUR VISIT TO BELL'S HEAD OFFICE'.

6.25in (16cm) high

£15-20   DSC

A 1950s full-length male painted advertising figure, possibly for 'Aertex' underwear, modelled standing, on a plinth base.

Male and female underwear advertising figures have become sought after in recent years. The eye-appeal of the figure is important to value. Modelling, facial features and hair style that are typical of their time add to desirability. Always examine a piece closely, as many have become worn.

19.75in (50cm) high

£550-750   **SAS**

A CLOSER LOOK AT A STORE DISPLAY

These would have been used as dramatic store displays, or even parade figures, at a time when exotic animals such as tigers were fashionable.

Rare surivors, a pair is extremely unusual, and these are in excellent condition, and complete with their packing cases which bear amusing wording.

With their crouching poses and bared, snarling teeth, the tigers are full of drama and would make superb display pieces today.

Learbury Clothes was based in Syrcacuse, New York, and produced fine quality menswear which often bore the labels of other brands. As it was a lesser known brand, few of these expensive displays would have been produced.

A pair of crated papier mâché advertising tigers, on moulded naturalistic bases, marked 'Learbury Tiger', with original packing crates marked 'Handle With Care This Box Contains Learbury Fashion Display', in excellent condition.

c1910-20

£10,000-15,000   **JDJ**

A 1930s possibly French male mannequin head, naturalistically painted with applied hair.

12.5in (32cm) high

£200-300   **SAS**

An Art Deco Harley Sport plaster male display bust, with painted features in composition plaster, the bust inscribed 'Harley Sport' in painted blue, on a rectangular plinth and square base.

23.5in (60cm) high

£400-600   **SAS**

An Art Deco French jewellery display bust, the cut-out bust modelled as a glamorous young woman, on a square wooden plinth, with an Art Deco green and white beadwork fringe necklace.

£300-500   **SAS**

A 1950s-60s French Lalique moulded glass shop display sign, with moulded and gilded lettering.

£70-100   **CARS**

JUNKTION

Early Advertising Bought and Sold

Enamel signs, tin/card advertisements, neon signs, pictorial posters, early biscuit/ toffee/ tobacco tins, display figures. Also advertising chairs, dog bowls, etc. Vending machines.Chemist shop drawers, seedsman drawers, drapers shop shirt drawers, shop display cabinets, Fry's etc. Biscuit display racks, ornate shop tills, shop counters, bar fittings, cast iron pub tables, tradesman's hand carts, bicycles, etc.

Always a large interesting quality stock

JUNKTION ANTIQUES
The Old Railway Station, New Bolingbroke, Boston, Lincs
Tel: +44 (0)1205 480068
Mobile: 07836 345491
Email: junktionantiques@hotmail.com
Web: www.junktionantiques.co.uk
OPEN WED, THURS & SATURDAY

A 1940s 'Drink SamBo Chocolate Malted Milk' printed tin advertising sign.

£250-350   MAS

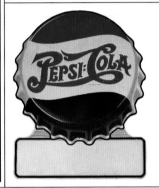

A 1950s Pepsi Cola transfer-printed tinplate shop large sign.

49in (124cm) high

£300-500   QU

Insure your collection at home and away - apply online at

www.connoisseurpolicies.com

Follow the simple instructions on the "buy online" pages on our website and you should be able to buy up to £50,000 of specialist insurance cover within a matter of minutes

Connoisseur Policies Ltd is a wholly owned subsidiary and appointed representative of Anthony Wakefield and Company Ltd, which is authorised and regulated by the Financial Services Authority

Telephone: 0870-241-0-142
information@connoisseurpolicies.com

'Connoisseur'® is a registered trademark of Connoisseur Policies Limited

A Coca Cola printed tinplate advertising tray, made by The H.D. Beech Co., of Coshocton, Ohio.

Coca Cola trays are highly sought after, particularly if made before 1930 or bearing artwork by Hamilton King. This very early example is known as 'The Exhibition Girl' as the 1909 World's Fair in Seattle can be seen behind her.

1909   13.25in (33.5cm) high

£600-900   SOTT

A very rare 1940s 12-sized aluminium Coca Cola bottle carrier.

This is very rare as most bottle carriers were made for 6-packs. Aluminium was a typical material used during this period as large supplies were produced for the war effort and were turned over for civilian use after the end of World War II.

16.25in (41cm) wide

£70-100   SOTT

A CLOSER LOOK AT AN ADVERTISING CALENDAR

This is a very early and very rare advertising calendar, but the truly superb condition makes it even rarer and more desirable.

The Daisy BB gun subject matter also contributes to the value – in the US, where this was sold, vintage guns and related memorabilia are highly collectable.

The printing is very fine, with a good level of detail and several colours – note how one of the daisies has been drawn over the inset of the boys in a skiff to add perspective.

The first Daisy BB gun was given away by the Plymouth Iron Windmill Co. as a promotion to farmers who bought a windmill. In 1895 the nearly bankrupt company changed its name to Daisy and limited itself to manufacturing guns.

A very rare Daisy Manufacturing Co. 'Model 96' air rifle calendar, lithographed in colours by Calvert Lith. Co., with illustration of two boys in a skiff with a gun, and complete with 12 date sheets and brass ring grommet, in excellent condition with only a few scuffs.

1896

£4,000-6,000   JDJ

A 1950s-60s Royal Alma circular Double Diamond Advertising Dish, the back with black printed mark.

5in (12.5cm) diam

£12-18   RET

A Hamleys 'The Finest Toy Shop In the World' catalogue, illustrated with sepia overprinted primary colours showing toys, games, activities including Meccano, FROG, Schuco and Trix products.

1938

£30-50   SAS

A Hires Munimaker marble, nickel, and glass syrup dispenser, the square marble base with brass Hires plaques on four sides and topped with a flared white milk glass globe.

c1900-10   35in (89cm) high

£1,500-2,500   JDJ

A chrome plated steel Schneider Trophy commemorative ashtray, the plane based on the Rolls Royce powered Supermarine S6B Schneider Trophy seaplane, with rotating propeller.

4.5in (11.5cm) high

£100-150   CARS

A De Havilland DH 106 Comet silver plated presentation model, mounted on an onyx ashtray base, with a good level of detailing.

Factors that influence values of airplane ashtrays include the model of plane, the size, materials used, and the level of detail. If the piece is connected to a famous event or aviator, the price can rise.

10in (25.5cm) wide

£200-250   GROB

A World War II onyx and metal airplane ashtray, with a Supermarine Spitfire mounted on top of a chome plated sphere.

8.25in (21cm) long

£80-120   CW

A World War II aluminium 'Trench Art' airplane ashtray with Supermarine Spitfire model with moving propellor, mounted on a machine component, possibly a cylinder head.

c1945   6.5in (16cm) high

£70-90   GCHI

A 1930s chrome plated airplane ashtray, with seaplane model, the base with with 'SP' within a shield mark.

6in (15cm) high

£60-90   CW

A Skyland Models showroom Concorde model, F-BVFA, with Air France livery, in excellent condition and with original display stand.

Concorde made its maiden flight in 1975, and was retired in 2003. It can now be seen at Dulles Airport, Washington DC. In 1998 it completed a round-the-world trip in 41 hours and 27 minutes.

48in (122cm) long

£400-600   TCA

A B&M Ceramics United States Navy 'Tactical Support Center' transfer-printed souvenir mug, with 'Tobias' transfer.

3.5in (9cm) high

£3-4   AEM

An unusual Schneider Trophy commemorative vase, probably made by Bough, with panels of anthropomorphic birds in blue, between Scottish rose and foliate borders on a yellow ground, the base painted 'EJMJ Mifflin, SOUTHAMPTON SEPTEMBER 1929, Schneider Trophy won by G Brit Waghorn'.

The origins of this cup or trophy are unclear. The name Mifflin cannot be found connected with this event, which was held over the Solent some distance away from the city of Southampton. Waghorn did, however, win the event. The Art & Crafts styling is unusual for this date.

10in (25.5cm) high

£300-400   W&W

A rare 1920-30s South Coast Flying Club member's car badge, decorated with four colours of enamel, with some repairs, the back stamped with 'COLLINS LONDON' makers mark.

If the enamel was undamaged, the value might rise to £500.

4.25in (10cm) high

£350-450   CARS

A Brooklands Aero Club octagonal enamelled metal member badge for 1937, numbered '255', with original cord, the back moulded 'NOT TRANSFERABLE' and with ' W.O. LEWIS B'HAM' maker's mark.

1.5in (3.5cm) high

£200-250   CARS

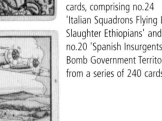

Two American Gum Inc 'Horrors of War' colour printed cards, comprising no.24 'Italian Squadrons Flying Low Slaughter Ethiopians' and no.20 'Spanish Insurgents Bomb Government Territory', from a series of 240 cards.

1936   *3.25in (8cm) wide*

£5-8 EACH   SOTT

A Bishops & Stonier ceramic child's bowl with a transfer-printed scene of Blériot's plane.

9.25in (23.5cm) diam.

£150-200   PC

A 1930s Art Deco cast spelter figurine of a dancing lady with outstretched arms, mounted on an onyx socle, and with spray-painted details.

11.5in (29cm) high

£100-150   **CARS**

A CLOSER LOOK AT AN ART DECO STATUE

Inexpensive statuettes made from moulded plastic and a lightweight metal alloy called spelter were produced during the 1920s and 30s to imitate more expensive carved ivory and cast bronze statues by Ferdinand Preiss, Demêtre Chiparus and others.

Pieces can be found for around £30-150 depending on the quality, size and pose, and offer the look of more expensive figurines, without the high prices

This is one of the better examples, with a lively pose, a sense of movement to the dress, a necklace, and fashionably bobbed hair.

The detail is not as fine as the pieces it was designed to imitate, and examples are frequently damaged or stained.

A 1930s Art Deco spelter statuette of a lady leaning backwards in a dance, with spray painted details and cream moulded plastic head and hands, mounted on an onyx socle.

9in (23cm) high

£100-150   **CARS**

A 1930s Art Deco spelter statuette, with draped shawl under her arms and spray painted details, the onyx base with a striker cigarette or cigar lighter, with some wear to the spray paint.

10in (25.5cm) high

£50-70   **CARS**

An Art Deco gilt bronze figure, modelled as a naked female dancer upon a circular green onyx socle, signed 'Renz', gilding badly damaged.

Although little is known about the designer, this figurine is gilt bronze suggesting a quality figure and the pose is desirable.

10in (25.5cm) high

£500-600   **GHOU**

A 1930s Art Deco spelter statuette, of a standing girl, with flower-like skirt, fan, and disc-shaped hat, mounted on a marble base.

10in (25.5cm) high

£80-120   **CARS**

A 1930s Art Deco spelter statuette of a kneeling girl with an onyx ball, mounted on an oval onyx base.

This may have been one of a pair of bookends.

7in (17.5cm) high

£150-200   **CARS**

AUTOMOBILIA

QUICK REFERENCE

- Automobilia is a diverse global collecting area, surrounding the lively vintage car market and encompassing everything from car parts to advertising to works of art. In general, appealing pieces that look good on display from the major marques are at the higher end of the market. These marques include Bentley, Rolls Royce, Jaguar, Buick, Ferrari and Chevrolet. Collectors tend to focus on one marque, or on a particular type of item.

- Apart from the cars themselves, car mascots usually fetch the largest sums of money. These were mounted on the front of the bonnet of a car, and can be found in many different shapes. Types include 'manufacturer mascots', made by the company that made the car, 'advertising mascots' made by a company such as Michelin to advertise its products, and 'accessory mascots' which include animals, figures and characters.

- Look for examples that conjure up feelings of the excitement and speed of motoring. Novelty forms can also be popular. Names to look for include Lalique, Red Ashay, Sabino and A & E Lejeune. Condition counts, and reproductions are known, so try to view and handle as many authentic examples as possible.

- Car badges, which adorned car grilles, are also popular and often more affordable. Most showed membership of an association such as an enthusiasts club. They are usually made from nickel- or chrome-plated cast brass, which may then be enamelled with a colourful design. Appealing pieces from major marques, or smaller but well-known clubs from the 1900s-30s, tend to be the most desirable.

- Many associations also produced badges for their members, and these have been rising in value recently. As before, appeal and marque are key factors to desirability and value. Also look out for lamps and advertising pieces, such as enamel signs. Items related to famous drivers, such as Stirling Moss, or events, such as Grand Prix, are also desirable due to their association.

A 1920s French A.E. Lejeune Bentley 'Flying B' chrome plated brass car mascot, stamped 'AEL' and mounted on a mottled brown Bakelite stand, made for a Pacific Open Tourer.

3.5in (9cm) high

£250-300   CARS

A large 1920s Joseph Fray chrome plated brass Bentley 'Flying B' car mascot, stamped 'JOS. FRAY B'HAM' and mounted on a Bakelite stand.

This mascot is smaller than similar examples. It may have been designed for an opening bonnet.

2.75in (7cm) high

£350-450   CARS

A 1920s Joseph Fray chrome plated brass Bentley 'Flying B' car mascot, mounted on a brown Bakelite stand, stamped 'JOS. FRAY B'HAM'.

Made for, and generally seen on, a Bentley Open Tourer. This example would have been worth more had it not been over-polished, leading to its plating being polished away and becoming 'brassed'.

Mascot 2in (5cm) high

£250-300   CARS

A late 1930s Bentley 'Flying B' car mascot, with the 'B' leaning back and stamped with registered design no. 'REG8211907' for 1937, mounted on a rectangular Bakelite plinth.

This example is quite worn, with much of the detail on the feathers having been worn away through excessive polishing. If it was crisper, the value would be around £250-300.

5.25in (13cm) long

£200-250   CARS

A CLOSER LOOK AT A BENTLEY CAR MASCOT

This is a rare prototype design that did not go into production and was never used on a car – very few examples exist.

The style reflects the Art Deco tastes of the period, but lacks the elegance and sense of speed of other designs.

It may have been designed by Frederick Gordon Crosby, who designed the logo for the first car in 1921.

It was probably made by Joseph Fray, who made most of Bentley's mascots.

A 1930s Bentley chrome plated brass 'Flying B' car mascot, with long wings, mounted on a brown Bakelite stand.

This was not used for a long period as it was deemed too large, particularly the wings. Look out for examples with only one wing behind, as these are very rare.

5.25in (13cm) long

£550-600   **CARS**

A rare 1930s chrome plated brass prototype Bentley 'Flying B' car mascot, possibly designed by Frederick Gordon Crosby and made by Joseph Fray, unmarked and mounted on a metal stand.

3.5in (9cm) high

£550-600   **CARS**

Lalique 'Chrysis' shown in frosted christal adoring & adorning the radiator of the fabulous Dusenberg, both reflecting the Art Deco period beautifully. By the French motoring artist Francois Vanaret

The complete collection of R.Lalique car mascots using the Lalique factory catalogue numbers along with the date of introduction of each piece:

Sirene/Small Mermaid 831 introduced in 1920 as a statuette adapted and used as a car mascot from 1925
Naïade/Large Mermaid 832 ditto as above
Cinque Chevaux/Five Horses 1122 introduced on 26/8/1925
Comète Etoile Filante/Comet Shooting Star 1123 24/8/25
Faucon/Falcon 1124 5/8/25
Tireur d'Arc/Archer 1126 3/8/26
Coq Nain/Cockeral 1135 10/2/28
Tête de Bélier/Rams Head 1136 3/2/28
Tête de Coq/Cockerals Head 1137 3/2/28
Tête d'Aigle/Eagles Head 1138 14/3/28
Tête d'Épervier/Hawks Head 1139 21/1/28
Tête de Peon/Peacocks Head 1140 3/2/28
Lévrier/Greyhound 1141 14/3/28
Saint Christophe/St Christopher 1142 1/3/28
Hirondelle/Swallow 1143 10/2/28
Petite Libellule/Small Dragonfly 1144 12/4/28
Grande Libellule/Large Dragonfly 1145 23/4/28
Grenouille/Frog 1146 3/5/28
Victoire/Victory Spirit of the Wind 1147 18/4/28
Longchamp A/Horse A 1152A 12/6/29
Longchamp B/Horse B 1152B 10/9/29
Epsom/Horse 1153 5/6/29
Sanglier/Wild Boer 1157 3/10/29
Perche Poisson/Perch Fish 1158 20/4/29
Vitesse/Speed Goddess 1160 17/9/29
Coq Houdan/Proud Cock 1161 30/4/29
Pintade/Guinea Fowl 1164 28/9/29
Hibou/Owl 1181 27/1/31
Renard/Fox 1182 9/12/30
Chrysis/Nude Female 1183 21/3/31

A late 1920s French Lalique 'Cinque Chevaux' (Five Horses) moulded glass car mascot, no.1122, moulded 'R.LALIQUE FRANCE' mark, mounted on a period display base.

This design was introduced on 26th August 1925, and was originally mounted on an illuminated radiator fitting made by Brèves Galleries of Knightsbridge. This example has a couple of internal air bubbles, which may deter some collectors. Without bubbles the value could increase by around £500.

5.5in (14cm) long

£6,000-6,500   **CARS**

A CLOSER LOOK AT A LALIQUE CAR MASCOT

Beaks were often damaged, as the mascot is top heavy. If the beak is not damaged the value can rise to £2,500-3,500.

This dramatic and evocative mascot was model no.1124, and was introduced on the 5th August 1925.

Very few Lalique car mascots were produced in coloured glass, with tinted glass being slightly more common.

Beware of modern fakes, where a colourless mascot has been treated with radiation to add a tint – these are usually darker: lilac examples are more purple in tone.

A late 1920s French Lalique 'Faucon' (Falcon) moulded glass car mascot, with a faint lilac tint, moulded 'R.LALIQUE' and etched 'FRANCE' marks.

6in (15cm) high

£2,000-2,500   **CARS**

A 1930s French Lalique 'Sirene' (Mermaid) opalescent moulded glass car mascot, moulded 'R.LALIQUE' mark.

This example has a chipped base, a common problem with vintage car mascots, but luckily the damage does not affect the figure itself. In perfect condition, it might fetch up to £1,500. Sirene was numbered 831 as a statuette in 1920. It was turned into a car mascot in 1925.

4in (10cm) high

£900-1,200   **CARS**

A 1950s-60s French Lalique colourless glass 'Perche Poisson' (Perch) moulded glass car mascot, no.1158, introduced on the 20th April 1929, the base with 'LALIQUE FRANCE' acid stamp.

Note that the glass on mascots from this period is slighty darker in tone than more modern examples, such as the one to the right, which are brighter and cleaner. This shape was discontinued in 2006.

3.75in (9.5cm) high

£550-650   **CARS**

A 1980s-90s French Lalique colourless glass 'Perche Poisson' (Perch) moulded glass car mascot, no.1158, introduced on the 20th April 1929, the base with diamond point engraved 'LALIQUE FRANCE' inscription and factory labels.

3.75in (9.5cm) high

£550-650   **CARS**

A 1980s-90s French Lalique clear and frosted moulded glass 'Sanglier' (Wild Boar) car mascot, no.1157 introduced on the 3rd October 1929, the base with diamond point engraved 'Lalique France' script mark.

2.75in (6.5cm) high

£350-450   **CARS**

A CLOSER LOOK AT A GORDON CROSBY JAGUAR CAR MASCOT

Known as the 'mottled cat', this was designed by Gordon Crosby, who designed the famous 'Leaping Cat' mascot for Jaguar in 1937.

It was used for one year from 1935-36 only on a Jaguar car, before being relaced by the more familiar design as Jaguar founder Sir William Lyons did not like it.

It was re-used on the Panther J72 built by Jankel during the late 1970s and early 1980s, which itself was loosely based on a Jaguar SS100 from the late 1930s.

The value given is for the mascot only, the cap itself is worth around £50.

A large Panther chrome plated car mascot, for a Jaguar model J72, designed by Gordon Crosby, on a radiator cap with an applied black enamel Panther winged logo.

7.25in (8cm) high

£350-450   **CARS**

A 1950s Jaguar chrome plated brass 'Leaping Cat' car mascot, with longer tail, designed by Gordon Crosby, for an Mk6, on a cylindrical mount stamped 7/2645/0, the base of the mascot ground down.

If the base had not been ground down, the value might have been £450-550. If the shaft is missing, the value falls by around £50.

8in (20.5cm) long

£300-350   **CARS**

A 1960s Jaguar chome plated brass 'Leaping Cat' car mascot, designed by Gordon Crosby, for S-Type models, on a long mount with two fixing screws.

7.75in (19.5cm) long

£100-150   **CARS**

A Singer Gazelle chrome plated car mascot, mounted on a wooden plinth.

Mascot 6in (15cm) long

£100-150   **CHT**

A modern reproduction chrome plated flying stork car mascot, in the style of Frederick Bazin, mounted on a radiator cap.

5.5in (14cm) high

£70-100   **CHT**

A Rolls Royce nickel-plated brass large 'Spirit of Ecstasy' car mascot, for a Phantom II, stamped with copyright marks and 'Charles Sykes', mounted on a wooden base.

1919-25

6in (15cm) high

£900-1,200   **CARS**

A late 1950s-60s Automobile Association (AA) enamelled and chromed car grille badge, in original condition with double screw fitting for a grille, numbered '38774Z'.

3.5in (9cm) high

£25-30   **CARS**

A Royal Automobile Club (RAC) Centenary commemorative chrome plated and enamelled car grille badge.

Only available in the centenary year of 1997, members were allowed to buy two examples, at a cost of £29.95 each.

1997   *4.75in (12cm) high*

£65-75   **CARS**

A 1950s-60s Company of Veteran Motorists member's grille badge, awarded to a member of 49 years standing, the back marked 'THE PROPERTY OF C.V.M.'.

THE CVM was founded in 1932 and promoted safe driving. In 1983 it became GEM, and then GEM Motoring Assist.

3.75in (9.5cm) high

£7-10   **CARS**

An Automobile Association type 1B nickel plated brass full member's badge, impressed 'Stenson Cooke Secretary', numbered '4410'.

6in (15cm) high

£100-150   **CHT**

An Royal Automobile Club of Italy type 3B badge, enamelled in blue, white, red and black, with some enamel losses.

4.5in (11.5cm) wide

£35-45   **CHT**

A 1960s Sussex Car Club enamelled pressed steel car grille badge.

As this was a smaller regional club, fewer badges would have been made, meaning they are harder to find today even though demand for them is limited.

4.5in (11.5cm) high

£40-50   **CARS**

A 1960s Aston Martin Owner's Club enamelled chromed brass car grille badge.

The original owner has removed his name under the enamelled area with a drill, revealing the brassy metal. If this had not been done, the value may have risen to £40-50. Also look out for more decorative vitreous enamelled examples, as these can fetch £70-100.

6in (15cm) high

£30-40   **CARS**

A Brooklands Automobile Racing Club member's enamel badge set, comprising member's badge on cord and two guest badges, each numbered '404'.

1926   1.25in (3cm) high

£280-320   CHT

A Brooklands Automobile Racing Club blue enamelled gold-metal member's badge for 1929, together with a bow-shaped guest pin, each numbered 189, the back moulded 'W.O. LEWIS B'HAM'. *Introduced in 1907, these sets have become highly sought after. A full set comprises one member's badge and two guest pins. If this set had been complete, it could have been worth up to £100 more.*

1928   1.5in (3.5cm) high

£200-250   CARS

A CLOSER LOOK AT A MEMBER'S BADGE SET

The brightly coloured geometric Art Deco style, and the design shaped like the front of a car, makes this set highly desirable.

The design was changed every year, so that current members could be quickly and easily identified.

This is a complete set. Always look for matching numbers on each piece – the original box adds up to 50% of the value of the pins.

1939 was the last year these sets of badges were made. Members' badges were produced from 1941-42, before they too were phased out.

Look out for sets of 1916 badges made in cream Bakelite as a complete set can fetch up to £2,000.

A Brooklands Automobile Racing Club member's enamel badge set, comprising member's badge on cord and two guest badges, each numbered 805, in original box, with printed membership number and rules to lid.

1939   1.25in (3cm) high

£500-700   CHT

A Charlie Chaplin signed manuscript letter and photograph, the letter addressed from Los Angeles, California, with stamped hand written envelope, mounted in composite frame.

£450-540   AH

A Pete Best signed photograph of the Beatles.

Best was the original drummer for the Beatles, from 1960-1962. He was replaced by Ringo Starr.

10in (25.5cm) wide

£30-40   ACOG

A Maria Teresa de Filippis signed Silverstone motor racing programme

9in (23cm) high.

£25-35   COC

A Gerald Ford signed presidential portrait.

£450-550   MAS

A Harrison Ford as Han Solo signed photograph.

The signature isn' t his best as it runs across a dark area of the photograph and appears lost.

c1980

£150-250   PC

STEPHEN FRY

A Stephen Fry signed postcard.

Dedications are less desirable.

6in (15cm) high

£10-15   PC

A Whoopi Goldberg signed photograph.

£35-45   ACOG

An Audrey Hepburn signature, mounted with a photograph from the film 'Breakfast at Tiffany's'.

16in (40.5cm) wide

£180-200   PC

BANKNOTES

A British one pound note for use by the British Military Expeditionary Forces in the Mediterranean and the Naval Expeditionary Forces in 1915, signed by John Bradbury, Secretary to the Treasury, overprinted in Arabic.

£1,800-2,400   PAMW

A Bank of England five pound note, signed by E.M.Harvey, issued in Hull.

1918

£700-800   PAMW

An British Treasury ten shilling note, signed by John Bradbury.

Treasury notes signed with Bradbury's name are known as 'Bradburys'.

£100-150   CWD

A Bank of England Britannia series ten shilling note, signed by L.K. O'Brien.

This note has a million serial number.

1955

£40-60   PAMW

A first issue Bank of England fifty pound note, A01 prefix.

1981   £100-150   CWD

A French Revolutionary assignat five livres note, year 2.

£5-10   CWD

A German fifty million mark note, from the Hyper Inflation period.

£2-3   CWD

A French one hundred new francs note, with Napoleon portrait.

£20-25   CWD

A Munster & Leinster five pound Ploughman note, signed by J.L. Gubbins, dated.

1929

£700-900   PAMW

A Japanese occupation of Malaya one thousand dollar note.

£1-2   CWD

A USA Confederate States fifty dollar note, with Lincoln portrait.

1864

£40-60   CWD

A USA five dollar Pioneer Family series note,.

1907

£100-150   CWD

BEADS

QUICK REFERENCE

- Beads were one of the earliest types of personal adornment. The very earliest beads were made from natural materials, such as shells, pebbles, bone fragments, seeds and feathers. The oldest examples known are shells dating from approximately 100,000 years ago. Many cultures attached social or cultural importance to beads, and status to those who made and wore them.
- As human societies developed, so did the forms, designs and materials used for beads. Glass beads were introduced around 30,000 years ago, with perhaps the oldest being Egyptian. Glass bead-making grew during the Phoenician and Roman periods.
- The value of a bead depends on a number of factors including its age, material, size, quality of decoration, rarity and desirability to collectors. Due to this wide variation, beads make an ideal collecting field to suit a wide range of budgets and tastes.
- A necklace does not always have to have its original stringing as most of the value is often in the beads themselves. However, if the original stringing was metal, or unique in some way, then it will be important to value.
- Examine beads for wear or damage, although a degree of wear is acceptable in older examples.
- Beads have been made in nearly every country at some point, and many are being reproduced today, so consulting a reliable dealer and buying a comprehensive reference book is highly recommended to help differentitate originals and copies.

Two early Venetian glass elongated barrel-shaped beads, with applied combed red and white striped trails on opaque dark bodies.

largest 0.75in (2cm) long

£15-25 EACH   VC

An early Venetian glass bead, with spiralling pink, white and green striped trail over a 'coiled' opaque dark body.

0.5in (1.5cm) long

£25-35   VC

Two early Venetian glass spherical beads, with applied white and multicoloured spots on opaque dark bodies.

0.5in (1cm) long

£15-25 EACH   VC

A 1930s Venetian lamp-wound 'Wedding Cake' blue spherical glass bead.

0.5in (1.5cm) long

£3-5   VC

Three 1950s Murano glass beads, teardrop-shaped with multicoloured millefiori.

0.75in (2cm) long

£2-3 EACH   VC

BEADS

A CLOSER LOOK AT A VENETIAN BEAD NECKLACE

The beads are complex, with more details than on other examples.

These are known as 'Wedding Cake' beads as the details are built up individually, using molten glass, much like the icing on a wedding cake.

This necklace has more beads, and so is more valuable than an example with fewer beads.

Each bead in handmade, with flowers, curling and swirling lines and spots being typical decoration – check that there is no damage and look for signs of age as they are being reproduced.

A 1930s necklace with Venetian lamp-wound 'Wedding Cake' green spherical glass beads.

Necklace 15in (38cm) long

£50-70 **VC**

A 1930s necklace with Venetian lamp-wound 'Wedding Cake' green spherical glass beads.

Necklace 15in (38cm) long

£70-90 **VC**

A 1930s necklace with Venetian lamp-wound 'Wedding Cake' green, red and blue spherical glass beads.

Necklace 15in (38cm) long

£60-80 **VC**

Four Parthian period shaped 'etched' carnelian beads, from Ur.

Four Parthian period shaped 'etched' carnelian spherical beads, from Ur.

c2,500 BC   largest 0.5in (1.5cm) long

£35-45 EACH **VC**

Despite being known as 'etched', the pattern was not carved at all, but was instead painted on using an alkaline solution. Each bead was then baked to set and fix the pattern.

c2,500 BC   largest 0.75in (2cm) long

£35-45 EACH **VC**

QUICK REFERENCE

- A true first edition will be from the first print run (impression) of the first published hardback edition. First editions can then have subsequent impressions, in which errors are corrected, but these are less desirable. A small first edition print run is likely to make a book more desirable. Consequently, although famous, iconic titles will always be prized, first edition books written at the height of an author's power may be worth less than early/less-well received books, as fewer were published. Those with an eye for the future may choose to buy (preferably) signed first editions of up-and-coming authors nominated for major prizes, such as the Man Booker, before the winner is announced.
- Learn how to recognise the different styles of numbering. This often takes the form of a '1' in the series of numbers on the inside copyright page that indicates the edition of the book. Other publishers state that a book is the first edition or use a sequence of letters. Check that the publishing date and copyright date match, and that these match the original publishing date and publisher for the title in a reference book.
- Though there are consistently popular classic authors, such as Ian Fleming and Agatha Christie, fashion can dictate which authors are most desirable. The popular rediscovery of a classic or a successful film or TV series adaptation will usually increase value of first editions.
- The author's signature adds value, particularly if on a limited special edition. Dedications are typically less desirable, unless the recipient is famous or connected to the author. Book signings are becoming more common, so this may become less of a factor in future.
- Condition is extremely important: mint condition commands a premium. Dust jackets should be clean, un-faded and un-damaged, though many can be restored. If the jacket is missing, value can fall by over 50 per cent. You should also check that the book is complete and has not been defaced or damaged.

Edgar Rice Burroughs, 'The Eternal Lover', first American edition, published by A.C. McClurg and Co. of Chicago, with illustrations by St John, original black-stamped blue cloth boards with faded spine and dust jacket with light wear.
1925
£1,000-1,500 BLNY

Edgar Rice Burroughs, 'Tarzan and the Jewels of Opar', first edition, published by A.C. McClurg and Co. of Chicago, with frontispiece and illustrations by St John, dark green gilt-stamped cloth and dust jacket with minor losses, and corners clipped.
1918
£1,000-1,500 BLNY

Pearl S. Buck, 'The Good Earth', first American edition, first issue, with pictorial endpapers, modern full brown morocco and gilt binding by Bayntun-Riviere.

The misspelling of 'fleas' as 'flees' on p.100 identifies this as the first issue of the first edition. This novel won a Pulitzer prize in 1932, and returned to the bestseller list after being included on Oprah Winfrey's Book Club in 2004.
1931
£350-450 BLO

John Le Carré, 'The Spy Who Came in from the Cold', first edition, first impression, published by Gollancz, London, signed presentation copy, dust jacket, with small chips.
1963
£1,800-2,200 BLO

Robert Bloch, 'Psycho', first American edition, published by Simon and Schuster, New York, with original half cloth in dust jacket.
1959
£600-900 BLNY

Agatha Christie, 'Evil Under The Sun', first edition, published by Collins, London, with original orange cloth, pictorial dust wrapper, price '7s 6d.', backstrip slightly faded and with small chips to head and tail.
1941

£400-600   **L&T**

G.K. Chesterton, 'The Father Brown Stories', first edition, published by Cassell & Co., London, with inked name on front free endpaper, original cloth, dust jacket, price clipped, and with rubbed corners.
1929

£250-300   **BLO**

A CLOSER LOOK AT A BURROUGHS FIRST EDITION

Burroughs' seminal work was first published by Olympia Press in Paris in 1959, titled 'The Naked Lunch'.

The first American edition was published three years later as it had been deemed pornographic. 'The' was dropped from the title, as the author never intended it to be there.

Colin Dexter, 'Last Seen Wearing', first edition, first impression publisher's sample copy, published by Macmillan, signed by the author on the title page, with publisher's stamp on front endpaper, with original boards and dust jacket.

This is Dexter's second novel in the popular Inspector Morse series. It is also the scarcest first edition in the series.

1976

£1,000-1,500   **BLO**

This American edition is also different from the Olympia Press edition as it was based on an earlier manuscript from 1958 owned by Burroughs' friend, the poet Allen Ginsberg.

Time magazine included the book in its list of '100 Best English-language Novels from 1923 to 2005'. It was made into a film by David Cronenberg in 1991, reigniting interest in it.

William Burroughs, 'Naked Lunch', first American edition, third printing, published by Grove Press, with black cloth over grey boards, dust jacket with very light rubbing to top and head of spine.
1962

£150-250   **BLNY**

Arthur Conan Doyle, 'The Hound of the Baskervilles', first edition, first issue, published by George Newnes, London, with 16 plates by Sidney Paget, cut signature of the author mounted on title page, original pictorial cloth, spine slightly dulled, in modern custom-made drop-back box replicating the book cover design.
1902

£1,800–2,200   **BLO**

Arthur Conan Doyle, 'The Hound of the Baskervilles, Another Adventure of Sherlock Holmes', first edition, published by George Newnes, London, illustrated with frontispiece and 15 plates, one plate detached but present, endpapers foxed and page edges lightly browned, cloth with few small stains.
1902

£1,000-1,500   **BLNY**

BOOKS

Oliver La Farge, 'Laughing Boy', first American edition, published by Houghton Mifflin Company, Cambridge, with publisher's thickly woven yellow cloth, maroon lettering to spine and upper cover, in slightly rubbed dust jacket, with slightly faded spine.

This novel won a Pulitzer Prize in 1930.

1929

£300-400   **BLNY**

A CLOSER LOOK AT A T. PRATCHETT FIRST EDITION

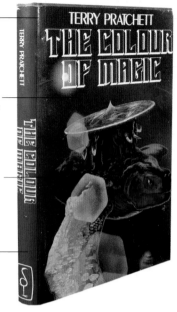

This is the scarce first edition of the first book of the internationally popular Discworld series.

This copy was bought direct from the publisher at the time of publication – reputedly only 506 copies were printed.

This true first impression of the first edition has no price, but bears a sticker reading ' Publisher' s Price £7.95' .

Later issues had overlays, or stickers, with book reviews on the flaps, this copy does not.

Mervyn Peake, 'The Gormenghast trilogy', comprising three first editions, published by Eyre & Spottiswoode, London, comprising 'Titus Groan', 'Gormenghast', and 'Titus Alone', original red cloth, dust wrappers, some slight offsetting to endpapers.

1946-59

£900-1,200   **L&T**

Terry Pratchett, 'The Colour of Magic', first edition, first impression, published by Colin Smythe, Gerrards Cross, original boards, dust jacket, with price sticker on inside front flap, slight rubbing to fore edges and corners.

1983

£4,000-6,000   **BLO**

Terry Pratchett, 'Mort', first edition, published by Gollancz, London, with original boards and dust jacket, in excellent condition.

The fourth book of the Discworld series and many readers' favourite, ensuring a strong following.

1987

£300-500   **BLO**

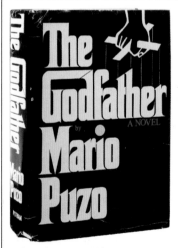

Philip Pullman, 'The Subtle Knife', first edition, published by Scholastic Press, London, with full number line, original green cloth and gilt stamp of dagger, dust jacket, and bookplate of The Children's Book Award on front free endpaper.

1997

£300-500   **L&T**

Mario Puzo, 'The Godfather', first edition, first impression, published by Putnam, New York, with red endpapers, original black and off-white cloth lettered in gilt, dust jacket, slight staining and creasing to jacket.

As the jacket is priced '$6.95' and bears the code numbering '6903', it is a first edition jacket. This copy is made more desirable as it is signed by Puzo. This was his first 'commercial' fiction book, following two moderately successful titles – it went on to outsell every other book during the 1970s.

1969

£1,200-1,800   **BLO**

QUICK REFERENCE – HARRY POTTER

J. K. Rowling's Harry Potter titles are among the most widely prized first editions on today's market. The first title in the series, 'Harry Potter and the Philosopher's Stone' has gained an almost legendary status. According to the publisher Bloomsbury, only 500 copies of the first print run of the first edition were produced, most of which were sold to British libraries or schools. This copy is one of those, and shows the level of wear and damage that can be expected from use in a school, as well as bearing the school library's stamp. Had it been in mint condition, the price could have risen to over £10,000. The true first editions have a full line of numbers on the imprint page, leading down to a '1', and do not have a dust jacket. Even the first British paperback issue of this title, also published in 1997, is sought after – copies have fetched over £1,500, as reputedly only 200 were printed.

J.K. Rowling, 'Harry Potter and the Philosopher's Stone', first edition, first impression, published by Bloomsbury, London, with unusual slight browning, ex-library copy with stamp and small sticker to verso of title, new endpapers, original pictorial boards, worn at edges and corners, loss and tape repairs around spine.

1997
£1,500-2,000 BLO

J.K. Rowling, 'Harry Potter and the Chamber of Secrets', uncorrected proof copy, original blue and white printed wrappers.

A 'proof copy' is sent out by a publisher to people including major booksellers, literary editors, and reviewers. The purpose is to promote the book before the final version is printed, and to give the author and publisher the chance to make final corrections or revisions. However, by this stage, the text is usually the closest version to the final product.
1998
£800–1,200 BLO

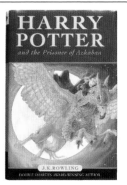

J.K. Rowling, 'Harry Potter and the Prisoner of Azkaban', first edition, first issue, published by Bloomsbury, London, with original pictorial boards and dust jacket.

This can be identified as the first issue due to the copyright wording reading 'Joanne Rowling' rather than 'J.K. Rowling', and the dropped text on p.7.
1999
£500-700 BLO

Siegfried Sassoon, 'Memoirs of a Fox-Hunting Man', Faber & Faber, London, first English illustrated edition, published by Faber & Faber, London, no.224 from a limited edition of 300 signed by the author and illustrator, illustrations by William Nicholson, original vellum lettered in black with designs in red and black.

1929
£700-1,000 L&T

Victoria (Vita) Sackville-West, 'Challenge', first edition, second American issue, published by Doran, New York, with original titled red cloth, dust jacket with light surface marking, and spine slightly dulled, with some tears.

This book was scheduled to be published by Collins in the UK, but Sackville-West withdrew it after pressure from her mother and her husband, Harold Nicolson. Doran used Collins' sheets, insert a new title page, to produce 2,000 copies. Supposedly written with Vita's female lover Violet Trefusis, the lead character is called Julian, which was the name used by Vita when she dressed as a man while travelling with Trefusis. Due to this connection, Vita's mother banned the British version, which was not published until 1974, 12 years after Vita's death.

1923
£350-450 BLO

Mickey Spillane, 'I, the Jury', first edition, published by E. P. Dutton & Co., New York, with original black cloth and slightly creased and rubbed dust jacket, with some tape residue.

1947
£800-1,200 BLNY

CAMERAS

QUICK REFERENCE

- The first photography dates from 1839, when Louis Daguerre launched the daguerreotype: the first commercially viable photographic process. However, these early cameras were bulky, expensive and difficult to use. By the 1880s, with the ready availability of prepared 'dry' photographic plates and advances in camera design, the market was opened to many more people. A large number of these wood- and brass- bodied, dry-plate cameras survive and they are often desirable (though less than the earlier wet-plate cameras). Collectors should look for names including Sanderson, Watson and Lancaster.

- The world's most collectable camera is perhaps the Leica, made by Leitz, in Wetzlar, Germany. Developed in 1913, the Leica used 35mm film and was small, light and easy to use. It had a fixed lens until 1930, when interchangeable screw-fit lenses were introduced. This system only changed in 1954, with the bayonet lens mounts of the 'M' series. Many are still usable, or can be repaired due to Leitz's fine quality engineering

- Each Leica has a unique serial number on its top plate, which you can use to identify the model and year of manufacture. Prices range from around £100 for more common models, such as the Model IIIa, to tens of thousands. Variations and unusual engravings add value, as will accessories such as lenses. Scratches, dents, and damaged mechanisms will seriously affect value, with most Leica collectors looking to buy in mint condition.

- With other mass-produced cameras, look for fine quality construction and well known brand names, such as Nikon Voigtlander, Canon and Zeiss Ikon. Condition is important, but usually not as much as for Leicas. Variation in colour and features, such as lenses, adds value.

A Canon S-II camera, no.15326, chrome, engraved 'Seiki-Kogaku, Tokyo', with shutter speeds 20–500, slow speeds dial, with a 'Nippon Kogaku' Nikkor-Q.C. f/3.5 5cm lens no. 570999, body covering replaced.

This can be dated to 1946, as in 1947 the company name changed to 'Canon Camera Company Ltd', replacing the 'Seiki Kogaku' wording.
1946

£300-400   SK

A Franke & Heidecke Wide-Angle Rolleiflex Reflex twin lens reflex camera, no.W2490135, with Zeiss Distagon 1:4 f=55mm lens.

£600-900   ROS

A Franke & Heidecke Tele Rolleiflex twin lens reflex camera, no.S2302261, with Zeiss Sonnar 1:4 f=135mm lens.

£120-180   ROS

A Hasselblad 1000F camera, with a Tessar 1:2.8 f=80mm lens.

Of fine and functional quality, the 1000F, and its predecessor the 1600F, can be hard to find in working order.

1953-57

£250-300   ROS

A Kodak no.5 Cirkut revolving back cycle view 360 degree panoramic roll film camera, no.46969, patented by William Folmer.
c1915-1917

£200-300   ROS

A Kodak 3A Panoram panoramic roll film camera.
c1926-1928

£60-80   **ROS**

A Leica IIIC camera, no.502557, chrome, with Leitz f3.5 Elmar lens and cap, with leather case, some faults.
1950

£150-250   **TOV**

A Leica MI camera, no.967287, chrome, with Leitz 50mm Elmar lens, and leather case.
1959

£200-300   **TOV**

A CLOSER LOOK AT A LEICA CAMERA

Leica cameras are hotly sought after by many collectors across the world. Those produced in strictly limited numbers are among the most desirable and valuable.

As well as model and age, condition is key – those in truly mint condition will always fetch more than used examples, particularly when they have their paperwork and box, as here.

This example is from a limited edition of 150 cameras, but only 30 had this lens type, commemorating the 150th anniversary of the Wetzlar Optisches Institut.

This is no ordinary M6 with a commemorative engraving – each one is platinum plated, covered with karung leather, and has a unique, special serial number relating to a year from 1849-1999.

A Leica M6 platinum 150th anniversary camera, no. 2490145, commemorative no.1994, the top-plate engraved '150 Jahre Optik 1849–1999 Summilux-M f/1.4 35 ASPH', with diced green-grey leather body covering, with a commemorative Leitz Summilux-M f/1.4 35mm lens, in silk-lined polished walnut root case, with warranty, manual, commemorative booklet, receipt, hood, caps, and strap.
1999

£3,500-5,000   **SK**

A Leica M4 50th anniversary camera, no.1412936, black, the front with commemorative '50 Jahre' laurel leaf motif, the back numbered '136-E', complete with manual, registration certificate and card box.

According to Leitz records, 1,730 units of this model were made, 350 each with the letters L, E, I and C, and 330 with the letter A.
1974

£2,200-2,800   **SK**

A rare Japanese chrome Muley Leica-type camera, no.102, the base plate engraved 'Made in Occupied Japan', leather-covered body, speed-housing engraved in script 'Muley' and in capitals 'G.T.S.'

A rare Japanese copy of a Lecia Standard by an unknown (and presumably small) Japanese workshop.
c1946-52

£2,000-3,000   **SK**

A Nikon F2, with chrome body, and Nikkor 50mm F.1.4 lens.
c1971

£100-150   ROS

A Zeiss Ikon Kolibri 523/18 compact camera, with rimset Compur shutter, and Tessar f=3.5 lens.
1930-35

£50-80   ROS

A CLOSER LOOK AT A NIKON CAMERA

Like Leica, Nikon has a large following of collectors around the world, which means demand is high for rare models.

This first civilian Nikon camera is the 'holy grail' for many collectors, and only around 700 examples are thought to have been produced.

Its serial number, 609117, dates from early on in the production, dating from before some 200 additional Nikon Is were converted into Nikon Ms by changing the focal plane, top and base plates and adding a sprocket wheel.

Examples in such excellent condition are rare and this affects value.

A Nikon I camera, no.609117, chrome with leather-covered body, with back numbered internally '609117', base-plate engraved 'Made in Occupied Japan', with a Nippon Kogaku W-Nikkor C f/3.5 3.5cm lens no.9101079.
1948

£6,000-9,000   SK

A rare black Nikon S 'Life Magazine' camera, no.6101424, black with leather-covered body, the top plate engraved 'Nippon Kogaku, Tokyo', enlarged wind and rewind knobs for field use, chrome lens and tripod mounts and a Nippon Kogaku Nikkor-H.C. f/2 5cm lens no.625463.

This Nikon S was produced for 'Life' magazine photographers and is extremely rare. Only 20 examples were commissioned by the magazine after they were impressed by photographs of the Korean war taken by war photographers such as David Douglas Duncan and Carl Mydams – this is one of only two surviving cameras known.

£15,000-20,000   SK

A Zeiss Ikon, Contarex Special camera, no meter, interchangeable reflex or prism view hood, with a Planar 1:2 f=50mm lens.
c1966

£300-400   ROS

A Zeiss Ikon Contarex Super Second 35mm camera, chrome, with a Zeiss 1:4 f=35mm lens.

c1970

£180-220   ROS

A late 19thC Sanderson mahogany and brass quarter plate field folding camera, with black leather bellows, spare plates, tripod, and other accessories.

£280-320   **FLD**

A Paillard Bolex H8 Reflex cine camera, the C mount fitted with 1:1.3 f=12.5mm, 1:1.4 f=36mm and Cine-Tele-Xenar 1:2.8/75 lenses in fitted leather maker's case, with accessories and instruction leaflets.

£60-80   **ROS**

A CLOSER LOOK AT A ZEISS CAMERA

Introduced in 1935, many consider this to be one of the most technically impressive cameras ever built, but it was heavy and tricky to use.

It was the first camera to have a built-in light meter, and was extremely expensive in its day, costing £233 including a Sonnar lens in 1939.

This camera is in excellent, working condition – if it is worn through use, or the shutter or light meter do not work, the value will be reduced by over a half as it is complex to repair.

This example has its original Sonnar lens plus a Tessar lens, manual, case, and a collection of accessories, many of which can be hard to find today and add value.

A Zeiss Contaflex twin lens reflex camera, no.A46226, chrome with leather-covered body, with a Zeiss f/2.8 8cm viewing lens no.1724131 and a Zeiss Tessar f/2.8 5cm taking lens no.1514331, in maker's case, together with a Zeiss Sonnar f/2 8.5cm taking lens no.2401465 in leather pouch and maker's box, manual, leather hood and accessories.

£1,200-1,800   **SK**

A Houghton-Butcher 'Ensign Special' Reflex Tropical model camera with brass-bound teak body.

'Tropical' cameras were made using teak and the fabric bellows were treated so they repelled insects when used in tropical climes.

£200-300   **ROS**

A Paillard Bolex H-16 cine camera, the C mount fitted with a Yvar 1:2.8 f=75mm, a Trioplan 1:2.8 Foc 3in, and a Ross 1in F 1.9 cine lens.

£50-70   **ROS**

A 1960s-70s Kodak shop display over-sized model of an Instamatic camera, with attached 'flash bulb' fitting.

£60-80   **ROS**

A carved walking cane, by 'Schtockschnitzler' Simmons, with bird whistle grip.

29in (73.5cm) high

£600-900   POOK

A carved cane, by 'Schtockschnitzler' Simmons, with bird grip.

£500-800   POOK

A carved cane with bird grip, by 'Schtockschnitzler' Simmons.

£800-1,200   POOK

A Bally carver cane, with painted bird grip.

33in (84cm) high

£2,500-3,500   POOK

QUICK REFERENCE – FOLK ART CANES

'Folk Art' is the term given to unique works by untrained or self-trained, usually country-based, artisans. This varied area has become immensely popular with collectors over the past few years, after being largely ignored for decades. Although folk art is now collected all over the world, the US market is the strongest and generally sees the highest prices. Prices paid for folk art walking canes have now even exceeded those paid for gadget canes containing functional items. Although the level of detail, condition, subject and date count, the primary consideration is the artist. 'Schtockschnitzler' Simmons was an itinerant German, whose nickname means 'cane carver'. He paid for his bed and board around Pennsylvania from c1895-1910 by selling his carvings, which also included decorative trees with seated birds. This rare and desirable example (below) retains its original paint, which is also unusually bright and unworn; for a functional item this is very rare. Birds are his hallmark design and are highly sought after, and this is a particularly desirable 'bird in hand' design.

A carved and painted cane, by 'Schtockschnitzler' Simmons, the grip in the form of a hand clasping a bird.

38.25in (97cm) high

£4,000-6,000   POOK

A carved and painted cane, by 'Schtockschnitzler' Simmons, the grip in the form of a hand supporting a bird on a basket.

38.25in (97cm) high

£6,000-9,000   POOK

A Bally carver cane, the handle carved as a bird and leaves.

33in (84cm) high

£400-600   POOK

A folk art carved cane, with grip in the form of a dog with a turtle in its mouth, the stock carved with various animal heads, and silver band and tip.

c1900   *33.25in (84.5cm) high*

£300-400   POOK

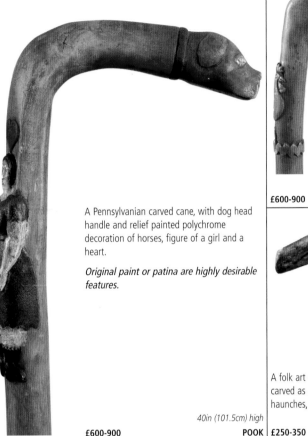

A Pennsylvanian carved cane, with dog head handle and relief painted polychrome decoration of horses, figure of a girl and a heart.

Original paint or patina are highly desirable features.

40in (101.5cm) high

£600-900   POOK

A carved cane with hound head grip, by 'Schtockschnitzler' Simmons, above a cockerel and sawtooth band.

33in (84cm) high

£600-900   POOK

A folk art carved cane, the handle carved as a seated dog on its haunches, wearing a long hat.

37in (94cm) high

£250-350   POOK

A carved cane, the handle carved as a charging elephant with raised trunk.

34.75in (88cm) high

£200-300   POOK

A 'Schtockschnitzler' Simmons carved cane, the handle carved as a whistle in the form of a hunting horn.

The inclusion of whistles in cane handles is not unusual.

38in (35.5cm) high

£400-500   POOK

CERAMICS

QUICK REFERENCE

- The Beswick Pottery was founded in Loughton, Staffordshire in 1894. The animal figurines for which Beswick is now best known began to appear as early as 1900. By 1930, they had become a major part of production. The company was sold to Royal Doulton in 1969, but the Beswick name was in use until 1989, when the production of Beswick and Doulton animal figurines was merged under the Royal Doulton name. The Beswick name was used again from 1999 until the factory closed in 2002. Prices rose after the closure and remain strong.

- Collectors tend to focus on one type of animal, with cattle currently one of the most popular. Other popular figurines include the series of Beatrix Potter characters launched in 1946 and the subsequent range of Disney figurines.

- The work of Arthur Gredington, who joined in 1939, is desirable. Other notable modellers include Colin Melbourne, Graham Tongue, Albert Hallam and Alan Maslankowski.

- Look for variation in colour, glaze, form (i.e. differently positioned legs), as these will affect value. 'Roan' and 'Rocking horse grey' are typically valuable. Similarly, matt glazes can be more valuable than glossy. Early pieces are generally the most desirable, but can be hard to identify as the Beswick backstamp and shape numbers were only used from 1934. Limited editions from as late as 1990 can be valuable if the edition was small. Condition is important. Examine protruding horns, thin legs and tails for breakages.

A Beswick 'Leghorn Cockerel' figurine, model 1892, designed by Arthur Gredington, the base with impressed mark.

1963-83   *9.75in (25cm) high*

£150-200   **LOC**

A Beswick 'Green Woodpecker' bird figure, model 1218, designed by Arthur Gredington, with gloss finish, the base with impressed marks and applied paper label.

The original version, produced from 1961-67, had high relief flowers applied to the base, and can be worth up to twice the value of this example.

1967-89   *8.75in (22cm) high*

£150-200   **WW**

A Beswick 'Songthrush' bird figure, model 2308, designed by Albert Hallam, with gloss finish, the base with impressed mark.

1970-89   *5.75in (14.5cm) high*

£100-150   **WW**

A Beswick 'Grouse (pair)' figure, model 2063, designed by Albert Hallam, impressed factory marks.

1966-75   *6in (15cm) high*

£350-450   **WW**

A Beswick 'Fan-tailed Dove' figure, model 1614, designed by Arthur Gredington, the base with impressed and printed mark.

1959-69   *6in (15.5cm) high*

£180-220   **WW**

A set of three Beswick 'Mallard' graduated wall plaques, model 596, designed by Mr Watkin, with gloss finish, the backs with impressed and printed marks.

1938-73   Largest 11.75in (30cm) wide
£100-150   WW

A Beswick 'Bird' figurine, model 1415, designed by Colin Melbourne, from the CM series, the base with factory marks.

1956-1962   5.25in (13.5cm) high
£150-200   W&W

A rare Beswick 'Huntsman Standing' figurine, model 1501, designed by Arthur Gredington, with a gloss glaze, sitting on a Palomino horse and wearing a red jacket.

1965-71   8.25in (21cm) high
£4,000-5,000   TEN

A rare Beswick 'Huntsman Standing' figurine, model 1501, designed by Arthur Gredington, with a gloss glaze, on a Skewbald horse and wearing a red jacket.

The horse in this model is an exceptionally rare colour, and is not listed in any standard reference books on Beswick. Nevertheless, this very high price shows what can happen when a small number of collectors in a specialist market compete to own a rare piece.

8.25in (21cm) high
£5,000-6,000   TEN

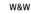

A Beswick 'Huntswoman' figurine, model 982, designed by Arthur Gredington, with gloss finish and factory marks to base.
1942-67   10.25in (26cm) high
£200-250   LOC

A Beswick 'Huntsman on Rearing Horse', model 868, designed by Arthur Gredington, with a dark chestnut horse, red jacket and factory marks to base.

1940-52   9.5in (24cm) high
£180-220   LOC

CERAMICS

A Beswick 'King Charles Spaniel Josephine of Blagreaves' figurine, model 2107B, designed by Arthur Gredington, with gloss finish.

1967-94   *7.5in (19cm) long*

£20-30   **SAS**

A Beswick 'Elephant And Tiger' figurine, model 1720, designed by Arthur Gredington, with a gloss finish, and circular printed mark.

1960-75   *11.75in (30cm) high*

£200-300   **SWO**

A CLOSER LOOK AT A BEATRIX POTTER CHARACTER FIGURINE

This is the rare, first model of Duchess, the second has her holding a pie rather than flowers and was produced from 1979-82.

When released, she was not popular with collectors or the buying public, so very few examples were sold at the time, making her hard to find today.

The value of this model varies widely depending on the location and demand at the time of sale – prices have ranged from £500 to over £2,000 during the past five to seven years.

The base has an oval shaped printed 'Beswick England' mark – those with circular marks are even rarer and were the earliest of this model ever produced.

A Beswick Beatrix Potter 'Duchess' figurine, model 1355, designed by Graham Orwell, with gloss finish and printed gold oval factory mark.

1955-67   *3.75in (9.5cm) high*

£1,000-1,500   **FLD**

A Beswick Beatrix Potter 'Benjamin Bunny' figurine, model 1105/3, third version with brown shoes, and ears and shoes tucked in, the base with printed factory mark.

Earlier models had arms extended with shoes held out and protruding ears, but as these parts were often broken the design was changed on later models.

c1980-2000   *4in (10cm) high*

£20-30   **SAS**

A Beswick Beatrix Potter 'Anna Maria' figurine, model 1851, designed by Albert Hallam, the base with printed brown five line mark.

1974-83

£50-70   **PC**

A Beswick Beatrix Potter 'Mr Alderman Ptolemy' figurine, model 2424, designed by Graham Tongue, with printed brown five line mark to base.

1974-1985

£25-35   **PC**

QUICK REFERENCE – BRIGLIN POTTERY

The Briglin Pottery was founded in central London in 1948 by Brigitte Appleby and Eileen Lewenstein. Each piece was potted and decorated by hand, with sgraffito and wax-resist techniques being used, often with a manganese oxide glaze. Colours tend towards earthy browns, beiges and creams, sometimes with a light blue, or greeny-blue. Patterns focus on the natural world, with stylisation being common and desirable to collectors. A white clay gave way to a more common red clay in the late 1950s. Pieces are generally marked with a 'BRIGLIN' impressed mark. Despite being highly successful in the 1960s and 70s, the pottery closed in 1990.

A 1970s Briglin vase, with wax-resist and manganese oxide black flowers with incised detail, the base impressed 'BRIGLIN'.
7.75in (19.5cm) high
£30-40   GC

A Briglin waisted cylindrical vase with wax-resist leaf design, the base with impressed 'BRIGLIN' mark.
9.75in (24.5cm) high
£60-80   GC

A Briglin baluster vase, with design of green leaves on a cream ground, the base impressed 'BRIGLIN'.
7.75in (19.5cm) high
£40-60   GC

A 1970s Briglin cylinder vase, with wax-resist design of a seeding flower in cream and blue glazes, the base impressed 'BRIGLIN'.
7.25in (18.5cm) high
£50-70   GC

A very large Briglin bowl, with wax-resist design of seeding country flowers, and covered with a transparent glaze, the base impressed 'BRIGLIN'.
12.75in (32cm) diam
£200-250   GC

A very large Briglin bowl, with wax-resist design of country flowers with a brushed brown glaze, and covered with a transparent glaze, the base inscribed 'BRIGLIN POTTERY AP'.

The 'AP' may stand for Alan Pett, a thrower at the London pottery. These bowls must have been among the largest pieces made at the pottery.
12.75in (32cm) diam
£200-250   GC

CERAMICS

QUICK REFERENCE

- The Carlton Works were established in Stoke-on-Trent in 1890 by Wiltshaw & Robinson. Pieces were produced under the name 'Carlton Ware' from 1894 and this became the company's name in 1958, although most production before this is generally known as Carlton Ware.
- In the 1920s and 1930s, Carlton Ware became known for its rich Art-Deco-styled lustre pieces, created in response to Wedgwood's more expensive Fairyland Lustre range.
- The factory also introduced a completely different style of ceramic in the 1930s, which became a mainstay of Carlton Ware for nearly two decades. This pastel-coloured, moulded range used flowers, leaves and fruit either as decorative motifs or as the main shape of the piece. Certain motifs,

such as 'Cherries', and colours are rare, as are some combinations. For example, 'Buttercup' is easy to find in yellow, but relatively rare in pink and consequently more desirable. As a large number of pieces were produced, condition is very important – inspect lids, rims and bases as these are often damaged. Look for boxed gift sets, and even empty boxes, as these add value.

- Carlton Ware went bankrupt in 1989, but the name and some moulds were bought by Francis Joseph in 1997, who continues to sell ceramics under the brand. There are Carlton Ware fakes on the market, so you should examine pieces closely and ensure the back stamp is appropriate for the item and period of manufacture.

A Carlton Ware embossed yellow and pink 'Waterlily' mug, the base impressed '1787'.

4.25in (11cm) high

£60-80   BEV

A Carlton Ware embossed yellow and green 'Waterlily' mug, the base with printed factory mark and impressed '1783'.

4.25in (11cm) high

£60-80   BEV

A Carlton Ware embossed pink 'Buttercup' mug, the base with printed marks and impressed '1585'.

This is a more desirable colour.

4.25in (11cm) high

£80-100   BEV

A Carlton Ware embossed yellow cabbage leaf milk jug, with printed factory mark and impressed '1524'.

4.25in (11cm) high

£80-120   BAD

A 1930s Carlton Ware embossed green and yellow 'Lily' teapot, the base with printed factory mark and impressed '1786'.

5.25in (13.5cm) high

£80-120   BAD

A CLOSER LOOK AT A CARLTON WARE BISCUIT BARREL

This is one of the rarest and most desirable items from the fruit and floral embossed ranges.

The geometric, Art Deco shape is unusual within the range, and is highly desirable.

This shape was only used for this biscuit jar and a small jam pot, and in Raspberry and Blackberry only.

Always check the corners, handles and lid for damage – note how the foot and knob on the lid are modelled as a raspberries.

A 1930s Carlton Ware large embossed yellow 'Apple Blossom' jug, the base with printed factory mark and impressed '1700/1'.

This the largest of three sizes.

14.5in (37cm) high

£200-300   BAD

A 1930s Carlton Ware Art Deco pink fruit embossed Raspberry biscuit jar, the base with factory marks and impressed '1565'.

5.5in (14cm) high

£200-250   BEV

A Carlton Ware Salad Ware embossed pink 'Buttercup' dish, the base with printed mark and impressed '1395'.

4.5in (11.5cm) long

£35-45   BAD

A Carlton Ware Salad Ware yellow embossed 'Buttercup' crescent dish, the base with printed factory mark and impressed '1529/3'.

7.5in (19cm) long

£35-45   BAD

A Carlton Ware embossed green 'Foxglove' handled basket, with printed and impressed marks to base.

10.25in (26cm) long

£80-120   BEV

A Carlton Ware yellow embossed 'Lily' Salad Ware toast rack, the base with printed marks and impressed '1861'.

4in (10cm) long

£80-120   BEV

A 1930s Carlton Ware 'Handcraft' plate, hand painted with a longboat, the back with printed and painted marks.

Introduced in 1928 and produced until the late 1930s, this entirely hand painted range is usually found with a matte finish. Colours tend to be bright, and the more Art Deco the pattern is, the more valuable it is likely to be.

10.5in (27cm) diam

£350-450   **WW**

A 1930s Carlton Ware 'Hollyhocks' bowl, pattern no.3973, printed and painted in colours and gilt on a green lustre ground, printed and painted marks.

£100-150

10.75in (27cm) wide

WW

A 1930s Carlton Ware 'Secretary Bird' twin-handled oval dish, pattern 4017, decorated on an orange lustre ground with gilded highlights.

The Japanese-inspired Secretary Bird pattern is scarce and sought after.

12in (30.5cm) wide

£200-300   **GHOU**

A 1930s Carlton Ware hand painted novelty 'Humpty Dumpty' toby jug.

These can also be found with musical mechanisms, but these are even rarer and can fetch up to £500-800.

7.5in (19cm) high

£300-500   **BAD**

A scarce 1930s Carlton Ware hand painted mushroom-shaped cruet set, with printed marks to base, lacking spoon.

Always examine all parts carefully as cracks or chips are common.

5in (12.5cm) diam

£150-200   **BEV**

A 1970s Carlton Ware orange owl money box, the base printed 'Carltonware made in England' and with trademark.

5in (12.5cm) high

£30-40   **CANS**

A 1970s Carlton Ware yellow-lime green lidded butter dish, with black printed mark to base.

5.75in (14.5cm) long

£18-22   **RET**

QUICK REFERENCE

- Clarice Cliff is one of the most desirable names in Art Deco ceramics. Prices can start as low as £50, but can rise into many thousands for rare and sought-after designs. Born in 1899 in Tunstall in the heart of the Staffordshire Potteries, Cliff began her career as an apprentice decorator at Linguard Webster & Co. in 1912, before joining A.J. Wilkinson in 1916.
- Her talents became obvious at Wilkinson, and the company's owner, Colley Shorter, gave Cliff her own studio in 1920 at the recently acquired Newport Pottery. There, she hand-painted defective blank wares with striking geometric or stylised floral patterns in bright colours, which covered the flaws. These developed into the now legendary 'Bizarre' series, launched in 1928.
- Neither 'Bizarre' (used until 1935) nor 'Fantasque' (used 1928-34) are range names, but are instead general titles, with patterns usually having their own names. Cliff trained a team of women, known as the 'Bizarre Girls' to produce these designs, which were applied to modern shapes.
- When evaluating desirability and value, consider the shape and size of the piece, the pattern and the colours used. Some patterns, and colourways within these patterns, are rarer than others. Orange tends to be more commonly found, while blue and purple are often rarer. Muted colours and more traditional floral designs are less sought after.
- In general, Cliff's brightly coloured, highly stylised Art Deco designs from 1928-c1934 are the most sought-after. If the shape is modern and Art Deco too, so much the better. Always look at the mark, and ensure that it is under the glaze. Beware as fakes do exist – experience of handling authentic pieces will help you to spot them.

A Clarice Cliff Bizarre 'Autumn Crocus' pattern Stamford shape milk jug and sugar bowl, with printed marks to base.

2.75in (7cm) high

£280-320   WW

A Clarice Cliff Bizarre 'Autumn Crocus' pattern Perth shape jug, printed mark to base and some wear to glaze.

5in (13cm) high

£80-120   WW

A Clarice Cliff Bizarre 'Blue Crocus' pattern ribbed beer tankard, with printed mark to base, minor scuffs to banding.

c1935   6.25in (16cm) high

£200-300   FLD

A pair of Clarice Cliff Bizarre 'Autumn Crocus' pattern square-section candlesticks, with 'Bizarre' and 'CROCUS' printed marks.

Candlesticks are comparatively scarce, and the corners are often chipped through use.

c1930   7.75in (20cm) high

£350-450   FLD

A Clarice Cliff Bizarre 'Autumn Crocus' pattern Isis shape vase, with large script printed mark.

c1929   9.75in (25cm) high

£750-950   FLD

A Clarice Cliff Fantasque Bizarre 'Pastel Melon' pattern Athens shape jug, with combined printed 'FANTASQUE' and 'Bizarre' mark.

c1930   *7in (18cm) high*

£350-450   **FLD**

A Clarice Cliff Fantasque 'Melon' pattern vase, shape 376.

7in (18cm) high

£800-1,200   **GHOU**

A CLOSER LOOK AT A CLARICE CLIFF MELON JUG

Melon was produced from 1930-32 in orange, green, red and pastel colourways – orange is the most common with pastel being rarer.

The pattern of stylised fruit may have been inspired by Cubist paintings, as well as the geometric Art Deco style of the time.

The Lotus jug (the handle is not seen here) is a very popular form and displays the pattern well. It tends to be hard to find.

Note how the shapes are outlined in yellow rather than black to give more emphasis to the coloured forms rather than the outlines.

A Clarice Cliff 'Pastel Melon' single-handled Lotus jug, with combined printed 'FANTASQUE' and 'Bizarre' mark, with a few minor paint scuffs.

c1931   *11.5in (29cm) high*

£800-1,200   **FLD**

A Clarice Cliff Fantasque 'Melon' pattern circular plate, with printed 'Fantasque' mark, few minor scuffs.

c1930   *10in (25.5cm) diam*

£120-180   **FLD**

A Clarice Cliff Fantasque 'Melon' pattern vase, shape no.358.

8in (20cm) high

£650-850   **GHOU**

A Clarice Cliff 'Green Melon' pattern octagonal plate, with printed 'Fantasque' mark and 'Lawleys' gold back stamp, with broken body and chips to rim.

Lawleys were a specialist retailer of ceramics who dealt with many leading ceramics factories.

c1930   *8in (20.5cm) high*

£60-90   **FLD**

A Clarice Cliff Bizarre 'Rhodanthe' pattern Tyrol shape bowl, with printed 'Bizarre' mark, and a few minor scuffs to decoration.
c1934   *4in (10cm) wide*
£480-520   **FLD**

QUICK REFERENCE – RHODANTHE PATTERN

Rhodanthe was introduced in 1934 and shows stylised trees with flower-like foliage and sinuous trunks and branches. It became very popular and took over from Crocus as Cliff's best-selling pattern. As this design was still produced after World War II, it is comparatively common today. It shows a move away from the typical Bizarre style – the pattern is not banded, geometric or heavily outlined. Also, the hand-painted colours were blended into each other in a process known as 'etching'. The most common colourway is shown here, with dominant orange tones. Variations in colour have different names – the pink Viscaria and the blue Aurea. Both are less common, Viscaria particularly so.

A Clarice Cliff Bizarre 'Rhodanthe' pattern Conical sugar sifter, with printed 'Bizarre' mark, restored chips.
c1934   *4in (10cm) wide*
£480-520   **FLD**

A Clarice Cliff Bizarre 'Aurea' Mei Ping vase, shape 14, with printed 'Bizarre' mark.
c1936   *8.75in (22.5cm) high*
£450-550   **FLD**

A Clarice Cliff Bizarre 'Rhodanthe' vase, shape 212, with Delecia glazed interior, and plain 'Claire Cliff' script printed mark.
c1935-6   *5.5in (14cm) high*
                          FLD
£350-450

A large Clarice Cliff Bizarre 'Aurea' pattern conical footed bowl, shape 383, with Delecia streaked glazed exterior, and painted green 'Clarice Cliff' and 'Bizarre' mark, chip to foot and some scratching.
9in (23cm) wide
£180-220   **FLD**

A Clarice Cliff Bizarre 'Viscaria' pattern Leda plate, with printed mark to underside.
9in (23cm) wide
£100-150   **GORL**

CERAMICS

A Clarice Cliff Fantasque Bizarre 'Pastel Autumn' pattern vase, shape 362, painted with a stylized tree and cottage landscape, with printed marks and light crazing to the glaze.
c1932   *8.25in (21cm) high*
£1,200-1,500   **FLD**

A CLOSER LOOK AT AN ORANGE AUTUMN WALL PLAQUE

Clarice Cliff's plaques were pressed from solid clay making them one of the most easily broken pieces – few have survived compared to the number made.

Made in 10.5in (25.5cm), 13in (33cm) and 18in (46cm) sizes, they display the pattern extremely well and are popular with collectors. The footrim was drilled for hanging.

Autumn was produced in many different colourways, with Red being the earliest and first made in 1931, and Pastel being scarcer. Variations abound.

A Clarice Cliff Bizarre 'Orange Autumn' large wall plaque, with printed 'Bizarre' mark.
c1932   *13in (33cm) diam*
£1,800-2,200   **FLD**

A Clarice Cliff 'Pastel Autumn' small pedestal nut bowl, shape 260, with combined 'FANTASQUE' and 'Bizarre' printed marks.
c1931   *2.25in (6cm) high*
£350-450   **FLD**

A Clarice Cliff Fantasque Bizarre 'Blue Autumn' large cauldron, with printed 'FANTASQUE' and 'Bizarre' marks, with a few minor scuffs.
c1931   *4.25in (11cm) high*
£350-450   **FLD**

A Clarice Cliff Bizarre 'Green Autumn' pattern flying swan flower block, shape 423, with a brightly coloured relief moulded bird, and printed 'Bizarre' mark.
c1931   *6.25in (16cm) high*
£400-600   **FLD**

A Clarice Cliff Bizarre 'Broth' globe vase, shape 370, with printed 'Bizarre' mark, with a few minor scuffs and light crazing to glaze.
c1930   *5.5in (14cm) high*
£1,200-1,800   **FLD**

A Clarice Cliff 'Cloud Flowers' vase, shape 896, the base with relief moulded script signature mark.

The cloud-like design recalls Chinese textiles, showing the breadth of Cliff's sources of inspiration. It is also sometimes known as Nemesia and can be found in other colours.

c1935   8.75in (22.5cm) high

£350-450   **FLD**

A Clarice Cliff Fantasque 'Comets' sandwich tray, shape 334, with printed 'Fantasque' mark, with minor scuffs.

This is a desirable and early abstract pattern.

c1929

£550-650   **FLD**

A Clarice Cliff Bizarre 'Delecia' range shape no.451 vase, with dripped glazes and printed marks.

8in (20.5cm) high

£180-220   **WW**

A Clarice Cliff 'Orange Erin' pattern rectangular Biarritz shape plate, with Royal Staffordshire 'Biarritz' mark, a few minor scuffs.

c1933   9in (23cm) wide

£300-400   **FLD**

A Clarice Cliff 'Green Erin' pattern circular plate, with printed 'Bizarre' mark.

c1933   9in (23cm) diam

£300-400   **FLD**

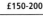

A Clarice Cliff Fantasque Bizarre 'Red Gardenia' pattern Coronet shape jug, with some fading.

7in (18cm) high

£150-200   **GHOU**

A Clarice Cliff 'Latona Dahlia' pattern fruit bowl, with 'Bizarre' and 'LATONA' printed marks.

c1931   7in (18cm) wide

£280-320   **FLD**

CERAMICS

A Clarice Cliff oval lily bowl, shape no.973, with printed marks to base.

Designed to hold flower bulbs, this shape was introduced in 1938 and produced until the late 1950s. Reputedly over 250,000 were sold.

9in (23cm) wide

£50-70 GHOU

A Clarice Cliff Bizarre nursery ware bowl, the rim modelled as a rabbit, with printed factory mark and wear to blue band.

8.5in (21.5cm) wide

£250-300 WW

A Clarice Cliff pipe holder, modelled as a small bird, with printed 'Clarice Cliff' script mark.

3in (7.5cm) high

£50-70 FLD

A Clarice Cliff tree stump planter, with two moulded budgerigars, and brown printed script signature, and small hairline crack to bowl.

10.75in (27.5cm) long

£45-55 FLD

A Clarice Cliff 'Circus' breakfast cup and saucer, with transfer-printed clown pattern designed by Laura Knight, and pink printed 'Laura Knight' signature and 'Bizarre' marks.

c1935

£200-250 FLD

ESSENTIAL REFERENCE - ART IN INDUSTRY

The influential 'Modern Art for the Table' exhibition held at Harrods department store, London in late 1934 aimed to showcase the work of leading artists in ceramic and glass. Dame Laura Knight's 'Circus' pattern was a central display and other contributors included Frank Brangwyn and Duncan Grant. All the earthenware was produced by Wilkinson's and unusually included Clarice's name alongside the artist's. Although many designs were shown again at the prominent Royal Academy 'Art In Industry' exhibition in 1935, they were not successful commercially and were withdrawn from sale.

A Clarice Cliff 'Circus' circular side plate, with transfer-printed clown pattern designed by Laura Knight, and pink printed 'Laura Knight' signature and 'Bizarre' marks, with two scuffs to banding.

c1935

6in (15cm) diam

£250-350 FLD

FIND OUT MORE...

Greg Slater and Jonathan Brough ' Comprehensively Clarice Cliff' . London: Thames & Hudson, 2005.

Sevi Guatelli, ' The Best of Clarice Cliff' . Edinburgh: Best 50 Limited, 2008; www.thebestofclaricecliff.com

A first edition Clarice Cliff 'Circus' circular side plate, with transfer-printed horse pattern designed by Laura Knight, and pink printed 'Laura Knight' signature and 'Bizarre' marks.

1934

6.75in (17cm) diam

£250-350 FLD

QUICK REFERENCE – CUPS & SAUCERS

- Cups and saucers dating from the 1860s to the 1930s have risen in desirability again. Their popularity as part of 19thC tableware sets fell sharply for a few years as fashions moved away from a chintzy, floral look. As such, even fine quality sets could often be found at auction for under £100. Today the story is different, with people mixing patterns and shapes to create 'harlequin' sets to use at tea parties, causing a renewal in collecting interest.
- Look out first for major makers by checking marks on the base, as this will usually indicate fine quality. Pieces by factories such as Royal Doulton, Coalport, Royal Worcester, Hammersley, Paragon and Shelley will typically be priced at the higher end of the market. Many of these names have large and loyal bands of collectors, ensuring prices remain high. Popular designer names such as Susie Cooper, Clarice Cliff and others will also command higher prices.

- Always look for signs of quality in the decoration. Many pieces have hand-painted details, often highlighted in gilt – a fact that surprises many considering the time and skill required to decorate by hand. Sets with finely detailed and well-executed patterns will be more desirable and valuable, as will those that have shapes or patterns that exemplify the style of the day – for example, the Art Deco style of the 1920s and 30s.
- Many of the most decorative examples with gilt interiors were intended for display rather than use. These 'cabinet' cups are also rising in desirability again, although not as sharply as examples that can be used. Always examine the pieces closely – items that were in regular use may have been damaged over time. Worn patterns or gilding, and particularly cracks and chips, will reduce desirability and value.

An Aynsley cup and saucer, with gilt rim.

Saucer 4.5in (11cm) diam

£30-50   MA

A 1920s Aynsley transfer and hand-painted teacup and saucer, decorated with orange flowers and cobalt and orange panels.

Saucer 5.25in (13.5cm) diam

£20-25   W&L

An Aynsley teacup and saucer, with pink transfer-printed flowers and yellow hand-painted butterfly handle, the back with printed marks.

Saucer 5.25in (13.5cm) diam

£100-150   BEV

An Aynsley bone china transfer-printed tea cup and saucer, with blue cornflower or love-in-a-mist flowers, and lavender scalloped rim, with yellow butterfly handle, the back with reg no.765788 for 1931.

Saucer 5.25in (13.5cm) diam

£120-160   BEV

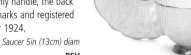

An Aynsley teacup and saucer, with yellow exterior, gilt rim and hand-painted butterfly handle, the back with printed marks and registered no.705789 for 1924.

Saucer 5in (13cm) diam

£120-180   BEV

A CLOSER LOOK AT AN AYNSLEY CUP & SAUCER

Note that the butterfly motif has been repeated on the inside of the cup as well – this is a rare and sought-after feature.

The butterfly handle is very well painted and detailed, with its legs and antennae painted onto the bowl.

Known as the 'Tulip' shape, the cup and saucer are moulded to represent petals or leaves.

Three colour examples, such as this with green, yellow and white, are more decorative, desirable and valuable.

An Aynsley 'Tulip' shape teacup and saucer, moulded and painted in white, yellow and green, and with hand-painted butterfly handle, the base with printed marks and registered no.765788 for 1931.

Saucer 5.25in (13.5cm) diam

£180-220 **BEV**

A 1920s Royal Bayreuth teacup and saucer, with transfer-printed sprays of flowers in panels, and green ground with gilt floral, scrolling and hatched pattern.

Saucer 5in (12.5cm) diam

£50-70 **BAD**

A Brown Westhead Moore & Co. Cauldon Ware cup and saucer, with a yellow scalloped border with scrolling birds and flower garlands.

Saucer 4.75in (12cm) diam

£70-90 **BEV**

A 1930s Burleigh 'Belvedere' shape teacup and saucer, with hand-painted green band and sprays of multicoloured flowers on a cream background, marked 'no.309992 MADE IN ENGLAND BELVEDERE REGD'.

Saucer 5.75in (14.5cm) diam

£30-50 **BEV**

A 1930s Burleigh Zenith shape teacup and saucer, with hand-painted 'Lemon Tree' pattern with blue border, the cup with angular and shaped handle, the base with printed marks and registered no.769495, for 1931.

This is a rare and desirable pattern, on a quintessential Art Deco shape.

5.75in (14.5cm) diam

£55-65 **BEV**

A 1930s Burleigh Ware Imperial shape teacup and saucer, with hand-painted floral and foliate design and shaped handle.

5.75in (14.5cm) diam

£30-40 **BEV**

QUICK REFERENCE – BURGESS & LEIGH

Founded in 1851 as Hulme & Booth, the company became Burgess & Leigh (later shortened to Burleigh) in 1877. It was known for toilet sets and tablewares until the 1920s, when the focus moved to tea sets and tablewares. During the 1920s and 1930s, it became associated with brightly hand-painted tea sets and jugs, which often had shaped or figural handles as on this teacup. Many shapes were designed by Ernest Bailey, with patterns by Harold Bennett. Charlotte Rhead also produced designs from 1926-31. The company remained in the family of the co-founding Leigh family until 1999, when it was rescued from bankruptcy by the Dorling family, and was renamed Burgess, Dorling & Leigh.

A 1930s Burleigh Ware Imperial shape teacup and saucer, designed by Ernest Bailey, with hand-painted garden scene with balustrade, the back painted with no.11516 and with printed factory and Australian registration marks.

5.75in (14.5cm) diam

£30-40   BEV

A W&L teacup and saucer, with transfer-printed foliate and floral pattern on a mottled blue band, with scrolling and panels, the back with factory mark and registered no.152134 for 1890.

5.5in (14cm) diam

£18-22   W&L

A Carltonware Rita shape teacup and saucer, decorated with green raised dots on a cream ground, and with gilt interior.

This pattern, no.4225, can be found in a number of different colour combinations including white on Rouge Royale.

Saucer 4.5in (11.5cm) diam

£80-120   BEV

A 1930s Carltonware blue 'Barge' pattern Rita shape cabinet cup and saucer, with gilt interior.

Exotic hand-painted patterns on lustre grounds were first introduced in the 1920s.

Saucer 4.5in (11.5cm) diam

£100-150   BEV

A 1920s Carltonware yellow 'Mikado' pattern coffee can and saucer, with gilt interior, with 'W&R' printed mark.

The presence of the Wiltshaw & Robinson mark indicates that this is an early piece from the 1920s.

Saucer 4.25in (10.5cm) diam

£80-120   BEV

A Coalport quatrefoil-shaped cabinet teacup and saucer, with gilt interior, with panels of red with raised applied gilt with turquoise glazed dots, and hand-painted landscapes, with some wear.

Saucer 4.75in (12cm) wide

£80-120   BAD

A Copeland Spode cup and saucer, of scalloped form, with hand-painted and transfer-printed flowers inside and out, gilt scallop edged rim and reeded bodies, with printed mark and painted mark '571'.

Saucer 4.75in (12cm) diam

£40-60   BEV

CERAMICS

A Davenport Imari-style hand-painted and transfer-printed teacup and saucer, with gilt highlights.

Imari is the name given to a type of porcelain made at Arita in Japan, and exported via the port of Imari. Cobalt blue, red and gilt are characteristic colours, often arranged in panels containing stylised natural motifs.

c1880s

Saucer 5.5in (14cm) diam

£60-80   BEV

A 1920s Crown Staffordshire teacup and saucer, with hand-painted and transfer-printed green mottled rim and pagoda on a cliff design, and with black handle.

Saucer 5.5in (14cm) diam

£30-35   W&L

A 1930s Royal Doulton hand-painted 'Aspen' pattern teacup and saucer.

The style of this tree, cliff and sea landscape was clearly inspired by Clarice Cliff's landscape patterns. However, note that the shape was not, being much more traditional.

5.25in (13.5cm) diam

£25-35   BEV

A 1930s Royal Doulton Art Deco 'Deluxe' pattern teacup and saucer, with hand-painted green and black geometric design with silver details.

This set is typically Art Deco in style, from the conical shape of the cup, to the angular handle and geometric pattern in light green and black and picked out in silver.

Saucer 5.5in (14cm) diam

£70-100   BAD

An Art Deco Fielding's Crown Devon fully hand-painted cup and saucer, decorated with arrows and sun design on a beige ground, the back with printed mark and painted 'A195'.

Saucer 4.5in (11.5cm) diam

£75-85   BEV

A Foley cup and saucer, with transfer-printed chintz pattern on a green ground, the base painted 'V1770' and printed 'English Bone China FB7 '.

c1932 5.5in (14cm) diam

£30-40   BEV

A Foley China octagonal cup and saucer, with blue transfer-printed pattern of urns and scrolling vines, the back with printed factory mark, painted '10024' and with registered no.447136 for December 1904.

c1895-97   5.25in (13.5cm) diam

£55-65   W&L

A Foley Bone China 'Montrose' pattern teacup and saucer, with blue panels with pheasant and gold scrolling pattern, and sprays of pink roses, with shaped and gilded handle.

Saucer 5.75in (14.5cm) diam

£15-20 **W&L**

A Grafton China teacup and saucer, with hand-painted orange four-leaf clovers and clumps of primroses amid trees, the back with printed marks and painted '5432' pattern number.

5.5in (14cm) diam

£20-25 **W&L**

A CLOSER LOOK AT A ROYAL WINTON TEACUP AND SAUCER

Royal Winton became renowned for their transfer-printed chintz wares after they developed a process allowing the transfer to be applied to a complex curving surface.

Chintzware was inspired by paisley and similar patterned textiles being imported during the 19thC. It enjoyed two heights of popularity, during the 1930s and the 1950s. The shape and mark can often help date a piece, with this ornate handle signifying an early date.

Hazel is a desirable and comparatively scarce pattern. Other patterns with black backgrounds include 'Black Crocus', 'Cromer' and James Kent's 'Florita'.

A 1930s Grimwades Royal Winton chintzware teacup and saucer, with transfer-printed 'Hazel' pattern and printed marks to reverse.

5.75in (14.5cm) diam

£55-65 **W&L**

An A.B. Jones & Sons Ltd Royal Grafton Bone China light blue transfer-printed cup and saucer, with scrolling rim, decorated with beige/gold diagonal leaf shapes containing sprays of pink and purple roses.

Saucer 5.5in (14cm) diam

£20-25 **W&L**

A Hammersley scalloped edge teacup and saucer, with ornate handle and transfer-printed and hand-painted scene of flowers in front of trellis, with printed marks to base.

6in (15cm) diam

£25-35 **W&L**

A Hammersley & Co. cylindrical coffee can and saucer, with floral gilt border and large pink roses.

1900-18 *Saucer 4.5in (11.5cm) diam*

£45-55 **BEV**

A Haviland & Co. Limoges teacup and saucer, with moulded panels and transfer-printed blue cornflowers and corn ears.

1876-79   Saucer 4.75in (12cm) diam

£20-30   **BEV**

A George Jones & Sons 'Abbey 1790' blue and white transfer-printed teacup and saucer, with printed marks to reverse.

Saucer 5.75in (14.5cm) diam

£30-40   **BEV**

A C.T. Maling cup and saucer, with pink fringed gilt scrolls, transfer-printed pink roses, with printed tower mark and painted 'A3122/4'. c1895 Saucer

5.5in (14cm) diam

£30-50   **BAD**

A Midwinter Fashion shape cup and saucer, with transfer-printed 'Bali H'ai' pattern on saucer, designed by John Russell in 1960.

Saucer 4.75in (12cm) wide

£15-18   **RET**

A Noritake Imari-style teacup and saucer, decorated with orange chrysanthemums and foliage in panels, with gilt detailing, the back with printed leaf marks.

This is both an early mark and an early pattern based on traditional Japanese ceramics, but modified for Western tastes.

c1908   Saucer 5.25in (13.5cm) diam

£30-40   **W&L**

A Minton Haddon Hall pattern ribbed teacup and saucer, designed by John Wadworth, pattern B4451, with green vines with pink and blue flowers, with printed mark to back.

The double 'S' mark through the factory mark on the back indicates that this was a factory second. Other factories, such as Royal Doulton, score marks through with lines. Be aware of how factories identify seconds, as they will never be as desirable or valuable as first quality pieces in the same condition.

Saucer 4.5in (11.5cm) diam

£18-22   **W&L**

A 1980s Paragon teacup and saucer, with the transfer-printed and hand-painted 'Rockingham' pattern of floral sprays surrounded by a burgundy border with gold scrolling patterns.

6in (15cm) diam

£22-28   **W&L**

A Paragon double-handled teacup and saucer, with transfer-printed sprays of flowers in panels surrounded by gold flowers on a burgundy background, with scrolling patterns around, the back with printed marks.

c1939   5.75in (14cm) diam

£20-25   **W&L**

A CLOSER LOOK AT A SHELLEY CUP AND SAUCER

Produced from 1930-33 only, Shelley's Vogue shape is one of the most desirable and valuable Art Deco teacup forms.

The solid handle caused some problems for buyers as it was difficult to hold, leading to the similar Eve shape, with an open handle, being introduced in 1932.

The geometric, footed conical shape with a triangular handle is quintessentially Art Deco.

The bright 'Sunray' pattern makes this example even more desirable – Art Deco patterns on Art Deco shapes are highly sought after.

A 1930s Paragon Art Deco hand-painted china cup and saucer, decorated with yellow crocuses, the base with registration no.766514 for 1931.

Saucer 5.25in (13.5cm) diam

£30-40   **BEV**

A 1930s Shelley Art Deco Vogue shape teacup and saucer, with the hand-painted 'Sunray' pattern, no.11742, the base with printed factory mark and registered design no.756538 for 1930.

5.5in (14cm) diam

£80-120   **BEV**

A 1930s Shelley scalloped octagonal Queen Anne shape teacup and saucer, with hand-painted and transfer-printed foxglove and grey tall trees pattern and blue rim, the base with printed marks and registered no.723404 for 1926.

This popular shape was produced from 1926-33, and again in the 1950s, and can be found with over 170 different patterns.

Saucer 5.25in (13.5cm) wide

£40-60   **BAD**

A 1920s-30s Rosenthal teacup and saucer, with the transfer-printed 'Donatello' pattern of flowers and a gilt scrolling border.

4.25in (11cm) diam

£55-65   **BEV**

An R.H. & S.L. Plant 'Tuscan China' teacup and saucer, with hand-painted and transfer-printed pattern of foxgloves, flowers and a garden wall.

5.5in (14cm) diam

£20-25   **W&L**

CERAMICS

An R.H. & S.L. Plant Ltd 'Tuscan China' trio set, decorated with a transfer-printed and hand-painted pattern of garlands and plums, with a black edged rim.

Saucer 6.75in (17cm) diam

£22-28   W&L

A late 1930s R.H. & S.L. Plant 'Tuscan China' teacup and saucer, with transfer-printed and hand-painted flowers and blue rim, the base with printed marks and registered no.771590 for 1932.

5.75in (14.5cm) diam

£20-25   W&L

A late 19thC H.M. Williamson & Sons 'Kaiser' pattern teacup and saucer, with hand-painted and transfer-printed scrolling and mottled pattern with blue, yellow and pink flowers, with 'W & Sons' printed marks.

Saucer 5.25in (13.5cm) diam

£18-22   W&L

A Royal Worcester armorial cup and saucer, decorated with gilded panels containing a coat of arms, a monogram, butterflies and flower sprays, printed marks and date codes, the saucer with a restored stress crack.

1895   Saucer 6.25in (16cm) diam

£55-65   WW

A 1930s Sampson Smith Ltd 'Wetley China' cup and saucer, with hand-painted pattern of irises and blue rim, the back with printed marks and registered no.731211 for 1927.

Saucer 4.25in (11cm) diam

£30-50   BEV

A 1920s Royal Worcester cabinet teacup and saucer, with hand-painted flowers and transfer-printed green bows and flowers, with gilt interior, with printed factory mark.

Saucer 3.75in (9.5cm) diam

£80-120   BEV

A Royal Worcester teacup and saucer, pattern no.333, decorated with blue Classical panels and laurel rim.

Saucer 5in (13cm) diam

£30-40   W&L

QUICK REFERENCE

- Founded in 1815 by John Doulton, Martha Jones and John Watts in Lambeth, south London, Doulton initially produced utilitarian ceramics, such as chimney pots and pipes. The company began producing decorative wares from around 1871. Many of these pieces were designed and decorated by students from the nearby Lambeth School of Art. Look for the typical motifs and artists' monograms of notable artists, including Lambeth-trained sisters Florence and Hannah Barlow, and brothers Arthur and George Tinworth. These 'Doulton Lambeth' pieces included stoneware, which was often made in the Art Nouveau style, a 'faience' range, which featured naturalistic hand painting, and a 'Silicon' ware range.
- In 1877, Doulton took over the Pinder, Bourne & Co. factory in Burslem, Staffordshire, which produced earthenware and bone china. Its name was changed to Doulton and Company Ltd in 1882, and the company soon became known for fine porcelain. The title 'royal' was granted in 1901 by Edward VII and 'Royal Doulton' marks appeared in 1902. The Lambeth factory closed in 1956, but production continues at Burslem.
- The production of figures, for which Royal Doulton is now well known, took off in 1913, under the direction of modeller Charles Noke. These figures were all given an individual 'HN' number, after Harry Nixon, then manager of the painting department. More than 4,000 of these numbers have subsequently been assigned to different models and colourways, many of which were designed by Leslie Harradine. In general, the most desirable figures are those produced for a short time only, usually before WWII, particularly if finely modelled and in a rare colourway.
- Vases are often worth more than bowls or jardinières. Pairs are more desirable than singles or matched pairs. Those in a High Victorian style typical of the factory and period, like the piece shown bottom right, may be worth investing in as prices are lower than 10 years ago and quality is high.
- Condition is important, particularly with figures, as damage reduces value considerably, so check all over for chips, scratches and cracks. Over the past decade, value and demand for Doulton pieces have declined, though the finest pieces, particularly stoneware and very rare figurines, are still sought after. Now may, therefore, be a good time to buy, as a potential revival in the future would cause prices to rise.

A Doulton Lambeth stoneware ovoid vase, by Hannah Barlow, sgraffito-decorated with ponies and sheep in a landscape with oxide tint between repeat carved foliate borders in tan and tonal blue, impressed and incised marks.

10.5in (27cm) high

£600-900　　　　　**FLD**

A Doulton Lambeth stoneware ovoid vase, by Hannah Barlow, sgraffito-decorated with ponies and sheep in a landscape setting, between carved foliate borders, with impressed and incised marks, restored neck.

10.5in (27cm) high

£200-300　　　　　**FLD**

A pair of Doulton Lambeth stoneware pedestal vases, by Louisa Edwards, carved with a stylised Classical-inspired stiff leaf design within repeat borders, the base with impressed and incised marks.

11in (27.5cm) high

£500-700　　　　　**FLD**

A Doulton Lambeth vase, by Hannah Barlow, sgraffito-decorated with a deep band of ponies and cattle with oxide glaze between carved borders with a repeat palmette design, impressed and incised marks.

11in (28cm) high

£600-900　　　　　**FLD**

A Doulton Lambeth stoneware vase, by Elisa Simmance, incised and applied with scrolling flowers and foliage with beadwork decoration, the base with impressed mark, incised monogram, damaged.

18.5in (47cm) high

£150-200　　　　　**WW**

CERAMICS

A pair of Doulton Lambeth stoneware vases, by Hannah Barlow, incised with a continuous band of horses between stiff and scrolling leaf collars, the bases with incised marks.

9.25in (23.5cm) high

£700-1,000   **FLD**

A pair of Doulton Lambeth waisted and footed vases, bearing monograms for Frank Butler, Ernest Bishop and Elizabeth Atkins, and incised '524' and '523', decorated with stylised, entwined foliage and flower heads.

1879   *10.25in (26cm) high*

£300-500   **HALL**

A CLOSER LOOK AT A DOULTON VASE

The vase was decorated by Hannah Barlow (1851-1916), who is celebrated for her lively and life-like animal designs.

Barlow used the sgrafitto technique, where a sharp point scratches a design into the wet clay – the body is then wiped with an oxide stain, which settles in the lines to highlight them.

It is an unusually large size, and would have cost a considerable sum in its day, making it rare today.

The price would have more than doubled if it was part of an original, matching pair.

A Doulton Lambeth stoneware floor vase, by Hannah Barlow, decorated with a deep sgraffito band of sheep in a highland setting with oxide tint between carved and tube-line foliate borders, the base with incised and impressed marks.

18in (46cm) high

£800-1,200   **FLD**

A pair of Doulton Lambeth stoneware vases, by Hannah Barlow, each incised with a continuous band of cows in pasture between stiff and scrolling leaf collars, the bases with incised marks.

9.25in (23.5cm) high

£700-1,000   **FLD**

A pair of Doutlon Lambeth vases, by George Tinworth, incised with scrolling and raised beads, on a shaded brown glaze, signed with initials on the body, one with a firing crack.

11.75in (30cm) diam

£600-800   **SWO**

A Victorian Doulton Lambeth stoneware vase, by Emily Stormer, decorated overall with raised rosettes, beading and stylised leaves, impressed marks and signature to base.

6in (15cm) high

£400-600   **DUK**

A Royal Doulton 'Brangwyn Ware' slender ovoid vase, designed by Frank Brangwyn, numbered 'D5081', incised with stylised leaves and buds, the base with printed mark, moulded '7936'.

Sir Frank William Brangwyn (1867-1956) was a progressive artist, illustrator, and designer, who was a member of the Royal Academy and the Royal Watercolour Society.

11.5in (29.5cm) high

£200-300   DN

A CLOSER LOOK AT A ROYAL DOULTON VASE

The Titanian range used titanium oxide to give a green or blue glaze ranging from light grey-blue to a deep royal blue – it is typically speckled, cloudy or streaked.

Birds are typical motifs, as are Oriental figures, and the treatment was used by Harry Tittensor, Harry Allen and other notable decorators.

This range was produced from 1915-c1930. Look out for Egpyptian motifs inspired by the discovery of Tutankhamun's tomb in 1922 as these fetch higher sums than birds.

Bases are generally marked with the factory mark and also the name of the range.

A Royal Doulton blue 'Titanian' cylindrical vase, decorated and gilded with a perched peacock and peahen, with printed mark to base.

10.25in (26cm) high

£400-600   DA&H

A Royal Doulton Veined Flambé vase, the ovoid body decorated with cobalt over red glazes, numbered '1622'.

15.75in (40cm) high

£150-250   FLD

A Royal Doulton porcelain twin-handled ovoid vase, with transfer-printed scene titled 'Ophelia', and printed factory mark to base.

8.25in (21cm) high

£70-100   SAS

A Royal Doulton bottle neck bulbous jug, of green ground with incised leaf decoration in brown and incised initials 'JB', with impressed mark to base with decorator's initials 'MVM'.

9in (23cm) high

£250-300   LOC

A Royal Doulton 'Titanian' vase, painted with a young coal tit on a green ground, signed 'H. Allen' for Harry Allen.

Although this example is hand-painted, not all Titanian wares were – many were transfer-printed and highlighted in gilt.

3.5in (9cm) high

£200-300   LT

A Royal Doulton 'Titanian' large bowl, the mottled grey-green ground decorated with gilt exotic birds on branches of chrysanthemums, with jewelled rim with additional floral sprays.

14.5in (37cm) diam

£450-550   **LT**

A Royal Doulton plate, decorated with a portrait of an Art Nouveau maiden, the back with impressed and printed marks.

9.25in (23.5cm) diam

£70-100   **WW**

A Royal Doulton 'John Peel' loving cup, with fox and whip handles, numbered 293 from a limited edition of 500, moulded on one side with figures, on the other with hounds.

1923   *9in (23cm) high*

£400-600   **BE**

A Royal Doulton Robin Hood loving cup, designed by Charles Noke and Harry Fenton, numbered 393 from a limited edition of 600, relief decorated with scenes in Sherwood Forest, with printed marks to base.

Introduced in 1938, this was part of a range of limited edition jugs or cups produced from 1930-38.

8.5in (21.5cm) high

£650-750   **LT**

A CLOSER LOOK AT A DOULTON CHARACTER JUG

This example can be identified as a prototype rather than a variation as the base is printed ' Design Original Sample and Decorating Sample 1' .

The handle on this prototype is modelled slightly differently to the production piece, and has the Flag of St. George to the reverse of the Union Jack.

The production model had a beige, not green, balaclava, the coat was brown not buff, and the face was painted differently.

Prices for trials and unique pieces have remained strong, despite the general downturn in the Doulton market.

A Royal Doulton large 'Bacchus' character jug, D6499, designed by Max Henk, with rare City of Stoke-on-Trent Jubilee Year backstamp.

1959   *7in (18cm) high*

£700-1,000   **TOV**

A Royal Doulton prototype 'Captain Scott of the Antarctic' large character jug, similar to D7116, wearing olive green balaclava and buff coat, with printing to base.

7in (18cm) high

£3,000-5,000   **LT**

A Royal Doulton 'King Charles' figure, HN404, designed by Charles Noke and Harry Tittensor, with an unusual buff base, the base with printed green mark and initialled 'PS'.

Note the large size of this desirable figurine, which is valuable in all three of its variations.

1920-51	16.75in (42.5cm) high
£750-950	**TEN**

A Royal Doulton 'Sir Walter Raleigh' figure, HN1751, designed by Leslie Harradine, with printed marks to base.

1936-49	12.25in (31cm) high
£400-500	**A&G**

A Royal Doulton 'Vice Admiral Lord Nelson' figure, HN3489, designed by Alan Maslankowski, numbered 351 from a limited edition of 950, with certificate.

1993	12.5in (31.5cm) high
£500-700	**LT**

A Royal Doulton 'The Moor' large figurine, HN3642, with a flambé glaze, designed by Charles Noke in 1929.

1994-95	17.25in (44cm) high
£800-1,200	**FLD**

A CLOSER LOOK AT A ROYAL DOULTON FIGURINE

Figures produced for long periods of time are usually the most affordable and have also have fallen in value recently, as so many exist.

This example has a grey skirt, violet blouse and green and purple tartan shawl, all of which are different to the standard production model.

The biggest difference between this and the standard model is the fact that she is meant to be a balloon seller, but here she has no balloons.

She has a hairline crack to her skirt, but this does not deter collectors who are keen to collect as many rare variations as possible.

A Royal Doulton 'In the Stocks' figure, HN1474, designed by Leslie Harradine, some restoration.

1931-38	5in (12.5cm) high
£600-800	**LT**

A Royal Doulton 'Biddy Penny Farthing' figure, HN1843 without balloons, designed by Leslie Harradine (1938-present).

	9in (23cm) high
£2,000-3,000	**LT**

CERAMICS

A Royal Doulton 'Pierette' figure, HN1749, designed by Leslie Harradine.

Although she can also be found with a red skirt, (HN1391), values are roughly the same.

1936-49   9.5in (24cm) high

£600-800   LT

A Royal Doulton protoype 'Charity' figure, HN3087, designed by Eric Griffiths, with a different purple blanket and yellow dress, Lawley's in a limited edition of 9,500 for the NSPCC.

1987   8.5in (21.5cm) high

£80-120   SAS

A Royal Doulton protoype 'Faith' figure, HN3082, designed by Eric Griffiths, with a different coloured pink and red coat, commissioned by Lawley's in a limited edition of 9,500 for the NSPCC.

8.5in (21.5cm) high

£80-120   SAS

A Royal Doulton 'Lambing Time' figure, HN1890, designed by W.M. Chance, with printed marks to base.

1938-81   9.25in (23.5cm) high

£35-45   SAS

A Royal Doulton 'Gandalf' figurine, HN2911, with blue cloak, designed by D. Lyttleton, from the Middle Earth series.

1980-84   7in (18cm) high

£40-60   PC

A Royal Doulton 'The Homecoming' figure, HN3295, and a 'Welcome Home' figure, HN3299, designed by A. Hughes from the Children of the Blitz series, both numbered 1944 from a limited edition of 9,500.

1990-91   *Tallest 8.5in (21.5cm) high*

£150-200   HT

A Royal Doulton 'The Boy Evacuee' figure, HN3202, and a 'The Girl Evacuee' figure, HN3203, designed by A. Hughes from the Children of the Blitz series, both numbered 7809 from a limited edition of 9,500.

1989   *Tallest 8.25in (21cm) high*

£250-350   HT

A Royal Doulton Archives Collection 'T'ang Horse' figurine, BA25, with flambé glaze, designed by Alan Maslankowski from a limited edition of 250 from the Burslem Artwares series.
2001   *10.5in (27cm) high*
£250-300   **FLD**

A Royal Doulton Archives Collection 'Hebei Goat', BA36, in a flambé glaze, designed by Alan Maslankowski from a limited edition of 250 from the Burslem Artwares Collection.
2002   *10.5in (26.5cm) high*
£200-250   **FLD**

QUICK REFERENCE - DOULTON FLAMBÉ GLAZE

The ancient Chinese 'sang-de-boeuf' glaze was much admired by John Slater and Charles Noke, who attempted to copy it in the 1890s. Cuthbert Bailey joined Doulton in 1901 and Bernard Moore, in 1902. Together they made a breakthrough and their results won prizes when first exhibited at the St Louis World's Fair in 1904, and the glaze is still popular and desirable today. Animals are highly sought after, particularly those designed by Noke. This is the largest elephant from a series of three, and also the most valuable.

A Royal Doulton frog, with a flambé Sung glaze, mottled crimson, green, yellow glazes, impressed '1162'.

The Sung glaze is highly sought after, particularly in combination with the flambé glaze. This shape is different from the standard frog numbered HN1162, more closely resembling HN905. This combination also suggests an early date.
                          4.5in (11.5cm) wide
£3,200-3,800   **LT**

A Royal Doulton large elephant, HN1121, with flambé glaze and trunk down, designed by Charles Noke.
c1938-57   *13in (33cm) wide*
£2,000-3,000   **LT**

A Royal Doulton 'Lop Eared Rabbit', HN1165B, with flambé and Sung glazes, the base impressed '1165B' and dated.
1923   *4in (10cm) long*
£3,000-4,000   **LT**

A Royal Doulton 'Lion on rock' figurine, HN2641, designed by Charles Noke from the Prestige series.
1952-92
                          10.25in (26cm) wide
£150-250   **FLD**

A Royal Doulton 'Bulldog with Tam O'Shanter & Haversack', HN153, designed by an unknown modeller, and with khaki glaze and printed registered no.663408 for 1918, one fore paw re-glued and chipped.

The values for these wartime commemoratives have fallen, and continue to do so, as highly accurate, very good quality reproductions are being made. Look out for the examples in the Titanian glaze, as values for these are holding strong.
1918-c1925
£250-300   **DN**

QUICK REFERENCE

- The Fulper Pottery Co. was founded in 1814 in Flemington, New Jersey by Samuel Hill. It operated until 1935, when it was acquired by Stangl. It initially produced utilitarian wares, introducing art pottery in 1909. Wares were slip-moulded and Fulper became renowned for its varied range of rich glazes.
- Their first art pottery line, produced from 1909 until WWI, was known as 'Vasecraft'. Many forms were Germanic in their solid and architectural feel, and glazes were of a particularly high quality. Production from this early period is usually the most sought-after and valuable.
- After c1914, shapes became more curved, with inspiration drawn from Oriental forms. Glaze quality began to deteriorate gradually, particularly during the late 1920s. From the late 1920s until the factory closed, the Art Deco movement influenced forms, and glazes were of considerably poorer quality.
- Bodies also became lighter in weight over time, and although heavy examples are not always better quality, light examples are almost always lower quality. Always consider the glaze as every piece was glazed by a skilled decorator, making each unique. The more complex and interesting the glaze and shape, the better the piece is likely to be.

A Fulper two-handled vase, covered in Copperdust Crystalline and Mirrored Black flambé glaze, with paper label over vertical mark.

9.75in (25cm) high

£350-450   **DRA**

A Fulper corseted two-handled vase, with frothy Copperdust Crystalline glaze over Flemington Green flambé, with vertical mark.

9.5in (24cm) high

£250-350   **DRA**

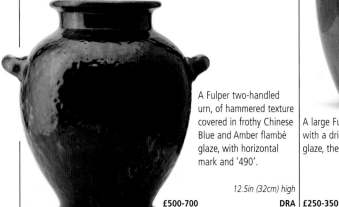

A Fulper two-handled urn, of hammered texture covered in frothy Chinese Blue and Amber flambé glaze, with horizontal mark and '490'.

12.5in (32cm) high

£500-700   **DRA**

A large Fulper bullet vase, covered with a dripped Cat's Eye flambé glaze, the base with factory mark.

10in (25.5cm) high

£250-350   **DRA**

A Fulper baluster vase, covered in a fine frothy Cucumber Matt glaze, with vertical mark.

12in (30.5cm) high

£700-900   **DRA**

A Fulper melon-shaped vase, covered in a Cat's Eye flambé glaze, with vertical mark.

7in (18cm) high

£300-400 DRA

A CLOSER LOOK AT A FULPER VASE

At 16in (40.5cm) high, this is a large piece, with superb visual impact.

The form was inspired by Chinese ceramics, and can be dated to a period from the late 1910s to the mid-1920s.

Fulper is known for its complex, specially produced glazes that vary from being 'mirrored' to mottled to micro-crystalline – the former and the latter effects are particularly desirable.

Although some examples from this period do not bear the highest quality glazes, this example is very well-glazed.

A tall Fulper ovoid vase, covered in Cucumber Crystalline glaze, the base with raised racetrack mark.

16in (40.5cm) high

£1,500-2,500 DRA

A large Fulper squat vessel, covered in brown crystalline glaze dripping over Mustard Matt, small chip to foot ring, with vertical mark.

10in (25.5cm) wide

£800-1,200 DRA

An early Fulper lamp base, covered in Mouse Grey to blue flambé glaze, the base with '17' ink stamp.

Fulper lamps were only made for a short period from c1910-15, making them scarce today. They were produced under the strictest production standards, meaning quality was high. Lamps with their original shades with glass inserts are particularly prized, even more so if they have geometric or natural motifs.

17.25in (44cm) high

£800-1,200 DRA

A rare Fulper factory lamp base, in Cat's Eye flambé glaze, with vertical mark and numbered '107'.

11.25in (28.5cm) high

£300-400 DRA

A Fulper cat figure, in White Matt glaze, with horizontal mark.

8.5in (21.5cm) high

£500-700 DRA

QUICK REFERENCE – HORNSEA

Hornsea Pottery was founded by Colin and Desmond Rawson in a large house in East Riding, Yorkshire in 1949. In 1954, the successful pottery moved into an old brick factory. Around this time, they also began to employ designers, including John Clappison, the son of an investor in the company. Hornsea's success grew into the 1960s with ranges such as 'Home Decor' (introduced 1960-62), 'Slipware' (introduced 1963), 'Heirloom' (1967-87), and others, all designed by Clappison, who was appointed chief designer in 1958 and continued to be so until the company closed in 1984. Some ranges, such as 'Heirloom', were so successful that the many examples on the market mean that prices are low. Rarer ranges and unusual colourways or shapes tend to fetch higher prices.

A mid-late 1960s Hornsea grey glazed 'Slipware' jardiniere, designed by John Clappison in 1963, the base with printed mark.

10in (25.5cm) wide

£70-100   GC

A mid-late 1960s Hornsea Mustard glazed 'Slipware' jardiniere, designed by John Clappison in 1963, the base with printed mark.

10in (25.5cm) wide

£70-100   GC

A mid-late 1960s Hornsea mauve glazed 'Slipware' baluster vase, designed by John Clappison in 1963, the base with printed mark.

Always examine these appealing period pieces all over as the glaze can craze easily, and small chips or glaze flakes are often found on the rim or base. Both factors devalue a piece considerably.

9.25in (23.5cm) high

£60-80   GC

A mid-late 1960s Hornsea light green glazed 'Slipware' baluster vase, designed by John Clappison in 1963, the base with printed mark.

7.5in (19cm) high

£40-60   GC

A mid-late 1960s Hornsea light blue glazed 'Slipware' squat baluster vase, designed by John Clappison in 1963, the base with printed mark.

4in (10cm) high

£20-30   GC

A small Hornsea pottery 'White Bud' jardinière, from the Home Decor range designed by John Clappison c1961, with moulded spot design.

9.5in (24cm) wide

£35-45   SAS

A Hornsea Pottery dish, in the form of a Viking longboat, from the Home Decor range designed by John Clappison c1961, with a cream glaze and printed Studiocraft marks.

c1965   11in (28cm) wide
£50-70   MHT

A Hornsea Pottery 'Coastline' pattern sugar bowl, with white crackle glaze on a black ground.

The curving asymmetric form is typical of the 1950s, and the pattern is very similar to the 'Cortina' range released in 1955 by West German factory Jasba.

c1957   3.35 in (8.5cm) high
£18-22   PC

A Hornsea Pottery cruet set on tray, comprising a salt and pepper shaker, mustard pot and oil bottle, lacking mustard-spoon, the base with black printed factory marks.

9in (23cm) long
£40-50   RET

A Hornsea black and white cruet set, on a black dish, designed by John Clappison.

c1962   5.25in (13.5cm) high
£10-15   TCM

A Hornsea Pottery tapering vase with moulded stylised foliate design on a grey ground, with printed Hornsea mark, and impressed '422'.

6.75in (17cm) high
£28-32   RET

A late 1960s Hornsea Pottery 'Springtime' pattern white square box with beige impressed flower design and turquoise lid, designed by John Clappison in 1964, the base impressed '280', and with printed factory and 'SPRINGTIME' marks.

3.25in (8cm) high
£18-22   RET

A rare 1960s Hornsea Pottery 'Studiocraft' waisted vase, designed by John Clappison in 1966, with screen-printed stylised leaves and printed marks to base.

This is a very rare range and is not connected with the earlier Studio Craft range of 1960-62.

7.75in (19.5cm) high
£40-60   RET

CERAMICS

QUICK REFERENCE

- Addis Emmett Hull founded the A.E. Hull Pottery in Crooksville, Ohio in 1905. Initially he produced utilitarian stonewares, and from 1907, dinnerwares, following the purchase of the Acme Pottery Co. Although some decorative vases were produced in the 1920s, it is the colourful matte glazed art pottery introduced in the 1930s that is collected today.

- Using moulds, wares were mass-produced with floral patterns. Although gloss glazes were produced, glazes are typically soft and matte, and were sprayed on to give a graduated effect. Colours are typically light and pastel-based, although a vibrant pink is commonly found.

- In 1950, the pottery burnt down and was rebuilt, opening again in 1952. The new machinery could not replicate the matte glazes, so the company was forced to concentrate on gloss glazes. By the late 1970s, the focus of production had moved to dinnerware, which was made until the company closed in 1986.

- Look out for well-moulded forms with even, graduated effects to the glazes. Glazes should be free of crazing. Inspect pieces all-over for any damage such as cracks or chips as this reduces value considerably. Pieces produced before 1950 tend to be the most desirable, with sought-after ranges including 'Calla Lily', 'Woodland' and 'Tokay'.

A Hull 'Water Lily' pattern double-handled vase, in pink and green, marked 'Hull Art USA L-4-6 1/2'.

6.75in (17cm) high

£30-40   BEL

A Hull 'Magnolia' pattern matte graduated pink and blue double handled urn vase, the base molded 'Hull Art U.S.A. 46 1/4'.

6.5in (16.5cm) high

£30-40   AEM

A Hull 'Calla Lily' pattern graduated light green and cream glazed vase, the base marked '340/33-6'.

6.25in (16cm) high

£70-90   BEL

A Hull pink 'Magnolia' pattern vase, with blue flowers, the base impressed 'H-13-10 1/2'.

11in (28cm) high

£30-40   TSIS

A Hull 'Magnolia' pattern matte glazed cornucopia, the base marked 'Hull Art USA 19-8 1/2"'.

8.75in (22cm) high

£20-30   BEL

A CLOSER LOOK AT A HULL LITTLE RED RIDING HOOD BUTTER DISH

A range of Little Red Riding Hood items was produced during the 1940s and early 50s, including a lamp, salt and pepper shakers and the famous cookie jar.

This range is very popular and fakes are known – these are often made from a brighter white ceramic, and have larger flower transfers and more heavily applied gilt, than originals.

The butter dish, with Little Red Riding Hood appearing to curtsey, is among the rarest items in the range.

Look out for different transfers on this range as the value can be affected – poinsettia transfers are particularly desirable and valuable.

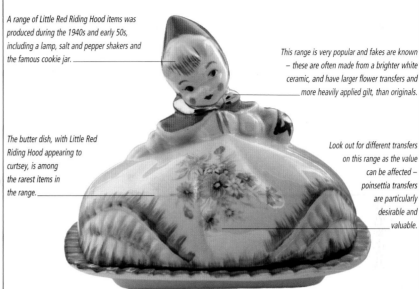

A very rare Hull Little Red Riding Hood butterdish, the base marked 'Pat. Des. No. 135889'.

Most pieces from this range were made by Hull and decorated by Royal China (part of Regal China), before being sent back to Hull for sale, but Regal also produced examples themselves.

7in (17.5cm) long

£300-400   BB

A pair of Hull 'Tokay' pattern gloss glazed cornucopia vases, the bases impressed 'Tokay U.S.A.'.

The 'Tokay' range, with its grapes and moulded vine-like handles, was introduced in 1958.

6.25in (16cm) high

£50-70   AEM

A Hull double handled urn vase, with green dripped glaze, the base unmarked.

This is a typical Arts & Crafts form and glaze.

4.75in (12cm) high

£50-70   TSIS

A Hull 'Water Lily' pattern flower pot with attached saucer, the base marked 'Hull Art USA L-25-5 3/4"', in mint condition.

5.75in (14.5cm) high

£30-50   BEL

A Hull 'Tokay' pattern pink and green glazed fruit bowl, the base marked '7 Tokay USA', with restored rim.

9.75in (24.5cm) wide

£30-50   BEL

A rare Hull 'Little Red Riding Hood' teapot, with transfer-printed daisy and poppy pattern and gilt and hand-painted detailing, the base moulded 'U.S.A.'.

1943-57   8in (20cm) long

£200-250   BB

CERAMICS

QUICK REFERENCE

- Italian ceramics of the 1950s and 1960s have risen in popularity in recent years, and are colourful and relatively affordable. They can be found anywhere from car boot sales to specialist auctions, and prices range from a few pounds to over £2,000. The highest prices tend to be paid for pieces by notable designers such as Guide Gambone (1909-1969) and Marcello Fantoni (b.1915).
- After WWII Italy enjoyed an influx of money and a renewal of confidence that caused a boom in many industries. A large number of potteries produced affordable decorative ceramics for export. Forms were moulded, but decorated by hand. Colours are typically bright with abstract, stylised designs, and the influence of contemporary modern art can be seen in geometric and figurative patterns.
- Shapes included vases, lampbases, dishes and bowls and, depending on the quality and price, were sold in a range of shops from discount outlets to high end department stores such as Macy's or Heal's. Distributors included Raymor in the US and Hutcheson & Son Ltd in the UK. Many distributors applied their own labels to pieces.
- Look out for well-formed, well-decorated examples that show skill in execution and detail in design. Colours and patterns should be representative of the period and style. Larger pieces are usually worth more, particularly if they are well made, and damage reduces value dramatically.
- Currently, very little is known about the majority of designers or factories. Bases are marked only 'Italy' followed by a number, possibly indicating the pattern, shape, or order number. Many names indicate towns, with these pieces being sold as tourist souvenirs. Bitossi's 'Rimini Blue' range, designed by Aldo Londi in 1953, is currently popular with collectors, particularly animal forms.

A 1950s-60s Italian vase with hand-painted multi-coloured squares and random white streaks on a textured pink ground, the base painted 'ITALY 6801'

8in (20.5cm) high

£40-60   GC

A 1950s-60s Italian vase with hand-painted multi-coloured squares and random white streaks on a textured light blue ground, the base painted 'ITALY 6514'

9in (23cm) high

£60-80   GC

A 1950s-60s Italian large conical vase, the body decorated with a panel of a sgraffito design of a stylised musician, the top and base covered with a beige lava-like glaze, the base inscribed 'Sestri Levante'.

Sestri Levante is a seaside resort and fishing port on the Italian Riviera. It is likely that these bottles were tourist souvenirs.

A 1950s-60s Italian floor vase, hand-painted with lozenges in different colours, the base painted 'ITALY 40/200 56'.

16.25in (41cm) high

£60-80   M20C

A 1950s-60s Italian large bottle vase, the body decorated with a sgraffito design of stylised people, the top and base covered with a beige lava-like glaze, the base inscribed 'Sestri Levante'.

16.25in (41.5cm) high

£150-200   GC

15.75in (40cm) high

£150-200   GC

A CLOSER LOOK AT A FANTONI VASE

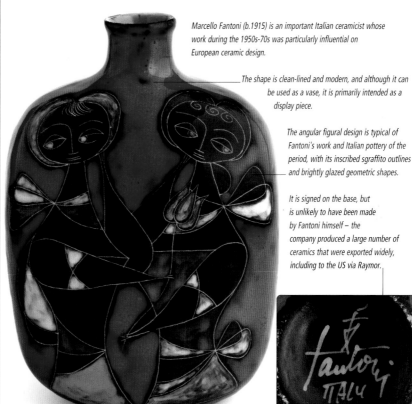

Marcello Fantoni (b.1915) is an important Italian ceramicist whose work during the 1950s-70s was particularly influential on European ceramic design.

The shape is clean-lined and modern, and although it can be used as a vase, it is primarily intended as a display piece.

The angular figural design is typical of Fantoni's work and Italian pottery of the period, with its inscribed sgraffito outlines and brightly glazed geometric shapes.

It is signed on the base, but is unlikely to have been made by Fantoni himself – the company produced a large number of ceramics that were exported widely, including to the US via Raymor.

An Italian Fantoni bottle vase, with a sgraffito and glazed gossiping women design on a glossy red glazed background, with turquoise glazed interior, the base painted 'Fantoni Italy', with hairline crack to rim.

6.75in (17cm) high

£300-500   **W&W**

A 1960s Italian vase, with hand-painted stylised flowers or peacock feather eyes, and trefoil rim, the base painted 'ITALY 5Z'.

9.75in (24.5cm) high

£60-80   **GC**

A 1950s Italian vase, hand-painted and sgraffito image of two women, the base painted 'ITALY 692'.

The asymmetric shape is typically 1950s. The figures are very similar to those used by Marcello Fantoni, as seen on the vase above.

12in (30.5cm) high

£60-100   **GROB**

A 1960s-70s Italian Bitossi green glazed footed cylindrical vase, impressed with geometric and runic symbols, the base painted '711 ITALY'

10in (25cm) high

£40-60   **RET**

A 1950s-70s Italian blue glazed torpedo vase, impressed with geometric symbols, probably by Bitossi.

10in (25cm) high

£40-60   **RET**

A 1960s-70s Italian Bitossi dark blue glazed low vase, impressed with geomtric and runic symbols, the base painted 'H-67/72 ITALY'.

£20-30   **RET**

QUICK REFERENCE

- The Lotus Pottery was founded in Devon by Michael and Elizabeth Skipwith in 1958 after they met at the Leeds College of Art. Initially known as Loversal Pottery, after Michael's birthplace in Doncaster, the couple changed the name when they moved to Old Stoke Farm in Stoke Gabriel in Devon. Although some decorative wares were made, the mainstay of production was kitchen and tablewares.

- By 1968, a number of glazes were in use, the most popular of which was the then-fashionable olive green shown here. Patterns differed widely and were based on natural themes, with the stylised daisy being the most popular, and the most common today. Other glazes included 'Dartside Green', white on red, and the blue on white 'Loire' range introduced in 1974. Look out for unusual glazes and patterns, as these tend to be popular.

- Bulls and larger decorative wares tend to fetch the highest prices, with tableware being generally affordable – few items fetch over £80 and most are under £30. Look out for the 'Alpine' range, decorated in sage green at the top and white at the bottom and inside. Introduced in 1966, it was accepted for the Design Council's Index of British Design.

- Most examples are marked around the base with the impressed 'LP' pottery monogram, although this is rarely found on the smallest pieces. The company prospered in the early 1970s, but suffered from increased competition from other potteries later in the decade. The Lotus Pottery closed in 1982, but Michael and Elizabeth Skipwith continued to pot individually.

A Lotus Pottery medium sized bull, designed by Elizabeth Skipwith, with a pattern of repeated g's or circles with curves on an olive green glaze, and with moulded hair to head.

Note the moulded hair on this example – not all Lotus bulls have this feature.

9in (22.5cm) long

£30-40   M20C

A Lotus Pottery small bull, designed by Elizabeth Skipwith, with mottled cream circle design on an olive green glaze.

6in (15cm) long

£20-30   DSC

A Lotus Pottery small bull, designed by Elizabeth Skipwith, with a hand-painted foliate seaweed-like design on an olive green glaze.

3in (7.5cm) high

£10-15   M20C

A Lotus Pottery small bull, designed by Elizabeth Skipwith, with a cream flower on an olive green glossy glaze.

5in (12.5cm) long

£20-25   M20C

A Lotus Pottery large bull, designed by Elizabeth Skipwith, with star-like stylised flower on an olive green glaze.

12.75in (32.5cm) long

£50-70   M20C

QUICK REFERENCE – LOTUS POTTERY BULLS

The bull is the most collectable and best-loved form produced by the pottery. It was made from the late 1960s to the mid-1970s in four different sizes from 5in (12.5cm) long to 13in (32.5cm) long. Stylised bulls in general from this period have become highly desirable. Lotus bulls can be differentiated from those produced by Bitossi, Beswick (see p41) and other makers by their glazes and bulky form, even though they are typically unmarked. This is a very unusual and scarce glaze that recalls patterns used by Briglin (see p43). If it was in a more common glaze, such as the typical flower on an olive ground, the value would be around £20-30.

A Lotus Pottery bird figurine, with mottled cream flower on an olive green glaze.

This is a rare shape, and very similar to 'folk art' pottery whistles produced in US states such as Pennsylvania by early settlers.
6.25in (16cm) high

£30-40 DSC

A Lotus Pottery medium sized bull, designed by Elizabeth Skipwith, with wax-resist spirals and a cream glaze.

6.25in (16cm) long

£30-40 M20C

A Lotus Pottery vase, with a mottled cream flower on an olive green glaze, the side with impressed marks.

£25-35

8in (20cm) high

DSC

A Lotus Pottery triangular dish, with stylised flower motif on a glossy olive glaze.

4.5in (11.5cm) wide

£7-10 RET

A Lotus Pottery salt shaker, with mottled cream flower on an olive green glaze.

3.25in (8cm) high

£3-5 DSC

A Lotus Pottery pebble-shaped sugar sifter, with mottled cream flower on an olive green glaze, the centre with holes.

3.5in (8cm) diam

£8-12 DSC

CERAMICS

QUICK REFERENCE

- The eccentric Martin Brothers are best known for their pottery bird-shaped jars, which can fetch anything from around £10,000 upwards at auction today. As well as these, they also produced salt-glazed stoneware pottery, including vases, jugs and dishes, which can be more affordable. Damage and restoration reduces values considerably, with pieces often being available for under £1,000.

- Robert Wallace Martin founded his first pottery in the 1860s, making terracotta sculpture. In 1873, he opened a new pottery in Fulham, London with his brothers Charles, Walter and Edwin. In 1877, they moved to Southall where most of their work was produced. The pottery prospered producing Gothic Revival style wares until the 1910s when deaths in the family left it foundering, until it closed in 1915.

- Look for the complex, unusual and sometimes 'grotesque' patterns and forms based on natural and mythological themes for which the brothers are best known. Robert Wallace was responsible for most of the grotesque figural jars and face jugs, Charles managed the business, Walter brought technical expertise, particularly with glazes, and Edwin was the thrower and decorator, having previously worked at Doulton.

- The brothers often signed the pieces they were responsible for, and most pieces are also dated. Marks can also help date pieces. From 1873-74 marks included the Fulham address, from 1874-78 the mark was simply 'London', from 1878-79 it was 'Southall', and from 1879-1915 it included 'London' and 'Southall'. The word 'Bros' or 'Brothers' was used after 1882.

A Martin Brothers stoneware miniature vase, incised and painted with blossom in white and brown on a buff ground, the base incised 'Martin London'.

2.25in (6cm) high

£350-450   WW

A Martin Brothers stoneware vase, by Robert Wallace Martin, with flowering plants, the base incised 'R W Martin & Bros., London & Southall 2.1886', extensive cracking.

Undamaged this vase may have fetched over three times as much.

1886   9.5in (24cm) high

£280-320   DN

A Martin Brothers stoneware vase, incised with scrolling foliage, painted in shades of brown and ochre, incised '9-1890, Martin Bros, London & Southall', cracked.

8.5in (21.5cm) high

£500-700   WW

A pair of early Martin Brothers stoneware vases, by Robert Wallace Martin, incised with simple foliage and berries on a banded design, incised 'R W Martin Southall, 1878', hairline crack to one, repair to rim of other.

1878   10in (25.5cm) high

£600-900   WW

A tall Martin Brothers stoneware vase, of slender form, incised and painted with simple grasses, the base incised 'Martin Bros, London & Southall, 10-1903', hairline crack to top rim.

1903 9.25in (23.5cm) high

£300-500   WW

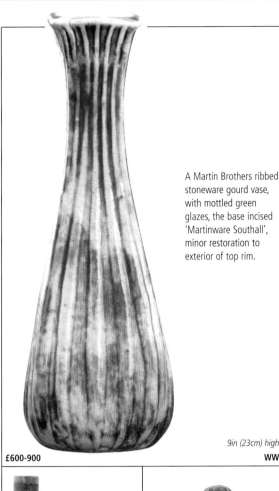

A Martin Brothers ribbed stoneware gourd vase, with mottled green glazes, the base incised 'Martinware Southall', minor restoration to exterior of top rim.

9in (23cm) high

£600-900   WW

A CLOSER LOOK AT A MARTIN BROTHERS JUG

The decoration is typical in terms of its concern with the Medieval 'grotesque', as well as the Far and Middle Eastern influences seen in the curling arabesques.

As well as being well-potted, the inscribed and painted design is extremely well-executed.

Although jugs are less popular than vases, particularly birds and figural forms, they are becoming more sought after as prices for the best pieces continue to rise.

It dates from 1895, which can be considered a highpoint of the brothers' output.

A Martin Brothers square section stoneware dragon jug, each side incised and painted with a ferocious dragon on an ochre ground, the base incised 'Martin Brothers London & Southall, 4-1895', professional restoration to the top rim.

1895   9.75in (24.5cm) high

£2,000-3,000   WW

A large Martin Brothers footed vase, with a tall collar neck incised with humming birds and lilies over a tonal blue ground, incised mark and date to base, restored.

1898   12.5in (32cm) high

£300-500   FLD

A small Martin Brothers stoneware bottle vase, incised with a ruffle shoulder band in green with a blue neck and brown body, the base incised 'Martin London'.

5in (12.5cm) high

£300-500   DN

A Martin Brothers stoneware vase, by Robert Wallace Martin, of lobed form with four cylindrical necks, incised with weave decoration, the base incised 'R W Martin D38', chips.

6in (15cm) high

£400-600   WW

A Martin Brothers stoneware jug, incised with finches flying and resting in boughs, incised 'R W Martin & Bros, London & Southall, 1-1887', restored base rim.

1887   8.75in (22cm) high

£400-600   WW

CERAMICS

QUICK REFERENCE

- William Moorcroft (1872–1945) began working as a designer at James MacIntyre & Company, Burslem in 1897, and was promoted to Manager of Ornamental Ware in 1898. His first designs were the 'Florian' and 'Aurelian' ranges, typified by their complex Moorish-inspired symmetrical patterns of natural themes including leaves and flowers. Highly stylised, they are typical of the Art Nouveau style prevalent at the time.

- Moorcroft's hand-thrown shapes were decorated with a tube-lining process, where an outline of liquid clay was piped onto the surface and then filled with liquid glaze. After great success, Moorcroft left MacIntyre in 1912 in order to found his own company with backing from London retailer Liberty. His success continued and, in 1929, Moorcroft was awarded the Royal Warrant.

- Colours are typically rich and deep, and patterns continued to be inspired by the natural world, although as the Art Nouveau style went out of fashion new ranges were created. After William's death, his son Walter took over and continued many of his father's designs, as well as introducing some of his own.

- The most desirable and valuable ranges tend to be early, from 1900–20s, and include 'Florian', 'Aurelian' and any of the landscape or mushroom patterns. However, more modern ranges produced by designers including Sally Tuffin (at Moorcroft from 1986–92) and Rachel Bishop (joined 1993) are also growing in value on the 'secondary market', particularly if they are from a limited edition or in an unusual colour or pattern variation.

- Patterns produced for long periods tend to be the most affordable, particularly if the piece is small. The pattern, shape, size and type of marks on the base can help to date a piece, and always examine the entire body for signs of damage.

A Macintyre & Co. 'Aurelian' pattern part tea service, designed by William Moorcroft, comprising a hot water jug, two plates, three saucers and five cups, the bases with registration no.314901 for 1898, and 308931 for 1897.

c1899   *Jug 5.75in (14.5cm) high*

£250-350   DN

A Moorcroft 'Flamminian' pattern small baluster vase, for Liberty & Co., designed by William Moorcroft, the red ground with foliate roundels, with incised signature and printed marks.

1906-1913   *4.75in (14.5cm) high*

£200-300   DN

A Macintyre & Co. twin-handled jar, with blue Forget-me-not flower pattern, designed by William Moorcroft, printed mark, missing lid.

c1903   *4.25in (11cm) high*

£70-100   SAS

A MacIntyre & Co. miniature vase, with the 'Poppy' design, designed by William Moorcroft, the base impressed '28', and brown printed 'MacIntyre' mark and 'WM' in green.

Probably produced from c1910-20 as salesman's samples, miniatures are very rare and desirable. The idea was revived in the 1970s, but backstamps and patterns differ. These later pieces are worth from around a tenth of this value.

2.25in (6cm) high

£1,000-1,500   SWO

An MacIntyre & Co. Florian ware 'Seaweed' pattern biscuit barrel and cover, designed by William Moorcroft, the base with script 'WM' mark.

c1902   *6.25in (16cm) high*

£300-500   SWO

QUICK REFERENCE – POMEGRANATE

'Pomegranate' was designed by William Moorcroft and introduced in 1910. Along with 'Pansy', introduced a year later, it marked a sea-change in Moorcroft's designs. Background colours were mottled and merged together, and motifs were limited to one area of the piece, usually arranged in a band around the body – often the shoulder. First retailed by Liberty & Co., it became Moorcroft's most successful design by the 1920s, sold around the world. Examples made from 1910-c1919 had yellow or green backgrounds, while later examples had deeper blue and purple backgrounds.

A Moorcroft 'Pomegranate' pattern baluster vase, designed by William Moorcroft, on a dark blue and green ground, with signed and printed marks to base.

7in (17.5cm) high

£50-80   SAS

A Moorcroft 'Celadon Pomegranate' pattern large bowl, designed by William Moorcroft, with a pale green glazed ground, the base with painted signature.

10.25in (26cm) diam

£1,800-2,200   FLD

A Moorcroft 'Pomegranate' pattern spherical vase, designed by William Moorcroft, on a blue ground, with impressed signature and 'Potter to H M The Queen', with blue painted initials.

5.25in (13.5cm) high

£400-600   DN

A Moorcroft 'Pomegranate' pattern slender ovoid tall vase, designed by William Moorcroft, on a shaded blue ground, with impressed mark, cracked.

12.5in (31.5cm) high

£200-300   DN

A Moorcroft 'Pomegranate' pattern trumpet-shaped vase, designed by William Moorcroft, the base impressed 'Moorcroft Made in England' and with painted signature.

c1937   *7.25in (18.5cm) high*

£400-600   SWO

A miniature William Moorcroft pomegranate and berry pattern vase, with a dark blue ground, green initials and impressed marks.

3.5in (9cm) high

£150-200   SWO

A Moorcroft 'Amazon Twilight' pattern ovoid vase, designed by Nicola Slaney, with impressed mark, artist signed and dated '17.9.98'.

This was Slaney's first design for Moorcroft; it was enormously successful.

1998   8.25in (21cm) high

£300-500   DN

A Moorcroft 'Anna Lily' pattern double-handled vase, designed by Nicola Slaney, the base with printed and script marks.

1998   10.25in (26cm) high

£300-500   SWO

A Moorcroft 'Coneflower' pattern vase, designed by Anji Davenport, the base with factory and artist's marks, paw stamp, and mushroom stamp.

2001   7.5in (19cm) tall

£80-100   BEL

A Moorcroft 'Cotton Top' pattern baluster vase, designed by Sian Leeper, with impressed and painted marks, numbered 111 from a limited edition of 150.

2002   8.75in (22.5cm) high

£150-250   DN

A Moorcroft trial 'D'Larch' pattern ginger jar and cover, with stylised trees in yellow and green, on a graduated navy blue ground, initialled to reverse, dated '3.10.2000'.

2000

£350-450   LT

A Moorcroft 'Finches' pattern baluster vase, designed by Sally Tuffin, on a blue ground, with painted initials and date code.

1993   7.25in (18.5cm) high

£200-300   DN

A Moorcroft 'Kyoto' pattern vase, designed by Rachel Bishop, numbered 70 from a limited edition of 100, the base with printed and painted marks, and with certificate.

The design is based on that found on the gate to the Imperial Palace in the ancient Japanese capital of Kyoto. Along with Sally Tuffin, Bishop is one of Moorcroft's most sought-after contemporary designers.

c1994/95   24in (61cm) high

£1,200-1,800   LT

A Moorcroft 'Pohutukawa' pattern baluster vase, designed by Sally Tuffin, from a limited edition of 100 for Tanfield Potter, with impressed mark and date code, with Tanfield Potter retailer's label.

Tanfield Potter are a historic and respected ceramics and glass retailer in Auckland, New Zealand. They commissioned this design, which was also produced on a charger made in 1992 in a limited edition of 220. Related to the myrtle, the evergreen flowering Pohutukawa is also called the 'New Zealand Christmas Tree'.

1900   13in (33cm) high

£150-200   **DN**

A Moorcroft 'Siberian Iris' pattern vase, designed by Sian Leeper, numbered 208 from a limited edition of 250, the base with impressed and painted marks.

2003   8.75in (22cm) high

£250-350   **DN**

A Moorcroft 'Torridon' pattern ovoid vase, designed by Philip Gibson, with impressed and painted marks.

2004   8in (20.5cm) high

£250-350   **DN**

QUICK REFERENCE – SALLY TUFFIN

Sally Tuffin (b.1938) studied at the Royal College of Art's fashion school before co-founding the fashion and textile design company 'Tuffin & Foale' that became synonymous with fashion during the Swinging Sixties. In 1986, after bringing up two children, she returned to design as Moorcroft's third ever designer – and the first from outside the Moorcroft family. She remained there until 1993, when she founded the Dennis Chinaworks with her husband Richard Dennis, a thriving company that she still runs today. From 1995-98, she also designed for Poole Pottery. Her work is hotly sought after by collectors, with five figure prices being paid for unique items and scarce, desirable ranges.

A Moorcroft 'Raincloud' pattern vase, designed by Sally Tuffin, numbered 147 from a limited edition of 150, initialled and dated 'Sally Tuffin' and signed 'J. Moorcroft' 1993'.

1993 16.75in (45.5cm) high

£1,000-1,500   **LT**

A Moorcroft 'H.M.S. Sirius' pattern charger, designed by Sally Tuffin, numbered 9 from a limited edition of 150, together with original box.

This pattern was originally made to commemorate the Australian Bicentenary in 1988, but opened up to a wider audience later. The edition size was 250, with 100 being made specially for the Australian market.

1988   14in (35.5cm) diam

£350-450   **WW**

A Moorcroft 'Underwood' pattern ovoid vase, designed and decorated by Debbie Hancock, numbered 235 from a limited edition of 350 produced for MacIntyre of Leeds, with impressed and printed marks, and painted initials.

7in (18cm) high

£200-300   **DN**

FIND OUT MORE...

Paul Atterbury ' Moorcroft' , *published by Richard Dennis, 1996*

A Poole Pottery orange, green and yellow 'Delphis' large spear dish, with printed black POOLE dolphin mark, stamped '82', and with painted 'iY or CY' monogram.

17.5in (44cm) long

£40-50   **M20C**

A 1950s Poole Pottery 'Contemporary' range bowl, shape 338 designed by Alfred Read, decorated with the FSU pattern designed by Ruth Pavely, the base with printed mark.

This mark was used from 1955-59. A more rectangular version was used 1959-67.

17.5in (44cm) wide

£60-90   **WW**

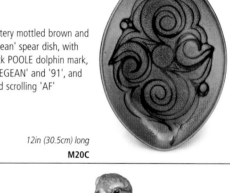

A Poole Pottery mottled brown and yellow 'Aegean' spear dish, with printed black POOLE dolphin mark, stamped 'AEGEAN' and '91', and with painted scrolling 'AF' monogram.

12in (30.5cm) long

£30-40   **M20C**

A Poole Pottery mottled brown and yellow 'Aegean' large spear dish, with printed black POOLE dolphin mark, stamped 'AEGEAN' and '82', and with painted 'iY or CY' monogram.

17.5in (44cm) long

£40-50   **M20C**

A Poole Pottery white glazed vase with wax resist band of a spiralling pattern, covered all over with a glossy transparent glaze, the base with black printed 'POOLE ENGLAND' mark, with painted ABC monogram and painted JM monogram for Jacqueline MacKenzie.

A Poole Pottery 'Delphis' bowl, with printed factory mark, stamped '3', and with painted 'MA' monogram for Mary Albon.

1972-74   *8in (20.5cm) diam*

£30-40   **M20C**

1972-77   *12in (30.5cm) high*

£30-40   **M20C**

A Poole Pottery stoneware 'Grouse' group figurine, designed by Barbara Linley Adams, together with a bird on a pinecone figurine, each with impressed and printed marks.

These figurines are believed to have been produced as test samples, and are in addition to the limited edtion of 1,000 pieces. From the collection of Roy Holland, Managing Director of Poole Pottery.

13in (33cm) wide

£150-250   **W&W**

QUICK REFERENCE

- Rookwood was founded in Cincinnati, Ohio in 1880 by Maria Longworth Nichols, a wealthy heiress who decorated ceramics as a hobby. Initially, the pottery lost money, until Nichols invited William Watts Tyler to run the company in 1883. Tyler set about organising the structure of the company and standardising lines. When Nichols moved abroad in 1890, Tyler took over the now profitable pottery.
- Well-proportioned and balanced shapes were thrown and decorated by hand. These shapes were then glazed with one of the many different glazes developed by Rookwood from the mid-1880s onwards. Tyler encouraged experimentation: glaze technicians were employed to reproduce ancient techniques and glazes, and develop new ones. The first to be produced is known as Standard, which is typified by a graduated brown background, usually painted with flowers. Portraits are rare and desirable.
- Much of the interest for collectors lies in Rookwood's glazes, many of which were inspired by Japanese ceramics. Following the success of Standard, the clear, glossy Iris glaze and the green-tinted Sea Green glaze were introduced in 1894. Vellum, which creates an Impressionistic appearance by diffusing the painted decoration (usually plants or landscapes) it covers, was launched in 1900. Matte glazes followed in 1901. As the glaze is so important, crazing (a fine network of lines) will reduce value, as will damage that detracts from the glaze or design.
- Rookwood employed many highly skilled decorators, such as Matthew Daly, Sara Sax and Maria Storer, and their work can be highly desirable. Pieces tend to be signed, so look out for marks.

A Rookwood Standard glaze vase, decorated by Edith Felten with floral decoration, marked with Rookwood logo, 'IV', shape no.914F and the artist's initials, restored top rim.

1904   4.25in (11cm) high
£100-150   BEL

A rare tall Rookwood Standard glaze vase, decorated by Sallie Toohey, with poppies on a graduated brown and beige ground, the base with flame mark, '856B' and artist's cipher.

1899   15.5in (39.5cm) high
£2,500-3,500   DRA

A Rookwood Iris Glaze vase, by Lenore Asbury, with white clematis, the base with flame mark and 'VI/951C/W./L.A'.

Rookwood's 'Iris' glaze was introduced in 1894, and was exhibited at the 1900 Paris Exposition.

1906   9.5in (24cm) high
£2,000-3,000   DRA

A Rookwood vase, decorated by Carl Schmidt with white roses, the base with the Rookwood flame mark, dated 'IV', impressed '612EZ', and artist's initials 'CS'.

7.75in (19.5cm) high
£800-1,200   JDJ

A Rookwood Iris glaze bulbous vase, decorated by Clara Lindeman with a branch of pink apple blossoms on shaded ground, the base with flame mark and 'VIII/654C/C.C.L.'

1908   5in (12.5cm) high
£800-1,200   DRA

QUICK REFERENCE – ROSEVILLE MARKS

Roseville used many different marks over time, but many pieces were left unmarked. The word 'USA' was only used on raised, moulded marks. Beware of faintly moulded examples, as these may be fakes. Also consider the style of the wording and individual letters, as this can help identify fakes made primarily in the Far East. If in doubt, compare to a piece you are sure is original, also taking the colours and form of the body into account.

Early Rozane Ware 'wafer' mark with 'Woodland' range name.

Stamped 'RV' ink mark, c1923-c1927.

Foil or paper label and handwritten shape number, c1927-35.

Impressed Roseville mark and shape number, 1936-40.

Moulded Roseville USA mark, shape number and size, 1940 onwards.

A 1940s-Roseville pink 'Apple Blossom' basket, 309-8", marked 'Roseville USA 309-8"'.

8.5in (20.5cm) high

£150-250   **BEL**

A Roseville blue 'Bleeding Heart' vase, 961-4", marked 'Roseville USA 961-4"'.

4.75in (12cm) wide.

£100-150   **BEL**

A Roseville 'Blackberry' vase, 567-4", with glaze flake and an area of branch handle repaired.

4in (10cm) high

£200-300   **BEL**

A Roseville blue 'Bushberry' vase, marked 'USA 32-7'.

7.25in (18.5cm) high

£180-220   **BEL**

QUICK REFERENCE – ROYAL COPENHAGEN

Royal Copenhagen was founded under Danish Royal patronage in 1775. Although it is well known for its fine tableware (such as 'Flora Danica'), it is 20thC decorative wares that attract the most interest from collectors today. Important designers include Axel Salto, Knud Kyhn, Arnold Krog, Johanne Gerber, and the long-serving Nils Thorsson. Forms tend to be simple, with much inspiration for the pattern taken from nature. The pieces are subject to strongly modern stylisation. The base of the popular 'Baca' and similar ranges of the 1950s-70s bear monograms for each designer, which are known as 'chop' marks. The one shown here is for Johanne Gerber.

A Royal Copenhagen Baca Fajance bottle vase, with a handpainted pattern of leaves and branches, no.780/3259, designed by Johanne Gerber, the base with printed and painted marks.

7.75in (19.5cm) high

£50-80　　　　　　　　　GC

A Danish Royal Copenhagen Fajance vase, no. 711/3755, designed by Nils Thorsson, with painted and printed factory marks to base.

7.5in (19cm) high

£40-60　　　　　　　　　RET

A Royal Copenhagen Fajance pottery vase, no.726/3259, designed by Nils Thorsson, with painted and printed factory marks to base.

8.75in (22.5cm) high

£60-80　　　　　SAS

A Danish Royal Copenhagen Baca Fajance chimney vase, no. 635/3121, designed by Ellen Malmer, with printed and painted marks to base.

7.75in (19.5cm) high

£50-60　　　　　　　　　M20C

A Danish Royal Copenhagen Baca Fajance dish, no.730/2883, designed by Nils Thorsson, the base with printed factory marks.

6.75in (17cm) wide

£30-40　　　　　　　　　RET

A Royal Copenhagen Fajance square dish, no.704/2883, designed by Nils Thorsson, with painted and printed factory marks to base.

6.5in (16.5cm) wide

£50-70　　　　　SAS

CERAMICS

A Royal Copenhagen celadon lidded fluted bowl, no.457/2939, the finial modelled as a seated figure and with crackle glaze, with gilt highlights, the base with printed and painted marks.

6in (15.5cm) high

£80-120　　　　　　**W&W**

A Royal Copenhagen spherical stoneware vase, designed by Axel Salto, embossed with a tree pattern under black and mahogany glaze, the base incised 'Salto 1243 'with factory mark.

7.75in (19.5cm) high

£2,000-2,500　　　　　**DRA**

A Royal Copenhagen bear cub, no. 21434, designed by Knud Kyhn.

Earlier glazes are lighter in tone, being more creamy in colour, sometimes with green tones.

3.25in (8cm) high

£50-80　　　　　　　**WW**

An Art Deco Royal Copenhagan celadon glaze free standing mask, 'Medusa', designed by Hans Henrik Hansen in 1927, model no. 1/2950, the base with impressed and painted marks.

1927　　　　　　*10.5in (27cm) high*

£500-700　　　　　　**WW**

A CLOSER LOOK AT AN AXEL SALTO ROYAL COPENHAGEN VASE

Axel Salto (1889-1961) is regarded by many as most influential Danish ceramics designer. He worked for the company from 1933 onwards.

Beginning to pot in the mid-1920s, he won numerous awards including the Grand Prix at the Milan Triennale 1951.

Salto' s powerfully modelled 'budding', 'sprouting' or 'living' themed stonewares were inspired by organic forms such as buds and tree cones. They cross the boundary between functional vase and decorative sculpture.

His dark and rich glazes match the natural form perfectly, and were inspired by ancient Chinese examples such as Sung period wares.

A 1950s-60s Royal Copenhagen bowl, designed by Gerd Bogelund, the interior decorated with a fine brown haresfur glaze, the exterior with impressed and sgrafitto stylised motifs of ears of wheat, the base with printed three wave mark and painted 'GB'.

4.75in (12cm) high

£120-180　　　　　　**UCT**

A Royal Copenhagen stoneware 'budding' vase, designed by Axel Salto, covered in mottled brown glaze, the base incised 'SALTO', with factory marks, and numbered '20559'.

10in (25.5cm) wide

£6,000-8,000　　　　　**DRA**

QUICK REFERENCE

- The Worcester porcelain factory (established in 1751) first began operating under the name Worcester Royal Porcelain Company in 1862. George III had granted the first of several royal warrants in Worcester's illustrious history in 1789.
- The late Victorian period was very successful for Royal Worcester. The company became known for the colour of its porcelain: soft ivory and pink tints, which echoed art glass. Key designers include George Owen and James Hadley.
- The early years of 20thC saw a simplification of forms and decorative styles. There was a greater output of everyday ware, but hand-painted porcelain was still produced and contributed to the company's success. Vases, plates and other forms were decorated by well-known painters, including Harry Davies and the Stinton family (the best known are Harry Stinton, his father John Stinton Jnr., and uncle James Stinton). By this time all major Royal Worcester artists were signing their work, so look for marks, as a well-known artist may add value.
- Naturalistically painted, modelled ceramic sculptures were introduced in the 1930s. Dorothy Doughty's bird and flower models (produced from 1935) are popular with collectors, as are Doris Lindner's animal figures. Look for small limited editions, as these may be rare and desirable.
- Royal Worcester became a public company in 1954 and merged with Spode in 1978. From this period, Royal Worcester stopped their decorative pieces, focusing on high-quality tableware and figure modelling. In 2009, having gone into administration, Royal Worcester was bought by rival company, Portmeirion Pottery.
- Pieces are marked 'Royal Worcester', with a dot added to this mark for every year between 1892 and 1916. After this, an asterisk was added to the dots.

A Royal Worcester miniature vase, painted by James Stinton with a pheasant in a landscape, with gilt scrolling handles, puce mark to the base and no.'287'.

5.5in (14cm) high

£250-350   DUK

A Royal Worcester 'blush' double-handled vase, with pierced collar and painted with flowers and a butterfly, on gilt-painted and moulded base.

13.5in (38.5cm) high

£180-220   A&G

A Royal Worcester porcelain two-handled pedestal ovoid vase, shape no.2277, painted by Ernest Philips with two panels of summer flowers and a pink ribbon bow, within blue and gilt striped bands, signed, printed mark in puce, date cipher.
1912

£350-450   TEN

A Royal Worcester prismatic enamel pedestal urn, decorated with trailing gilt blossom and enamelled flowers on pink-blush-tinted ivory ground below mask head handles strung with 'silk' swags below short pierced neck, restored.

11.75in (30cm) high

£300-400   FLD

A Royal Worcester two-handled pedestal vase, shape 998/G, painted by G.H. Cole with lilies within green and gilt stiff-leaf band borders, with green printed marks, dated.

£300-500   DN

A Royal Worcester pedestal vase, the globular body decorated with brightly coloured clover, buttercups and forget-me-nots, the base with printed mark and date code.

1903 *9.75in (25cm) high*

£180-220   **WW**

A CLOSER LOOK AT A PAIR OF ROYAL WORCESTER VASES

Miniature vases are scarce and desirable. The fact that they are an original pair adds to the value.

They required great skill to decorate due to their size. This traditional shape shows off the pattern very well.

They were decorated by Harry Stinton (1883-1968), who is considered to be the best of the famed Stinton family of decorators at Worcester.

Stinton is particularly celebrated for his Highland cattle scenes, which were similar to those produced by his father John, but use a more purple palette.

A pair of Royal Worcester baluster vases, shape no.461, painted with Highland cattle in a mountainous setting by Harry Stinton, signed 'H. Stinton', green mark, bearing retailer's stamp of John Ford & Co., 39 Princes Street, Edinburgh.

4in (10cm) high

£800-1,000   **A&G**

A Royal Worcester trumpet vase, painted with roses and buds by Millie Hunt, signed 'M Hunt', within sponged gold borders, dated.

1931

£220-280   **FLD**

A pair of Royal Worcester trumpet vases, each painted with pink and claret roses by Millie Hunt, signed 'M Hunt', within gilt sponged collars, dated, 1934 and 1937

7.5in (19cm) high

£500-600   **FLD**

A pair of Royal Worcester small baluster vases, painted with fruit by Albert J. Shuck, shape no.2491, one with two apples and blackberries with reverse blackberries vignette, the other with two apples and cherries, the reverse with fruiting strawberry vignette, both signed, one with indistinct date code.

c1937 *4in (10cm) high*

£600-700   **TEN**

An early 20thC Royal Worcester footed vase, painted by James Stinton with a cock pheasant and flying hen bird in a landscape setting, with pierced collar, signed, green printed mark, pattern '42/G'.

5.75in (14.5cm) high

£250-350   **L&T**

A Royal Worcester porcelain 'Warwick Vase', shape 2130, painted with landscape scenes and signed 'H. Davies' within raised gilt pendant husk and floral swag borders on a white and apple green ground, dated, restored.

9.75in (25cm) diam

£400-500   **FLD**

A Royal Worcester tyg, painted with pink and claret rose sprays below a moulded border reading 'Auld Lang Syne', restored.

9.5in (24cm) high

£300-400   **FLD**

A Royal Worcester jug, with hand-painted floral pattern and gilded dragon-shaped handle, the base with printed factory marks, also printed '11048' and with registered no.21627 for 1893.

6in (15.5cm) high

£100-150   **BAD**

A late 20thC Royal Worcester teapot, painted by Terence Nutt on one side with two apples and blackberries, on the other with a peach, blackberries and green grapes, with gilded and gadrooned rim, spout, handle and circular foot, printed crown and wheel mark in black, initialled 'RB/BB', signed.

6in (15cm) high

£1,000-1,500   **TEN**

A late 19thC Royal Worcester Persian-style ewer, painted with a study of an owl on a branch and moonlit clouds by Charles Baldwyn, restored.

10.25in (26cm) high

£100-150   **FLD**

A late 19thC Royal Worcester sugar bowl and sparrow beak milk jug, hand-decorated with bamboo and geometric Oriental motifs in floral blue and gilt.

3.5in (9cm) high

£120-180   **LOC**

A Royal Worcester bonbon dish, in the form of a conch shell, with coral and weed stem with a circular base, in gilt, bronze and ivory effect, puce printed mark to the base, with impressed mark and 'no. 94'.

8.75in (22cm) high

£250-300   **DUK**

A Royal Worcester 'British Friesian bull', RW3746, modelled by Doris Lindner, numbered 268 from a limited edition of 500, with black printed marks, wood stand and certificate.

Issued 1962

£450-550   DN

A Royal Worcester 'Dairy Shorthorn bull', RW3781, modelled by Doris Lindner, numbered 106 from a limited edition of 500, with black printed marks, wood stand and certificate.

Issued 1965

£450-550   DN

A Royal Worcester 'Jersey bull', RW3776, modelled by Doris Lindner, numbered 167 from an edition of 500, with black printed marks, wood stand and certificate.

£450-550   DN

A Royal Worcester 'Jersey Cow', modelled by Doris Lindner, numbered 357 from a limited edition of 500, with stand and certificate.

7in (18cm) high

£400-600   LOC

A Royal Worcester 'Dairy Shorthorn Bull', modelled by Doris Lindner, numbered 250 from a limited edition of 500, with stand and certificate.

8.75in (22cm) high

£350-450   LOC

QUICK REFERENCE – DORIS LINDNER

Sculptor Doris Lindner (1896-1979) became one of Royal Worcester's most notable modellers after she was asked to contribute to an exhibition in London in 1931. Her first model was of a polar bear, followed by dogs and other animals such as foxes, some in the Art Deco style of the day. In 1935, she began modelling horses and produced her first limited edition, of 'Princess Elizabeth on Tommy', in 1948. The 1960s were her heyday, and she produced more than 20 limited edition figurines, modelled from life. Most edition sizes were 500, with a few smaller (and scarcer) editions of 100 or 150. Today, her work is sought after by a dedicated group of collectors, meaning prices have remained strong, even during the economic downturn. The model should retain its wooden plinth and certificate.

A Royal Worcester 'Aberdeen Angus' bull, RW3697, modelled by Doris Lindner, numbered '286' from a limited edition of 500, with wooden stand and certificate. Issued 1959

7.5in (19cm) high

£700-900   LOC

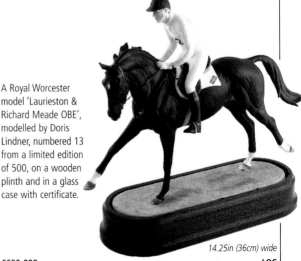

A Royal Worcester model 'Laurieston & Richard Meade OBE', modelled by Doris Lindner, numbered 13 from a limited edition of 500, on a wooden plinth and in a glass case with certificate.

14.25in (36cm) wide

£600-800   LOC

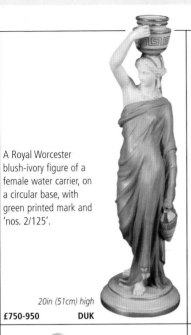

A Royal Worcester blush-ivory figure of a female water carrier, on a circular base, with green printed mark and 'nos. 2/125'.

20in (51cm) high
£750-950   DUK

A Royal Worcester 'The Tea Party' figure group, RW3700, modelled by Ruth Esther van Ruyckevelt, from a limited edition of 250, from the Victorian Figures series, in colours and gilt, black printed crown and wheel mark, title and facsimile signature, impressed '42', in original box with certificate.

1960   8in (20cm) high
£700-1,000   TEN

A Royal Worcester candle snuffer, modelled as a nun, with printed mark and date code.

1924   4in (10cm) high
£70-100   WW

A Royal Worcester blush-ivory figure of a rustic girl at a spring, model no.1810, partially coloured and gilt, with green marks.

1900   6.75in (17cm) high
£200-300   DN

A Royal Worcester 'Mephistopheles' Toby jug, shape 2850, the base with printed marks.

3.25in (8.5cm) high
£50-60   FLD

A Royal Worcester 'Spitfire' figure group, RW3352, designed by Eileen Soper from the Wartime series, dated, minor restoration.

This is the rare coloured version, which is worth considerably more than plain white. During the war, when this was produced, raw materials were strictly limited and could not generally be used on decorative pieces.
1941
£1,000-1,500   FLD

A pair of late 19thC Royal Worcester 'Irish Navvy and Wife' figures, by James Hadley, shape no.1810, typically modelled, in shades of green and pink, printed and impressed marked.

Tallest 7in (18cm) high
£300-400   HT

CERAMICS

A pair of Finnish Arabia salt and pepper shakers, designed by Kaj Franck in 1955, glazed in glossy black or red.

2.75in (7cm) high

£40-60   QU

A Danish Soholm Stentoj rectangular wall plaque, with stylised floral design, designed by Joseph Simmonds, with impressed mark on back, numbered '3540', and with painted 'LE' monogram.

17.5in (44.5cm) long

£100-150   RET

A 1970s Swedish Elbogen Pottery 'Marg' figure, the base with painted marks.

This was part of a range of different handmade female figures, each with its own name.

13.5in (34cm) high

£80-120   M20C

A CLOSER LOOK AT BJORN WIINBLAD CANDELABRA

Bjorn Wiinblad (1918-2006) was a Danish artist, illustrator, designer and ceramicist whose work has attracted a worldwide reputation and group of collectors.

Bjørn Wiinblad was born in Copenhagen and was educated at the Royal Academy of Arts in Copenhagen. He first started working with ceramics at Lars Syberg's studio, and set up his own studio in 1952.

From 1946, he worked at (and subsequently owned) the Danish factory Nymolle, and also worked with Germany's Rosenthal from 1956 onwards. He designed mass-produced transfer printed ceramics for both companies. He also ran his own pottery studio, from 1952, and it was there that these handmade, hand-painted candelabra were made.

His work is inspired by traditional Danish myths, music and nature, and often features whimsical characters in his individual and eccentric style.

A Norwegian Figgjo Flint Turi Design 'Lotte' pattern transfer-printed and painted beaker, with printed marks to base.

3in (7.5cm) high

£12-18   RET

A Swedish Gustavsberg stoneware poodle, from the 'Kennel' series designed by Lisa Larson in 1972, with painted and impressed marks to base.

3.5in (9cm) high

£50-70   SAS

Two Danish studio earthenware candelabra, by Bjorn Winblad, each of conical form, modelled as figures beneath a bowl and sconces, dated.

1972   *Tallest 15.75in (40cm) high*

£500-700   SWO

QUICK REFERENCE

- The Shelley brand was devised c1910 by the Wileman & Co. pottery in Staffordshire, England, but was not used officially until 1925. The company was founded c1892 and became known for its art pottery. However, it became world famous for its tea and tablewares during the 1920s and '30s. The pottery closed in 1966.

- Notable designers who produced important ranges which are sought after by collectors today, include Frederick Alfred Rhead, Walter Slater and his son Eric; and illustrators Hilda Cowham and Mabel Lucie Attwell, who are known for their desirable nursery ware (see p86-88).

- Among the most collectable and valuable Shelley designs are the two Art Deco geometric teaware ranges, 'Mode' and 'Vogue' designed by Eric Slater, and produced from 1930-33. The teacups had solid handles, which made them difficult to hold, and this led to the development of the hollow-handled 'Eve' shape in 1932. Also look out for the 'Queen Anne'

shape, which was decorated with over 170 different patterns, and the popular 'Dainty' shape, which was designed in 1896.

- The most desirable and valuable patterns are Art Deco in style, typically executed in the bright colours typical of the era. Values vary depending on the pattern. Desirability is maximised when these are found on a strongly Art Deco shape, such as 'Vogue' or 'Mode'. Transfer-printed floral 'chintz' wares are also sought after, but values for them have fallen over the past five years. More attention is being paid to Eric Slater's banded and dripped 'Harmony' ranges.

- Look out for complete teasets as these tend to fetch the largest sums. Teapots and individual teacups are also desirable, and are always worth considering when undamaged. Rhead's late 19thC art pottery ranges are also well worth looking out for as prices tend to be high due to their scarcity and his increased popularity among collectors in the UK and the US.

A Shelley blue lustre vase, designed by Walter Slater, printed and painted with a Chinese dragon, highlighted in gilt, with printed mark and facsimile signature to base.

Walter Slater replaced F. A. Rhead as Art Director, working there from 1905-37.

15in (38cm) high

£1,200-1,800   WW

A very rare Shelley Intarsio range 'Pomegranate' pattern vase, with printed marks to base.

Shelley were forced to withdraw this pattern by Moorcroft as it was similar to their Pomegranate pattern. A ginger jar in the same pattern can fetch up to £1,800.

8in (20.5cm) high

£700-1,000   GOL

A Wileman & Co. Intarsio range temple jar, with the 'Rabbits' pattern, designed by Frederick Alfred Rhead.

Notable ceramics designer Frederick Alfred Rhead (1856-1933) was Art Director at Wileman & Co. from 1896-1905. He produced a number of innovative ranges, the most desirable of which was Intarsio. This is a very scarce pattern on a rare and highly desirable form.

c1900

£2,000-2,500   GOL

A Shelley Intarsio range 'Native Americans' pattern vase, no.3411, with printed marks to base.

This stylised pattern is extremely rare on any form, and is especially desirable on large impressive vase forms such as this.

11in (28cm) high

£2,800-3,300   GOL

CERAMICS

A 1930s Shelley cake stand with handpainted circle design and shaped chrome stand, the base with green printed factory mark.

10in (25.5cm) high

£50-60   **RET**

A 1930s Shelley Vogue shape part coffee set, comprising coffee pot, four cups and saucers and milk jug, handpainted with the very rare 'Coral Martian' pattern, no.11867, with printed marks to bases.

The pattern name has been applied by collectors, and was not the original name. The pattern was also available in green, which is worth around the same amount.

1931-33   *7in (18cm) high*

£2,000-2,500   **GOL**

A very scarce Shelley lemonade set, with jug and six beakers, decorated with the 'Apples' pattern, with printed marks to the base.

The jug is very similar to Clarice Cliff's iconic Art Deco 'Conical' shape, showing how popular styles were reproduced by different makers.

8in (23cm) high

£800-1,200   **GOL**

A 1930s Shelley Mode shape teaset for two, hand-painted with the yellow butterfly wing pattern, no.11758, with printed marks to base.

Teapot 5in (12.5cm) high

£2,000-2,500   **GOL**

A CLOSER LOOK AT A SHELLEY TEA SERVICE

The Harmony range of Dripware was discovered 'by accident' when Eric Slater mixed too much turpentine in glazes, which dripped in an attractive manner.

Evenly distributed banding is highly desirable, particularly on the desirable Art Deco 'Eve' shape.

Purple Harmony is very rare – yellows, blues and greens are more common.

A Shelley Harmony waisted vase, with dripping bands of orange and green.

c1930   *21cm high*

£130-160   **BEV**

Slater accentuated the effects and widened it into a range of decorative wares – tablewares are harder to find, particularly in sets.

FIND OUT MORE...

' Shelley Potteries' , by Chris Watkins, William Harvey and Robert Senft, published by Barrie & Jenkins, 1980. The Shelley Group, www.shelley.co.uk or The National Shelley Club, www.nationalshelleychinaclub.com

A 1930s Shelley 'Harmony' range Eve shape teaset, designed by Eric Slater, comprising teapot, six cups and saucers, milk jug and sugar bowl, decorated with the purple Harmony pattern no.12084.

Teapot 7in (18cm) high

£2,500-3,000   **GOL**

A Stangl Pottery 'Bluebird', no.3276, with 'STANGL' brown oval mark, incised '3276' and with artist's initials 'ES'.

5.25in (13.5cm) high

£50-70   BEL

A Stangl Pottery 'Western Bluebird' figurine, no.3815, with printed factory marks and decorator's initials.

7in (17.5cm) high

£75-95   BH

A Stangl Pottery 'Key West Quail Dove', no.3454, marked 'STANGL 3454' in blue ink and artist signed 'RV' initials.

9.25in (23.5cm) high

£150-200   BEL

A Stangl Pottery 'Cardinal' in matte finish, no.3444, with small brown oval 'STANGL' mark, incised '3444' and with artist's initials, a small glaze flaw at the tip of the tail.

6.75in (17cm) high

£100-150   BEL

QUICK REFERENCE – STANGL BIRDS

Partly inspired by Audubon's famous 'Birds of America', Stangl's birds were originally produced from 1940-72. Values are based on the size and complexity of the figurine, and how well it has been decorated. Decorators, whose numbers were swelled with homeworkers at busy times, were able to choose their own colours, and their level of skill varied widely. Even though artists often signed their work with initials, the work of individual artists does not really affect value, so this information is only of use for dating. In 1972, some models were re-released, and these are often signed and dated. As with 'vintage' Stangl, they can still be desirable and valuable if they are well decorated. This pair of woodpeckers is an excellent example of a good design that has been well decorated.

A Stangl Pottery 'Gray Cardinal', no.3596, marked with partial small black 'STANGL POTTERY BIRDS' mark, incised '3596' and with 'BM' artist's initials.

4.75in (12cm) high

£45-55   BEL

A Stangl Pottery large 'Cockatoo', no.3584, with large black oval 'STANGL POTTERY BIRDS' mark and '3584' in black.

12.25in (31cm) high

£150-200   BEL

A Stangl 'Woodpeckers' figurine, no.8752, with inscribed number and printed factory mark.

8in (20.5cm) high

£300-400   BH

QUICK REFERENCE

- The term 'studio pottery' is used to describe pottery made by the owner of an independent pottery, or under their supervision. Quantities are typically limited, and each piece is, in effect, unique as it was handmade or hand-decorated. Although some studio pottery was made in the 19thC, it developed into a movement of its own after World War II.
- Key figures include forerunners Bernard Leach, his colleague Shoji Hamada, Lucie Rie, and Hans Coper. Later names, many of whom studied with or were inspired by one of these influential potters, include Alan Caiger-Smith, David Leach, Marianne de Trey and John Maltby.
  In the US, leading potters such as the Natzlers, Peter Voulkos, Maija Grotell, Beatrice Wood and others were also highly influential.

- Although the work of these important potters is usually very expensive, look out for the work of their students, as this is often more affordable and just as important when put in context. Similarly, the work of many potters is yet to be 'discovered'. Learn how to recognise styles of certain potters and find out a little about their backgrounds.
- Always consider the form, glaze and size. Look for pieces that are well made, and of good quality. Collecting by theme, such as glaze, is often rewarding as there are many variations to be found. Consider a potter's work in context of his time – those that innovated or led a new style, or exemplified the 'look' of the day, are often worth considering. Invest in a book of marks (often called 'seals') to help you learn how to identify particular potters.

An Aldermaston Pottery bowl, by Alan Caiger-Smith, with green, blue and black curving lines and painted monogram.

10.75in (27.5cm) diam

£500-700   WW

An Aldermaston Pottery bowl, by Alan Caiger-Smith, the interior with stylised panels in blue and ochre, the exterior with a simple blue band, the base with painted marks.

11.75in (30cm) diam

£300-500   WW

An 1960s Ambleside footed vase, designed and possibly made by George Cook, with sgrafitto geometric pattern, the base inscribed 'Ambleside'.

4.75in (12cm) high

£30-50   GC

A Richard Batterham stoneware jar, in a pale celadon glaze over impressed dot and line decoration.

9.75in (25cm) high

£150-200   WW

An Aldermaston Pottery waisted cylindrical vase, by Alan Caiger-Smith, with red lustre panels and printed and painted marks to base.

Caiger-Smith founded the Aldermaston Pottery in 1955. Considered a key training ground for a new generation of potters, it closed in 2006 when he retired. He is known for his tin and lustre glazes, which are often combined with Hispano-Moresque patterns and styles.

9.25in (23.5cm) high

£350-450   WW

A Carn Pottery fan vase, with low relief moulded curving and circular design to one side and stylised flower design to the other, the base with factory black printed mark.

Along with cats, fan vases are the most desirable shapes.

6in (15cm) high

£20-30   UCT

A Seth Cardew stoneware jug, with a tenmoku gaze and inscribed with bands and wavy lines, with impressed 'SC' seal mark.

6.25in (16cm) high

£30-50   W&W

A Carn Pottery asymmetric vase, with moulded low relief stylised designs, the base with black printed factory mark.

5.25in (13cm) high

£15-25   UCT

A Michael Casson basket, with a mottled brown salt glaze, the base with impressed seal.

13.25in (33.5cm) high

£120-180   W&W

A Deichman Pottery jardinière bowl, decorated with fish in a green glaze on a cream ground, the base painted with 'EKD' and 'NB' monograms.

Danish-born Kjeld and Erica Deichmann founded a pottery in New Brunswick, Canada in 1935. Inspired by Scandinavian pottery they had grown up around, they pioneered studio pottery and the craft tradition in Canada. Erica was responsible for the glazes, whilst Kjeld produced the forms. The pottery closed in 1963, when Kjeld died. This pattern is unusual, most pieces are plain.

6in (15cm) high CAD

£700-1,000   TAC

A Coldrum Pottery baluster vase, by Reginald Wells, covered with a mottled blue and lavender glaze, the base stamped 'Coldrum'.

9.25in (23.5cm) high

£100-150   W&W

A Canadian Deichmann mug, with green dripped glaze, the base inscribed 'Deichmann 45' and with 'NB' monogram, damaged handle.

5.25in (13cm) high CAD

£80-120   TAC

CERAMICS

A Farnham Pottery owl money bank, with incised and applied decoration and green glaze, minor chips.

Founded in Surrey in 1872, the company produced art pottery from 1880 onwards. Typically covered in a green glaze, wares were sold by Liberty and Heal's among others. Owls are typical motifs, but jugs are more common and were produced into the 1950s.

2.25in (6cm) high

£300-400   **WW**

An earthenware animal-shaped shower caddy, by Deborah Halpern, with painted 'Deborah D Halpern' signature.

Australian artist and ceramicist Halpern (b.1957) is known for her quirky and colourful animals inspired by Picasso.

14.25in (36cm) high

£300-500   **JA**

A large David Leach Lowerdown Pottery cut-sided vase, covered in a dolomite glaze, with impressed seal marks.

7.5in (19cm) high

£450-550   **WW**

An early St Ives stoneware bowl, by Bernard Leach, incised to interior and exterior with cloud motif under an ash glaze, impressed 'St Ives' and 'BL' script seal marks.

5.5in (14cm) diam

£300-500   **WW**

A CLOSER LOOK AT A STUDIO POTTERY SCULPTURE

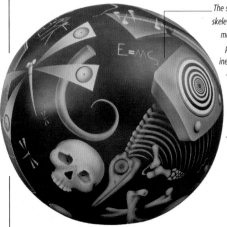

The skull and dinosaur skeleton are 'momento mori', hinting at the passing of life and inevitability of death – a theme used in art since the Renaissance.

The spherical form suggests the world, with objects in it showing developments across time, such as bacteria under a microscope, and a television.

It is well-designed and finely painted, being an excellent example of ceramics used as an art form to convey a message.

A Steven Gunderson ceramic sphere, decorated with geometric biological forms in black, white and red, with ball inside.

19in (48cm) diam

£800-1,200   **SK**

A Bernard Leach stoneware tea bowl, with tenmoku glaze outside and khaki glaze inside, and impressed 'BL' and 'St Ives' seals.

Pieces by Leach (1887-1979) are highly sought after. Generally considered to be the 'father' of studio ceramics, he founded the influential St Ives pottery with Shoji Hamada in 1910, from where he trained many of the great names in studio pottery.

4.75in (12cm) diam

£700-1,000   TEN

A Bernard Leach stoneware tea bowl, blue glaze with khaki on one side, with impressed 'BL' and 'St Ives' seals.

c1960   3.25in (8.5cm) high

£500-600   TEN

A John Maltby stoneware unomi, octagonal with painted panels, impressed seal.

Born in 1936, Maltby is one of the UK's most celebrated living studio potters. He trained in sculpture under David Leach and founded his own pottery in 1964. He is known today for his unique sculptural forms, simple geometric motifs and creating contrasts between light and dark. A unomi is a traditional Japanese tea bowl.

3.75in (9.5cm) high

£250-300   WW

A Bernard Leach earthenware mug, inscribed 'S.S. White Heather 1921' and decorated with a view of the boat with an 'X4' brown glaze, incised 'BL' and 'St Ives'.

The S.S. White Heather was a herring boat. This mug was made by Leach as part of a set.

4.25in (10.5cm) high

£200–300   TEN

One of a pair of Lorenzen salt and pepper shakers, decorated with abstract fish and waves on a mottled grey ground, the bases inscribed 'Lorenzen's Lanz Nova Scotia'.

c1960   2.25in (5.5cm) high

£20-30 PAIR   MHC

A John Maltby stoneware elliptical vase, decorated with diamond motifs, with impressed seal mark.

5in (12.5cm) high

£80-120   WW

A Paul Metcalfe early figural bottle vase, decorated with a stylised figure of a robed lady in green and white oxide glazes, the base with painted monogram and date.

1962   17in (44.5cm) high

£100-150   FLD

CERAMICS

QUICK REFERENCE – NATZLER

Viennese born Otto (b.1908) and Gertrud (1908-71) Natzler founded their pottery in Los Angeles upon their arrival in the US in 1938. Forms, produced by Gertrud, were typically simple with bowls being the first shapes produced. Otto devised the glazes, and it is primarily for these that the couple have become celebrated. The most desirable (and valuable) glazes resemble bubbled and cratered lava, but complex crystalline glazes, as seen on this bowl, are also sought after. The Natzler name is typically inscribed into the base.

A Natzler earthenware footed small bowl, in a blue and brown glaze, signed on the base.

4.5in (11.5cm) diam

£2,000-3,000   DRA

A Natzler footed bowl, in olive-green, turquoise and brown mottled semi-matte glaze, the base signed 'NATZLER'.

8.5in (21.5cm) diam

£1,200-1,800   DRA

A Natzler earthenware footed bowl, in a blue crystalline glaze, signed 'Natzler'.

6.25in (16cm) diam

£7,000-10,000   SDR

A Natzler beaker-shaped earthenware vase, with indented lip, covered in grey sea glaze, signed 'Natzler'.

5.5in (14cm) high

£3,500-4,500   SDR

A Natzler free-form earthenware bowl, covered in matte stone grey glaze, signed 'Natzler'.

This mottled and striated glaze, and the one on the blue bowl above, bear many similarities to the 'hare' s-fur' glazes used by Scandinavian ceramics companies such as Palshus and Gustavsberg.

6.25in (16cm) high

£3,000-4,000   SDR

A Natzler earthenware cup, covered in glossy mottled turquoise and lavender glazes, signed 'Natzler'.

c1962   3.75in (9.5cm) high

£2,500-3,500   SDR

A William Newland earthenware bull, slip-trailed with geometric motifs in cream on an ochre ground, with painted signature and dated '58', repaired horn.

Newland (1919-98), along with Margaret Hine and Nicola Vergette, was part of a group known as the 'Picassoettes' since they took their inspiration from Picasso. Bulls and other animal forms, decorated with exotic motifs, are typical.

1958   12.25in (31cm) wide

£700-900   **WW**

A CLOSER LOOK AT A PARKINSON SCULPTURE

Parkinson pottery, which is hard to find, has become highly sought-after since a book and exhibition in 2004.

It has a surreal appearance, recalling glove display hands in department stores, and accentuated by the chess board design.

Black and white painted slip-cast domestic and sculptural animals and figures are typical – this is an extremely rare design.

Susan studied at the Royal College of Art. The pottery was active for only eleven years from 1952-63.

A Richard Parkinson Ltd 'Hand in Glove' sculpture, designed by Susan Parkinson, painted with geometric panels of chess pieces, minor restoration on base rim.

13.75in (35cm) high

£1,000-1,500   **WW**

A Richard Parkinson Ltd slip cast porcelain bust of schoolboy, designed by Susan Parkinson, with black enamel decoration, the base with impressed marks.

6in (15cm) high

£550-650   **FLD**

A Richard Parkinson Ltd heraldic lion, designed by Susan Parkinson, painted in dark grey-blue on a white ground, with impressed mark.

9.5in (24cm) wide

£380-420   **WW**

A Katharine Pleydell-Bouverie stoneware cut-sided vase, covered in a green glaze, impressed seal mark, painted 'BX'.

2.25in (5.5cm) high

£100-150   **WW**

A tin-glazed earthenware jug, decorated by Alfred Powell with a lakeside landscape scene in blue, the reverse with a similar scene of a country house, the base with painted monogram.

Athough better known for his work with Wedgwood, Powell and his wife Louise also decorated a series of blanks.

5.25in (13.5cm) high

£150-200   **W&W**

CERAMICS

A CLOSER LOOK AT A SUSIE COOPER VASE

This spherical shape is typical of the geometricity of the Art Deco movement. This shape was hard to make and is rare today.

The right angles and straight lines of the hand-painted pattern contrast against the curving shape, but are also typical of the Art Deco movement.

This is typical of Cooper's most desirable Art Deco designs from c1928-30. Had it been in brighter colours and not cracked, it would have fetched more

A Gray's Pottery ball vase, designed by Susie Cooper, pattern no.8215, painted with geometric design in shades of yellow, black and grey, printed factory mark, painted number, hairline crack to base.

c1929   7in (18cm) high

£450-650   **WW**

The mark on the base shows a galleon amidst waves with yellow sails – this style of mark was used from 1921-31.

A late 1930s Susie Cooper Kestrel shape coffee set for six, decorated in the 'Crescents' pattern, no.1543, comprising coffee pot, milk jug, sugar bowl, ten cups, saucers and side plates and others, the bases with printed and painted marks, minor damages.

Coffee Pot 7.5in (19cm) high

£100-150   **WW**

A late 1930s Susie Cooper 'Panel Spray' part service, pattern no.1690, comprising milk jug and sugar bowl, six cups, saucers and side plates and a sandwich plate, the bases with printed marks.

This is a very rare pattern, probably as production was interrupted by the onset of war in 1939. Each of the six 'trio' sets, which comprise a cup and saucer and side plate, are commercial and collectable. The scarcer milk jug and sugar bowl are an additional bonus.

£1,000-1,500   **WW**

A late 1930s Susie Cooper 'Blue Crescent' Kestrel bachelor set, comprising teapot, two hot-water pots, milk jug and sugar basin, cup, saucer and side plate, a muffin dish and cover, cruet and a toast rack, the bases with printed factory marks, minor damages.

Teapot 5in (12.5cm) high

£200-300   **WW**

A Grays Pottery hand painted circular plate, designed by Susie Cooper, with an abstract geometric pattern in yellow, black and red with overlapping geometric forms.

c1929   10in (25.5cm) diam

£80-120   **FLD**

A Susie Cooper 'Endon' pattern 'Spiral' shape dinner service, comprising six dinner plates, six dessert plates, six side plates, two meat plates, five side plates, five dessert plates, six fruit bowls, six saucers and two tureens, one lidded.

The 'Spiral' shape was introduced in 1938, and the 'Endon' pattern dates from a similar time.

£120-180   **SWO**

QUICK REFERENCE

- Joseph Szeiler (1924–1986) was born in Hungary and studied to become a veterinary surgeon before emigrating to England, via Austria, in 1948. He first worked for J&G Meakin as a mould runner, later gaining more experience at Wade Heath & Co. In 1951, he took the decision to found his own company, renting a room in Hanley, Staffordshire. His first production included animals and figures: Szeiler created the designs and moulds, then made and glazed the figurines.

- In 1955, his business had expanded enough to allow him to buy larger premises in Burslem, where his company remained until his death and its closure in 1986.
- Animal figurines are the most common and most desirable designs, with many being highly stylised and elongated. Fawn and cream, sometimes with a light blue, are typical colours. Prices have begun to rise, as more collectors are drawn to Szeiler's work, but rarely fetch over £50.

A Szeiler elongated dog figurine, with printed mark to base.

3in (7.5cm) high

£7-10   DSC

A Szeiler sleeping dog in a basket.

Animals in woven baskets are a hallmark range for Szeiler, and can be found in many different variations.

Basket 1.5in (4cm) high

£5-8   DSC

A Szeiler long-eared small donkey figurine, in repose, with printed mark to base.

The long ears are a typical feature of many Szeiler animals. The mark is earlier in date, although no precise date ranges are yet known.

3.25in (8cm) long

£8-10   DSC

A Szeiler-type 'Bengo' figurine, with blue collar and tag, the base with 'UNIVERSAL MADE IN ENGLAND' printed mark.

This figurine is worth more as it represents Bengo, a popular cartoon character. Universal and Zalpark marks indicate that a piece may have been made as part of a joint venture.

3.25in (8.2cm) high

£20-25   DSC

A Szeiler blue and white donkey figurine, with elongated ears, the base with printed mark.

4.75in (12cm) high

£25-30   DSC

A Szeiler donkey and cart figurine, with printed mark to base.

6in (15cm) long

£15-20   DSC

A Szeiler koala and cub figurine, with printed mark to base.

3.5in (9cm) high

£15-20   DSC

CERAMICS

A Copeland Spode blue and white transfer printed 'Italian' pattern teapot.

9.75in (24.5cm) long

£60-80   **BAD**

QUICK REFERENCE – SADLER CAR TEAPOTS

Sadler's car teapots were first released in 1937 and produced again after WWII. Green, cream or yellow are the most commonly found single colours. Produced in the 1930s only, black, grey, maroon, blue or pink are scarcer colours. They have platinum luste details. The rarest variation from the 1930s has transfer-printed patterns of pixies and animals in the style of (but not by) Mabel Lucie Attwell, along with orange detailing, and can fetch over £500. When present, the numberplate is 'OKT42' indicating 'Okay, tea for two', but this was generally only applied to pre-war examples. After the war, single colour and mottled examples were produced, and impressed marks included the Sadler name. Prices have remained stable, due to their appeal to collectors of teapots and automobilia.

A 1920s-30s handpainted 'cottage ware' teapot, unmarked but possibly by Price Bros., with two chips to the corner of the lid and knob.

c1930s   *8.5in (21.5cm) wide*

£7-10   **PC**

A 1930s Royal Doulton handpainted 'Aspen' pattern teapot, with gilded foot, handle, rim and spout.

5.25in (13.5cm) diam

£50-60   **BEV**

A 1930s-50s Sadler novelty motor car teapot, with a green glaze, the base with impressed marks and registered number 820236 for 1937.

8.75in (22.5cm) wide

£30-50   **WW**

A 1930s Royal Doulton teapot, with handpainted arabesque pattern in green yellow, black and gold, the base marked 'V.1289'.

c1934   *5in (12.5cm) high*

£80-100   **BEV**

A Shelley 'Mode' shape teapot and cover, pattern number 11754, in green and gold, the base with printed and painted marks.

Designed by Eric Slater and produced from 1930-33, Mode is one of Shelley's two strongest Art Deco forms. This popular pattern was also available in yellow, red, black, blue or pink – all with similar gold handles and details.

5in (13cm) high

£300-400   **WW**

A Shelley fine bone china transfer printed 'Anemone' pattern 35oz teapot.

7in (17.5cm) high

£70-100   **W&L**

A CLOSER LOOK AT A TEAPOT

A Royal Grafton Fine Bone China teapot, handpainted with large brown flower and blue leaves.

7in (17.5cm) high

£20-30 **W&L**

Crossed legs from the 'Walking Ware' range are scarcer than others.

Pay attention to the colours and patterns of the shoes and, if applicable, the socks – some colours or colour combinations can be very rare.

Teapots, particularly in smaller sizes like this, are typically more valuable than cups or eggcups, unless the pattern is rare.

The bodies are usually white, those with transfer printed patterns, such as tropical islands, are rarer.

A Grindley small teapot, transfer printed with sprays of colourful flowers, with black detail and rims.

3.5in (9cm) high

£25-35 **W&L**

A Carltonware 'crossed legs' teapot with yellow shoes and green and brown socks, designed by Roger Michell of the Lustre Pottery, with printed marks to base.

1978 *8.25in (21cm) high*

£100-150 **BEV**

A 1950s Sadler teapot, with sprial ribbed body and transfer printed with roses, with impressed marks to base.

4.75in (12cm) high

£18-22 **W&L**

A Midwinter 'Fashion' shape coffee pot, with the transfer-printed 'Bali H'ai' design, designed by John Russell, with printed marks to base.

7.5in (19cm) high

£40-60 **RET**

A Midwinter 'HMS Mary' novelty teapot and cover, the base with impressed and printed marks.

c1940 *9.5in (24cm) wide*

£250-350 **WW**

A Grueby tile, decorated in cuenca with a yellow tulip and green leaves on a green ground, marked 'KY', with two corner chips.

6in (15cm) wide

£1,000-1,500　　　　　**DRA**

A W.B. Simpson tile panel of a knight, painted in colours, the back with impressed marks and paper label, cracked into twopieces.

24.5in (62cm) high

£280-320　　　　　**WW**

A Batchelder horizontal tile, depicting a Dutch boy and girl with dog-drawn carriage in typical Dutch landscape, the back covered with grout, hiding probable mark.

17.75in (45cm) wide

£450-550　　　　　**DRA**

A CLOSER LOOK AT A SET OF EAST GERMAN TILES

This set, and the others on this page, were part of a series produced for an East German holiday home as part of a series showing the power and modernity of the Communist block.

Communist bloc.

The angular, brightly coloured design is appealing and typical of the period – the shapes of the tiles themselves echo and creatre the lines of the design.

The design includes a TV tower, which were considered important statement buildings – examples were built in Moscow, Stuttgart, Riga and Berlin amongst other cities.

The sputnik satellite can also be seen amid the dots that represent stars in outer space – furthermore, the sun shines on the

A set of East German enamelled copper wall tiles, showing the Alexander TV tower in Berlin, the Sputnik satellite, and a radiating sun, framed in metal.

c1975　　　　　*28in (71cm) high*

£700-900　　　　　**VZ**

A set of East German enamelled copper wall tiles, showing an idyllic countryside landscape in the background with a dam, power station and a crane, framed in metal.

c1975　　　*30.5in (76.5cm) wide*

£650-750　　　　　**VZ**

A set of East German enamelled copper wall tiles, showing an industrial landscape with factory chimneys, a chemical plant, a modern high speed train and a flowery meadow with trees, framed in metal.

c1975　　　　　*40in (101cm) wide*

£650-750　　　　　**VZ**

QUICK REFERENCE

- The Troika Pottery was founded in 1963, at the Wells Pottery in Wheal Dream, St Ives, Cornwall, by potter Benny Sirota, painter Leslie Illsley and architect Jan Thompson (who left in 1965). Early pieces were smooth and glossy, often in white. Shapes were slip-moulded using liquid clay poured into moulds to ensure uniformity and ease of production.
- New shapes were introduced 1965. Illsley was influenced by Scandinavian ceramics as well as the work of Paul Klee and Constantin Brancusi, therefore circle and geometric designs in earthy muted colours were common. Success followed, due in part to the tourist industry, and in part because several high-profile London stores began stocking Troika wares.
- In 1970 the pottery expanded and moved to Newlyn. The characteristic matte, textured glaze became the main glaze around 1974.
- Consider the form, size, colours and the style of decoration. Practical, rectangular vases were produced in large numbers and are more common today. Meanwhile, scarcer hallmark shapes, such as 'wheel', 'anvil' and 'chimney' vases, remain popular with collectors. Well-executed, complex geometric patterns are desirable. Figural and pictorial images are extremely rare. Damage will reduce value considerably.
- From 1963 to 1967, pieces were usually marked 'St Ives' with a stylised trident in a square. The trident was phased out after 1967, and when the pottery moved to Newlyn, the 'St Ives' was also dropped.

A rare early Troika St Ives rectangular wall plaque, with abstract geometric decoration of squares and raised circles within a black border, with printed Trident mark.

7.5in (19cm) high

£200-300   GORL

A Troika St Ives 'Thames' wall plaque, modelled with a stylised curve of the river with two dimensional buildings surrounding, with Trident mark.

9.75in (25cm) high

£800-1,200   GORL

CERAMICS

A Troika 'Chimney' vase, relief decorated to each side with abstract carved motifs, and with white tin-glazed sides, painted mark and initialled for Avril Bennett.

1973-79   *8in (20.5cm) high*

£250-350   **FLD**

A Troika St Ives 'Chimney' vase, decorated with a gingerbread man in black oxide over a blue ground with an abstract pattern, with a black oxide glazed shoulder, hand painted St Ives mark.

7.75in (20cm) high

£300-500   **FLD**

A CLOSER LOOK AT A TROIKA MASK

Troika's masks are rare because they were complex to make and took up space in the kiln, making them expensive to buy and so comparatively few were sold.

Always inspect the corners and the base, which are often cracked or chipped. Prices have fallen slightly over the past few years, even for those in mint condition.

They were inspired by the work of artist Paul Klee, Aztec designs and also sometimes African or Oceanic tribal art and masks.

The backs of these masks are also decorated, but any decoration is usually much simpler than on the front.

A rare Troika pottery mask, doubled sided with typical geometric moulded decoration, with a brown ground, the base with painted mark and indistinct decorator's initials.

10in (25.5cm) high

£600-900   **GORL**

A Troika Pottery 'Chimney' vase, incised with sun and keypad motif, with a panel of 'Studio St Ives' stamped decoration, glazed in purple, blue and bronze, the base with painted marks and unidentified decorator's monogram.

7.75in (20cm) high

£350-450   **WW**

A Troika Pottery 'Rectangle' vase, decorated by Avril Bennett in relief and washed with oxide glazes in a palette of green and brown, the base with painted marks.

1973-79   *12.75in (33cm) high*

£280-320   **FLD**

A Troika Pottery square jardinière, decorated by Louise Jinks, the base with painted factory marks, and with hairline crack to the rim.

Jinks was a senior decorator from 1979-81.

1976-81   *7.5in (19cm) high*

£180-220   **GHOU**

CERAMICS

ESSENTIAL REFERENCE

- Wade was founded by Henry Hallam in 1810, and produced industrial ceramic fittings. In 1867, it moved to Burslem, Staffordshire, becoming known as Wade & Colcough. By the mid-1940s, the three Wade brothers each owned a factory in England; a fourth was founded in Ireland in the 1950s. In 1958, the three factories were combined into Wade Potteries Ltd by Sir George Wade. The company still exists, although the Irish factory closed in the 1990s.

- Wade is perhaps best known for its ranges of miniature, moulded porcelain figurines known as 'Whimsies'. The company had produced miniature figurines since the 1930s, and Whimsies were introduced in 1954. Sold in boxed sets, they were available until 1959, when they were given away as free gifts with products such as Red Rose tea or Christmas crackers. They were offered as premiums in Canada from 1967, and the US from 1983.

- In 1971, they were re-introduced for sale, but were sold individually in boxes. This continued until 1984, when they were withdrawn once again, to be re-introduced recently. Although millions have been made, they have become highly sought-after, with higher prices paid for scarcer,

earlier examples, or unusual variations in glaze or form. Excepting the most recent release, earlier examples are considered as being more finely modelled and decorated.

- The company also produced other ranges of figurines, trays and small ceramic items from the mid-1950s into the 1980s, which are also collectable. These include 'Minikins', 'Whoppas', and the two very popular 'Hat Box' ranges of cartoon film characters, licensed by Disney. Available from 1956-65 and again from 1981-85, the ranges also attract interest from Disney collectors.

- Always consider condition, as this is important to value, as so many examples exist. Run your fingers all over a Whimsie to check for chips and examine them closely to look for repair – either can reduce value by as much as 70 per cent or more. Excellent condition original boxes can double the value.

- In the selection shown here, range names and numbers have been taken from the Charlton Standard Catalogue and, unless otherwise indicated, precise date ranges given refer to the range, or a combination between a figure's introduction date and the production dates of the range.

A Wade 'St Bernard' Whimsie, from Set Seven, the Pedigree Dogs range.

Many early Whimsies have separate legs – these were abandoned on later examples, presumably as they were too fragile and easily broken.

1957-61   1.75in (4.5cm) long

£25-30   DSC

A Wade 'Alsatian' Whimsie, from Set Seven, the Pedigree Dogs range.

1957-61   1.5in (4cm) long

£20-25   DSC

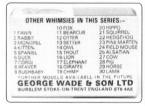

OTHER WHIMSIES IN THIS SERIES:-		
	10 FOX	20 HIPPO
1 FAWN	11 BEARCUB	21 SQUIRREL
2 RABBIT	12 OTTER	22 HEDGEHOG
3 MONGREL	13 SETTER	23 PINE MARTEN
4 KITTEN	14 OWL	24 FIELD MOUSE
5 SPANIEL	15 TROUT	25 ALSATIAN
6 DUCK	16 LION	27 COW
7 CORGI	17 ELEPHANT	28 PIG
8 BEAVER	18 GIRAFFE	29 HORSE
9 BUSHBABY	19 CHIMP	30 LAMB

FURTHER MODELS AVAILABLE IN THE FUTURE

GEORGE WADE & SON LTD
BURSLEM STOKE-ON-TRENT ENGLAND ST6 4AE

A Wade 'Collie' Whimsie, from the English Whimsies range, complete with original box.

The figure on its own is usually worth around £3-4.

1975-84   1.5in (3.5cm) high

£5-8   DSC

A Wade 'Spaniel With Ball' Whimsie, finished in white, from Set One, the English Animals range.

A rarer variation has a beige glazed rump. Perhaps made as prototypes, examples can fetch twice this value or more.

1954-58   2in (5cm) long

£15-20   DSC

A Wade 'Jock' figurine, with no tartan coat, from Set One of the original Disney 'Lady and the Tramp' Hat Box range.

This is the rarest and most valuable variation of the three Jocks from the first issue of this range.

1956-65   1.75in (4.5cm) high
£30-35   DSC

A Wade 'Jock' figurine, with green tartan coat, from Set One of the original Disney 'Lady and the Tramp' Hat Box range.

1956-65   1.75in (4.5cm) high
£15-20   DSC

A Wade 'Jock' figurine, with blue tartan coat, from Set One of the original Disney 'Lady and the Tramp' Hat Box range.

1956-65   1.75in (4.5cm) high
£15-20   DSC

A Wade 'Scamp' figurine, from the re-issued Disney 'Lady and the Tramp' Hat Box range, with original plastic 'hat box' with paper labels.

1981-85   1.75in (4cm) long
£20-25   DSC

A Wade 'Lady' figurine from the re-issued Disney 'Lady and the Tramp' Hat Box series, with gilt label to stomach and plastic 'hat box' with paper labels.

Original moulds were used for many figurines in the second series, and it can be hard to tell which period they were made in without the box. However, as some moulds were worn through use, details on re-issues can be flatter. Painted details may also differ e.g. later versions of Lady (like this one) lack a blue collar.

1981-85   1.75in (4cm) long
£20-25   DSC

MILLERS COMPARES

This is the first version of Tramp. In the second version he is seated, as the legs on the earlier version proved fragile and easily broken.

Like many Whimsies, the modelling and painting on this earlier version are better.

This simpler second version was introduced in 1985 to complete the re-issued set in the last year of its production.

The base is ridged, which is a hallmark of authentic Whimsies, and this style of label was used 1981-1985.

A Wade 'Tramp' figurine, from Set One of the original Disney 'Lady and the Tramp' Hat Box range.

1956-6   52.25in (5.5cm) high
£20-25   DSC

A Wade 'Tramp' figurine, from the re-issued Disney 'Lady and the Tramp' Hat Box range, the base with gilt label.

1985   2in (5cm) high
£15-20   DSC

CERAMICS

A Wade 'Peg' figurine, from the re-issued Disney 'Lady and the Tramp' Hat Box range, with original printed card box.

Card boxes replaced plastic 'hat boxes' towards the end of the production period, with Peg only being sold in a card box.

1985   1.75in (4cm) long

£20-25   DSC

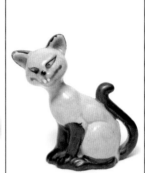

A Wade 'Si' figurine from Set Two of the Disney 'Lady and the Tramp' Hat Box range.

1956-65   2in (5cm) high

£30-35   DSC

A Wade 'Am' figurine from Set Two of the Disney 'Lady and the Tramp' Hat Box range.

1956-65   2in (5cm) high

£30-35   DSC

A rare Wade 'Tod' figurine from the re-issued Disney 'Fox & The Hound' Hat Box range.

Tod was not as popular as other characters with buyers at the time, making him rare today.

1982-85   2in (5cm) high

£40-50   DSC

A Wade 'Dumbo' figurine, from Set Two of the the Disney Hat Box range.

As well as being a desirable character, undamaged examples of ' Dumbo' are scarce.

1956-65   1.5in (4cm) high

£30-35   DSC

A Wade 'Bambi' figurine from the first issue of Set Two of the Disney 'Bambi' Hat Box range, with original printed card 'hat box'.

This is the original card 'hat box' packaging from the 1950s and 60s.

1956-65   1.75in (4cm) high

£30-35   DSC

A Wade 'Pegasus' figurine, from Set Two of the Disney Hat Box range.

Always examine the wings carefully as they are often damaged. Pegasus is from Dinsey's 'Fantasia'.

1956-65   2in (5cm) high

£40-50   DSC

ESSENTIAL REFERENCE – MINIKINS

A Wade 'Cat Walking' Minikin, from Series One, with blue tail and ears.
1955-58   *1.5in (4cm) long*
£10-15   **DSC**

A Wade 'Cow' Minikin, from Series Two, with 'L-plate' motif to front and musical notes to back.

Minikins were issued from 1955-58 in three different series, each comprising differently shaped figurines modelled by William Harper. All are unmarked and covered in a glossy white glaze, but bear different combinations of motifs and coloured facial features. In all, these differences created 48 variations per set. At an original cost of 1/- each, they were sold to retailers in boxes of 48. With its 'L' plate and musical notes on a cow, this model is a scarce combination.
1956-58   *1.25in 93cm) long*
£20-25   **DSC**

A Wade 'Cat Standing' Minikin, from Series One, with green star and yellow ears.
1955-58   *1.25in (3cm) high*
£10-15   **DSC**

A Wade 'Dog' Minikin, from Series Three, with red collar and yellow ears.
1957-58   *1.25in 93cm) high*
£20-25   **DSC**

A Wade 'Mouse' Minikin, from Series Two, with blue spot.
1956-58   *1in (2.5cm) high*
£10-15   **DSC**

A Wade 'Rabbit' Minikin, from Series Two, with musical note decoration.
1956-58   *1.25in (3cm) long*
£10-15   **DSC**

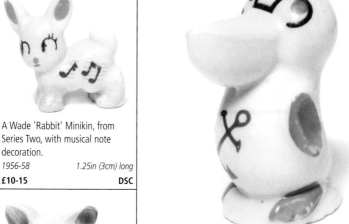

A Wade 'Fawn' Minikin, from Series Three, with flower to chest and pink ears.

This model is quite rare as it was only produced for one year. Note the oversized head, which is typically 1950s in style and also hinted at Disney's 'Bambi'.
1957-58   *1.25in (3cm) high*
£25-30   **DSC**

A very rare Wade 'Pelican' Minikin, from Series Three, with anchor decoration.

This is rare as it was produced for only one year before the Minikin range was discontinued. The Pelican was also less popular than other more 'cuddly' and collected animals such as dogs and cats.
1957-58   *1.25in (3cm) high*
£30-35   **DSC**

CERAMICS

A CLOSER LOOK AT A NATWEST PIGGY BANK

Many believe these unmarked Woody versions are fakes – all Wade banks are marked 'WADE ENGLAND' on the base.

The deeper pink skin colour and the unmarked base indicate that this example was made by Sunshine Ceramics.

Sunshine Ceramics received the initial commission to manufacture the piggy banks, but could not keep up with demand and consquently it lost the commission to Wade in 1983.

Although they are rarer than Wade's version, over 100,000 Woodies were reputed to have been made, but only 400 full sets of the family were made.

A Sunshine Ceramics 'Woody' piggy bank, modelled by Paul Cardew, and produced for the National Westminster Bank, the base unmarked.

1982   *5.25in (13cm) high*

£5-8   DSC

A Wade 'Woody' piggy bank, modelled by Paul Cardew, produced for the National Westminster Bank, the base moulded 'WADE ENGLAND'.

1983-88   *5.25in (13cm) high*

£10-15   DSC

A Wade 'Annabel' piggy bank, modelled by Paul Cardew, produced for the National Westminster Bank, the base moulded 'WADE ENGLAND'.

1983-88   *6in (15cm) high*

£15-20   DSC

A Wade 'Maxwell' piggy bank, modelled by Paul Cardew, produced for the National Westminster Bank, the base moulded 'WADE ENGLAND'.

1983-88   *6.5in (16cm) high*

£25-30   DSC

A Wade 'Lady Hilary' piggy bank, modelled by Paul Cardew, produced for the National Westminster Bank, the base moulded 'WADE ENGLAND'.

1983-88   *6.75in (17cm) high*

£35-40   DSC

ESSENTIAL REFERENCE: NATWEST PIGGY BANKS

A Wade 'Sir Nathaniel' piggy bank, modelled by Paul Cardew, produced for the National Westminster Bank, the base moulded 'WADE ENGLAND'.

The National Westminster bank offered these piggy banks from 1982-88 as an incentive for children to save. Woody was given when a child opened an account, with Annabel being given when the balance had reached £25, Maxwell when the balance reached £50, Lady Hilary when it reached £75, and Sir Nathaniel when it reached £100. As £100 was a large sum of money for a child in the 1980s, far fewer examples of Sir Nathaniel were given away compared to Woody. 'Cousin Wesley', modelled by Ken Holmes, was given away in 1998, expanding the family to six. Only 5,000 examples were made and he can fetch £300 or more today with box and slip. Also look out for the 'Gold Woody', decorated with 22 carat gold leaf, of which only only around 30 examples were made, each accompanied by a certificate of authenticty. Fakes are known. These include the 'Gold Woody', and a 'Gold Annabel' which was never made by Wade. Sir Nathaniel banks in white coats are also fakes. In 2007, Paul Cardew's Rame Pottery re-released the pig family with silver detailing to celebrate its 25th anniversary. A new full set costs £200.

1983-88   *7in (17.5cm) high*

£50-60   DSC

A 1950s Wade set of four transfer printed ballet dancer dishes, complete with original box.

Dishes 4.75in (10.5cm) wide

£30-40   DSC

A Wade 'Alsation Puppy Lying' pup in a basket dish, with an Alsatian Puppy Lying Whimsy figurine, from the Cat and Puppy Dishes range.

1974-8   1 3.25in (8cm) wide

£10-15   DSC

A 1950s-60s Wade Viking longboat dish, with green and beige glazes and moulded marks to base.

7.5in (19cm) long

£10-15   DSC

A 1950s Wade Mermaid vase, with moulded mermaids on two sides.

The shape and design was perhaps inspired by similar 1930s Art Deco pressed glass vases from Czechoslovakia, Germany and England.

4.25in (10.5cm) wide

£20-25   DSC

A 1950s-60s posy vase, with a Koala on a branch.

2.5in (6.5cm) high

£20-25   DSC

An Irish Wade trinket box, with moulded shamrocks and transfer printed horse racing scene, with moulded marks and grey-blue glaze to base.

The grey glaze, often with greeny-blue tones, is typical of Wade's Irish production.

5in (12.5cm) wide

£15-20   DSC

A 1930s Wade jug vase, in the form of a budgerigar perched on a branch curling up a column, the base printed 'WADE ENGLAND'.

10.25in (26cm) high

£25-30   DSC

FIND OUT MORE...

www.wade.co.uk – *the official company website*

Pat Murray, Wade Whimsical Collectable, *The Charlton Press, 2004*

CERAMICS

QUICK REFERENCE

- Wedgwood was founded by Josiah Wedgwood (1730-1796) in Burslem, Staffordshire in 1759. Success came quickly, and he expanded in 1764, and again in 1768. After meeting the businessman Thomas Bentley, who became his partner in 1769, Wedgwood became fascinated by Classical Greek and Roman designs, and these influenced the company's designs from then on. Although all types of pottery were made, the company is famous for its matte Jasper ware developed c1774-75 and produced in blue, black or green with applied white friezes of Classical scenes.

- The company continued to be an important and innovative pottery during the 20th century, and employed a number of notable designers from the 1930s onwards. Perhaps the most important of these was New Zealand architect and Modernist designer Keith Murray (1892-1981). His geometric Art Deco designs in cool, Classical matte glazes have become highly sought after today. Forms are simple, with moulded ribs, or plain bands cut into the bodies with a lathe. They were produced in a range of colours including 'Moonstone' white, 'Straw Yellow' and green.

- Other notable designers included Daisy Makeig-Jones (1881-1945) who is known for her complex 'Fairyland Lustre' range of the late 1910s and 1920s, and illustrator Eric Ravilious (1903-42) who designed nursery and table ware from c1936 to 1940. Norman Wilson (1902-85), John Skeaping (1901-80) and Millicent Taplin (1902-80) are other notable names whose various designs from the 1920-60s are worth looking out for.

- Wedgwood has attracted a huge following of collectors, and prices are strong, particularly for 20thC designs. It will be interesting to see how the company's recent insolvency affects values over the coming years.

A Wedgwood matte green ball vase, shape 4197, designed by Keith Murray, the base with printed full signature mark.

6in (15.5cm) high

£350-400   BEV

A Wedgwood Straw yellow tapering cylindrical vase, shape 4315, designed by Keith Murray, the base with printed 'KM' mark.

7.5in (19cm) high

£450-550   BEV

A 1930s Wedgwood matte green horizontally fluted globe vase, shape 4324, designed by Keith Murray, the base with impressed 'KM' mark.

This is an extremely rare design. This mark was introduced in 1934. It is more commonly seen printed, rather than impressed.

7in (17.5cm) high

£500-700   PC

A Wedgwood Straw yellow ball vase, shape 4197, designed by Keith Murray, the base with printed full signature mark.

This mark was introduced 1932.

6in (15cm) high

£350-450   BEV

A Wedgwood Black Basalt bowl, by Norman Wilson, of fluted form, glazed black, impressed marks, minor chips to top rim.

10in (25.5cm) diam

£380-480   WW

A rare Wedgwood earthenware bowl, by Norman Wilson, sky blue cut back to black, the interior black, impressed marks, 'NW' monogram.

6.25in (16cm) diam

£420-480   WW

A Wedgwood bowl, designed by Norman Wilson, of fluted form, glazed black and white, impressed marks, printed 'NW'.

Here, a Black Basalt slip has been applied to a Moonstone white glazed body, which has then been cut back on a lathe to reveal the underlying colour.

10.75in (27cm) diam

£280-380   WW

QUICK REFERENCE – NORMAN WILSON

Norman Wilson (1902-1985) was invited to join Wedgwood as Works Manager in 1926. Part of a young, dynamic team, he became Production Director in 1946, having introduced new production processes including the installation of a tunnel kiln. Among collectors, he is best known for his glaze experiments, and matte glazes that were used by Keith Murray. After studying ancient Chinese Sung glazes, Wilson developed a range of unique experimental glazes that were applied to production and specially commissioned forms. Known as 'Norman Wilson Unique Ware', these were produced erratically from 1928-63, with no two pieces being exactly the same.

A Wedgwood Dragon Lustre dish, designed by Daisy Makeig-Jones, with mythical beast printed in gilt on a pearl lustre ground, the base with printed and painted marks.

3.5in (9cm) diam

£100-150   WW

A Wedgwood earthenware bowl, designed by Norman Wilson, the exterior salmon pink, the interior mottled pink, the base with impressed marks and 'NM' monogram.

8in (20.5cm) diam

£400-500   WW

A Wedgwood Fairyland Lustre 'Candlemas' pattern vase, designed by Daisy Makeig-Jones, shape 2410, printed and painted in colours and gilt on a black ground, the base with printed factory mark, and 'NJW Baker' retailer's paper label.

'Candlemas' was introduced in 1918, and was based on the ritual ceremony of the blessing of candles, which would then be carried in a procession. Produced in four different colour variations, it was made until 1929.

7.5in (19.5cm) high

£800-1,200   WW

A Weller scenic 'Hudson' vase, painted by Hester Pillsbury with a cabin in the woods, against a mountainous landscape, repair to two cracks through body, kiln stamp.

Scenic Hudson vases are scarcer than floral patterns. Had this vase not been cracked it might have been worth double this price.

9in (23cm) high

£600-800　　　　**CRA**

A CLOSER LOOK AT A WELLER VASE

The Sicard range was designed by Frenchman Jacques Sicard, who had previously worked for notable French potter Clement Massier.

One of Weller's most sought-after ranges among collectors, this example is enhanced by a decorative shape typical of the period.

Developed under great secrecy with the aim of putting Weller back among the top pottery companies in the US, the range was sold from 1902-12.

The range is typified by iridescent glazes and motifs derived from nature. This example displays a superb range of colours and a complex and detailed pattern.

A Weller 'Sicard' two-handled vase, painted with blossoms on a rich purple lustred ground, signed 'Weller Sicard'.

9in (23cm) high

£1,500-2,500　　　　**DRA**

A Weller 'Etna' vase, moulded with pink daisies against a shaded dark grey ground, the base stamped 'WELLER WARE ETNA'.

10.75in (27.5cm) high

£250-350　　　　**DRA**

A Weller 'Sicard' vase with scrolling leaf and daisy pattern, the base with script factory mark, glaze chip to bottom, possibly from grinding.

5.5in (14cm) high

£450-550　　　　**DRA**

A Weller 'Sicard' cabinet vase, decorated with an all-over star pattern, the base stamped '6'.

4in (10cm) high

£350-450　　　　**DRA**

A Weller 'Turada' bowl, with heavy slip decoration and black glaze, the base marked 'Weller Turada 44'.

Turada was designed by Samuel Weller.

c1898

4.5in (11.4cm) diam

£60-80　　　　**BEL**

A Weller 'Knifewood' vase, with owls, squirrels and birds on oak branches, the base stamped 'Weller'.

7in (18cm) high

£450-550   **DRA**

A rare Weller Matt Green-glazed basket vase, on a 'Silvertone' blank, crisply decorated, unmarked, and with restoration to handle.

Such green glazes were typical of Arts and Crafts potteries, and are desirable among collectors today.

9in (23cm) high

£200-300   **DRA**

A rare Weller 'Fru Russett' tapering vase, with pierced rim, large applied yellow flowers and green leaves on a pale purple ground, restored rim, the base with impressed mark.

The Arts and Crafts style Fru Russett range was introduced in 1905 and is very rare today. Typical colours include matte green, brown, or blue and motifs are usually floral.

10.5in (26.5cm) high

£1,200-1,800   **CRA**

A very rare Weller 'Muskota' wall hanging 'Tree Squirrel', with restored paws.

The Muskota line of animals was produced from 1915-28 and is very popular with collectors today. The range also included butterflies, birds and fish, with this form being very scarce.

13.75in (35cm) long

£450-550   **BH**

A Weller 'Tutone' chalice vase, with green highlights, the base with Weller Pottery full kiln stamp, and three tight lines at the rim.

5.5in (14cm) high

£15-25   **BEL**

A Weller 'Velva' vase, in brown with floral panel, the base with script Weller Pottery mark.

7.5in (19cm) high

£60-80   **BEL**

A Weller 'Woodcraft' tree-shaped vase, with climbing squirrel and owl, with tight crack to rim, and second restored crack.

18in (45.5cm) high

£600-800   **DRA**

A rare Weller Art Deco owl figurine, in a semi-matte blue glaze, the Greek letters 'Kappa Kappa Gamma' on the base.

9.75in (25cm) high

£400-600   **BEL**

CERAMICS

QUICK REFERENCE

- Wemyss ware was produced by the Fife Pottery in Kirkaldy Scotland from 1882, after the owner's son, Robert Methven Heron, invited Bohemian decorators to join the pottery. The pottery had its origins in the 18thC producing objects in muted colours, but when Karel Nekola, one of the new staff, decorated pieces with flowers and leaves inspired by his love of nature, production changed direction and Wemyss ware was born.

- Popularity grew rapidly, and pieces were sold by top London retailer Thomas Goode & Son, whose marks can often be found on pieces.

- Following Nekola's death in 1915. Edwin Sandland took over decoration. After his death in 1928 he was in turn succeeded by Nekola's son Joe. A loss in popularity due to changing public tastes forced the pottery to close in 1930. Joe Nekola moved to the Bovey Tracey pottery in Devon, taking the Wemyss moulds with him. After his death in 1952, Esther Weeks took over until 1957. She is still decorating Wemyss today at the Griselda Pottery, Fife (established 1985).

- The colourful, cheery and quirky style of Wemyss ware has attracted a legion of loyal collectors, including personalities such as Elton John, the late HM Queen Elizabeth the Queen Mother, and HRH Prince Charles. Most collectors collect Wemyss ware by pattern and some patterns and shapes are more desirable than others. The work of Karel Nekola is particularly sought after.

- Examine pieces all over for signs of damage, as this reduces value dramatically. Wares made in Fife are particularly prone to crazing and chipping. Devon-produced pieces have a cleaner white 'glassy' glaze, and are lighter in weight than examples from Fife. They are also generally less valuable, giving a more affordable entry point to the market.

A Wemyss basket jardinière, decorated with cabbage roses, the base with impressed 'Wemyss' mark.

c1900   11.5in (29.5cm) diam

£280-320   **L&T**

A small Wemyss loving cup, decorated with dog roses, with impressed 'Wemyss Ware R. H. & S.' mark, and 'T. Goode & Co.' retailer's mark, glaze losses on rim.

c1900   4.25in (10.5cm) high

£280-320   **L&T**

An early 20thC Wemyss dog bowl, decorated with cabbage roses and inscription 'Plus je connais les hommes/Plus j'admire les chiens', with painted and impressed marks 'Wemyss', restoration to rim, cracks.

The charming inscription means "The more I know [about] men, the more I admire dogs." Dog bowls are scarce and valuable.

4.25in (11cm) diam

£300-500   **L&T**

A small Wemyss basket, decorated with cabbage roses, with impressed 'Wemyss Ware R. H. & S.' mark, and 'T Goode & Co.' retailer's mark.

c1900   8in (20.5cm) long

£250-300   **L&T**

An early 20thC Wemyss low pomade and cover, with dog roses, possibly by Karel Nekola, with impressed and painted 'Wemyss' mark, chip to rim.

3.75in (9.5cm) diam

£350-400   **L&T**

A Wemyss 'Cabbage Rose' biscuit box and cover, painted in colours, impressed and painted 'Wemyss' painted and printed marks.

5in (12.5cm) diam

£220-280   WW

A large early 20thC Wemyss mug, decorated with cabbage roses, with impressed mark 'Wemyss'.

5.5in (14cm) high

£280-320   L&T

A 1920s Wemyss biscuit barrel and cover, decorated in the 'Jazzy' pattern with cabbage roses, the cover inscribed 'Biscuits', with painted 'Wemyss 213' mark.

'Jazzy' is the name given to the multi-coloured, brushed background, which replaces the standard white on other pieces.

4.75in (12cm) diam

£250-350   L&T

A Wemyss 'Cabbage Rose' jug and a basin, painted in colours, the bases with various marks, damaged.

Had this not been damaged, it may have fetched over £800.

Jug 6.25in (16cm) high

£150-200   WW

A CLOSER LOOK AT A WEMYSS GOBLET

The rose, shamrock and thistle motifs are typical of decoration on Wemyss, but are rarely found together on one piece.

The rose can be read as indicating England, the thistle Scotland, and the shamrock Ireland.

The goblet bears the VR monogram for 'Victoria Regina' – royal commemoratives are widely collected, which widens the market.

The goblet shape is appealing, and the decoration is very detailed.

An early 20thC Wemyss pin tray, decorated by Karel Nekola with dog roses and bearing the inscription "Sois satisfait des fruits, des fleurs, même des feuilles/ Si c'est dans ton jardin à toi que tu les cueilles", impressed and painted mark "Wemyss", hairline crack.

The wording reads, 'Be satisfied with the fruits, flowers, and same with the leaves/If it is in your garden that you picked them'. Plaques are scarce and desirable.

5.75in (14.5cm) wide

£500-700   L&T

A small Wemyss Victoria goblet, with decoration of roses, thistles and shamrock, and bearing crown and cipher, impressed mark 'Wemyss Ware R. H. & S.', 'T. Goode & Co.' retailer's mark.

c1900

5.5in (14cm) high

£200-300   L&T

CERAMICS

A small early 20thC Wemyss pig, covered in a green glaze.

6.25in (16cm) long

£350-450   L&T

A Wemyss pottery pig, covered in a pink glaze, with impressed mark.

6.25in (16cm) high

£320-380   WW

A small Wemyss pig figure, covered in a white glaze, with impressed 'Wemyss' mark.

c1900   6.25in (16cm) long

£350-450   L&T

A Wemyss pig, painted in shades of black and white, its snout and toes painted pink, painted 'Wemyss', and printed 'Made in England'.

6.5in (16.5cm) wide

£350-450   WW

A CLOSER LOOK AT A WEMYSS PIG

Pigs can be found in a number of different patterns and plain glazes, but beware of fakes which have glossier glazes in different tones when compared to authentic examples.

Plump seated pigs are perhaps the most celebrated and recognisable of Wemyss' shapes and are highly sought after.

Smaller Plichta pigs dating from after 1930, such as this one, tend to be more affordable than earlier examples.

In 2004, Sotheby's sold a rare sleeping piglet painted with roses for a record price of £34,800.

A small post-1930 Wemyss pig figure, decorated by Joe Nekola with shamrocks, printed marks 'Plichta London England', painted marks 'Nekola/pinx'.

6.25in (16cm) long

£320-380   L&T

A Wemyss goose flower holder, naturalistically painted in typical colours, on an oval foot, impressed 'Wemyss Ware R.H. & S.' and a pink stamped mark for T. Goode & Co.

c1900   8in (20.5cm) high

£320-380   DN

QUICK REFERENCE

- West German ceramics from the 1950s-1970s have recently become highly collectable. Interest in this field is understandable, as this period enjoyed an explosion of innovation and design in West German pottery, which changed dramatically from decade to decade. Established companies, such as Bay Keramik, Dümler & Breiden, Emons & Söhne and Ruscha, underwent a revival, as new companies, such as Scheurich and Otto Keramik, opened.

- The ceramics of the 1950s are typified by curving, organic or geometric forms, and painted in bright, primary colours, often outlined in black. Patterns comprised ovals, circles, lines and stylised, curving, natural motifs. Angled or asymmetric curving handles or rims were common. Largely ornamental, jug vases with handles were particularly popular. These handles were often strongly angled in the 1950s, taking on ring forms in the 1960s.

- There was a complete change of style in the 1960s-70s. Colour and texture became extremely important. Rather than forming planned patterns, glazes were trailed, dripped or daubed over the body of the piece. Many of these glazes were thick 'lava' glazes, arranged in bands or stripes of bright colours, such as orange or red.

- Look for wilder, thick glazes, known by collectors as 'Fat Lava', as these tend to be more desirable, particularly in unusual forms. Many 'Fat Lava' pieces were produced in limited numbers, as opposed to tamer designs in less exuberant colours, which are more common.

- Makers can be identified by considering shape, colour, type of glaze and style of moulded marks on the base. Some pieces were inscribed or had impressed marks: some even have labels. Handle as many identified pieces, ideally those with labels, as possible.

A 1950s Marzi & Remi 'sugarglaze' vase, with inscribed curving lines through a brick coloured glaze, the base marked '2015-50'.

19.75in (50cm) high

£80-120   **OUT**

A 1960s Bay Keramik floor vase, with hand-painted cell-like design, introduced in 1961, the base with moulded numbers.

Many have attributed this design to Bodo Mans due to the abstract nature and bright colours of the design, but this has not been confirmed.

£100-150   **OUT**

A 1950s West German Conradt Gebrüder vase, with hand-painted round and curving line design, the base marked "100/5".

10in (25cm) high

£40-60   **OUT**

A 1950s West German Bay Keramik torpedo vase, with white textured glaze and hand-decorated multicoloured crescent and curving line decoration, the base moulded '529 38'.

15.25in (38.5cm) high

£20-30   **RET**

A 1950s West German Bay Keramik baluster vase, with hand-painted yellow and blue bands and black dashes, designed by Bodo Mans, the base moulded '584-25'.

10in (25cm) high

£30-50   **OUT**

CERAMICS

A 1950s West German Fürstenberg porcelain bull, with black glaze, the base marked 'F'.

6in (15cm) high

£40-60   OUT

A 1950s Keto 'Komposition' vase, with hand-painted multicoloured triangles and inscribed lines, the base printed 'Keto Keramik Handarbeit Komposition 1004'.

9in (23cm) high

£40-60   OUT

A CLOSER LOOK AT A BAY VASE

Defined areas of bright, saturated colour combined with inscribed 'sgrafitto' or painted lines are typical of 1950s designs.

Patterns were often named after romantic, foreign places as the 1950s was the age of the jet plane and an increase in foreign travel.

Bodo Mans was one of the most notable designers during the 1950s, and produced many similar designs inspired by modern art.

Despite the pattern being modern, the shape is more traditional – had that been more modern as well, the value would have been higher.

A West German Bay Keramik 'Paris' pattern urn vase, designed by Bodo Mans in 1960, the base moulded '1014-25 WEST-GERMANY'.

10in (25cm) high

£30-40   MA

A 1960s West German Marzi & Remy blue and white arabesque patterned jug vase, with impressed 'MR' monogram used from 1960-67, numbered '2027/32A'.

Marzi & Remy (1879-1994) are best known for their beer steins, which were mostly decorated with the design protruding through the coloured glaze, as in this example. This moulded pattern recalls tiles of the Arts and Crafts movement of the late 19thC and early 20thC.

1960-67   *12.5in (32cm) high*

£20-30   M20C

A 1970s Ruscha wall plate, decorated with a sgraffito and glazed design of grazing fawns on a mottled cream ground, the back printed 'RUSCHA HANDARBEIT' and moulded '717/1'.

1969-78   *7.25in (18.5cm) diam*

£22-28   RET

A 1950s West German Schramberg Majolika Fabrik hand-painted 'Cuba' pattern dish, the base marked '4370 Cuba'.

5in (12cm) wide

£15-20   OUT

A West German Scheurich floor vase, the grey bubbly 'lava' glaze cut through to reveal the red underglaze in the form of horses, the base with moulded marks.

18in (46cm) high

£100-150   **WW**

A West German Scheurich 'Lora' pattern floor vase, with a copper-coloured micro-crystalline glaze over a glossy red glaze, the base moulded '517 45 W.GERMANY'.

This type of coppery micro-crystalline glaze was developed by Oswald Kleudgen and became a signature glaze of his.

17in (43cm) high

£80-100   **M20C**

A CLOSER LOOK AT A SCHEURICH VASE

Known to collectors as the 'Flame' pattern, the range was actually called 'Lora'.

This is a comparatively large size, had it been a floor vase, the value could have been doubled.

This particular colour combination is very unusual, particularly the green.

Before firing, layers of glaze are cut away by hand to reveal underlying colours, making the pattern on each unique.

A West German Scheurich 'Lora' pattern floor vase with three layers of glaze, comprising a beige lava glaze over glossy orange over glossy green, the base with indistinct numbering.

15in (38cm) high

£70-100   **M20C**

A 1970s West German Scheurich torpedo vase, with thin grey lava glaze and glossy white and dripped blue bands, the base moulded '522-20'.

8in (20cm) high

£40-60   **OUT**

A West German Scheurich floor vase, with banded orange and green design and tube-lined curlicue designs in a lava glaze.

20in (51cm) high

£30-50   **SAS**

A 1970s Scheurich cylinder vase with orange band and tube-lined grey 'lava' glaze design, with beige and grey 'lava' glaze top and base, the base moulded '231 15 W GERMANY'.

This form number was used on three different shapes by Scheurich, showing how shape numbers were reused at different times.

6in (15cm) high

£15-20   **RET**

A 1970s Scheurich 'Wien' series bulb vase, designed by A. Seide, with lava glazed ribbed top and dripped glazed body designed by Oswald Kleudgen, the base with indistinct moulded marks.

7in (17.5cm) high

£20-30   **RET**

A 1970s West-German Scheurich 'Wien' series jug vase, designed by A. Seide, covered with a dripped orangey red glaze over a bronze-brown ground, the base numbered '269-27'.

10.5in (27cm) high

£40-60   **OUT**

A mid-late 1970s West German Scheurich jug vase, with glossy orange and brown glazes, the base moulded 400-22 W.GERMANY.

8.75in (22cm) high

£15-20   **M20C**

A West German Scheurich jug vase, with glossy mottled red central band and cream foamy glaze over a brown ground, the base moulded 400-22 W.GERMANY.

8.75in (22cm) high

£20-25   **M20C**

QUICK REFERENCE - GLAZES AND SHAPES

Ruscha were one of the many companies to produce one shape and then apply a myriad of different glaze treatments, known as the 'decor' to collectors, with the famed 313 jug designed by Kurt Tschörner in 1954. The practice was taken up by many other companies, with Scheurich being a the most prolific practitioner. Given the vast choice available in the marketplace, many collectors choose to focus on one shape by one maker and then aim to collect as many different variations on the decor as possible. This particular example is more valuable than the other two on this page as it has the most appealing lava glaze. In many cases, shapes can fetch more if they have been focused on by a large number of collectors.

A West German Scheurich jug vase, with heavy cream and brown lava glaze over a matte cobalt blue ground, the base moulded '400-22 W.GERMANY'.

8.75in (22cm) high

£25-30   **M20C**

A 1970s West German Scheurich 'Montignac' pattern, Linie 72 series bottle vase, with bull outlined in a lava glaze, the base moulded 281-19.

By the 1950s, ceramic design began to show the influence of the prehistoric cave paintings found in the Lascaux caves, France, 1940. Montignac is the nearest town to the caves. The decoration is rare.

7.5 (19cm) high

£40-60   **OUT**

A 1970s Bay cylindrical footed vase, moulded decoration, blue glaze, base moulded '604-11 BAY W.-GERMANY', with silver foil manufacturer's label.

This design imitates Aldo Londi's popular 1953 'Rimini Blue' design for Bitossi, although the pattern is moulded, not impressed.

7in (17.5cm) high

£20-25   RET

A 1970s West German Bay Keramik jug vase, with white speckled glaze and orange and brown 'lava' glazed band, the base moulded 'W.-GERMANY 2 20'.

8in (20.5cm) high

£25-30   RET

A Carstens glossy lime green footed cylinder vase, with grey salt glaze swirls, the base moulded '147-28' and with printed white semi-circular 'WEST-GERMANY' mark.

11.5in (29cm) high

£30-40   RET

A 1970s Carstens Luxus series vase, with green, orange and red glazes and stylised floral design, designed by Dieter Peter, the base with moulded factory logo and numbered '7692-45 W.-GERMANY'.

17.75in (45cm) high

£100-150   RET

A 1970s Austrian Carstens small handled jug vase, with orange, beige and green glazes and stylised floral design, designed by Dieter Peter, the base moulded '3967-18 AUSTRIA'.

7.25in (18.5cm) high

£35-45   RET

A West German Carstens waisted vase, with alternating bands of a brown glaze with copper inclusions and orange salt-glaze, with factory silver foil label, the base moulded '3643-30 W.-GERMANY'.

12in (30.5cm) high

£30-35   RET

A 1960s West German Carstens 'Ankara' pattern vase, designed by Scholtis, the base with moulded Carstens mark, numbered '1236-23'.

Although prices for many West German ceramics of this period can vary widely, this design seems to fetch consistently good prices when offered at modern design auctions.

9in (23cm) high

£40-60   OUT

CERAMICS

A 1970s West German Roth Keramik double-handled disc vase, shape no.314, with glossy red and black lava glazes, base unmarked.

This is also found in a smaller size.

15.5in (39cm) high

£300-350 **GC**

An extremely rare 1970s Roth Keramik red dish, with red glossy curving shapes between black 'lava' glazes, unmarked.

8in (20cm) long

£300-500 **OUT**

A CLOSER LOOK AT A ROTH VASE

Known as the 'Guitar' to collectors, this is arguably the rarest and most dramatic of Roth's designs, with no clear precedent.

It can be found in a number of different colours, including red, purple, yellow, blue, and different green tones – values rise in that order to as much as £600.

An extremely rare 'reverse' variation is also known, with glossy red glazed lines between 'lava' glazed shapes.

Roth's pieces are not marked with the company name on the base, but are sometimes labelled.

A 1970s West German Roth Keramik orange and black lava glaze 'guitar' vase, shape no.312, by an unknown designer, the base unmarked.

12.25in (31cm) high

£250-300 **GC**

A 1970s West German Ruscha no.717 dish, with red stylised flower pattern, crystalline copper glaze and tubelined lava glaze, the base moulded '717/2'.

11in (27.5cm) diam

£40-50 **M20C**

A late 1970s-early 1980s West German Ruscha no.717 dish, with orange stylised flower and leaf pattern and tube-lined lava glaze, the base moulded '717/2'.

11in (27.5cm) diam

£35-45 **M20C**

A 1970s Ruscha wall charger with applied discs and rectangles and mottled and cloudy brown, beige and orange glazes, inscribed on back '717/2'.

The 717 dish is one of the most common dish shapes found today, and was produced from the 1950s onwards in a variety of decor types. This design is not too hard to find. The discs are often raised, almost resembling mushrooms.

11in (28cm) diam

£50-70 **RET**

An extremely rare Ruscha vase, shape 816/1, with tube-lined gun-metal grey lava glaze in a grid pattern, and a glossy turquoise glaze, the base unmarked.

Both the glaze and the shape are very hard to find – this combination is extremely rare.

8.5in (21.5cm) high

£120-180   MHC

QUICK REFERENCE - RUSCHA'S VULKANO GLAZE

The 'Vulkano' glaze marks the turning point in West German ceramics design between the linear, abstract designs in primary colours of the 1950s, and the freely applied, dripping and 'volcanic' lava glazes of the 1960s and 70s. Designed for leading factory Ruscha by talented glaze technician Otto Gerharz Snr in 1959, the focus became the glaze itself, rather than the patterns that could be created with it. Look out for a good variety of strong colours including green, as shown here, as these tend to be popular with collectors.

A 1960s West German Ruscha 'Vulkano' glaze vase, the shape designed by Kurt Tscörner, the glaze by Otto Gerharz Snr, the base marked 320/2.

7in (18cm) high

£30-50   OUT

A 1960s Ruscha 'Vulkano' glaze jug, the form designed by Kurt Tschörner, the glaze by Otto Gerharz Snr, the base moulded '314/2'.

10.75in (27cm) high

£80-100   GC

A 1970s East German Strehla waisted, footed vase with tube-lined lava glaze on a red ground, unmarked.

East German companies were keen to cash in on the success of West German ceramics, and produced their own, very similar, versions.

8.25in (21cm) high

A 1970s West German Ruscha 'Antique' vase with a moulded pattern of charioteers, and red glaze over a brown background, the base marked '508-18'.

7in (18cm) high

£40-60   OUT   £22-28   RET

A 1960s West German Übelacker Keramik jug vase, with mottled blue glaze and red and green band, the base impressed with an Ü motif and numbered 1628/30, and with silver manufacturer's label.

12in (30.5cm) high

£35-45   RET

FIND OUT MORE...

Fat Lava: West German Pottery From the 1960s & 70s, *by Mark Hill, published by www.markhillpublishing.com*

From Spritzdekor to Fat Lava and West & East German Pottery: Makers' Marks & Form Numbers, *by Kevin Graham, published privately, kj_graham@gmx.de*

CERAMICS

QUICK REFERENCE

- This section is arranged alphabetically by manufacturer, with the final page comprising ceramics by as yet unidentified factories. Unlike glass, most ceramics are marked on the base. Marks may include the factory name, and possibly the designer's name as well, although this generally only appears on 20thC ceramics. Other marks may include an impressed number identifying the shape, and a painted or printed number or name to indicate the pattern or range.

- In 1890, the American McKinley Tariff Act required the name of the country of orgin to be marked on goods, including ceramics. This lead to the appearance of marks such as 'England', 'Bavaria' and 'Nippon' (Japan). In 1921 the act was amended, requiring the words 'Made in' to appear before the country. There are some exceptions, including Wedgwood, who used 'Made in England' from 1898.

- Other marks can help identify a country of origin. For example, 'Déposé would indicate manufacture in France and 'Gesetzlich Geschütz' (Ges.Gesch) in Germany. Look out for 'Reg'd' (registered) design numbers and diamond marks as these can both supply further information when researched in reference books. 'Trademark' and 'Limited' or 'Ltd' were not used before c1861-62, and are often much later.

- Be aware that the styles and shapes of marks often changed over time, which can help with dating. If a piece is unmarked, consider the way it was made: was it hand-potted or moulded, or decorated by hand? Compare the style of the form and the decoration with examples in reference books or on websites, but always cross-reference any possible identifications with other sources, particularly if found online.

An Arequipa ovoid vase, finely carved with an iris under a matte green glaze, the base with stamped mark, restoration to a small area at rim.

7.75in (19.5cm) high

£800-1,200   DRA

A Canadian Beauce Pottery wine carafe, shape G-121, and four goblets, shape G-119, with ribbed cog-like decoration and green glaze, designed by Jacques Garnier in 1964, the base with 'arrow heads' factory mark.

This is typical of the geometric, almost Modernist, solid forms produced by Garnier.

9in (23cm) high

£50-80   TWF

An early 1970s Canadian Blue Mountain Pottery tall bottle vase with flared neck and rim, with 'Flame' glaze with some orange dripping/mottling, the base with moulded 'three tree' mark.

8.25in (21cm) high

£20-40   TWF

A 1960s-70s Canadian Blue Mountain Pottery jug, with a dripped and mottled cobalt and light blue glaze, the base with moulded three tree mark.

10.25in (26.5cm) high

£30-50   TWF

A 1970s Canadian Blue Mountain Pottery 'Spitoon' vase, shape 32A, with scarce brown glaze overlaid with randomly trailed foam-effect white glaze.

5.25in (13cm) high

£20-40   TWF

A modern Burleigh Ware 'Guardsmen' jug, modelled in low relief with marching guardsmen and a sentry box, the base with printed factory marks.

This stunning jug was designed and first released in the early 1930s. Very few original examples survive today, and these can fetch over £1,000 in undamaged condition. Beware, as reproductions have been made since the late 1970s, and are considerably less valuable. Authentic Burleigh reproductions like this, which are better painted and moulded than copies by other factories, are more desirable.

7.75in (20cm) high

£120-180 WW

A Bursley Ware rectangular tray, designed by Charlotte Rhead, pattern TL43, painted with flower designs in pastel shades.

13in (33cm) wide

£150-200 GHOU

A C. & Co. Ltd slip decorated planter, painted with white 'Glasgow Rose' motif, on a green ground, printed mark.

7.5in (19cm) diam

£80-120 WW

A 19thC Capo di Monte oval box and cover, with gilt-metal mounts, decorated with moulded cherubs at play.

5in (13cm) wide

£80-120 L&T

A Cauldon 'Chariots' pattern blue and white transfer-printed octagonal vase.

5in (12.5cm) high

£75-85 BAD

QUICK REFERENCE - CANDY WARE

Candy & Co. Ltd was founded in 1875 in Newton Abbott in Devon, England and began by producing bricks and tiles. In 1922, it launched its 'Wescontree Ware' range of art pottery, changing the name to 'Candy Ware' in 1936. Comprising vases, jugs, bowls, lamp bases, chargers, ashtrays and others, a hand-thrown and hand-decorated range was introduced in 1936. Primarily filling the kiln around the core production of utilitarian products, the art pottery range was discontinued in the 1950s when a new kiln was installed. The company itself closed in 1998.

A Clermont Fine China limited edition model of the Cleveland Bay stallion 'Mulgrave Supreme', modelled by Robert Donaldson, numbered 17/100, contained in a mahogany and glazed display case, together with certificate.

12in (30.5cm) high

£700-900 A&G

A late 1930s Candy Ware ribbed vase, with light blue and beige dripped glaze, silver embossed Candy Ware label and indistinct circular printed mark to the base.

7.5in (19cm) high

£20-30 M20C

CERAMICS

A 1920s Clews & Co. Ltd 'Chameleon Ware' vase with hand-painted stylised leaf design.

Chameleon ware was designed by David Capper, Works Manager at Clews. Introduced from 1913-14, Capper developed experimental semi-matte glazes to imitate the popular Ruskin art pottery glazes, and applied them to Oriental inspired forms. The affordable range won a gold medal at the Philadelphia Exposition in 1926, and grew to make up 80 per cent of the factory's output. Look out for Egyptian, Middle Eastern and Oriental patterns, inspired by archaeological finds at the time.

6.25in (15.5cm) high

£40-60   **P&I**

A 1930s Clews & Co. 'Chameleon Ware' squat vase with mottled blue and green glaze, with tripod firing mark to base.

4in (10cm) diam

£20-30   **P&I**

A 1960s Crown Devon ovoid jardinière, handpainted with a geometric design possibly designed by Colin Melbourne, the base impressed '1508'.

9in (23cm) long

£8-10   **M20C**

A Crown Devon 'Delph' vase, pattern no. 2055, painted in colours with factory marks to base.

8.75in (22cm) high

£30-40   **WW**

A CLOSER LOOK AT A COWAN PLATE

Viktor Schreckengost (1906-2008) was an important American artist, industrial designer and ceramics designer who worked through the Art Deco and mid-century modern styles.

His best known work is the 'Jazz Bowl' created in 1930 for Eleanor Roosevelt which is now considered an Art Deco masterpiece, and an example is in the Cleveland Museum of Art.

This hand-painted charger is also recognisably Art Deco, and was part of a series of similar designs showing sporting activities that also includes 'Polo'.

Large, visually impressive and typical of his style, they are sought-after and hard to find.

A Cowan 'The Hunt' wall plate, with low-relief moulded and hand-painted pattern, designed by Viktor Schreckengost.

1930-31

11.5in (28.5cm) diam

£700-1,000   **ANT**

QUICK REFERENCE - COLIN MELBOURNE

Colin Melbourne is arguably one of the most ignored British modernist ceramic designers. A graduate of the Royal College of Art, he produced highly modern, stylised animal figurines for Beswick from 1955. Known as the 'CM' range, produced from 1956-66, their avant garde style was unpopular at the time, and they are comparatively rare today. In 1954, he formed a design consultancy with David Queensberry called Drumlanrig Melbourne, and also worked for Crown Devon, where he continued to produce highly modern designs. His work is still underrated today, and represents an excellent opportunity for collectors with an eye for the future.

A Crown Ducal 'Rhodian' pattern shape 150 ovoid vase, pattern no. 3272, designed by Charlotte Rhead, the base with printed and painted marks.
c1933   *4.5in (11.5cm) high*
£80-120   **GHOU**

A pair of Crown Ducal vases, of bulbous cylindrical form, with red glazed interior, cream ground with piped panels containing red and brown leaves, with printed mark.
                           6in (15cm) high
£60-80   **LOC**

A Crown Devon 'Memphis' range vase, designed by Colin Melbourne, with a gilt chevron transfer pattern over a black glazed ground, the base with printed and impressed marks.
7.75in (20cm) high
£80-120   **FLD**

A Crown Devon 'Memphis' range vase, designed by Colin Melbourne, with a gilt chevron transfer pattern over a black glazed ground, printed marks.
10.25in (26cm) high
£80-120   **FLD**

A Crown Lynn vase, by Frank Carpay, the vase thrown by Daniel Steenstra, decorated with bands of forest green, orange, black and teal, with stylised celestial spheres representing the Sputnik, and silver lustre glaze at the rim.

Crown Lynn was founded near Auckland, New Zealand, in 1854. Tableware production began in 1941, and the company produced wares for the war effort and for New Zealand railways. The company still produces table and decorative wares today. Dutchman Frank Carpay (1917-1985) studied under Picasso at Madoura in France, and also Roger Capron at Vallauris. He worked for Crown Lynn's 'Specials Department' from 1953-56, producing designs such as this, which was commissioned by the vendor during a visit to the pottery.
c1955   *9.75in (25cm) high*
£700-900   **WEB**

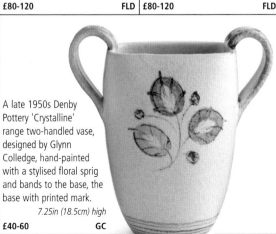

A late 1950s Denby Pottery 'Crystalline' range two-handled vase, designed by Glynn Colledge, hand-painted with a stylised floral sprig and bands to the base, the base with printed mark.
7.25in (18.5cm) high
£40-60   **GC**

CERAMICS

A Hammersley scalloped and gilded milk jug and sugar bowl, with hand-painted flowers.

The teacups are in the same shape as the sugar bowl.

c1900-14   Milk jug 3in (7.5cm) high

£40-60   **BAD**

A Haviland porcelain cake plate, decorated by Anna B. Leonard, with gourds and leaves in orange and green, stamped 'Haviland France' and painted 'Anna B. Leonard'.

14in (35.5cm) diam

£300-500   **DRA**

A 1970s Honiton Pottery rectangular dish with a hand-painted fish design, the base impressed 'HONITON ENGLAND' and painted 'DC'.

11.25in (27cm) long

£15-20   **M20C**

A 1960s-70s Dutch Jema bull, impressed with runic and geometric symbols and covered with a blue-green glaze, the stomach impressed 'JEMA HOLLAND 79'.

14.5in (36.5cm) long

£50-70   **M20C**

A tall Kenton Hills vase, with pink blossoms on pearl grey ground, the base drilled probably at the factory, with leaf stamp and '176'.

12.5in (32cm) high

£300-500   **DRA**

A Kenton Hills 'Unica' vase, by Alza Stratton, in brown butterfat on white ground, signed 'Alza Stratton Unica', stamped mark, restoration.

8.25in (21cm) high

£200-300   **DRA**

A large Katshutte Pottery figure of a Spanish dancer, painted in colours, printed factory mark, paper label, repaired fan.

20in (51cm) high

£400-600   **WW**

A Robert Lallemant elliptical pottery vase, blue and black painted marks, with damage.

Lallemant (1902-1954) studied at the Ecole des Beaux-Arts in Dijon and at Lachenal c1921, founding a pottery in Paris in 1923 producing modern and stylised patterns on clean-lined angular forms. If it had not been damaged, it may have fetched over three times this value.

6.75in (17cm) high

£100-150   **WW**

A Langley Pottery vase, designed by Glynn Colledge and hand-painted with a stylised foliate design, the base with printed windmill mark.

8in (20.5cm) high

£30-40   M20C

A 1960s-70s Langley Pottery bulbous vase hand-painted with a stylised natural motif in green, brown and orange glazes, designed by Glynn Colledge, the base with printed windmill factory mark and painted 'J.M.'.

Staffordshire based firm Lovatt & Lovatt, who made Langley pottery, was acquired by Denby in 1959, which explains how Denby designer Glynn Colledge came to design for them. This is a scarce shape and a desirable pattern.

7.75in (19.5cm) high

£80-120   GC

A 1960s-70s Langley Pottery footed cylindrical vase, hand-painted with a stylised natural motif, designed by Glynn Colledge, printed windmill factory mark.

7.75in (19.5cm) high

£50-70   GC

A Canadian Laurentian Pottery sculptural jug vase, with integral handle, organic curving rim and orange and brown dripped glaze.

11.75in (29.5cm) high

£20-40   TWF

A McCoy 'Loy-Nel-Art' vase, with loop handles and floral decoration, marked '02' on the base, glaze slightly scratched and flaked at base.

12.25in (31cm) high

£100-150   BEL

A French Longwy vase, the base painted 'F=3024-D:56907', with printed green factory mark.

4.5in (11cm) high

£80-120   BEV

A 19thC Meissen box and cover, painted with flowers, the cover formed as a shell with a cartouche of figures standing on the docks to the interior, cancelled crossed swords mark, damage and restoration.

4.75in (12cm) wide

£80-120   WW

A 20thC Meissen group of two songbirds, modelled perched on a stump, with blue crossed swords mark, incised '3071'.

£180-220   DN

CERAMICS

A 1960s Midwinter Fashion shape transfer-printed 'Petite Rose' cake stand, with chrome plated fittings, designed by John Russell.

9in (23cm) high

£20-30   **RET**

A Minton cabinet plate, with pierced Greek key gilt border and pâte-sur-pâte style border of dolphins and shells on a pale blue ground, with printed mark.

1891-1902   9.5in (24cm) diam

£30-40   **LOC**

A pair of Minton models of cockatoos, each perched on a branch.

£320-380   **L&T**

A Myott & Sons hand-painted 'Diamond' vase, with original flower frog, the base with gold printed factory mark and painted '9185' pattern mark.

6in (15cm) high

£120-180   **BAD**

A 1930s Myott 'Squareneck' jug, painted in beige, yellow, orange green and brown tones with a fruiting pattern, the base with gold printed mark, painted 9104 pattern mark and registered no. 739316 for 1928.

8.75in (22.5cm) high

£80-120   **BAD**

A CLOSER LOOK AT A MYOTT JUG

Myott was founded in 1898 but is best known for its colorful Art Deco ceramics produced in the 1930s. Records were destroyed in a fire in 1949, making it hard for collectors to find out more.

Autumnal oranges and browns are typical of Myott - red, blue and green are rarer - but watch out for flaking to the orange. Printed gold marks were used from 1930-42.

Prices are currently considerably lower than those for other Art Deco ceramics by Susie Cooper and Clarice Cliff – this is an area to watch as their appeal is obvious.

Pieces bearing the 'B.A.G.' mark were made for export by British American Glass. The quality of the design and painting is usually higher on such pieces, and the patterns may have been exclusive to them.

A 1930s Myott baluster shaped jug, with a hand-painted green and orange floral and geometric design, the base with gold printed 'BAG Co Ltd, HAND PAINTED' mark and stamped 'B.G 76'.

7.75in (19.5cm) high

£100-150   **BAD**

A 1960s-70s French Vallauris blue glazed mussel-shaped dish, with orange glazed spot.

13in (33cm) long

£15-25   M20C

A Volkmar three-handled vase, covered in mottled indigo matte glaze, incised 'V'.

7in (18cm) high

£600-900   DRA

A CLOSER LOOK AT A VALLAURIS VASE

The town of Vallauris is well-known for its many potteries which have attracted notable artists and designers, including Pablo Picasso who worked at the Madoura pottery from 1948-55.

Other designers include Roger Capron and Charles Voltz – the designer of this piece is not yet known, but the glaze type and colours link it to a Vallauris pottery.

The curving, asymmetric form, that even extends to the the shape of the rim and the body, which curves backwards, is typical of the period.

The base is unmarked but the light weight and clay type indicate that it was made by pouring liquid clay, known as slip, into a mould rather than being hand potted.

A late 1950s/early 1960s French Vallauris large floor vase, with curving asymmetric form, handle and rim.

15.5in (40cm) high

£40-60   MHC

A 1930s Wade Heath waisted cylindrical jug, handpainted with orange flowers, green leaves and grey and yellow patches, the base with printed lion mark, and impressed '127'.

7.75in (19.5cm) high

£30-50   BAD

A Watcombe Pottery terracotta jug, designed by Dr Christopher Dresser, of angular form with three serrated bands, printed "Watcombe Torquay" with registered diamond for 3rd June 1872.

8in (20.5cm) high

£120-180   WW

A Watcombe pottery model of a winking cat with long neck, covered in an ochre glaze and with one glass eye, the base with inscribed marks.

12in (30.5cm) high

£180-220   BE

A Wheatley vase, with four buttressed feet, the top embossed with leaves and buds, covered in matte green glaze, marked 'WP' and 'C102'.

10in (25.5cm) high

£1,000-1,500 DRA

A Wheatley tall tapering cylindrical vase, covered in a fine feathered matte green glaze, and with 'WP' mark.

10in (25.5cm) high

£800-1,200 DRA

A CLOSER LOOK AT A WALLEY VASE

William J. Walley (1852-1919) was born the son of a potter in Ohio. He travelled to England to study at Minton in the 1860s before founding his first pottery in Maine in 1873.

Hand-sculpted motifs are also typical and range from leaves in the manner of Grueby, to this famous and highly sought-after devil's head.

Following an important aspect of the Arts and Crafts movement, he believed that every pot should be made and decorated by hand rather than being moulded and produced on a factory production line.

Simple but strong greens and blue matte glazes are typical, gloss glazes are more unusual – particularly with this amount of colour variation.

A W.J. Walley vase with devil mask, losses and crude repair to glaze flaking, the base stamped 'WJW'.

12in (30.5cm) high

£1,700-2,000 DRA

A T.J. Wheatley 'Albertine' vase, modelled with applied hibiscus on a barbotine painted ground, stamped 'WHEATLEY' and artist signed 'KW', a few minor losses and touch-ups.

The three-dimensional underglaze slip decoration, called 'Barbotine', was derived from Limoges faience, and became extremely popular in the US, and particularly in Cincinnati. Thomas Jerome Wheatley was involved in several Cincinnati pottery businesses between 1879 and 1882. The Cincinnati Art Pottery was incorporated in Ohio at the end of 1880 with Wheatley as a partner, and operated under the name T. J. Wheatley & Company until he left the business in 1882. This particular example, from the range often known as 'Albertine', was exhibited in "From Our Native Clay," held by the American Ceramic Arts Society in New York in 1987.

c1880

19in (28cm) high

£600-900 CRA

A T.J. Wheatley vase with applied thistle, under matte green glaze, no visible mark, several flecks and nicks.

11.5in (29cm) high

£500-800 DRA

A late 19thC Hungarian Zsolnay Pecs earthenware vase, decorated with hand-painted red, green and blue Moorish or Turkish style flowers on a mustard ground.

10.25in (26cm) tall

£50-80 LOC

A Hungarian Zsolnay Pecs heart-shaped dish, painted with a central bird within Persian style foliage, in geometric borders, the back with printed spire mark.

10in (25.5cm) diam

£280-320   **GORL**

An Arts and Crafts earthenware charger, painted with a bird in a landscape in shades of blue and yellow, painted marks, dated, hairline crack to rim.

1881   *12in (30.5cm) diam*

£150-200   **WW**

A Continental tin-glazed earthenware Gallé-style seated cat figurine, probably Mosaic, painted with honey-coloured fur patches and green eyes, and pseudo 'De Roos' mark to base.

The shape is also very similar to figures by Wemyss.

c1900   11.75in (30cm) high

£500-800   **TOV**

An early 20thC Continental porcelain tazza, applied with flowers, the base mounted with a maiden.

Despite the large amount of skill and time that went into creating such a detailed piece, fashions and tastes have moved away from ornate, floral designs such as this. Tazzas are also largely impractical today. Considering its size and obvious decorative appeal, its price seems very reasonable.

13.25in (34cm) high

£50-80   **WW**

A 19thC majolica figure, possibly Vesta, wearing a laurel wreath and carrying an eternal flame.

10.25in (26cm) high

£120-180   **FLD**

A late 19thC Staffordshire copper lustre jug with moulded and hand-painted flowers, unmarked.

7.75in (19.5cm) high

£20-30   **BAD**

An early 20thC French beeware basket, with bee on handle, handpainted with people in a row holding hands in landscape, with an 'X' on the base, the side signed 'I Berty Nice'.

6in (15cm) high

£50-70   **BAD**

QUICK REFERENCE

- Collectors look for characters associated with happy times in their own childhood or those that are widely popular. Pieces associated with comic books, TV programmes and films, or those by major brands, are usually popular. Official, licensed products are usually more desirable and more accurately modelled.
- Famous characters will usually have enthusiastic collecting bases and therefore will often fetch the largest sums. Look for typical clothes, poses, accessories or phrases associated with that character. Pieces produced before a character became well known are typically rare and desirable, as they would have been made in smaller numbers. Do not ignore minor characters as these can be rarer than more popular characters, and collectors will often want to complete a set.

- Many character items were intended for promotional use. Most were not made to last and few pieces are likely to have survived in good condition, making a truly mint example highly desirable.
- Limited editions may become valuable if the demand exceeds supply. For this reason, it is preferable to invest in pieces from small production runs (for example, under 1,000). The maker and quality of moulding and decoration will add desirability, as will an accurate depiction of the character. Limited editions should ideally come with mint condition boxes and paperwork.
- With the nostalgic nature of the market, demand ebbs and flows as generations mature. It is therefore a good idea to hunt for new collectable characters. For example, Buzz Lightyear is likely to be popular in the future.

A 1960s large soft vinyl jointed Mickey Mouse figure, unmarked.

13.75in (35cm) high

£15-20   EWA

A 1960s Walt Disney Productions soft vinyl Mickey Mouse figure, with tail, marked 'C WALT DISNEY PRODUCTION MADE IN ITALY'.

9.75in (25cm) high

£20-25   EWA

A 1970s Walt Disney Productions Mickey Mouse poseable vinyl advertising figurine, in yellow shirt and red and white polka dot shorts, marked 'C WALT DISNEY PRODUCTIONS MADE IN HONG KONG', with woven tag.

7.5in (19cm) high

£10-15   EWA

A Mattel Walt Disney Productions speaking Mickey Mouse figure, with oversized head containing the mechanism, marked 'C 1971 MATTEL Inc WALT DISNEY PRODUCTIONS BURBANK TOYS INC'.

c1971   5in (13cm) high

£15-20   EWA

A Playcraft 'Squeeze 'N Squeak' Mickey Mouse figure, marked 'C WALT DISNEY PRODUCTION 1979'.

5in (12.5cm) high

£10-15   EWA

A Kohner plastic 'Mickey Mouse' Peppy Puppet, marked 'Walt Disney Productions', mint and unopened with original bubble packaging.

1970   *11in (28cm) high*

£25-35   **MTB**

A 1930s Britains 'Minnie Mouse' and 'Clarabelle', each with detachable heads, paintwork in fair condition, one head pin replaced by matchstick.

Britains' lead figures of Disney characters are hard to find. Minnie is scarcer than Mickey, and Clarabelle is even rarer. Although she was created in 1928, the same year Mickey Mouse made his debut in 'Steamboat Willie', she only appeared as a bit-character on screen afterwards. She was originally paired with Horace Horsecollar, Mickey's friend, but was later seen stepping out with Goofy. After 1942, she almost faded into obscurity, appearing in only four films. However, she appeared more frequently in Disney's comics.

£300-500   **SAS**

A Walt Disney Productions Goofy vinyl figure, marked 'C WALT DISNEY PRODUCTIONS MADE IN HONG KONG' and 'MADE FOR INGERSOLL MARKETING LTD'.

Ingersoll (now part of Timex) made its first Disney watch, featuring Mickey Mouse, in 1933. Since then it has been in continuous production, being made by a number of different watchmakers. This figurine is likely to have been made as part of a promotional countertop display. Well made, licenced and relatively detailed with his clothing, he seems likely to be a great bet for the future.

8.75in (22cm) high

£20-30   **EWA**

A Walt Disney Productions Pinocchio vinyl figure, marked 'WALT DISNEY PRODUCTIONS' on shoes and impressed on back of hat, with woven Ingersoll Marketing tag.

8in (20.5cm) high

£20-30   **EWA**

A scarce 1930s Wadeheath 'Donald Duck' child's teapot and cover, hand-painted in characteristic yellow, blue and black.

5in (12.5cm) long

£400-600   **LT**

A Snow White and the Seven Dwarfs ceramic musician band, of unidentified manufacture, each individually modelled, Doc has repaired left foot, otherwise minor chips and scratches.

Snow White 8in (20cm) high

£70-100 THE SET   **VEC**

COMMEMORATIVES

QUICK REFERENCE

- Although royal commemorative ware was made before Queen Victoria's reign, it was not until then that production boomed. Ceramics (the first and most common kind of royal memorabilia) could be produced and distributed economically due to the advent of transfer printing, canals and the railways. Popularity grew during the late 19thC and the early 20thC, and memorabilia is still produced today.
- As so much memorabilia was produced, collectors tend to focus on one monarch, or one event. Queen Victoria and the current Queen are among the most popular subjects, partly because of the number and variety of pieces produced during their long reigns. Some events commemorated within these reigns are scarcer than others. For example, many more pieces commemorating Queen Victoria's Golden Jubilee were produced than for her marriage. Interest in items celebrating the lives of younger members of current royal family is also growing.

- Value typically depends on the quality and maker of the piece. Well-known, high quality manufacturers, such as Royal Worcester, Royal Crown Derby, Minton and Copeland are consistently popular. You should also look out for the work of popular 20th century designers such as Eric Ravilious, Charlotte Rhead and Richard Guyatt. However, well decorated pieces that are not by major makers or designers are also often desirable. Brightly coloured and detailed pieces appeal are likely to appeal to a wide range of collectors.
- Look for limited editions, particularly pieces from editions of less than 250. Keep all paperwork and boxes as these are essential to value.
- Condition is very important. Many 19thC pieces were not made to last, so some wear is acceptable. However cracks and chips will reduce desirability. Damage on recent pieces reduces value considerably.

A Copeland & Garrett '1837/38 Victoria' miniature pottery plate, printed with a named portrait surmounted by flowers of the Union within a scrolling border, the reverse with impressed and printed marks.

4.25in (11cm) diam

£580-680   SAS

A Wedgwood & Co. earthenware tea bowl and saucer, printed in black and enamelled in colours, the reverse named 'Victoria', with impressed and printed marks.
c1838

£180-220   SAS

An '1840 Victoria & Albert Wedding' blue printed pottery jug, with named portraits, the reverse with a crown centred by the date.

4.5in (11.5cm) high

£100-150   SAS

An '1838 Victoria' commemorative octagonal nursery plate.

The portrait on this desirable plate was developed after a portrait painted by Sir George Hayter.
c1838

£200-300   SAS

A Hines Bros '1887 Victoria's Jubilee' octagonal pottery plate, printed in black, with gilt lined rim.

c1887   *9.75in (24.5cm) wide*

£50-70   SAS

A Doulton Lambeth '1897 Diamond Jubilee' blue glazed stoneware jug, moulded with green young and old oval portraits of Queen Victoria.

8.75in (22cm) high

£120-180   SAS

An Adderley '1937 George VI Coronation' loving cup, printed in colours with St. George slaying the dragon.

1936   *4.75in (12cm) high*

£200-250   SAS

A CLOSER LOOK AT A TILE

Founded in 1877, Sherwin & Cotton of Staffordshire was a well-known tile producer until its take-over by Johnsons in 1911, which continued to use the name for some time.

This was designed by George Cartlidge, and was part of a series of 'photographic' tiles he produced. Cartlidge also designed some Morrisware for S.Hancock & Sons.

Showing Victoria as most imagine her to have appeared, this was made to commemorate the Diamond Jubilee.

This series of tiles was renowned at the time for its translucent glazes and three-dimensional appearance.

A Sherwin & Cotton relief and intaglio moulded photographic dust-pressed tile panel, depicting Queen Victoria in sepia glaze, framed.

c1897   *9in (23cm) high*

£100-150   FLD

A Paragon '1937 Edward VIII Coronation' loving cup, with twin gilt lion handles, numbered 562 from an edition of 1,000.

Memorabilia for Edward VIII's (better known as the Duke of Windsor) proposed coronation is not as rare as many think. Although he abdicated in December 1936, manufacturers had nearly a year, from George V's death in January 1936, to produce commemorative wares.

1936   *4.5in (11.5cm) high*

£70-100   GHOU

A Copeland for Goode '1937 George VI Coronation' pottery tyg, printed with sepia portraits and decorated in colours, small hairline crack.

£200-300   SAS

A small Shelley George VI and Queen Elizabeth '1939 Visit to America' loving cup, decorated in colours and gilt, with printed marks to the base.

1939   *3.5in (8.5cm) high*

£120-180   SAS

COMMEMORATIVES

A Crown Devon '1937 George VI Coronation' musical tankard, moulded with superimposed portraits oval flags and flowers in colours, playing 'Here's a Health unto His Majesty'.

c1937   6in (15.5cm) high

£80-120   **SAS**

A transfer printed 'George VI Coronation' mug designed by Dame Laura Knight, the base with printed mark reading 'R.R. No.814375/6 DESIGNED & MODELLED BY DAME LAURA KNIGHT D.B.E. R.A.' and with GR cypher and facsimile Laura Knight signature, the inside of the rim printed 'PRESENTED ON CORONATION DAY BY SIR ARTHUR STANLEY TREASURER OF ST THOMAS HOSPITAL'.

1937   3.25in (8cm) high

£35-40   **CARS**

An Aynsley '1953 Elizabeth II Coronation' plate, with central printed portrait flanked by flags and flowers and inscribed border.

c1953   9in (23cm) diam

£200-300   **SAS**

An Aynsley '1953 Elizabeth II Coronation' plate, with printed colour portrait and profuse gilt decoration.

c1953   9in (23cm) diam

£100-150   **SAS**

A Paragon '1953 Elizabeth II Coronation' limited edition loving cup, set with twin gilt lion handles, numbered 555 from an edition of 1,000.

4.75in (12cm) high

£120-180   **SAS**

A Spode '1981 Price Charles & Lady Diana Wedding' limited edition loving cup, with sepia portrait ovals decorated in colors with flowers on a gilded cobalt blue ground, numbered 229 from an edition of 250, with certificate.

6.25in (16cm) high

£60-90   **SAS**

A Wedgwood '1953 Elizabeth II Coronation' mug, with printed design designed by Eric Ravilious, the base with printed factory mark.

c1953   4.25in (10.5cm) high

£180-220   **WW**

A 'Nelson in Memoriam' commemorative reverse handpainted glass picture, depicting Britannia with an oval portrait of Nelson beneath his battle honours with dates, framed.

c1805   16.25in (41cm) high

£2,500-3,500   **SAS**

An '1805 Nelson' death of Nelson pearlware jug, printed in brown and highlighted in colours with an inscribed portrait oval and on the reverse HMS Victory centred by an oval cartouche inscribed with honours, restored.

6.75in (17cm) high

£350-450   **SAS**

An unusual '1812 Constitution and Russian Campaign' silver lustre decorated pearlware jug, printed with loyal cartouche flanked by a lion and unicorn and on the reverse 'A. Cossack of the Oural Mountains'.

1812   5.25in (13.5cm) high

£250-350   **SAS**

A Copeland for Goode 'Transvaal Tyg', subscriber's copy, decorated in colours and gilt, cracked.

c1900   5.5in (14cm) high

£150-200   **SAS**

An Elliot pottery jug, commemorating the relief of 'Mafeking' on May 17th 1900, applied with monograms of Queen Victoria and Baden-Powell, hound handle.

1900   6.75in (17.5cm) high

£120-180   **FLD**

CERAMICS

A Booth '1914 Great War' cylindrical mug, printed in grey and decorated in colours with servicemen from the allied forces.

£80-120   **SAS**

A Paragon '1938 Munich Peace Conference' plate, printed with a named portrait of Chamberlain and inscribed on the reverse.

1938   *9in (21cm) diam*

£100-150   **SAS**

A Wilkinson Ltd Marechal Foch toby jug, designed by Sir Francis Carruthers Gould, seated with a glass of champagne, the bottle inscribed 'Au Diable Le Kaiser' (The Kaiser to the devil), the plinth with animals, the base with black printed marks and Carruthers Gould's facsimile signature.

A Wilkinson Ltd. 'Admiral Beatty - Dread Nought' character jug, designed by Sir Francis Carruthers Gould, decorated in underglaze colours, enamelled and gilded, the underside with printed manufacturer's and retailer's mark and facsimile signature of Carruthers Gould.

Issued by Soane & Smith Ltd during World War I.

10.75in (27cm) high

£250-350   **SAS**

This jug was produced for and distributed by Soane & Smith as a limited edition along with ten others to celebrate the allied leaders of World War I. The rarest is of General Louis Botha, as only 150 examples were produced. An example fetched over £1,500 at auction in 2005, and a complete set fetched £9,000 at auction in 2009.

1918   *11.75in (30cm) high*

£400-600   **DN**

A CLOSER LOOK AT A WINSTON CHURCHILL TOBY JUG

Churchill is an iconic British figure and commemorative pieces are still highly sought after by specialist collectors, especially items produced in his lifetime.

This is made more appealing due to the well-modelled, characterful face and his fingers which are posed in his famous 'V' for victory sign.

It is modelled and glazed in the manner of Ralph Wood, and is considered one of the best traditional toby jugs made in the 20thC, so it appeals to toby jug collectors too.

Examples are known decorated in more colours. In 2008 an undamaged, more finely decorated, example sold for over £1,800 at auction.

A 'The Rt Hon Winston S Churchill OM CH FRS MP' pottery toby jug, by Leonard Jarvis, modelled in relief and painted in colours, incised marks, chips to paint brushes.

c1946   *7in (18cm) high*

£350-450   **WW**

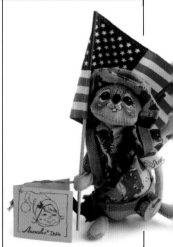

An Annalee Gulf War commemorative 'Desert Storm' mouse, in mint condition with card tag, clothing and flag.

1991   *8.25in (21cm) high*

£20-30   **BH**

COSTUME JEWELLERY

QUICK REFERENCE

- Costume jewellery has risen dramatically in popularity over the last ten years, and values have risen accordingly. However, while iconic pieces by well-known designers are now commanding prices close to those paid for precious jewellery, much costume jewellery is still comparatively affordable. With a great variety of pieces available, there is a look for every taste and occasion.
- Desirable makers include Trifari, Chanel, Christian Dior, Stanley Hagler, Schiaparelli, Miriam Haskell and Joseff of Hollywood, and their names are usually marked on the back of their pieces. Copies are becoming more common, particularly at the upper end of the market, so learn to recognise marks and the quality of materials.
- Style and eye-appeal are also very important to value. As many buy costume jewellery to wear, a great design with the 'sparkle' factor will generally be desirable and valuable, even without a renowned maker's name.
- During the 1930s and 1940s, many pieces were made from solid silver, sometimes plated with gold, and these are usually marked 'Sterling' to the reverse.
- The quality, colour and size of the stones are important to value: look out for chunky 'baroque' faux pearls, and Murano or Czech glass beads. The way the stones are set also helps indicate a piece's quality. The best examples are held in place with metal prongs, with work done by hand. Much costume jewellery has three-dimensional effects that may be hand-wired onto frame, and these pieces are particularly desirable.
- Missing stones will reduce value. Although they can be replaced, it is often hard to find an exact match of size or colour. The beads and faux pearls, used by designers like Miriam Haskell are even more difficult to find as they were exclusive designs and are no longer made to the same quality.

A mid-1950s Art wreath pin, gold tone metal set with pastel Lucite flowers and aurora borealis highlights, marked "Art".

1.75in (4.5cm) diam

£40-60   **PC**

A pair of Boucher holly wreath Christmas earrings, set with green and gold glass spheres.

1in (2.5cm) diam

£6-8 PAIR   **AEM**

A very rare 1980s Butler & Wilson Amy Johnson pin, plastic and chrome, the back with white painted "Butler & Wilson" mark.

2.75in (7cm) wide

£100-150   **TDG**

A Robert DeMario gilt metal flower and leaf pin, set with faux anthracite and pearls, some stones missing, the back marked "DeMario N.Y.".

2.5in (6.5cm) wide

£10-15   **PC**

A pair of Kramer clip-on earrings, with red, colourless and purple rhinestones, and faux pearls, the clip impressed KRAMER.

1in (2.5cm) high

£15-20   **PC**

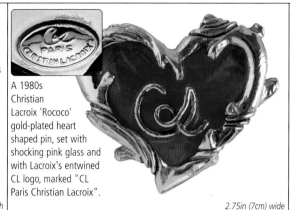

A 1980s Christian Lacroix 'Rococo' gold-plated heart shaped pin, set with shocking pink glass and with Lacroix's entwined CL logo, marked "CL Paris Christian Lacroix".

2.75in (7cm) wide

£30-50   **TDG**

A 1950s pair of earrings, attributed to Rousselet, comprised of multicoloured glass drops set on gold tone chains.

2.75in (7cm) long

£50-80   **PC**

A 1960s pair of Schreiner faux aquamarine earrings, the large central stones surrounded by circular and teardrop shaped rhinestones.

1.25in (3cm) high

£50-70 PAIR   **CRIS**

A Lea Stein Rhodoid small scottie dog pin, with applied black bow and eye and nose details, the clip marked 'LEA STEIN PARIS'

1.5in (3.5cm) high

£25-35   **PC**

A CLOSER LOOK AT A ROBERT NECKLACE AND EARRINGS

There are a number of different types of cut rhinestones, including the rectangular 'baguette', which also have many facets – both are signs of quality.

Blue is a very desirable colour, and the different, complimentary tones of blue add visual appeal.

The lighter blue stones are 'aurora borealis' stones, which have an applied iridescence that changes and sparkles as they move in the light.

The rhinestones are 'prong set', rather than being glued into a moulded setting – this is another sign of quality and also allows more light to enter the rhinestones.

A Robert necklace and pair of earrings, set with aquamarine and cobalt blue cut fax stones.

Earrings 1.25in (3cm) wide

£100-150   **PC**

COSTUME JEWELLERY

A 1950s Trifari gold-plated butterfly pin, the wings inset with 'plique à jour' style coloured glass ovoid beads.

2in (5cm) wide

£50-80　　　PC

A mid-1950s Trifari gold-plated pin in the form of a basket of flowers, the flowers inset with coloured rhinestones.

1.75in (4.5cm) high

£40-60　　　PC

A 1940s Trifari vermeil bow-shaped pin, with red ruby baguette and colourless pavé-set rhinestones.

3.5in (9cm) wide

£300-500　　　PC

A 1990s Vivienne Westwood silver tone metal bow and orb pin, pavé set with clear rhinestones.

1.5in (3.5cm) long

£50-80　　　PC

A late 1950s Trifari gold plated pin in the form of three fish, the eyes with inset ruby red cabouchon rhinestones.

2.25in (6.5cm) high

£70-100　　　ROX

A Vivienne Westwood gold-tone metal heart-shaped perfume holder pin, surmounted by a trademark orb and ribbon, with red enamel, and ring fitting to transform into necklace/choker, containing Boudoir perfume.

c2000　　　*2in (5cm) high*

£40-60　　　TDG

QUICK REFERENCE – TRIFARI

Trifari's origins lay in a company founded by Italian emigré Gustavo Trifari in New York around 1910. Success first came when sales manager Leo Krussman joined in 1917, and grew when salesman Carl Fishel joined in 1923, and 'Trifari, Krussman & Fishel (TKF) was founded in 1925. Designer Alfred Philippe joined in 1930, and his designs are amongst the most sought-after today. During the 1930s, the company designed pieces for a number of Broadway musicals, as well as for film and theatre stars, which cemented its success. Quality was always high, even after World War II, with only the best rhinestones being used in good quality settings. During the 1940s, a number of gold-plated sterling silver (vermeil) pieces were made, which are usually valuable. The company continues to produce innovative and sought-after designs today. This brightly coloured set has further appeal due to the patriotic colours used, as well as the all-important 'sparkle' factor, enhanced by the differently cut rhinestones.

A 1950s Trifari pin and earrings, set with colourless and blue baguette cut rhinestones and light blue rectangular rhinestones, the backs stamped 'TRIFARI PAT PEND'.

Pin 2.25 (5.5cm) high

£150-200　　　PC

A pair of unmarked clip earrings, set with cut faux aquamarines and teardrop shaped brown glass stones, in a gold tone mount.

1.25in (3cm) high

£20-25   **PC**

A pair of unmarked earrings, the gold tone mounts set with faceted aurora borealis stones and large faux amber teardrops.

1.25in (3cm) high

£30-40   **PC**

A pair of unmarked earrings and matching leaf shaped pin, the gold tone metal mounts with prong set striped 'tiger's eye' rhinestones.

Pin 2.75in (7cm) high

£70-90   **PC**

A pair of unmarked earrings, with vintage stones prong-set in a modern matte gold-tone metal mount.

1.5in (4cm) high

£20-30   **PC**

A 1920s unmarked cold enamelled orchid-shaped pin, set with faceted diamanté.

2in (5cm) high

£20-30   **PC**

A 1950s unmarked vintage gold plated patriotic US flag pin, prong-set with red, colourless and blue rhinestones.

1.5in (3.5cm) high

£5-8   **AEM**

A 1930s Art Deco Continental silver clip, with red plastic bar and inset diamanté, the back with Continental control marks, and stamped 'MD'.

1.5in (3.5cm) high

£50-80   **PC**

DOLLS

QUICK REFERENCE – SINDY

- Sindy was launched by Pedigree in 1963 as a competitor to Mattel's Barbie fashion doll. Rather than produce Barbie under license, Sindy was modelled on another American doll, Ideal's Tammy. Her 'girl next door' look made her instantly more popular than Barbie in Britain, and she became a bestseller in 1968 and 1970. Initially, Pedigree also produced a wider range of clothing and accessories than Mattel.

- In 1978 Sindy was launched in the US by Marx Toys, but as the company went into receivership in 1980, was discontinued. Fashions were updated in the 1980s, and in 1989 she was redesigned to look more like Barbie, who dominated the market during the late 1980s and '90s. In 1997, Sindy was removed from major retailers after a law suit from Mattel, until her successful relaunch in 1999.

- Look out for early dolls and outfits from the late 1960s and early 1970s. Some accessories were lost, making them rare today, and some outfits and dolls are more desirable than others. As with most plastic fashion and similar dolls, items must be in as close to shop-bought condition as possible. Stains, fading and cut or messy hair, reduce value. Although 'the doll you love to dress' is usually the most valuable item, values for some outfits can match those paid for the dolls.

A Pedigree Sindy doll, first issue with original 'Weekenders' outfit, with original original box.

First issue Sindy dolls are becoming increasingly hard to find, particularly with their original boxes and clothes. On this example, the original pink card band adds value as it is usually missing. This outfit was designed by Foale & Tuffin. Sally Tuffin went on to produce ceramic desgns for Poole and, ultimately, her own company.
c1964 *12in (30.5cm) high*
£120-180 **MTB**

A 1970s Pedigree 'Funtime' blonde Sindy doll, with original clothing, in mint, unopened condition in original window box.

12in (30.48cm) high
£100-150 **MTB**

A Pedigree 'Sweet Dreams' Sindy doll, with sleeping eyes, twist neck, twist body, bending knees, and original 'Good Morning' clothes, in mint condition in unopened card window box.
1978 *12in (30.48cm) high*
£100-150 **MTB**

A Marx Toys Sindy doll, with original clothes, in mint condition in unopened, worn card window box.

1978 *13in (33cm) high*
£50-80 **MTB**

A 1980s Pedigree 'Ballerina' Sindy doll, with original clothes, in mint condition, in unopened card window box.

13in (33cm) high
£50-70 **MTB**

A Pedigree Sindy 'Party Time' doll, with original blue dress and shoes and 'We're Havin' a Party' 45rpm record, in mint condition in unopened card window box.

'Party Time' Sindy was only sold with blonde hair and a choice of three coloured outfits in royal blue, yellow and pink.

1981   12in (30.5cm) high
£120-180   **MTB**

A CLOSER LOOK AT A PAUL SINDY DOLL

The first issue Paul from 1965 had moulded hair. This second issue, with rooted hair, was introduced in 1966.

He was named after Paul McCartney, since The Beatles were the most popular band at the time, and even his hair mimics the famous 'mop top'.

Even though he was also dubbed 'the well-dressed young man', Paul didn't sell well and was withdrawn shortly after his introduction.

Paul's white sneakers are rare as they were usually lost, as was his plastic stand.

A Pedigree Paul doll, in mint condition with original 'Casuals' clothing, plastic stand and box.
1966   12in (30.5cm) high
£100-150   **MTB**

A Hasbro 'Rainbow Sindy' doll, with multicoloured hair, original clothes and hair styling guide, in mint condition in unopened, original card window box.

1992
£20-25   **MTB**

A Pedigree 'Patch' doll, with original schoolgirl outfit with plastic satchel, complete and in mint condition.

Patch is Sindy's little sister.

1966   9in (23cm) high
£50-60   **DSC**

A Pedigree Sindy 'Seaside Sweetheart' outfit, complete in unopened box.

1964   12.5in (31.5cm) wide
£100-150   **MTB**

A Pedigree Sindy 'Country Walk' outfit, complete in unopened box.

This early set, which originally retailed for £19/11d, is sought after because it still has the original bone and dog bowl. A similar set was issued by Mattel for Barbie, but the dog was a terrier rather than a poodle.

1963   12.5in (31.5cm) high
£120-180   **MTB**

QUICK REFERENCE – DAISY DOLLS

The Daisy doll range was produced from 1973-83 in Hong Kong and distributed and marketed by Flair Toys in the UK, the US and Europe. Her unique selling point was that her clothes were designed by top fashion designer Mary Quant, with her name being taken from Quant's orange and white daisy company logo. Her outfits were themed around a world trip, and many were given names of activities associated with cities or named after the cities themselves. There are several variations: a budget 'Dizzy Daisy' without bendable legs or a twisting waist; a version with both features; and 'Dashing Daisy' with bendable waist and curved hands enabling her to hold things. From 1979, Daisy had centre-parted hair and rooted eyelashes. The small-headed version is preferred by collectors to the later large head, and this coloured leotard is a hard-to-find variant on the standard one.

A 1970s Flair Toys Ltd 'Daisy Long Legs' doll, complete with original clothes, stand, booklet and badge, and in mint condition in original card window box.

Daisy Long Legs was released in 1978, and at 15in (38cm) high, is taller than the standard 9in (23cm) high Daisy. As she was taller, a special range of clothes was produced to fit her.

1978-83   17in (43cm) high

£80-120   **MTB**

A 1970s American Gabriel Industries Inc. 'Dotty' Daisy doll, with large head, blonde hair, and original clothing, in complete and mint condition, in unopened original box.

10.5in (26.5cm) high

£65-75   **MTB**

An American Gabriel Industries Inc. 'St. Tropez' Daisy doll, with medium-sized head and original clothes, in complete and mint condition, in original unopened card window box.

10.5in (26.5cm) high

£120-180   **MTB**

A 1970s Flair Toys Ltd 'Dizzy Daisy' doll, with small head, blonde hair and original clothing, in complete and mint condition in unopened card window box.

9.5in (24cm) high

£100-150   **MTB**

A late 1970s Flair Toys Ltd 'Dashing Daisy' 'Skidoo' doll, complete with original clothes and skateboard, in mint condition in slightly damaged original card window box.

The back of the box shows a number of the accessories and different outfits designed by Mary Quant to accompany Daisy. As would be expected from such a fashion designer, she really was 'on trend' for her time!

12in (30.5cm) high

£150-200   **MTB**

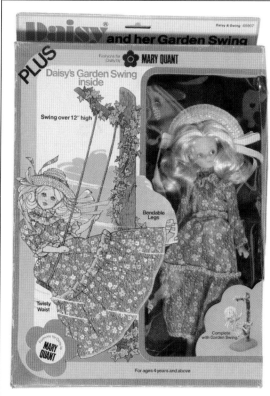

A 1970s Flair Toys Ltd 'Daisy & Swing' doll playset, complete with Daisy doll with bendable legs, clothes, and plastic garden swing, in mint condition in original card window box.

This set is hard to find, particularly complete and in its original box.

12in (30.5cm) high

£120-180   **MTB**

A 1970s Flair Toys Ltd Daisy 'Fandango' outfit, designed by Mary Quant, complete and in mint condition with original packaging.

8in (20cm) high

£35-45   **MTB**

A 1970s Flair Toys Ltd Daisy 'Bee-Bop' outfit, designed by Mary Quant, complete and in mint condition with original packaging.

8in (20cm) high

£30-40   **MTB**

A 1970s Flair Toys Ltd Daisy 'Hoedown' outfit, designed by Mary Quant, complete and in mint condition with original packaging.

11.5in (29cm) high

£32-38   **MTB**

A 1970s Flair Toys Ltd Daisy 'Guinevere' outfit, designed by Mary Quant, complete and in mint condition with original packaging.

12in (30.5cm) high

£32-38   **MTB**

A 1970s Flair Toys Ltd Daisy 'Showbiz' outfit, designed by Mary Quant, complete and in mint condition with original packaging.

12.5in (31.75cm) high

£20-30   **MTB**

A 1970s Flair Toys Ltd Daisy 'St. Moritz' outfit, designed by Mary Quant, complete and in mint condition with original packaging.

12in (30.5cm) high

£25-35   **MTB**

QUICK REFERENCE - PIPPA

Pippa, 'the pocket sized fashion doll' was produced by Palitoy from 1972-80. At only 7in (18cm) in height, she was smaller than her more famous competitors Barbie or Sindy, allowing little girls to carry her around in their pockets or bags. A couple of hundred different, colourful outfits were produced and these have become collectable today, particularly if complete, as many small pieces were lost. Pippa's condition is important to collectors. As she was carried around, she is often worn, and her honey blonde hair tended to yellow unappealingly with age. In 1979, this fourth issue was released and had much fairier hair. As with other variations, these can be of more interest to collectors looking to complete a collection. This particular dress (right) is also hard to find. Mint and boxed examples will fetch the higher values.

A Palitoy Pippa's friend 'Tammie' doll, third issue in gingham dress, in complete and mint condition, in original card window box.

Tammie's first issue outfit (1972) of blue trousers and a top printed with vines and leaves in blue tones is very hard to find.

A Palitoy Pippa doll, fourth issue in multicoloured daisy print yellow dress, in mint condition in original card window box.

1979   7in (18cm) high

£150-200   **MTB**

A Palitoy Princess Pippa doll, in mint condition, in unopened card window box.

c1974   7in (18cm) high

£200-250 **MTB**

1975   7in (18cm) high

£100-150 **MTB**

A rare Palitoy Pippa's friend 'Penny' doll, first issue with dungarees, in mint condition, in original card window box.

1976   7in (18cm) high

£200-300 **MTB**

A Palitoy Pippa's friend 'Mandy' doll, first issue with red pocket on dress, in complete and mint condition, in original card window box.

1976   7in (18cm) high

£100-150 **MTB**

A late 1970s Palitoy Princess Pippa doll, complete and in mint condition, in original card window box.

With long hair down to her feet, Princess Pippa was introduced in 1974, with this dancing version arriving in 1975. Look out for the almost 'Arctic blonde' fair-haired variation, which is very rare.

c1976 7in (18cm) h

£200-300 **MTB**

A Palitoy Pippa's friend 'Pete' doll, with original clothes, in mint and complete condition, in original card window box.

Pete is virtually identical to Topper's 'Gary' doll.

c1977   7in (18cm) high
£70-90   **MTB**

A Palitoy Pippa 'In the Pink' outfit from the Vienna Collection, in complete and mint condition in original box.

1974   8in (20cm) wide
£45-50   **MTB**

A Palitoy Pippa 'Monaco Collection' outfit, complete and in mint condition with original box.

The white, wide-brimmed hat is the rarest part as it was usually lost.

1976   8in (20cm) wide
£20-25   **MTB**

A Palitoy Pippa 'Riviera Collection' outfit, in complete and mint condition, in unopened original card box.

c1976   8in (20cm) wide
£45-50   **MTB**

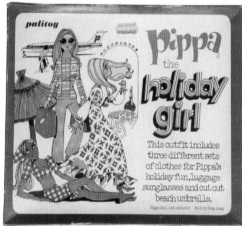

A Palitoy Pippa 'Holiday Girl' clothing set, comprising three outfits, in complete and mint condition with original box.

The 'Disco Fan' set released in the same year also contained three outfits.

1975   9in (23cm) high
£100-150   **MTB**

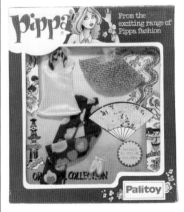

A Palitoy Pippa 'Oriental Collection' outfit, with fan, in complete and mint condition in original, unopened box.

c1977   7in (18cm) wide
£45-50   **MTB**

A Meccano Pippa 'Holiday Collection' outfit, for the French market, complete and in mint condition with unopened box.

1978   8in (20cm) wide
£40-50   **MTB**

DOLLS

A Mattel 'Midge' doll, with 'brownette' hair, 'bendable' legs and original clothing, complete and unopened in original card box.

This was the most expensive Midge doll produced, and is scarce today as she was also not as popular as Barbie herself. Midge is Barbie's best friend.

1964   12in (30.5cm) high

£400-500   **MTB**

A Mattel 'bubble-cut' Barbie doll, with blond hair, model 850, with original red swimsuit, stand and leaflet, in very good condition with original box.

Released in 1959, the ever youthful Barbie celebrated her 50th birthday last year. Vintage, pre-1973, dolls are as sought after today as they were by the little girls who played with Barbie originally.

1962-67   12in (30.5cm) high

£150-200   **MTB**

A Mattel Barbie doll, with 'Twist 'n Turn' waist, produced for the European market, in mint condition, in unopened slightly worn box.

These inexpensive versions of Barbie were bagged inside the box, but sold in the US without the box, leading to them being called 'baggies' by collectors.

1973   12in (30.5cm)

£40-60   **MTB**

A Mattel black 'Tropical Barbie', model 1022, with long hair and original clothes, in mint condition in unopened, original box.

Sold 'with the longest hair ever', she cost $6.99, and was a variant of the white Tropical Barbie released in the same year.

1985   12in (30.5cm) high

£20-30   **MTB**

A Mattel Barbie 'Solo in the Spotlight' special edition reproduction doll, model 13534, with brunette hair, in mint condition in unopened mint condition box.

This doll was also retailed in Hallmark card stores.

1994   13in (33cm) high

£40-60   **MTB**

A Mattel 'Skipper' doll, model 950, blonde hair, original swimsuit and shoes, card box with taped ends.

Although the doll is in very good condition overall, the box has been repaired, which reduces the overall value, which may have topped £150 in mint condition.

1964-66   10in (25.4cm) high

£80-120   **MTB**

A Mattel 'Talking Ken' doll, model 1111, with original red outfit, and sealed in original card window box.

1968   13in (33cm) high

£70-100   **MTB**

A scarce Mattel 'Barbie Ponytail' printed vinyl carrying case.

1961   10.75in (27cm) wide

£30-50   **BH**

QUICK REFERENCE - TRESSY

Released in 1964, Tressy's unique feature was her 'growing' hair, operated by pushing a button on her stomach, and wound back in using a key in a slot in her back. She was made by Palitoy in the UK, American Character in the US and Bella in France. Her sister was Toots (Cricket in the US), her friend was Mary Make-Up, and her clothing line was 'Budget Fashions'. This first issue had sideways glancing eyes and was boxed in a fragile, and now very rare, triangular box.

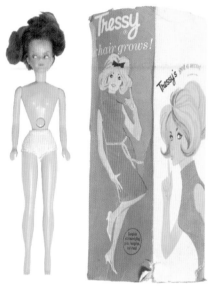

A Palitoy Tressy, first issue, with brown hair, and knickers, together with an original triangular cardboard box.
c1965   *15in (38cm) high*
£60-90   **MTB**

A Palitoy Tressy doll, fourth issue, with original clothing, in mint condition in unopened card window box.

Released in the mid-1970s, this version had gripping hands and a built-in key in her back to wind her hair. She was also available in an identical blue outfit.
                              15in (38cm) high
£100-150   **MTB**

A French Bella Tressy doll, with original clothing, in mint condition in unopened card window box.
c1966   *14in (35.5cm) high*
£55-65   **MTB**

A Palitoy 'Toots' doll, complete with ballet dress, style book and hairgrips, with rare red triangular box.
c1966   *10.5in (26.5cm) high*
£80-120   **MTB**

A late 1960s-70s Palitoy Tressy tennis or sports outfit, in complete and mint condition in original packaging.
                              12in (30.5cm) high
£10-15   **MTB**

A late 1960s Tressy 'Emerald Princess' outfit, in complete and mint condition in original packaging.
                              10.5in (26.5cm) high
£50-80   **MTB**

A 1960s Palitoy Tressy 'Mix n' Match' outfit, complete and in mint condition in original packaging.

                              9.5in (24cm) high
£15-20   **MTB**

DOLLS

An Ideal Tammy doll, first issue, with original skiing outfit and skis, complete with original card box.

Tammy was produced from 1962-66. This is and example of the first issue, with a first issue box. Intended as a competitor to the wildly successful Barbie, she also had an extensive wardrobe, and a set of friends and accessories, but was more wholesome than Barbie.

1962   13in (33cm) high

£100-150   **MTB**

An Ideal Tammy doll, with original blue jumpsuit and stand, in original card box.

c1964   13in (33cm) high

£100-150   **MTB**

An Ideal Dad doll, complete with original clothes, rare shoes and stand, and original card box.

Tammy's Mom is much harder to find than her Dad.

c1964   13in (33cm) high

£70-100   **MTB**

An American Mattel Rock Flowers 'Rosemary' doll, complete with original clothes, record and card window box.

8in (20.5cm)

£60-80   **MTB**

An Ideal Ted doll, complete with original clothes and stand, and original card box.

Ted was Tammy's brother, and is very similar to Tammy's boyfriend Bud. However, Bud has darker eyebrows and is the hardest doll of Tammy's friends and family to find.

c1964   13in (33cm) high

£70-100   **MTB**

An American Mattel Rock Flowers 'Heather' doll, complete with original clothes, record and card window box.

Produced from 1971-74, Mattel's Rock Flowers series were similar to Dawn dolls and had bendy bodies, rooted hair and painted faces. In total, five dolls, including Doug, were produced. The record played two songs that were typical of the period.

8in (20.5cm) high

£50-70   **MTB**

An American Mattel Rock Flowers 'Lilac' doll, complete with original clothes, record and card window box.

8in (20.5cm) high

£50-80 MTB

A Palitoy 'Dancing Tammie' pocket-sized doll, complete with original clothing, in mint condition in unopened original card window box.

7in (18cm) high

£50-80 MTB

A Palitoy 'Dancing Marie' pocket-sized doll, complete with original clothing, in mint condition in unopened original card window box.

Marie was one of Palitoy's miniature fashion dolls, like Pippa. Her novelty lies in her ability to dance – if her arms were moved, her body twisted.

7in (18cm) high

£160-180 MTB

A Dutch Otto Simon Fleur 'Showjumper' doll, with riding outfit, in complete and mint condition, in original card window box.

Fleur was a European 'clone' of Sindy, released in 1978 after Pedigree ceased sales of Sindy in the Netherlands. She proved to be highly successful in her home country and, although she met with some success internationally from 1983, sales were highest in the Netherlands. Fleur was redesigned in the late 1980s, and discontinued in 1988. This doll was one of the less expensive in the range, and packaged in a box to mimic Sindy.

14in (35.5cm) high

£20-30 MTB

An American Mattel 'Twiggy' doll, with twisting waist, and original clothes and plastic boots.

The boots in particular are scarce. Without the original clothing, the doll alone is usually worth up to £30.

1966-67

11in (28cm) high

£40-50 DSC

A Dutch Otto Simon & B.T. Toys International Fleur 'Mount Everest' doll, with mountain climbing outfit, in complete and mint condition, in original card window box.

14in (35.5cm) high

£20-30 MTB

An Ideal Dorothy Hamill doll, with original clothes and medal, in mint condition in original card window box.

Dorothy Hamill was the US Olympic figure skating champion who won a gold medal in the 1976 Innsbruck Winter Olympics.

1977

13in (33cm) high

£40-60 MTB

DOLLS

An Armand Marseille AM 996 doll, with sleeping blue eyes, painted eyebrows and eyelashes, open mouth with two teeth, and jointed composition body.

20in (51cm) high

£100-150   SAS

An Armand Marseille AM 996 doll, with sleeping blue eyes, painted eyebrows, hair eyelashes, open mouth with flicking tongue, two teeth, brown wig, and jointed composition body.

20in (51cm) high

£100-150   SAS

An Armand Marseille AM 351 'Dream Baby', with sleeping blue eyes, painted eyelashes, open mouth with two teeth, and composition body.

9.75in (25cm) high

£50-80   SAS

A Simon & Halbig 1078 doll, with sleeping blue eyes, painted eyebrows and eyelashes, open mouth with four teeth, pierced ear-lobes, and jointed composition body.

18in (46cm) high

£180-220   SAS

A Robert Carl 25 doll, with sleeping brown eyes, painted eyebrows and eyelashes, open mouth with four teeth, jointed composition body, dressed as a nurse.

16.25in (41cm) high

£80-120   SAS

A Bruno Schmidt 2097.2 baby doll, with sleeping blue eyes, painted eyebrows and eyelashes, open mouth with two teeth, joined composition body.

14.25in (36cm) high

£100-150   SAS

A Simon & Halbig 949 doll, with fixed blue eyes, painted eyebrows and eyelashes, closed mouth, pierced ear lobes, kid body with porcelain lower arms, four fingers incomplete, in original box.

18.5in (47cm) high

£250-350   SAS

A 1930s American sprayed composition 'Topsy' doll, with floral printed red clothing, unmarked.

9in (23cm) high

£30-40   DSC

A 1930s Canadian Reliable sprayed composition black doll, with later blue knitted cardigan, nappy and socks.

Many of Reliable's dolls were exported, including to the UK.

11in (28cm) high

£25-30   DSC

A 1930s American sprayed composition 'Topsy' doll, with cotton dress and woven socks, unmarked.

Composition is a hard material made up of glue, resin and wood particles. More resistant to damage and cheaper to produce than bisque, surfaces are often spray painted. Topsy dolls, with their hallmark top knots of hair, were popular in the US during the 1930s. The value depends on the maker, expression on the face, size and condition.

11in (28cm) high

£40-50   DSC

A Norah Wellings 'Welsh Girl' fabric doll, with original clothing, in mint condition with card tag.

As well as being desirable to Norah Wellings collectors, these are also sought after by costume doll collectors.

9in (23cm) high

£50-60   DSC

A 1920s-30s Norah Wellings 'Island Girl' fabric doll, with original clothes, in good condition, with some wear.

14.25in (36cm) high

£20-30   DSC

A 1930s Chad Valley 'Greek Boy' fabric doll, in original clothes, with red embroidered label to sole of left foot, very slight discoloration, otherwise in excellent condition.

17in (33cm) high

£100-150   VEC

A German Steiff 'Musician' brown felt 1911 replica doll, from a limited edition 1,200, with white tag numbered '411915', tags and certificate, in mint condition, with original box.

1997-98   *17in (43cm) high*

£50-80   VEC

DOLLS

A 1950s Linda hard plastic doll, with red corduroy dress and bonnet, the back moulded 'MADE IN HONG KONG', in original and excellent condition.

These dolls were copies of the popular, but comparatively expensive, Miss Rosebud dolls. They were sold in cornershops at prices which were more affordable to children saving pocket money. The style of bonnet and dress is a typical feature.

8in (20.5cm) high

£15-20   **DSC**

A 1950s Welsh Tudor Rose hard plastic 'Island Girl' Topsy-style black doll, with grass skirt and ribbons tied in her three hair knots.

Tudor Rose dolls have been increasing in value over the past few years.

8in (20.5cm) high

£25-30   **DSC**

A 1950s Amanda Jane 'Jinx' hard plastic doll, dressed as a sailor, in complete condition.

7.5in (19cm) high

£40-50   **DSC**

A 1950s Rosebud 'Miss Rosebud' hard plastic doll, with polka dot printed dress, the back moulded 'Miss Rosebud MADE IN ENGLAND'.

As well as considering condition, look at the clothes, as these make a difference to value. For example, the complete fairy outfit can mean the same doll may fetch around £150.

7.5in (19cm) high

£40-50   **DSC**

A 1950s Palitoy hard plastic 'Marcher' doll, in complete original condition with printed floral skirt, socks and plastic shoes.

This doll gained its name due to her unusual walking movement, which looks almost like marching.

19.25in (49cm) high

£40-50   **DSC**

A 1950-53 Vogue hard plastic Ginny, with factory purple ribbon trimmed dress and painted lashes.

7.5in (19cm) high

£120-180   **BH**

A 1950s hard plastic Roberta Walker, wearing a pink dress with grey trim.

8in (20cm) high

£20-30   **BH**

A late 19thC to early 20thC 'Smallest Doll In The World', the fully jointed, carved wooden miniature doll contained inside a wooden egg.

Despite its tiny size, the doll's feet are painted, as are her facial features and her hair.

Doll 0.5in (1.5cm) high

£80-120   DSC

A 1930s probably Japanese 'peanut baby', the celluloid miniature doll with fabric nappy contained inside a pressed pulp peanut shell.

Peanut 4in (10cm) high

£20-25   DSC

A 1920s Japanese painted moulded solid bisque 'My Little Pet' miniature doll, with felt clothes, mounted on original printed sales card.

Card 4.5in (11.5cm) high

£20-30   DSC

A 1930s Japanese 'Bathing Set' celluloid miniature doll, with celluloid bath, oversized dummy, and section of fabric, contained in a matchbox with original printed label.

Bath 1.5in (3.5cm) long

£25-30   DSC

A 1950s 'Smallest Baby In The World' plastic miniature doll, with red plastic bath and original box.

Bath 1.25in (3cm) long

£10-15   DSC

A CLOSER LOOK AT MINIATURE DOLLS

A 1950s Rodnoid hard plastic miniature doll, with jointed arms and legs.

The Rodnoid name could only be used for one year, as the company found that it was already in use by another company for one of its products.

2.75in (7cm) high

£10-15   DSC

The box is rare as most would have been thrown away as these were inexpensive dolls at the time.

These were often used in doll houses, due to their small size.

Note the wild statements about the dolls printed on the box.

On its own, each doll is worth around £5.

A 1950s boxed set of three Japanese moulded rubber 'Three Little Sisters' miniature dolls, imported by CODEG, complete with original box.

Dolls 2.25in (5.5cm) high

£25-30   DSC

QUICK REFERENCE

- Shallowpool Handicrafts were produced by Peggy Pryce, Joan Rickarby and Muriel Fogarty in Devon, England. After World War II, the three women bought a rural cottage and set up a business in fabric homewares, producing items such as rugs and lampshades. They began making dolls during the mid-1950s. Rickarby designed the painted plaster heads and hands, former hairdresser Pryce produced the wigs, and Fogarty assembled the dolls on wire armatures, and handled business matters.
- Dolls were based on Cornish or historical characters, painstakingly researched to ensure that costumes were as accurate and detailed as possible. They were sold in local shops, and gift and souvenir shops in Cornwall for tourists.

- The company grew to be very successful, employing 16 doll makers and exporting to shops in the US as well as around the UK. In the late 1970s, Pryce married and left the business, with Rickarby and Fogarty carrying on with production until the mid-1980s, when they both retired and Shallowpool Handicrafts was closed.
- To ensure you are buying a complete doll, it is helpful to familiarise yourself with the dolls produced, including their clothes and accessories. There may be variations, particularly in fabrics used for clothing, but this does not usually affect value. Avoid staining, fading, tears, or damage to the paint, especially on the faces, as these will reduce the desirability.

A Shallowpool 'Cornish Pasty Seller' doll, with painted plaster Cornish pasties on a plate and printed poem about pasties in her apron pocket.

This is one of the most commonly found dolls, undoubtedly due to the popularity of Cornish pasties.

8in (20.5cm) high

£15-20   DSC

A Shallowpool 'Bal Maiden' doll, with cane and plaster long-handled hammer stick and knitting in her apron pocket.

This Cornish character broke up rocks dug out of copper or tin mines, an activity known as 'spalling', to earn a living.

7.5in (19cm) high

£25-30   DSC

A Shallowpool 'Old Mother Hubbard' doll, with white painted plaster dog on a fabric ribbon.

9in (23cm) high

£40-50   DSC

A Shallowpool 'Fanny Wheeler' doll, holding a painted plaster lantern.

Fanny Wheeler assisted her father in his smuggling activities, taking a boat to France with him to bring back kegs of illicit spirits.

7.75in (19.5cm) high

£40-50   DSC

A Shallowpool 'Cornish Lady' dressed in early 17thC riding costume, with a feathered hat.

This figure was inspired by Lady Howard of Fitzford from Daphne du Maurier's 1964 novel 'The King's General'.

8in (20.5cm) high

£20-25   DSC

QUICK REFERENCE

- Although there are still collectors who buy vintage eyewear as a record of optical developments and changing styles, most of today's buyers are looking to wear their new purchases. The most popular frames are colourful and date from the 1950s onwards. Value depends on style, condition, the name of the maker or designer, and materials used.
- Frames that effectively represent their period are particularly desirable, with the 'cat's eye' style of the 1950s and oversized rounded frames of the 1960s being widely sought after. Rare 'wild' styles in bright or clashing colours and shapes that might have been unpopular or expensive at time are often the most valuable.
- Consider the material and work that has gone into making the frames. Hand-crafted elements, such as enamelling, painting or complex laminating or cutting, will generally add value.

- Look for the names or monograms of famous designers, as these will generally add value. Notable eyewear designers include Alain Mikli and Emmanuelle Khanh; frames were also designed for or by Christian Dior, Emilio Pucci and Pierre Cardin. Some designers' monograms changed over time, which can help with dating.
- Always examine frames for burn marks, cracks or splits, which cannot be repaired easily and will make the frames less attractive to prospective buyers. Warped or bent plastic can sometimes be corrected by professionals and is therefore often less problematic. Look for 'dead' unused shop stock, which is usually unworn.
- Scratched, cracked, or even missing lenses do not typically affect value, as buyers often intend to fit their own lenses. Unusual original lenses, such as those with a graduated tint in matching or contrasting colour, may add value, however, and should be kept even if they are replaced.

A pair of 1940s-60s small tortoiseshell plastic frames, with half hexagonal rims and curved arms.

A pair of 1930s-40s clear pink tinged plastic half-hexagonal frames, unmarked.
5in (12.5cm) wide

£40-60   VE

Retro styles such as this, particularly in tortoiseshell, have recently become fashionable again, after years of modern styles being popular.
5in (12.5cm) wide

£70-100   VE

A pair of 1960s French black plastic sunglasses with half hexagonal-shaped top rims, curved arms and "VERGO FILTRANT FRANCE" oval sticker on the original lenses.
5in (12.5cm) wide

£70-100   VE

A pair of 1950s plastic sunglasses, the frames of transparent light blue over opaque white.
5in (13cm) wide

£30-40   CANS

A pair of 1950s brown and white laminated plastic sunglasses.
5in (13cm) wide

£30-50   CANS

FASHION

QUICK REFERENCE

- Vintage fashion is still a hot collecting area. Examples are not only sought after by collectors, but also by fashionistas who follow the trend for wearing vintage set by celebrities such as Kate Moss and Sarah Jessica Parker. Although this rise in popularity has meant prices have risen too, there's plenty still available to suit every budget. Pieces can be found at auctions, vintage fashion dealers and even in charity shops.

- The top end of the market is dominated by the work of leading 20thC designers such as Christian Dior, Gianni Versace and Coco Chanel. These pieces can be divided into two categories: couture, made in limited quantities after pieces from seasonal collections, and 'diffusion' ranges that can be bought 'off the peg'. Couture examples are usually more desirable, particularly if they are from notable collections, and fetch higher sums. Learn to recognise the difference by researching the different labels used.

- Although the top end of the market may be the most stable area in terms of value, the middle and lower ends have seen similar rises, and can be more fun to collect. Clothes often cost the same as, or even less than, something from the high street. Currently, the 1950s, 60s and 70s are the most popular decades. Always check the label as some makers may have been 'cult' names. Look out for prestigious locations which can indicate good quality makers or retailers.

- Look for pieces that are well cut, made from high grade materials, well finished and which have good stitching. Avoid pieces that are torn or stained – unless this is intentional. Examine vintage photographs and fashion books to learn more about the styles of the period you are interested in. After the work of leading designers, pieces that epitomise the fashion of the age are the most sought after by collectors.

An early 20thC American cotton and lace day dress, with tapework and lace panels and trim, and embroidered flowers and leaves, with elasticated waist.

Dresses from this period are scarcer than most, due to their age and fragile material. The style came back into fashion in the 1970s, with names such as Gunne Saxe. More common in the US than the UK, if the condition is as good as this, it should make an excellent buy.
c1915   41.5in (105cm) high

£100-150   CANS

A 1920s brown corduroy coat, with a a detachable fox fur collar or stole, lined in cotton, and with ruched sleeves, unlabelled.
45.75in (116cm) high

£200-250   CANS

A 1930s-40s black crepe dress, with red and white beaded pockets with stylized flower within a shield design, in excellent condition.

As well as the dress fabric being in perfect condition, there is, surprisingly, no damage to the beaded pockets. Damage to beaded designs like these is almost impossible to repair satisfactorily and can reduce value by over 75 per cent.
39.5in (100cm) long

£80-120   CANS

A 1930s yellow chiffon or georgette tea dress, printed with red and yellow flowers and green leaves, with ruffled neck.

42.25in (107cm) long

£100-150   CANS

A late 1940s burgundy crushed velvet belted dress, with ruched shoulders and glass buttons, unlabelled.

£80-120   CANS

A late 1940s-50s Canadian Sty-Val silver-grey acetate dress, woven with roses in silver and gold coloured thread, labelled.

38.25in (97cm) high

£80-100   CANS

A 1940s green cotton dress, printed with black and white flowers, with bow to front, and matching jacket with cream lapels, unlabelled.

58in (147cm) long

£100-150   CANS

A 1940s Utility houndstooth coat with attached hood, original Bakelite buttons, matching belt, and deep cuffs.

A 1940s black crepe dress, with pleated fan effect to front, scooped neck line, and high split skirt.

47in (119cm) high

£60-80   CANS

A 1940s American Brookmar day dress, printed with red berries, purple leaves and green flowers, with torn label.

42.25in (107cm) long

£60-80   CANS

41in (104cm) high

£180-220   CANS

FASHION

A CLOSER LOOK AT A 1950S DRESS

The cut of the dress with its full skirt and bolero jacket, is typical of the 1950s.

The bright colours reflect the change from the austerity of wartime and post-war 1940s utility-wear.

The stylised pink rose and polka dot motifs are also typical of the period and add a whimsical touch.

The condition is excellent, making it very wearable today – an important factor in its valuation.

A 1950s 'London Town MADE IN MAYFAIR LONDON ENGLAND' purple, orange, brown and green floral printed halterneck dress, with boned and structured inside mesh petticoat underneath, and trail to the scoop back.

37in (94cm) long

£80-100   **CANS**

A 1950s American sleeveless halterneck cotton dress and matching bolero jacket, printed with pink roses in white wavy bands, and white polka dots on blue, with label reading 'LO ROCO MODEL in Marchington'.

45in (114cm) long

£80-100   **CANS**

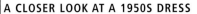

A 1950s cotton belted dress, printed with roses and polka dots, the pockets with black trim, unlabelled.

34.75in (88cm) long

£70-90   CANS

A 1950s green cotton belted maxi-dress, printed with white flowers and with 'angel' or 'flutter' sleeves.

51.75in (131cm) long

£40-50   CANS

A 1950s white cotton shirtwaister dress, printed with polka dots and with spherical buttons inset with rhinestones, unlabelled.

40.5in (103cm) long

£60-80   CANS

A 1950s American Kabro of Houston tonal blue, grey and purple cotton shirtwaister dress, with Tiki style print.

As American GIs returned to the US from overseas, Hawaiian inspired Tiki prints underwent a style revival in the 1950s and 60s, affecting everything from barware to fashion.

43.75in (111cm) long

£60-80   **CANS**

A mid-1950s Jeanne Lanvin black Chantilly lace cocktail dress, with boned strapless bodice, bouffant tiered skirt, large silk rose, horse-hair stiffened petticoat, bearing large woven label.

£420-480   **KT**

QUICK REFERENCE - CHRISTIAN DIOR

On February 12th 1947, a 42 year old Christian Dior (1905-57) exploded onto the international fashion scene with his first collection. Named 'Corolle', it brought elegance back to fashion with wasp-like waists, longer fuller skirts, a high bust and rounded shoulders. Within months the curvaceous style had become known as the 'New Look', and it went on to be copied across the world. Although the waist on this example is more relaxed, it still bears many of the hallmarks of Dior's original designs.

A Christian Dior Export slubbed silk cocktail dress, no.25713, with curving shoulders, boat neckline, large fringed bow to one hip, labelled 'Christian Dior Europe, manufacturé par Christian Dior Export'.

c1956–7   *Bust 34in (86cm)*

     KT

£380-420   **KT**

A 1950s ball gown, the cream ground embroidered with a floral pattern in green tones, with two green pleats and small bow to chest, unlabelled.

45.25in (115cm) long

£100-150   **CANS**

A 1950s jade green halterneck ball gown, woven with a vein-like design and bow to chest, with stiffened calico petticoat and and hooped layer underneath.

Ball gowns of this period make superb buys, as they are generally not hard to find, often of very good quality and are considerably less expensive than modern dresses. They also add a certain vintage style to an occasion. The pattern on this vibrantly coloured example is unusual.

47.75in (121cm) long

£150-200   **CANS**

A 1950s Liberty of London waisted Astrakhan collar wool coat, with 'Liberty of London' label to inside.

The waisted shape, buttons and Astrakhan collar give this a Victorian or Edwardian feel. Asktrakhan is the tightly curled fur from Persian or kerakul lambs.

39.5in (100cm) long

£150-200   **CANS**

An Ossie Clark printed velvet coat, with Russian-style button closure down one side, printed with multicoloured flowers designed by Celia Birtwell, with black on white printed label.

c1970   *Bust 34in (86cm)*

£450-550   **KT**

A late 1960s Pucci printed silk jersey evening gown, printed in shades of blue and green over a turquoise skirt, labelled.

Bust 36in (92cm)

£280-320   **KT**

A CLOSER LOOK AT A DOLLYROCKERS DRESS

DollyRockers was designed by Samuel Sherman, also known as 'Sambo' and was active from c1963-75.

They were promoted in conjunction with Dolcis shoes by Smith's Crisps model Pattie Boyd (b.1944), who married Beatle George Harrison and Eric Clapton.

Look out for dresses that are made from Liberty print, a fact indicated on the label, as these can fetch over £100.

Labels reading 'Dollyrockers London' are different, being new clothes made from vintage fabric, and sold today through London retailers.

A 1960s DollyRockers cotton dress, printed with brown, yellow and orange repeated flowers and foliage on a bright blue ground, with frill under bust, labelled.

32.75in (83cm) long

£60-80   **CANS**

A 1970s Emilio Pucci Kelly green cotton poplin skirt and blouse, printed with violet and blue floral pattern, with twill A-line skirt with welt pockets, with 'Emilio Pucci' label.

Now owned by luxury goods group LVMH, the Pucci name has never been out of fashion for long. Always look for the 'Emilio' name in the print as the company's classic 1960s and ' 70s look was widely copied. The colour and pattern of this suit are typical of Pucci's look.

size 6-8

£280-320   **FRE**

An early 1960s HF Couture of London pink cotton dress, printed with a green, black and white curving abstract pattern.

Despite dating from the 1960s, the shape is very 1950s and the pattern recalls the Art Deco period of the 1930s.

36in (91cm) long

£50-60   **CANS**

A 1960s Shifts International of Miami cotton dress, printed with blue fish and lime green seahorses on a white background, trimmed with lace.

The colours, pattern and shape are similar to dresses by Lily Pulitzer, which were also popular.

35in (89cm) long

£50-60   **CANS**

A 1950s Kittiwake swimsuit, with purple-brown and white wicker-like pattern, unworn.

22.75in (57.5cm) long

£30-40 CANS

An early 1960s Slix navy blue swimsuit, with diagonal red and white stripes, unworn.

18.5in (47cm) long

£40-50 CANS

ESSENTIAL REFERENCE - 1940S UTILITY CLOTHING

Utility clothing is the term used to describe clothes produced in Britain during the war, when materials were rationed and skilled labour was limited. The range was introduced in 1941, and bore the 'CC41' label shown here, which stood for Civilian Clothing 1941'. The government regulated the import, distribution and use of cloth, limiting the 'austere' styles and the range itself. They also controlled the price to ensure people could afford clothing of suitable quality. Much was worn out or altered, making surviving intact examples rare. Initial dislike turned into apathy, and the range was withdrawn in 1952.

A 1940s Capstan utility-wear woven pink cotton swimsuit, printed with seashells and fish, size 36, with Capstan and Utility labels.

18.5in (47cm) long

£60-80 CANS

An early 1960s Slix brown and white swimsuit, with diagonal stripe of alternating coloured leaves.

18.5in (47cm) long

£40-60 CANS

A mid 1960s Slix light blue swimsuit, with horizontal red stripe with woven white flowers, unworn.

18.5in (47cm) long

£35-45 CANS

A 1950s British Kittiwake swimsuit, with folded 'V' shape to front, unworn, size 34.

The label indicates that the elasticated material was tested by Courtaulds.

22.75in (57.5cm) high

£40-60 CANS

A pair of 1940s cork wedges with leopardskin fabric uppers, marked 'La Rose Jacksonville Florida'.

£150-200   GCHI

A 1950s blue leather shoe by Rayne, with leather tassel decoration, marked 'Rayne by Appointment'.

£20-30   LDY

One of a pair of 1950s brown suede peep-toe court shoes, with brown leather strapped decoration.

£20-30   LDY

A 1940s pair of mules, with burgundy suede uppers with embroidered flowers, and carved-wood platform soles, made in the Philippines.

Sometimes known as 'sweetheart souvenirs', these were sent or taken home to wives and girlfriends by American GIs stationed in the Philippines during and after WWII. Houses, foliage and flowers painted in bright colours are typical motifs. The use of coloured woven raffia is another common feature.

£150-200   GCHI

QUICK REFERENCE – SALVATORE FERRAGAMO

Salvatore Ferragamo (1898-1960) was one of the greatest innovators in shoe design. After an apprenticeship in Italy, he moved to Southern California in 1914, where he studied anatomy to ensure his shoes were comfortable. His handmade, innovative designs combined function with ornamental forms, and he rapidly gained a celebrity following including Rudolph Valentino and Mary Pickford. In 1927, he returned to Italy, where he continued his innovative work, introducing new materials such as the cork wedge, which was patented in 1937. He continued to attract celebrity clients, including Eva Peron and Marilyn Monroe, after the war. His reputation as a visionary designer of elegant and innovative shoes continued until his death.

One of a pair of late 1940s gold leather sandals, by Salvatore Ferragamo.

£300-500   LDY

A CLOSER LOOK AT A PAIR OF 1950S SHOES

The uppers and strap are made from clear flexible Perspex – plastics such as this were new and fashionable in the 1950s.

The choice of pink and the added sparkle from the diamanté complemented the fashions of the day.

The glamorous design contrasts with the austere fashions of the 1940s, which saw restrictions and rationing.

The stiletto is said to have been developed by French designer Charles Jordan in 1952 – two years later a more cost-effective plastic and metal version was developed, which began the trend.

A pair of 1950s Perspex and metallic pink 'Countess' last slingbacks, with diamanté detail on the toes and clear and diamanté-decorated heels, marked 'Mackay Starr New York'.

£120-180   GCHI

A pair of 1950s black suede court shoes, the toes decorated with red velvet ribbon bows, marked 'Michelé Fifth Avenue Paris custom made'.

£150-200   GCHI

A pair of 1950s Danbarale blue leather stilettos, with diamanté and fan detail.

£150-200   IVD

A pair of 1950s unworn American peep-toe slingbacks, with knot detail, marked 'The Guarantee Shoe Store'.

£35-45   CANS

A pair of 1950s flexible Perspex slingbacks, with Perspex 'bows', the painted heels decorated with diamanté, the shoes marked 'Jacqueline designed by Wohl'.

£70-100   GCHI

A pair of 1950s mink and black velvet slippers, marked 'Mandel's fascinating slippers' and 'Genuine Mink'.

£120-180   GCHI

A pair of 1950s Nina Original gold-coloured wood paltform mules, with black lace-effect plastic uppers.

£100-150 GCHI

A pair of 1950s faux-leopard skin fabric mules, with wing-shaped uppers.

£150-200 GCHI

A pair of 1950s Nylonette waterproof shoe protectors/galoshes, with black suedette flaps and a fastening button.

The hollow heels allowed the wearer to slip these over their shoes for protection.

£40-60 CANS

A pair of 1950s straw mules with wooden soles and Perspex heels, the heels inset with raffia flowers.

Always examine raffia closely, as it can be damaged very easily.

£200-250 GCHI

A pair of 1950s black suede zipped boots, with fur trim, marked 'Kickerino Alaskans', in excellent condition.

£100-150 GCHI

A pair of 1980s French Cassis, Cote d'Azur, black suede and gold leather court shoes, with chain detail at heel.

£70-100   LDY

QUICK REFERENCE - 1980S SHOES

The bold style of these shoes matches the dominant style of the period – power dressing. As more women entered executive jobs and strived for ever-increasing success in the working world, their clothes began to reflect their determination and power. Shoulder pads and suits in bold colours and patterns were typical. Examples include Signourney Weaver's character Katharine Parker in the 1988 film 'Working Girl', Prime Minister Margaret Thatcher, and Alexis Colby from the TV series 'Dynasty'. As many of today's designers are already beginning to look back to 1980s fashions, it will be interesting to see how this affects the value and desirability of original shoes and clothes.

A pair of 1980s R.P. Ellen green, white and navy blue slingbacks.

£20-30   CANS

A pair of 1980s 'Wild Pair' black sequin stilettos.

£45-55   IVD

A pair of 1980s Corsina grey leather peep-toe shoes, with applied cream leather butterfly detail.

£45-55   IVD

A 1980s Yves Saint Laurent suede and leather laced court shoe.

A pair of 1980s black and white swirl leather heels, by Gina.

£30-50   CANS

Saint Laurent updated the classic, clumpy brogue of the 1970s and devised a shoe that looks back to the early 20thC, reflects period fashions and is supremely elegant, with great proportions. With the Yves Saint Laurent label and high quality materials, these shoes are desirable and valuable.

£150-200   LDY

FASHION

QUICK REFERENCE

- It's not just collectors who are snapping up vintage handbags. With the surge of interest in vintage clothing seen over the past decade, fashionable people of all ages are buying handbags to give an individual touch.
- Prices range from as little as £20 to over £5,000 for a highly desirable Hermès 'Kelly' bag. However, most bags can be found for under £100 at vintage clothing stores, auctions, car boot sales and charity shops. When buying always look inside for designer labels, and examine a bag all over to assess its condition.
- Value depends on a number of factors including desirability, the maker, the quality of construction and the materials used, age and condition. Bags made from leather and the rarer animal skins are usually the most

valuable, although bags made of other materials that exemplify the style of the day or have novelty appeal can be equally valuable.
- Away from the best names such as Chanel, Hermès and Gucci, look out for labels of makers in desirable locations, such as Fifth Avenue, New York or Bond Street, London, as this usually indicates a high quality bag.
- Condition is very important. A bag in truly mint, shop-bought, condition will fetch a considerable premium over one that shows signs of use. Look inside as torn or stained interiors reduce desirability and value. Although bags from the 1950s and 60s are currently the most popular, iconic bags from the 1980s are beginning to see a surge of interest, so could be a good investment.

A 1920s Whiting & Davis chain mesh bag with embroidered pink fabric lining, metal frame, stamped inside.

Whiting & Davis, founded in 1876 in Massachusetts, is synonymous with high quality mesh bags. It made bags printed with brightly coloured Art Deco patterns. Although the company fell out of fashion in the mid20thC, it returned briefly during the 'disco' age in the 1970s. The companys's bags remain popular with collectors.

5in (12.5cm) wide

£70-100   CANS

A 1930s brown silk Art Deco bag, the clasp set with cut steel rhinestones, cream silk lined interior, metal frame, marked 'Made in England'.

6in (15cm) high

£30-40   CANS

A 1930s brown ruffled silk bag, pink satin lining, with original mirror, rhinestone clasp, marked 'Made in England'.

The quality and condition of the bag contribute to its value.

8.5in (22cm) wide

£40-60   CANS

A 1930s Art Deco woven Corde handbag, with brass fittings and frame covered with cream bakelite panels, marked 'Made in England'.

8.25in (21cm) high

£50-80   CANS

A 1930s woven silk clutch bag, the silk hand-printed with ducks and birds, with black silk lining and gold piping in and out, bevelled hand mirror and an Art Deco clasp.

7.5in (19.5cm) wide

£40-60   CANS

A 1930s Art Deco iridescent beaded bag, with black Lucite and chromed metal frame.

7in (18cm) wide

£120-180 **GCHI**

A 1940s bag, with a hand-painted and beaded garden and floral design, the padded handle with small floral motifs.

9in (23cm) wide

£150-200 **AHL**

A 1940s brown leather bag with crocodile skin panel decoration, with expandable front pocket and arrow-shaped catch.

10.5in (26.5cm) high

£60-90 **CANS**

A 1940s-50s British faux-snakeskin bag with wrist handle and purse.

6.75in (17cm) high

£30-50 **CANS**

A CLOSER LOOK AT A 1940S HANDBAG

During the post-war period, when many materials were expensive and hard to obtain, bags were decorated with all manner of different materials, such as telephone cable.

Box bags are also typical of the period. The bright, jaunty colours and pattern of the telephone cables added colour and cheer at a time of great austerity.

Avoid dirty or stained examples as they are hard to clean. Breaks in the cord also reduce value.

These bags were made in a variety of patterns and colour combinations – generally the more complex the pattern and the more colours are present, the better.

A 1940s blue felt bag, with applied posy of felt flowers and hearts.

15in (38cm) wide

£60-80 **GCHI**

A 1940s telephone cable covered box bag, lined with red woven fabric on a frame.

7.25in (18.5cm) wide

£60-80 **CANS**

FASHION

A 1950s-60s woven box bag, white plastic and yellow and black straw, metal clasp, unmarked.

11in (28cm) wide

£30-50   CANS

A CLOSER LOOK AT AN ENID COLLINS HANDBAG

Enid Collins founded her company in 1959 in Texas and quickly became a popular name with fashionable young women into the 1970s.

The most collectable and desirable bags are sturdy wooden box bags decorated with painted designs highlighted with rhinestones, faux jewels, sequins and other materials.

Authentic bags made before Collins sold the company in 1970 are stamped 'ec' on the outside, together with the name of the design, and also bear a stamp on the interior.

The more detailed and amusing the design, and the more materials and colours used, the more the bag is likely to be worth – but check carefully for missing parts.

A 1960s Enid Collins 'Night Owl' box bag, decorated with rhinestones, marked inside, with plastic handle.

8.5in (22cm) wide

£50-70   CANS

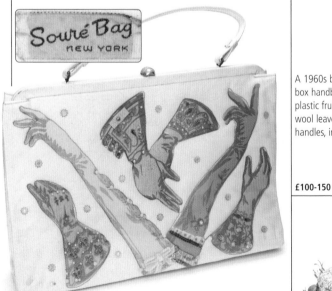

A 1950s-60s Souré Bag of New York, of plastic-covered printed cotton, decorated with embroidered multicoloured gloves, applied rhinestones and faux pearls.

15.25in (38.5cm) long

£220-280   GCHI

A 1960s basketwork box handbag, with applied plastic fruit and woven wool leaves and faux-leather handles, in excellent condition.

10.25in (26cm) high

£100-150   GCHI

A 1950s Hovland Swanson woven raffia drawstring bag, with applied raffia covered fruits and raffia 'grass', with original price and shop tickets.

8in (20cm) high

£50-70   GCHI

A 1980s enamelled 'kissing fish' belt buckle, with grey woven belt.

5in (12.5cm) wide

£15-20   CANS

A 1980s embossed metal buckle in the shape of a large fish eating a small fish, on a red elasticated belt.

5in (13cm) wide

£20-30   CANS

A set of 1950/60s Manderin Jiffy Juvenile Product elasticated permanently knotted ties for boys, in original shop display box.

Box 12.5in (32cm) wide

£40-60   CANS

A 1980s Valentino red and black chequered dyed fox stole, fully articulated with rhinestone eyes, labelled "Valentino Night/Made in Italy".

£75-95   FRE

A pair of 1930s Plaza silk stockings, in original, unopened packaging with dog shaped card, marked 'Made in England'.

The scarcity of an unopened pack, the dog motif and Art Deco font that make these appealing – some collectors even specialise in stockings.

6.75in (17cm) wide

£20-25   CANS

A set of six 1950s handpainted plastic Bobby Pins hairpins, on original shop display card.

Card 4.75in (12cm) high

£10-15   CANS

A set of six 1950s handpainted plastic Bobby Pins hairpins, on original shop display card.

Card 4.75in (12cm) high

£10-15   CANS

QUICK REFERENCE

- Caithness glass was founded near John O'Groats in Scotland in June 1961, primarily to create employment for local people. Talented Irish designer Domnhall O'Broin co-founded the company, and became its technical director and designer from 1961-1966, being responsible for many of their most successful designs. The company is now owned by Dartington Glass.

- O'Broin is arguably one of the over-looked names in 20th century glass design. He trained under Helen Monroe Turner at the Edinburgh College of Art and was one of the first apprentices at Waterford Crystal from 1950, where he worked under Miroslav Havel, and designed patterns such as 'Colleen'. O'Broin left Caithness in 1966, moving to the US where he worked for Pilgrim and Fenton before setting up on his own.

- His designs are typified by modern, yet elegant, shapes with clean lines. Scandinavian glass, being imported into Britain at the time in large numbers, was a strong inspiration. Rims were machine cut and the bases heavily cased in clear glass which 'lifted' and contrasted with the colour. Pieces were spun at high speed in moulds, giving an even, rounded base with a smooth central depression.

- The jewel-like colours used were inspired by the Scottish landscape, gaining patriotic and evocative names such as 'Loch Blue', 'moss' (green), 'Peat' and 'Heather' (purple). Pieces are generally unmarked, although 'CG' paper, or later 'Caithness Glass' labels may have survived.

- Avoid examples that are chipped or scuffed or have internal bubbles or limescale from water, as these factors detract from the purity of the colour and form. After O'Broin left, other designers worked for the company, including Charles Orr from 1967-72 and, notably, Colin Terris from 1972 onwards. Along with O'Broin's, their designs are becoming increasingly sought-after.

A 1960s-90s Caithness Glass footed fruit bowl, designed by Domhnall O'Broin in 1961.

7in (17.5cm) high

£20-30   GC

A 1960s-70s Caithness Glass Heather purple 'Cased' vase, no.4010/M, designed by Domhnall O'Broin in 1961.

7in (17.5cm) high

£30-50   GC

A 1960s-80s Caithness Glass small Loch blue 'Barrel' vase, no.4019/115, designed by Domhnall O'Broin in 1961.

5in (12.5cm) high

£15-20   GC

A Caithness Glass cased 'Moss Green' posy vase, by Domhnall O'Broin, factory and 'Design Centre London' paper labels.

4in (10cm) high

£10-15   MHC

A Caithness Glass Loch Blue 'Stroma' rose bowl, designed by Domhnall O'Broin in 1961.

The colour variation is brought about by the thickness of the glass – near the rim it is extremely thin.

XXin (XXcm) high

£20-30   GC

A 1960s Caithness Glass Loch Blue tall cylindrical mould blown vase, designed by Domhnall O'Broin in 1963, with paper label.

10.5in (26.5cm) high

£80-120 GC

A 1960s-70s Caithness Glass Peat brown 'Barrel' vase, no.4019/235, designed by Domhnall O'Broin in 1961.

9in (23cm) high

£50-70 GC

A 1960s-70s Caithness Glass Moss green lamp base, designed by Domhnall O'Broin in 1961, with original 'CG' paper label.

This was featured in the influential book 'Modern Glass' by Geoffrey Beard, as an example of a very modern design for the period. Larger pieces such as this are harder to find than smaller vases.

7.25in (18.5cm) high

£80-120 GC

A 1960s-70s Caithness Glass Heather lamp base, no.4010/LL, designed by Domhnall O'Broin in 1961.

10in (25.5cm) high

£70-100 GC

A 1960s-70s Caithness Glass Peat brown decanter with hollow blown stopper, designed by Domhnall O'Broin in 1961.

11.25in (28.5cm) high

£40-60 GC

A 1960s-70s Caithness Glass Heather cased purple decanter, with hollow stopper, designed by Domhnall O'Broin.

Colour tones can vary widely, and it can be hard to tell which colour a piece was intended to be. Clearly identifiable colours such as this are the most desirable.

11.25in (28.5cm) high

£60-80 GC

A Caithness Glass Peat brown Morven decanter, shape no.4025/D, designed by Domhnall O'Broin in 1961, with hollow stopper.

This starkly modern, squared off form is typical of O'Broin's forms. Unusually for a decanter, the inside of the rim is not ground, with the seal coming only from the weight of the well-fitted blown stopper.

9.75in (24cm) high

£30-40 M20C

A Caithness Glass Heather purple 'Morven' decanter, shape no.4025/D, designed by Domhnall O'Broin in 1961.

9.75in (25cm) high

£40-50   GAZE

A 1990s Caithness Glass cased mottled jade green 'Concerto' rose vase, with ribbed base and cellophane label.

Concerto was available in three colourways: Blue, Jade and Pink.

7in (17.5cm) high

£20-25   GC

A Caithness Glass graduated purple vase, engraved with a bird perched on a thorny branch.

A cutting and engraving department was founded at Caithness by Colin Terris in 1968, meaning all cut or engraved ranges date from after this year. Natural or animal motifs, and commemorative designs, are typical. Designs commemorating personal events, such as a wedding, usually devalue a piece.

9in (23cm) high

£10-15   GC

A Caithness Glass colourless cylindrical 'Oban' vase, designed by Charles Orr, with applied green and blue ribbon trails.

7in (17.5cm) high

£20-30   GC

A CLOSER LOOK AT A CAITHNESS GLASS VASE

Xanadu uses many layers of glass over an opaque white base to create a mottled, stone-like effect, and can be found in triangular, ovoid, rectangular and hexagonal forms.

The pattern was created by hand in a time-consuming process using coloured enamel frit and randomly applied hot glass trails, making each piece unique.

This range was expensive and comparatively unpopular at the time, so was withdrawn from sale only a few years after being introduced, meaning that it is comparatively scarce today.

It can be found in a range of colours including orange and red, green and blue, and purple and grey.

A Caithness Glass 'Xanadu' range ovoid vase, designed by Colin Terris in 1996, with layers of pulverised coloured enamel over an opaque white core and an applied blue trail.

7.25in (18.5cm) high

£70-100   GC

A Caithness Glass 'Xanadu' range bottle vase, designed by Colin Terris in 1996, with layers of pulverised coloured enamel over an opaque white core and an applied blue trail.

10in (25.5cm) high

£100-150   GC

QUICK REFERENCE

- Wines from the Champagne region have been prized since Roman times, and were often used at royal ceremonies. In 1662, English scientist Christopher Merret developed the first intentionally sparkling wine, although French Benedictine monk Dom Perignon is usually credited with this achievement. However, his version was developed some 40 years after Merret's.
- From the 17thC to the 20thC, champagne was sweet, often being served as a dessert. Dry 'brut' champagne only became popular in the late 19thC.
- Two types of glass are used to serve champagne: a tall flute with a rim that may curve slightly inwards, and a low, saucer-shaped dish. Both are mounted on stems to keep the hand from touching the bowl and warming the wine. The taller version is preferred by connoisseurs.
- The saucer, known as a 'coupe', was reputedly developed in 1663, although facts are scarce. Legend has it that its form

was based on the shape of the breasts of Madame de Pompadour or Queen Marie Antoinette. This is almost certainly false, as examples exist that predate both women. The style saw peaks in popularity during the mid-19thC and during the 1920s and 30s, when it was also used for cocktails.
- Value depends on the maker, glass, and the style and quality of any decoration. Prices for vintage examples can be lower than those for brand new glasses. Although unusual motifs can make a glass desirable, simple and almost 'modern', geometric cuts are often the most popular with collectors.
- Edwardian acid-etched examples are currently very affordable, and are typically made from a delicate, thin glass. Look for simpler classical or geometric patterns, as these may rise in value over time. Owning vintage glasses can add a stylish dash of originality to entertaining.

A 1930s-50s coupe champagne glass, cut with a pattern of stylised leaves and flowers.

Patterns like this tend to be less popular and desirable. The stem is also not cut.

4.5in (11.5cm) high

£10-12   **GROB**

A 19thC coupe champagne glass, the bowl copper wheel-cut with a pattern of leaves and ferns, with plain, waisted cylindrical stem.

4.5in (11.5cm) high

£12-15   **GROB**

A 19thC or early 20thC coupe champagne glass, the bowl cut with thistles and leaves, with straight faceted stem.

This is possibly by notable company Edinburgh & Leith.

4.75in (12cm) high

£20-25   **GROB**

A late 19thC or early 20thC coupe champagne glass, the bowl with acid-etched stylised floral swag and scrolling motif, with hatched band with stylised roses.

4.5in (11.5cm) high

£10-12   GROB

A mid 20thC coupe champagne glass, the bowl cut with trailing strawberry plants and strawberries, with conical baluster stem.

Strawberries are popular motifs – probably because of the luxurious association of strawberries and champagne.

4.5in (11.5cm) high

£10-12   GROB

GLASS

A late 19thC or early 20thC coupe champagne glass, with acid-etched bands of loops and interlaced circles, and tapering cylindrical stem.

4.75in (12cm) high

£8-12   **GROB**

A mid-20thC Continental coupe champagne glass, the bowl cut with a curving pattern of 'thumbprint' ovals, with conical baluster stem.

4.75in (12cm) high

£10-15   **GROB**

An early 20thC Continental coupe champagne glass, the bowl cut with a curving pattern of 'thumbprint' ovals, with conical baluster stem.

4.75in (12cm) high

£10-15   **GROB**

A late 19thC cut crystal coupe champagne glass, cut with diamonds and fans, and faceted, slightly waisted stem.

5in (12.5cm) high

£25-35   **W&L**

A 20thC Continental coupe champagne glass, the bowl cut with 'thumbprint' ovals and trefoil cuts, the conical baluster stem with annulated knop above.

Although this stem is comparatively complex compared with some examples, buyers often prefer the simpler, less ornate examples.

4.75in (12cm) high

£12-15   **GROB**

A 1920s-30s coupe champagne glass, the bowl with criss-cross diamond and star patterns, with facet-cut stem.

4.75in (12cm) high

£10-12   **GROB**

A 19thC coupe champagne glass, with heavy, hollow baluster stem, and bowl cut with large facets.

4.5in (11.5cm) high

£15-18   **GROB**

A 19thC coupe champagne glass, the hollow stem and base of the bowl cut with facets.

The hollow stem is a desirable feature for collectors.

5in (12.5cm) high

£25-30   GROB

GLASS

QUICK REFERENCE - CHANCE GLASS

Chance Brothers, founded in 1824 outside Birmingham, produced its first tableware in the 1930s. Its varied Fiesta range was introduced in 1951, and became immensely popular. Plate glass was heated until it 'slumped' into a mould, or over an object, to take its form. The 'handkerchief' vase was one of their most prolific and popular ranges. Look out for the rare reversed version of the pattern below, with red dots on a white background, as this can fetch over three times the value of this one. As with Gingham, the pattern continued to be produced by Fiesta Glass (successor to Chance Glass) from 1981.

A 1970s Chance Glass light blue 'Bandel II' pattern screen-printed small handkerchief vase.

4in (10cm) high

£7-10   RET

A Chance Glass small red 'Polka Dot' transfer-printed handkerchief vase.
1974-81   4in (10cm) high
£10-15   GC

A Chance Glass 'Large Flemish' handkerchief vase.

The lightly textured 'Large Flemish' pattern had been used for window glass at Chance since the late 19thC. It was allegedly inspired by the rippling effect of canals that ran through the factory.

7in (18cm) high

£15-25   GC

A 1980s Chance Glass small green and white 'Gingham' pattern transfer-printed handkerchief vase.
1978-81   4in (10cm) high
£15-20   GC

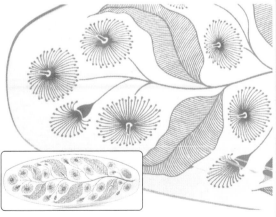

A 1970s Chance Glass screen-printed gold 'Calytpo' pattern ovoid tray, the pattern designed by Michael Harris in 1959.

The popularity of Calypto was long-lived as it was produced until at least 2000. Usually found in white, the gold colourway was introduced after 1970.

13.5in (34cm) long

£10-15   RET

QUICK REFERENCE

- The areas that make up much of today's Czech Republic have been renowned for glass design and production for centuries. The late 19thC and early 20thC saw much glass in the dominant Art Nouveau style being produced. Most pieces are commonly attributed to the company Loetz, but recent research has revealed that companies such as Kralik and Rindskopf also had a large output.
- As the country was 'behind the Iron Curtain' from 1945 until 1989, the major revolution in design has been largely ignored. As glass collectors and researchers have found more, prices have begun to rise.
- Complexity and rarity are currently the main indicators to value. The designer is also important, but as the market is so new many names are yet to become widely known. Hot-worked, enamelled and cut and engraved pieces that are unique and influential tend to fetch the highest sums.

- However, such pieces often inspired ranges that were mass-produced, and are more affordable.
- Many of these are hot-worked or pressed glass designs, and the modern, avant garde style developed from the late 1950s to the early 1970s are the most desirable. Leading designers, whose work is sought after by collectors, include Adolf Matura, Frantisek Vizner, and Frantisek Zemek, as well as the influential names known for producing more unique works such as Stanislav Libensky, Pavel Hlava, René Roubícek and Jirí Harcuba.
- As much glass is unmarked, it is best to consult a reference book to learn how to recognise designs. Many pieces are currently mistaken for the work of factories on Murano or in Scandinavia. A considerable amount of research is yet to be undertaken, and the area looks set to grow in importance over the next few years.

A Kralik 'Silveria' vase, the textured, mould blown lobed body with applied pink enamel to the base and randomly applied green trails, with a light iridescent surface.
c1900
£280-320   MDM

A Kralik red 'Banded' near-spherical vase, with pulled rim, reddish-pink enamel spots, and applied and melted in white trail and heavily iridised surface.
c1905
£350-450   MDM

A Czechoslovakian Kralik gold and amber 'Silberband' vase, with melted-in light green trails and heavy iridescent surface.

Both 'Silberband' and 'Silveria' (see right) are terms given by a collector, rather than the official range names. There are two variations: those with a combination of either cranberry and amber, or of green and amber, spots.
c1905   6in (15cm) diam
£350-450   MDM

A pair of tiny Kralik salts, in the 'Wavy' pattern, with silver rims.

1905
£140-160   MDM

A Kralik rare opalescent pink lobed bowl, of organic form, the exterior with heavy silvery iridescence.
c1905   6.5in (16.5cm) diam
£350-450   MDM

A Kralik 'Corrugated' tapered vase, with wavy rim, pulled pattern and heavy iridescent surface.
c1905

£350-450 MDM

A Kralik 'King Tut' vase, with green mottles and applied and pulled dark blue trails melted into the body.
c1905

£300-400 MDM

A Rindskopf waisted vase, applied pulled, 'feathered' trails over opaque body, iridescent surface.
c1900

£350-450 MDM

A Rindskopf floriform vase, applied, melted-in pulled and feathered white trails, and an iridised surface.
c1900

£450-550 MDM

A large tumbler vase, designed by Karel Poner, with hand-enamelled with Classically dressed female figures over a white cloudy ground, with engraved and enamelled signature with date.

Little is known about Poner, apart from that he studied under Professor Kysela at the School of Applied Arts in Prague. During the late 1930s and early 1940s he produced enamelled vessels in a modern, painterly style, featuring Classically dressed characters, or people going about their lives. Examples can be found in the Museum of Decorative Arts in Prague.

1941 *11.75in (30cm) high*

£350-450 FLD

A CLOSER LOOK AT A LOETZ VASE

The organic form and colour are typical of the Art Nouveau movement, and much of the glass produced by Loetz.

The iridescent, mottled green finish identifies it as being part of the successful 'Papillon' range, which was produced in quantity and was more affordable than other ranges.

It is further embellished with silver overlay, which was complex to apply. The overlay is also in the Art Nouveau style and is itself embellished with engravings.

This particular piece is visually stunning and would have been expensive and highly fashionable in its day.

A Loetz Creta 'Papillion' glass vase, swollen with a trefoil neck, the floral silver overlay with engraving.
c1900 *8.25in (21cm) high*

£1,000-1,500 DN

GLASS

A 1960s Czechoslovakian Msistov glassworks 'Rhapsody' range large vase, designed by Frantisek Zemek in 1960.

15.25in (38.5cm) high

£120-180   **TCF**

A Czechoslovakian Novy Bor mould blown ball vase, with optic moulded columns and iridescent surface effect, machine cut rim.

8.25in (22cm) high

£70-90   **GC**

A 1960s-70s Czechoslovakian Zelezny Brod Citrine tapered vase, with applied brown trails, designed by Frantisek Zemek.

This form was designed by Zemek in 1957 and was shown in the landmark publication 'Modern Bohemian Glass' by Josef Raban. The design, whilst typical of the 1950s obsession with curving organic forms, also hints at machinery, reminiscent of a screw or propeller.

8.25in (21cm) high

£50-70   **MHC**

A Czechoslovakian Moser vase, no.54303, designed by Jiri Suhajek in 1976, with applied light green side casing and stylised red and green flower to centre.

8.5in (21.5cm) high

£300-400   **VZ**

A Czechoslovakian Skrdlovice glassworks teardrop shaped vase, designed by Vladimir Jelinek or Zdenka Strobachovà, with graduated blue bands fading to rose pink, and 'kicked up' conical base.

c1960   *11.5in (29cm) high*

£1,200-1,800   **QU**

A CLOSER LOOK AT A CHLUM U TREBONE GLASS VASE

The colour variation is created by heating this heat-sensitive glass for different periods of time.

This type of glass was a speciality of the factory, with and orange-red 'Garnet' colourway being much more commonly found.

The UFO form is typical of its time, and the protrusion in the base recalls studio glass by fellow Czech designer Pavel Hlava.

The glass is blown into a ribbed mould before being blown to shape, which gives the linear optical effect.

A Czechoslovakian Chlum u Trebone glassworks optic mould blown 'Garnet & Blue' glass vase, designed by Jan Gabrhel in 1962, with protrusion in base.

4.5in (11.5cm) high

£100-150   **PC**

A 1970s Czechoslovakian Prachen glassworks amber glass cylindrical vase, applied blue prunts stamped with stylised floral motifs, designed by Josef Hospodka in 1969.

Although blue, the prunts appear green due to the transmitted light through the yellow-amber body.

9.75in (25cm) high

£80-120   SAS

A CLOSER LOOK AT A VÌZNER VASE

Frantisek Vi zner (b.1936) is one of Czechoslovakia's most influential and famous glass designers, with a global reputation.

Vi zner' s forms tend to be solid, with a monumental and almost industrial or architectural feel. They also hint at his later, simpler cut and polished studio works.

It was made using the challenging 'gathering on the post' technique, where the partially blown body is used to gather a second mass of differently coloured glass.

The 'peg' cased in a heavy base is recurring form in Vi zner' s work for Skrdlovice at the time – after 1977 he produced his own studio works.

A late 1970s Skrdlovice glassworks vase, no.7410 designed by Frantisek Vizner in 1974, the ribbed colourless body cased with a heavy green base, unmarked.

This design was produced in at least three sizes, being roughly 25cm, 19cm or 15cm in height, although sizes do vary as each piece was handmade.

£200-300   PC

A 1960s Borské Sklo colourless cased pink torpedo vase, with polished pontil to base.

9in (23cm) high

£22-28   RET

A 1960s-70s Czechoslovakian Skrdlovice glassworks cased bottle vase, with internal air bubbles, designed by Jaroslav Svoboda.

12in (30.5cm) high

£300-400   GC

A late 1960s-70s Czechoslovakian Borské Sklo green vase, designed by Pavel Hlava in 1967, with colourless casing.

Pavel Hlava (1924-2003) was one of the most notable Czech post-war glass designers. It is likely that this design was produced by blowing the molten glass into a modified wire cage, creating the undulating and warped bulges. It shows how his studio glass techniques were translated into glass produced in a factory.

10.25in (26cm) high

£70-100   M20C

A 1970s Czechoslovakian Berànek or Chribskà glassworks 'Niagara' range amber and blue bowl, with pulled rim and lobes.

9in (23cm) long

£25-30   RET

GLASS

QUICK REFERENCE - GALLÉ

Emile Gallé founded a glass decorating workshop in Nancy, France, in 1873. In 1874, he took over his father's glass and ceramics business and began producing his own designs, which won gold medals when exhibited at the International Exposition in Paris in 1878. His love of nature can be seen in his high quality floral and foliate designs which became the epitomy of the Art Nouveau style. The popularity of his work expanded, leading him to produce commercial cameo designs from 1899, which were made using acid-etched techniques. Gallé died in 1904, and from then a star was added next to his signature until 1914. The factory closed in 1936.

A Gallé cameo glass solifleur vase, purple overlay with wisteria flowers, cameo signature.

8.75in (22cm) high

£600-800   WW

A Gallé carved crystal Jack-in-the-Pulpit vase, etched 'Modèle et Decor Deposés Cristallerie Emile Gallé Nancy'.

13.25in (33.5cm) high

£1,200-1,500   DRA

An Emile Gallé vase, of colourless glass, with all-round opaque yellow and pink overlay decoration, etched five times, showing wisteria in bloom, relief-engraved 'Gallé' with three dots on side.

1904   *13.5in (34.5cm) high*

£3,500-4,500   WKA

A tall Gallé cameo glass vase, with amber nasturtium over a graduated yellow to amber and clear ground, signed 'Gallé' on body.

18in (46cm) high

£1,200-1,800   DRA

A Gallé cameo glass vase, with blue and purple dogwood blossoms on a frosted blue and yellow mottled ground, minor burst to rim.

10.75in (27.5cm) high

£1,200-1,800   DRA

A tall post-1904 Gallé cameo glass barrel vase, yellow tinted with pink berried branches, signed 'Gallé' and with a star, small chip to foot.

12.25in (31cm) high

£500-700   DN

QUICK REFERENCE

- Founded in Zealand, Denmark in 1825, Holmegaard initially produced bottles and other functional pieces. Early designers included Oluf Jensen and Orla Juul Nielsen, whose designs for tableware were exhibited at the 1925 Paris Exposition. However, it was the work of three designers who changed the company's fortunes.
- The first, Jacob Bang (1899-1965) joined Holmegaard in 1927, and was partly inspired by Nielsen's designs. His designs were predominantly period Modernist and austere in style with minimal surface decoration. Bang left Holmegaard in 1941 to design ceramics, but returned to glass in 1957 when he joined Kastrup, Holmegaard's sister company.
- The second was Per Lütken (1916-98), whose designs are the focus of many collectors today. Recruited from art school in 1942, Lütken is known for his asymmetric, organic and flowing designs from the 1950s. Curving bud-like or teardrop forms with heavy walls in grey or blue are typical of his work. Many of his designs are signed with a PL monogram, and dates were included up until 1962.
- In contrast to these, Lütken also designed the Carnaby range, which has a strong 'Pop Art' plastic appearance. This is similar to the 'Palet' range designed by the third key designer, Michael Bang (b1944), son of Jacob. Also popular are the 'Gulvvase' bottles, designed by Otto Brauer.
- The Kastrup factory was founded in 1847 to augment production at Holmegaard, and had a sister factory at Odense. In 1873, Kastrup was sold, but was merged with Holmegaard again in 1965. Generically, all pieces are known to collectors as 'Holmegaard'. Demand and prices for smaller and more common pieces have remained static, but unique pieces by the Bangs and designers other than Lütken may rise as more information is uncovered.

A Danish Kastrup Holmegaard 'Gulvvase', no. 540021, with transparent red cased opaque white body, designed by Otto Brauer in 1962.

Cased examples with opaque white interiors are the most desirable and valuable versions – red in particular. Transparent colours include cobalt blue, brown and olive green.

1965-80   17in (43cm) high

£180-220   **QU**

A 1970s English Cascade Glass kingfisher blue bottle, after Otto Brauer's 1962 Gulvvase.

This design was produced during the late 1970s. Cascade Glass can be identified by colour – this blue, colourless, pewter grey and smokey topaz.

10in (25.5cm) high

£10-15   **M20C**

A Danish Kastrup cobalt blue mid-size Gulvvase no.40230, designed by Otto Brauer in 1962.

12in (30.5cm) high

£50-70   **M20C**

A 1960s Danish Kastrup Glas blue bottle vase, from the Capri series designed by Jacob Bang in 1961, with original label.

6in (15cm) high

£30-50   **ZI**

A Danish Kastrup 'Capri' blue bottle vase, with applied prunt impressed 'JB', designed by Jacob Bang in 1961, catalogue number 32652.

8.75in (22cm) high

£50-70   **ZI**

A Danish Kastrup vase from the 'Antik Grøn' series, with applied prunt with impressed head, design no.32708 by Jacob Bang in 1964.

1964-70   6in (15cm) high
£50-70   ZI

A Danish Kastrup-Holmegaard candleholder from the 'Napoli' series, designed by Michael Bang in 1969.

1969-71   4in (10cm) high
£40-60   ZI

A 1960s Danish Holmegaard Majgron (May-Green) vase, no.46022, designed by Per Lütken, the base with inscribed factory marks.

11.5in (29cm) high
£40-60   GC

QUICK REFERENCE – KASTRUP

This design is often incorrectly attributed to Per Lütken and described as a 'Duckling' or 'Naebvase' (Beak vase). The designer of this piece is not known and, like the vase to the right, it is typical of a number of 'generic' vases produced by the company in response to popular tastes. This particular design can be found with this model number in the 1960 Kastrup catalogue, and was discontinued in 1965 after the company's merger with Holmegaard.

A Danish Holmegaard torpedo-shaped mould blown vase from the Grønland series, catalogue no.17706, designed by Per Lütken in 1960, the base signed 'Holmegaard 1961 PL'.

1961-64   9.75in
(24.5cm) high
£70-90   ZI

A Danish Kastrup cased blue large 'Orchidevase', shape no.32003, with internal controlled spiral of bubbles, designed by an unknown designer.

c1954-65   12.5in (32cm) high
£50-80   M20C

A Danish Kastrup small double cased swung-out vase, with opaque opal glass sandwiched between two layers of transparent sapphire blue, by an unknown designer.

c1960   9in (23cm) high
£50-80   ZI

A CLOSER LOOK AT A HOLMEGAARD VASE

A Danish Holmegaard light green 'Duckling' vase, cat. no. 14405, by Per Lütken in 1952, base signed 'Holmegaard 1954 PL'.

Produced from 1950 into the 1970s, these are wrongly called 'Naebvase' (Beak vases), which was a Danish nickname. Available in a range of sizes, colours include colourless, smoke grey and light green.

1954   8in (20cm) high

£30-50   **ZI**

This is a protype piece produced during the development of the 'Atlantis' range.

It was produced when the designer Michael Bang was discussing his ideas for the range with master glassblower Emanuel Anderson.

As it is freeblown with random patterning, it is unique – such early protoype examples are higly desirable.

These colours went on to be included in the 'Atlantis' factory production range.

A Danish Holmegaard free-blown test-piece vase made by Emanuel Andersen, designed by Michael Bang and Emanuel Andersen c1981.

8.25in (21cm) high

£300-350   **ZI**

A Danish Kastrup Holmegaard unique, free-blown abstract vase or sculpture, form no.2386, designed by Per Lütken for an exhibition in November 1970, the foot signed 'Holmegaard 2386 PL'.

1970   18.75in (47.5cm) high

£800-1,200   **ZI**

A Danish Holmegaard colourless cased green orchid vase, from the 'Flamingo' series, catalogue no.16028, designed by Per Lütken in 1956, the base inscribed 'Holmegaard 1958 PL'.

1958   6.25in (16cm) high

£80-£120   **ZI**

A 1960s Danish Kastrup Natblå (Night Blue) mould blown vase, catalogue no.32315, designed by Jacob Bang in 1959.

9in (23cm) high

£50-80   **ZI**

A Danish Holmegaard Sapphire blue large folded vase, designed by Per Lütken in 1955, the base signed 'Holmegaard 1955 PL'.

1955 8.25in (21cm) high

£150-200   **ZI**

GLASS

QUICK REFERENCE - CARNABY & PALET

There is much confusion over which brightly coloured opaque cased glass forms are from the 'Carnaby' and 'Palet' ranges, and which are by Holmegaard. Many examples attributed to Holmegaard are in fact by German factories such as Hirschberg or Friedrich. The 'Carnaby' range comprises only 16 shapes, which are vases, except for one pitcher (shown on this page), whilst the 'Palet' range is an extensive set of tablewares. Rims on 'Carnaby' pieces are not machine-cut, but are rounded. Values for 'Palet' vary widely, and depend on condition. As it was made to be used, it is often damaged or stained, meaning value is reduced.

A 1970s Kastrup-Holmegaard Coral Opal vase from the Carnaby series, designed by Per Lütken in 1969, catalogue no.341 10 94.
1969-76　　　　*4in (10cm) high*
£50-80　　　　**ZI**

A 1970s Kastrup-Holmegaard Coral Opal ball vase from the Carnaby series, catalogue no.56 03 16, designed by Per Lütken in 1969.
1969-76　　　　*5.25in (13.5cm) high*
£80-120　　　　**ZI**

A 1970s Danish Kastrup-Holmegaard Yellow Opal vase from the Carnaby series, catalogue no.341 10 67, designed by Per Lütken in 1969.
1969-76　　　　*5in (12.5cm) high*
£50-80　　　　**ZI**

A 1970s Danish Kastrup-Holmegaard Yellow Opal 120cl pitcher from the Palet series, catalogue no. 331 24 02, designed by Michael Bang in 1970.

The yellow colourway was introduced to the series in 1971.
8in (20.5cm) high
£50-70　　　　**ZI**

A 1970s Kastrup-Holmegaard Opal Blue sugar shaker, no. 392183, with cork stopper, designed by Michael Bang in 1970.

The use of a large cork stops the contents from falling out and also acts as a cushioned base for the thin glass body.
1970-75　　　　*5.5in (14cm) high*
£40-60　　　　**UCT**

A 1970s Kastrup-Holmegaard Jade Grøn 2.2ltr Cheese Jar from the Palet series, catalogue no.351 26 32, with applied prunt impressed 'OST', designed by Michael Bang in 1970.

6in (15cm) high
£150-200　　　　**ZI**

A 1970s Kastrup-Holmegaard Blue Opal pitcher, from the Carnaby series, designed by Per Lütken in 1969, catalogue no.39 13 00.

8in (20.5cm) high
£80-120　　　　**ZI**

A Holmegaard colourless 'Klukflaske' or 'Kuttrolf' decanter, with applied vines and rosettes, catalogue no.186, designed by an unknown designer.

c1900   *11in (28cm) high*
£80-120   **ZI**

A Danish Holmegaard colourless 'Klukflaske' or 'Kuttrolf' decanter from the Viol series, with black crown-shaped stopper, designed by Jacob Bang in 1938.

10in (25cm) high
£50-80   **ZI**

A 1990s Danish Holmegaard decanter, designed by Michael Bang, from the 'Amateur Schnappsmaker' series, with screen-printed 'Prunus spinosa L' sloe berry decoration designed by Finn Clausen in 1989, catalogue no.4 240 005.

1989-2005   *6.5in (16.5cm) high*
£20-30   **ZI**

A CLOSER LOOK AT A HOLMEGAARD DECANTER

The crown-shaped stopper indicates that this was from the 'Viol' series.

It is based on the traditional German 'kluk kluk' decanter made for centuries and so-named due to the glugging noise it makes when pouring.

With its crimped form, it is very practical to grip and handle. It can also be found with blue or colourless bodies.

Legend has it that the leaning 'drunken' form and crown hinted at an alcoholic Swedish king.

A 1950s-70s Danish Holmegaard Smoke grey 'tired' Klukflaske decanter from the Viol series, with crown-shaped knop, based on a design by Jacob Bang from 1928.

10in (25cm) high
£30-40   **ZI**

A Holmegaard 'Skaal' decanter and matching shot glasses, with handpainted sailor motif and 'Skaal' wording, catalogue no.M256, designed by Jacob Bang in 1937.

'Skaal!' is Danish for 'Cheers!' This schnapps set was also available with other hand-painted designs and finishes, including sandblasting.

1937-57   *7.75in (19.5cm) high*
£100-150   **ZI**

A Danish Holmegaard 'Fyldehund' or 'Snapsehund' decanter, in the form of a dog, with stoppered nose and tail handle, marked 'HG7'.

With its origins in the late 19thC, Holmegaard produced this form during the 1920s, reviving it again in the mid-1970s.

1977   *9in (23cm) long*
£60-90   **ZI**

GLASS

A Danish Kastrup pitcher from the Grøn Series, designed by Jacob Bang in 1960, catalogue no.7178.

This form was also available with a bamboo wrapping (cat. no. 7278). These examples are harder to find intact as the bamboo often becomes loose and damaged. When intact, these usually fetch a little more.

9.75in (24.5cm) high

£40-60   **ZI**

A CLOSER LOOK AT A HOLMEGAARD DECANTER

The impressed viking's head seal indicates this was made for Danish wine company Torben Anton. Other seals can be found; a CE under a crown for Cherry Elsinore, and with the logo of British wine merchants Stowells of Chelsea.

A taller blue version was also produced in 1955 – both have a hand-finished rim giving the effect that each is hand-blown.

The glasses are harder to find than the decanter.

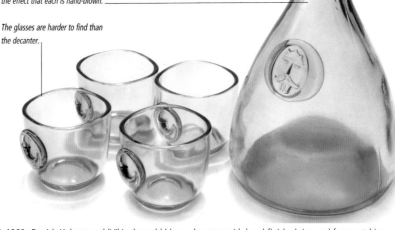

A 1960s Danish Holmegaard 'Viking' mould blown decanter with hand-finished rim, and four matching glasses, designed by Ole Winther.

1962-70   *9in (23cm) high*

£25-35   **M20C**

One of a set of six Holmegaard 'Labrador' grey sherry glasses, 'Atlantic' range, by Per Lütken, 1962.

'Labrador' was a favourite colour of of Lütken's from the 1950s.

4.25in (11cm) high

£30-50 SET   **ZI**

One of a set of six Holmegaard Smoke grey Dutch Cordial glasses.

Available in delgrun (Dark Green), Smoke (grey), clear and violet. Frequently found with klukflaskes on the secondary market, but they were not originally sold combined as sets.

c1958   *5.75in (14.5cm) high*

£30-50 SET   **ZI**

A 1950s Danish Holmegaard cordial or schnapps glass from the Mercur series, designed by Per Lütken in 1948.

2in (5cm) high

£50-80 FOR A SET OF SIX   **ZI**

A Danish Holmegaard blue-green sugar bowl and creamer from the 'Baltica' series, catalogue no.s 19765 and 19764 respectively.

The Mocca creamer set is available in blue-green, cobalt blue, ruby and clear glass.

Largest 2.75in (7cm) high

£30-50 PAIR   **ZI**

A Danish Holmegaard Sapphire blue mould-blown goblet-shaped vase, from the Saphir series, catalogue no.18163, designed by Per Lütken c1960, the base marked 'Holmegaard 18163 PL'.

3.5in (9cm) high

£40-60   ZI

A Danish Holmegaard Smoke grey ashtray, with pulled rim, catalogue no.16517, designed by Per Lütken c1960, the base inscribed 'Holmegaard 1962 PL'.

1962   6in (15cm) long

£30-50   ZI

A Danish Kastrup-Holmegaard 24% lead crystal fish sculpture, catalogue no.341 45 06, designed by Michael Bang c1974, marked 'HG5 MB'.

1975   3.5in (9cm) long

£30-50   ZI

A Danish Kastrup-Holmegaard furnace-worked bowl with random scalloped rim and knobbles, catalogue no.620719, from the Rosalin series, designed by Christer Holmgren in 1968, the base inscribed 'Holmegaard C. 620719'.

5.75in (14.5cm) diam

£40-60   ZI

An early 1970s Danish Kastrup-Holmegaard novelty bird figurine.

Sold as novelties through the shop in large quantities, these can be identified as Holmegaard by the colours used.

A Holmegaard bottle or decanter from the 'Apotekerflasker' series, with transfer printed design, marked 'HG80'.

2.5in (6cm) high

£30-50   ZI

Each year from 1975-99, Holmegaard produced a limited production copy of an late 18thC apothecary bottle from the Thisted Apotek (now Svane Apoteket) in Denmark. Each piece is marked 'HG for Holmegaard, followed by two digits for the year. As commissioned objects, they were not sold through Holmegaard's distributors.

1980   6.5in (16.5cm) high

£50-70   ZI

A Danish Kastrup-Holmegaard Smoke grey suncatcher with probably unique impressed abstract patterns, created using tools and objects in the factory.

c1970   4.75in (12cm) diam

£20-30   ZI

FIND OUT MORE...

www.holmegaardresource.com - *an independent online resource to vintage designs.*

www.glashistoriskselskab.dk - *Danish site providing a useful visual resource.*

QUICK REFERENCE - LALIQUE

René Lalique (1860-1945) began his career designing and making jewellery in the 1880s, turning to glass through perfume bottles he designed for Coty around 1906. By 1918, success led him to buy and to move into larger premises, where he designed quintessentially Art Deco style vases, bowls, lamps and perfume bottles using the mass-production techniques of pressing and moulding. Despite using these techniques, quality was high and Lalique's products were expensive. Over 150 designs were produced from 1920-30, with motifs focusing on stylised natural forms, animals and nudes. Lalique died in 1945, and from then all marks comprised his surname only, without the 'R' initial. The company still produces many of his original designs today.

A René Lalique 'Dentelle' clear and frosted vase, no.943, moulded 'R. LALIQUE', with chip to one rib.

c1912   7.5in (19cm) high

£400-600   **DRA**

A René Lalique 'Chamonix' opalescent vase, no.1090, stencilled 'R. LALIQUE FRANCE', with small nicks to buttresses.

c1933   6in (15cm) high

£500-800   **DRA**

A René Lalique 'Domremy' green vase, no. 979, moulded with thistles, etched mark 'R Lalique France No. 979', minor rim fault.

Green is a rarer colour than the much more common opalescent.

8.5in (21.5cm) high

£1,200-1,800   **TEN**

A Lalique 'Domremy' opalescent glass vase, no. 979, designed by René Lalique, stencil 'R Lalique', etched 'France'.

8.75in (22cm) high

£700-1,000   **WW**

4.5in (11.5cm) high

£1,500-2,000   **DRA**

A René Lalique 'Grenade' dark amber vase, no.1045, the base engraved 'R. Lalique France'.

A Lalique 'Nymphale' deep blue glass vase, the base engraved 'Lalique France'.

8.5in (21.5cm) high

£350-550   **DN**

A Lalique 'Rampillon' clear, frosted and blue-stained vase, no.991, the base with stencilled 'R Lalique' signature.

5in (13cm) high

£700-1,000   **WW**

A 1930s Lalique 'Saint Tropez' pattern blue-tinted opalescent glass vase, the tapering cylindrical body moulded with stems and berries, acid-etched mark 'R. Lalique, France' to base, minor chip to one berry.

7.5in (19cm) high

£1,500-2,000   **TOV**

A CLOSER LOOK AT A LALIQUE VASE

This is a comparatively scarce design, perhaps as it was less popular at the time meaning fewer were sold.

It retains some of its white patina, which helps to highlight the moulded pattern of peppercorns.

The dark topaz colour, which appears black here, is also scarce.

The shouldered urn shape and clean-lined form is typical of the Art Deco period.

A René Lalique deep topaz 'Poivre' vase, no.901, with whitish patina, the base moulded 'R. Lalique'.

c1921   *9.5in (24cm) high*

£2,000-3,000   **DRA**

A René Lalique 'Sauge' vase, no.1014, of clear and frosted glass with green patina, the base engraved 'R. Lalique'.

c1927   *9in (23cm) high*

£1,200-1,800   **DRA**

A René Lalique 'Sirenes' opalescent and blue stained glass perfume atomiser, no.660, the base marked 'R Lalique', metal fittings missing.

5.5in (14cm) high

£800-1,200   **WW**

A Lalique blue glass decanter, the reeded body with a blue glass stopper, marked 'Lalique made in France'.

11.25in (28.5cm) high

£150-250   **SWO**

A René Lalique 'Danseuses Egyptiennes no. 1' perfume burner, for Marcas et Bardel, with orange enamel and original chromium cap, moulded 'R. Lalique FRANCE'.

c1926   *5.25in (13.5cm) high*

£800-1,200   **DRA**

Two René Lalique 'Perles' clear and frosted glass perfume bottles, no.602, with brown patina, and moulded marks.

c1926   *5.75in (14.5cm) high*

£400-600   **DRA**

QUICK REFERENCE

- Mdina Glass was founded on Malta in 1968 by Michael Harris, an ex-Royal College of Art glass tutor. At Mdina Harris adapted new studio glass techniques acquired in the USA in 1966 to commercial production of art glass. His designs, often shallow dishes and bottle shaped vases, were made from thick glass and in colours that evoked the sea and the beach: turquoise, tan, aqua, greens and blues. Each piece is unique, as it was handmade.

- Production was aimed at the tourist and international gift market. Typical pieces were inexpensive and small, as these were easier to transport. Although much of Mdina's success was due to the tourist industry, it was helped by export sales to the UK, USA and Germany.

- Harris left Malta in 1972 and set up a glass factory on the Isle of Wight. Early pieces were similar to Mdina, but more finely blown. In 1978, saw the introduction of the Azurene range, designed by Harris and William Walker. It featured 22ct gold and silver leaf on coloured glass bodies. It was successful and continues to be desirable. Other popular ranges are Meadow Garden, Kyoto and Golden Peacock.

- Mdina pieces have 'Mdina' inscribed on their bases. Some may have their original stickers: paper stickers were earlier than plastic ones. Isle of Wight pieces can also be identified by a signature on the base or a sticker.

- Prices are rising, though affordable. Large, unusual designs and those signed by Michael Harris are the most desirable.

A Mdina Glass large stoppered bottle, designed by Michael Harris, of cylindrical form with swollen neck and spherical stopper with internal blue green and sandy ochre swirl, the base inscribed 'Mdina'.

Note the large size of this piece. These are considerably rarer than smaller examples, and seem only to have been produced until the mid-1970s.

16.25in (41cm) high

£350-450   **FLD**

A 1980s Mdina Glass bottle, the mottled ochre body with randomly applied green trails, the base inscribed 'Mdina'.

8in (20cm) high

£30-40   **M20C**

A 1980s Mdina Glass large bottle, with ochre mottling and applied colourless trails, the base inscirbed 'Mdina'.

13.5in (34cm) high

£40-60   **M20C**

A Mdina Glass 'Tiger' ovoid vase with flared neck, the base inscribed 'Mdina 1987'.

1987   *6in (15.5cm) high*

£50-70   **VZ**

A Mdina Glass vase, with flared rim and horizontal green trails outlined in sand brown over a colourless base with a fine network of ochre crackle lines, the base inscribed 'Mdina 1987'.

6in (15cm) high

£50-70   **VZ**

A 1970s Mdina Glass disc-shaped vase, with elongated neck and blue and green striated band, the base inscribed 'Mdina'.

6in (15.5cm) high

£50-70   **GC**

An extremely rare Mdina Glass 'Crizzle Stone', designed, made and signed by Michael Harris, with iridescent streak of silver chloride around the body, the base signed 'Michael Harris Mdina Glass Malta'.

Derived from his iconic 'Fish' vases, these are the rarest and most complex forms produced by Michael Harris at Mdina. See p.233 ' Miller's Collectables Price Guide 2009' for an example valued at £1,200-1,800 but unsigned by Harris – only two other signed examples are known.

7.5in (19cm) high

£2,800-3,400   **ART**

A large Mdina 'Cut Ice' Fish vase, designed by Michael Harris, the randomly strapped interior cased in colourless glass with two polished facets to one side.

c1971   9in (23cm) high

£250-350   **FLD**

A 1970s Mdina Glass 'Lollipop' vase, designed by Michael Harris, with green and blue curving forms with silver chloride colouring, cased in colourless glass, the base inscribed 'Mdina 1985', and with studio paper label.

1985   6.75in (17cm) high

£70-100   **VZ**

A mid-1970s Mdina 'Fish' vase, designed by Michael Harris, the purple and ochre core with silver chloride, cased in colourless glass with straps.

8.75in (22cm) high

£150-250   **FLD**

A 1980s Mdina Glass 'Fish' vase, with squared transparent blue wings over a mottled pink core, the base inscribed 'Mdina'.

7in (17.5cm) high

£40-60   **VZ**

A Mdina Glass object, comprising a 'Side Stripe' bottle vase embedded in a 'Sculpture' with green and ochre trails, the base signed 'Michael Harris Mdina Glass Malta', with annealing crack.

It is difficult to work out why this unusual and experimental piece was produced, and even more difficult to work out why it was signed by Michael Harris!

c1970   11in (28cm) long

£250-350   **SAS**

A Mdina Glass 'Tricorn' vase, designed by Michael Harris, with a mottled green and ochre body with silver chloride colouring, the base inscirbed 'Mdina'.

c1970-74   10.5in (27cm) diam

£250-350   **FLD**

GLASS

A Mdina Glass goblet, with blue straps applied over a mottled orange and yellow bowl, the foot engraved 'Mdina 1980'.

1980   *6.5in (16.5cm) high*

£40-50   **M20C**

A late 1970s-80s Mdina Glass random sculpture, with colourless and blue trails, the base inscribed 'Mdina'.

8.5in (21.5cm) high

£30-50   **M20C**

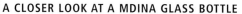

A CLOSER LOOK AT A MDINA GLASS BOTTLE

These are often mistaken for a Geoffrey Baxter design for Whitefriars due to the bark texture – Harris knew Baxter and had discussed the idea of a bark textured range with him around 1964.

It was made using the 'gathering on the post' technique, where the part blown neck was used to gather more glass, which was then blown into a mould to form the body.

These bottles are usually tall and thin, this wide form is very rare.

These bark textured bottles were only made from c1970, when metal moulds made in England had arrived in Malta, until c1972, when Harris left Mdina Glass.

A Mdina Glass mould blown bark textured bottle vase, designed by Michael Harris, the base with concave polished pontil mark.

c1971   *8.75in (22.5cm) high*

£150-200   **GC**

An Isle of Wight Studio Glass 'Tortoiseshell' low bottle vase, designed, made and signed by Michael Harris, the base with 'coachbolt' pontil mark and engraved 'Michael Harris Isle of Wight England'.

Although the Tortoiseshell range was produced from 1973-c82, the presence of a plain, concave 'coachbolt' pontil mark identifies this as coming from 1973.

1973   *6in (15cm) diam*

£180-220   **FLD**

An Isle of Wight Studio Glass 'Tortoiseshell' bell vase, designed by Michael Harris, with impressed 'flame' pontil mark to base and black triangular studio sticker.

c1978-80   *8in (20.5cm) high*

£120-180   **VZ**

An Isle of Wight Studio Glass 'Pink Azurene' cylinder vase, the mottled pink body overlaid with silver and 22ct gold leaf, the base engraved 'Michael Harris ENGLAND 11/500'.

This 'limited edition' style of signature shows that it was made for export to US department stores, such as JC Penney.

11.5in (29cm) high

£300-400   **FLD**

QUICK REFERENCE

- Glass has made on Murano since the 13thC, when glassmakers moved from Venice to protect the wealthy city from furnace fires. For centuries, traditional glass-making techniques were handed down through families and though design underwent a radical transformation in the 1950s, these historic techniques were simply used in new, innovative ways. Colours became brighter and exuberant, while forms became more abstract and sculptural. New designers were invited to the island and by the end of the decade the new movement was in full swing.
- The most desirable and valuable pieces are the work of influential designers, such as Paolo Venini, Fulvio Bianconi, Flavio Poli, Ercole Barovier and Dino Martens. As well as the designer, the factory is important. Notable factories include Venini (founded 1921), Seguso Vetri D'Arte (1933-92), Barovier & Toso (founded 1942) and A.V.E.M (founded

1932). Landmark designs include Dino Martens's 'Oriente', Flavio Poli's Sommerso, and Venini's 'fazzoletto' vases.
- Many pieces are not signed, so check reference books to help you identify the work of these factories and designers. Original labels will also help with identification, though these have usually been removed. Successful designs were widely copied or imitated by other designers and glass factories, so it is also advisable to study as many identified examples as you can, to get a feel for authentic pieces.
- Consider the technique used – the more visually appealing and complex it is, the more desirable your piece is likely to be. For example, with sommerso designs, brightly coloured, well-balanced forms with clearly demarcated layers are usually desirable. Bear in mind that the market is wider and often more affordable away from major designers, with some pieces available for £20.

A Seguso Vetri D'Arte sommerso glass vase, no.12024, with a brown core covered with a heavily ribbed honey yellow casing.

c1970   *12.75in (32cm) high*

£400-600   VZ

A Seguso Vetri d'Arte sommerso glass vase, designed by Flavio Poli, with graduated pink/red core, covered with layer of green and yellow glass and an outer layer of colourless glass.

c1965   *14in (35.5cm) high*

£1,800-2,200   DOR

A Seguso Vetri D'Arte sommerso torpedo shaped vase, designed by Flavio Poli, the light green core overlaid with an ice blue layer also forming the base, with factory label to base.

c1960   *17.5in (44.5cm) high*

£800-1,200   VZ

A Seguso Vetri D'Arte sommerso glass vase, designed by Flavio Poli, the tapering cylindrical green core cased in bright yellow, with heavy base.

c1960   *11.25in (28.5cm) high*

£300-500   GC

A Seguso Vetri D'Arte sommerso bottle vase with cylindrical neck, designed by Flavio Poli, the purple core covered with a light violet layer.

c1960   *10in (25.5cm) high*

£800-1,200   VZ

GLASS

A Seguso Vetri D'Arte sommerso vase, designed by Flavio Poli, the ovoid form triple cased in green, blue, red and colourless glass.

c1955   7in (18cm) high
£600-800   QU

A Seguso Vetri D'Arte sommerso vase, designed by Flavio Poli, of flattened conical form, the base of the blue core cased in a layer or pinky-red and with an outer layer of colourless glass.

c1958   10.75in (27.5cm) high
£800-1,200   VZ

A CLOSER LOOK AT A SEGUSO VASE

Appointed design director at Seguso in 1934, Poli went on to revolutionise the company's designs and became a key designer on post-war Murano.

The elliptical form and slit opening that is almost like a mussel, indicates this was from Poli's celebrated 'Valva' (valve) range.

The purity of the curving form and vivid colour is typical of his work at this time, and became enormously influential.

This range won grand prizes at the 1950 Biennale and the 1951 Triennale, and his sommerso designs won a Golden Compass award in 1954.

A Seguso Vetri D'Arte 'Valva' vase, designed by Flavio Poli, the light turquoise-blue core overlaid with two layers of different tones of violet glass, with outer colourless layer.

c1952   9.75in (24.5cm) high
£3,500-4,500   VZ

A Seguso Vetri D'Arte sommerso bowl, the pink core cased with a layer of yellow and with a thick colourless outer layer, with pulled rim.

c1950   13.75in (35cm) high
£300-500   DOR

A Seguso Vetri D'Arte sommerso bowl, the green core with yellow and orange casing, and a colourless outer layer, with asymmetrically pulled and curled rim.

c1950   11.5in (29cm) high
£1,200-1,800   DOR

A Seguso Vetri D'Arte textured light blue glass cubic paperweight, in the form of an ice block, with manufacturer's model number label reading '54461'.

c1978   3.5in (9cm) high
£250-300   VZ

A Barovier & Toso 'Crepuscolo' lampbase, the shaped clear glass body with iron wool inclusions, the applied foot and rings with gold foil inclusions, designed by Ercole Barovier.

c1950   *13.5in (34cm) high*
£400-600   **QU**

A Cenedese sommerso glass vase, the graduated blue and yellow core with layers of yellow, light blue and colourless glass.

c1950   *23in (60cm) h*
£1,000-1,500   **DOR**

A CLOSER LOOK AT AN A.V.E.M. JUG

The Ansa Volante range of jugs was exhibited at the 1952 Biennale exhibition in Venice, and the asymmetric form is a typical feature.

The term means 'flying handle', referring to the integral handle and dynamic form wih its sweeping lines – some have two handles.

The range was produced in red or green glass, both with an iridescent surface created by 'fuming' the piece in metallic salts.

A scarcer variation also included randomly placed aventurine filament inclusions.

An A.V.E.M. 'Ansa Volante' jug vase, designed by Giorgio Ferro in 1952, the organic, pulled deep red glass with a heavily iridised surface.

Ferro worked for A.V.E.M. from 1951-55 before leaving for Ferro Galliano.

13in (33cm) high
£800-1,200   **VZ**

A Barovier & Toso 'Neolitico' bowl, bands of trapped air bubbles and dark brown trails combed into columns, designed by Ercole Barovier.

The pattern is created by applying trails which are melted into the body and then 'combed' with tools in a similar way to Art Nouveau glass designs by Louis Comfort Tiffany.

1954   *10.5in (26.5cm) diam*
£800-1,200   **QU**

A Barovier & Toso 'Cordonato Oro' ovoid vase with pulled and curled rim, designed by Ercole Barovier, the red core with gold foil inclusions, covered with a colourless layer of ribbed glass, the ribs containing rope-twist effect gold foil inclusions, the base with factory label.

This range was shown by Barovier & Toso in the 1950 Biennale in Venice, and is a fusion between modern and traditional techniques and styles.

1950   *11.25in (28cm) high*
£450-550   **VZ**

A Cenedese sommerso vase, designed by Antonia da Ros, with cylindrical and flared neck and yellow casing over a blue core, the base inscribed 'Cenedese'.

c1968   *8.75in (22cm) high*
£700-1,000   **VZ**

GLASS

QUICK REFERENCE - MURRINES

A murrine is the term given to a small glass tile cut from a rod containing a pattern, typically in the form of a flower (for example a millefiori, or 'a thousand flowers'), lines, or other motifs. These are arranged in a pattern like a mosaic on a glassblower's table, and the part-blown hot glass body is rolled over them, picking them up. The whole is then inserted in the furnace, all the parts are melted together and the body finally blown into shape. The technique dates back to the Roman era, but in the post-war period it was revised and updated. Vittorio Ferro (b.1932) is one of the leading modern exponents of the style, and was the maestro at Fratelli Toso until the 1980s. Following his 'retirement', he continued to design and produce his individual style of murrines at the De Majo and Fratelli Pagnin factories. The brightly coloured, black-lined murrines and almost iridescent effect are hallmarks of his style, which is increasingly popular with collectors and looks to be a good bet for the future.

A Cenedese sommerso cylindrical vase, designed by Antonia da Ros, with cylindrical and flared neck and yellow casing over a green core, the base inscribed 'Cenedese'.

c1968   *12.5in (32cm) high*

£1,200-1,800   **VZ**

An Alberto Donà vase, of flattened ovoid form with pulled, curving neck, with yellow and turquoise green vertical stripes covered with a layer of colourless glass, the surface cut with shallow slices, the base signed 'Alberto Donà Murano 1993'.

1993   *19.5in (49.5cm) high*

£1,200-1,800   **VZ**

A De Majo 'Estate' baluster vase, designed and made by Vittorio Ferro, with grey and green murrines with internal black iridised veins, and red 'rose' murrines, the base inscribed 'Vittorio Ferro 1998'.

10.75in (27cm) high

£800-1,200   **VZ**

A Carlo Moretti ruby red glass vase, of double conical form, with applied rectangular shards of colourless glass with white stripes.

c1970   *6.5in (16.5cm) high*

£550-650   **DOR**

A 1950s Pustetto Zanetti 'Arte Nuova' sommerso glass vase, probably designed by Aldo Fuga, with green, yellow and colourless layers, with factory foil label.

The Arte Nuova glassworks was founded in 1954 by Itamo Pustetto and Mario Fuga and known for its sommerso designs, many by Pustetto and Nino D' Este. Designs by Aldo Fuga were acclaimed at the Brussels Exposition 1958. It closed in the mid-1960s. Works are often misattributed to Seguso.

11.75in (30cm) high

£400-600   **DOR**

A Fratelli Toso vase, the colourless glass body covered with stylised flower murrines with white metals and orange centres, designed by Ermanno Toso, with applied orange rim.

c1960   *6.75in (17cm) high*

£1,000-1,500   **VZ**

A 1950s-60s Fratelli Toso large cased blue 'splash' vase, with pulled arms and nodules, with 'MURANO CHAMBORD' gold foil label.

Chambord was a trade name used by Fratelli Toso, whose name appears at the bottom of the (usually) shield-shaped label, which is damaged on this example.

17in (43cm) diam

£120-180   **GC**

A Venini & C. 'Corroso' amber glass vase, in the form of a double-handled urn, with acid-etched textured surface, the base with three line 'venini murano italia' acid stamp.

The surface of this vase is treated with acid to give a mottled, lightly textured surface.

c1940   9.75in (24.5cm) h

£800-1,200   **VZ**

A scarce Venini & C. 'Foglia' leaf-shaped bowl, designed by Tyra Lundgren, the colourless glass with blue stripes, and iridescent surface, the base with 'venini murano MADE IN ITALY' three line mark.

Swedish glass designer Lundgren produced a number of prize-winning designs for Venini shortly before the war, which were exhibited in both Murano and Sweden.

c1938   8.8in (22cm) long

£1,200-1,800   **VZ**

A Venini & C. 'corroso' bowl, designed by Carlo Scarpa, of clear and turquoise-blue cased glass, with frosted exterior.

Corroso indicates a lightly textured matt exterior treated with acid.

c1940   7.8in (19.5cm) wide

£200-250   **VZ**

A Venini & C 'Tuuli' bottle, designed by Timo Sarpaneva, with opaque yellow and black bands, and black stopper, the base inscribed 'venini 90 Sarpaneva'.

This 'Tuuli' range was created using the complex and challenging 'incalmo' technique, where separate gathers of different glass were blown to precise sizes and joined together while hot. The austerity of design is typical of Sarpaneva's Finnish aesthetic.

1990   12.25in (31cm) high

£1,000-1,500   **VZ**

A Venini & C. 'Tuuli' bowl, designed by Timo Sarpaneva in 1988, the cylindrical form with applied opaque red and dark violet bands, with light violet tinted central band, the base inscribed 'venini 91 Sarpaneva'.

1991   5.25in (13.cm) high

£800-1,200   **VZ**

A Vittorio Zuffi & C. murrine vase, the urn-shaped colourless body with applied green handles and alternating columns of green star murrines and colourless glass with heavy aventurine inclusions.

c1895   5.25in (13cm) high

£400-500   **QU**

GLASS

QUICK REFERENCE - MEMPHIS AND MURANO

Eccentric and geometric forms in bright colours are typical of the Postmodern style promoted by the Memphis group in the 1980s. Although other designers and artists contributed to the group, Ettore Sottsass is considered their notional leader. Complex to make, and as much a piece of decorative sulpture as a functional form, each component of this bowl was separately blown before being joined together. Compagnia Vetreria Muranese produced Memphis glass designs from 1982 until c1992, becoming known as Toso Vetri D'Arte from 1982-90. Examples can be quite scarce as these were never mass-produced or inexpensive, and may be a good tip for the future if the style is re-appraised by more design collectors.

A Compagnia Vetreria Muranese 'Sol' bowl, designed by Ettore Sottsass for Memphis in 1982, comprised of transparent red, blue and green components, with an opaque lining, the base inscribed 'E. SOTTSASS PER MEMPHIS by COMPAGNIA VETRERIA MURANESE'.

8.5in (21.5cm) high

£1,000-1,500　　　　　　　　　　　　　　**VZ**

A Compagnia Vetreria Murano for Memphis 'Erinna' vase, designed by Ettore Sottsass, with pink, blue and orange components, the base inscribed 'E. SOTTSASS PER MEMPHIS'.

1986　　　19in (48cm) high

£1,000-1,500　　　**VZ**

A Compagnia Vetreria Muranese 'Pasifila' glass vase, designed by Ettore Sottsass in 1986, comprised of cone forms in blue, translucent white, pink and opal green, the base inscribed 'E.SOTTSASS PER MEMPHIS'.

18.25in (46cm) high

£1,000-1,500　　　**VZ**

A Vistosi limited edition 'Pink Cigar' table centrepiece, designed by Peter Shire, the asymmetric form comprised of blue, black (dark violet), pink and yellow geometric forms, the base inscribed 'PETER SHIRE X VISTOSI 2/4'.

c1985　　　16.5in (42cm) high

£1,000-1,500　　　　　　　**VZ**

A Vistosi limited edition table centrepiece, designed by Peter Shire, with green conical and light and dark blue disc and spherical forms on a colourless column with a brown spiralling trail, the base inscribed 'PETER SHIRE X VISTOSI 4/6'.

c1985　　　24in (61cm) high

£800-1,200　　　**VZ**

A Vistosi 'Faleria' limited edition lidded jar, designed by Ettore Sottsass in 1980, the yellow body with green hemispherical lid and lined in black, the base engraved 'E.SOTTSASS 150-250 VISTOSI'.

c1981 10.75in (27cm) high

£2,500-3,500　　　**QU**

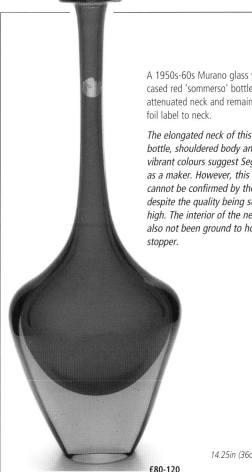

A 1950s-60s Murano glass yellow cased red 'sommerso' bottle, with attenuated neck and remains of foil label to neck.

The elongated neck of this bottle, shouldered body and vibrant colours suggest Seguso as a maker. However, this cannot be confirmed by the label despite the quality being suitably high. The interior of the neck has also not been ground to hold a stopper.

14.25in (36cm) high

£80-120   RET

A 1960s Murano glass yellow cased brown vase with colourless outer layer, elongated neck and winged body.

7.25in (18.5cm) high

£22-28   RET

A 1960s Murano 'sommerso' glass green cased red vase, with elongated neck and colourless outer casing.

17in (43cm) high

£60-80   RET

A 1960s Murano glass yellow cased green 'sommerso' vase with outer colourless casing, pulled rim and winged body.

These forms are often misattributed to Flavio Poli. A company called 'Turca' produced similar forms, and their link with Poli has not been confirmed.

11in (27.5cm) high

£65-75   RET

A 1960s Murano glass red and yellow cased bowl with curved and pulled rim.

13.5in (34cm) high

£45-55   RET

A 1960s Murano 'sommerso' glass yellow cased red bowl, with cut and pulled rim and 'MURANO MADE IN ITALY' red and silver foil label.

Similarly coloured circular foil labels with the same wording and scalloped edging can be attributed to Seguso during the 1950s.

11.25in (27cm) high

£45-55   RET

GLASS

A 1950s-60s Murano sommerso glass yellow cased green bowl, with wavy and pulled rim.

12.5in (31.5cm) wide

£20-30　　　　　　　　　　　　　　　　　　RET

A 1960s-70s Murano glass colourless cased orange-red heat sensitive glass bowl with pulled rim.

Here, a special chemical has been added to the glass so that it changes colour from orange to deep red when reheated in the furnace. The blue casing is unusual, as it would usually be colourless.

6in (15cm) diam

£30-40　　　　　　　　　　　　　　　　　　RET

A 1950s-60s Murano glass green 'Opaline' ashtray, with pulled and folded rim.

7.25in (18cm) high

£30-50　　　　　　　　　　　　　　　　　　MHT

A 1960s Murano sommerso glass yellow cased green oval bowl, with pinched thick rim.

These heavily rendered, vibrantly coloured bowls are sometimes known as 'geode' bowls after the geological rock forms containing crystal-lined cavities.

7.25in (18.5cm) high

£30-40　　　　　　　　　　　　　　　　　　RET

A 1960s Murano glass sommerso bowl with a red core, a layer of controlled bubbles and aventurine inclusions, cased with green tinged clear glass with pulled wings.

4.5in (11.5cm) diam

£30-40　　　　　　　　　　　　　　　RET

A 1960s Murano glass aqua green ashtray with colourless casing and pulled lobes.

9in (23cm) diam

£20-25　　　　　　　　　　　　　　　RET

A 1950s-70s Murano glass cased green and yellow ashtray, with pulled rim and network of controlled internal bubbles.

6.75in (17cm) diam

£10-15　　　　　　　　　　　　　　　M20C

A 1960s Murano glass yellow tinted cased red 'sommerso' bowl, cut with facets, the base cut with a hobnail pattern.

5.25in (13cm) wide

£35-45   **RET**

A 1960s-70s Murano 'sommerso' glass green and blue faceted ashtray, the outer layer tinged with violet.

A Murano glass dish, the graduated violet and colourless glass with applied cobalt blue abstract splash motif, and heavy colourless base.

The designer and maker of this bowl remain unknown. Some collectors have attributed it to Czechoslovakia, although this has not been confirmed and a Muranese origin is more likely. Regardless, it would have been very complex and hard to make.

c1960   6.75in (17cm) diam

£120-180   **QU**

5.25in (13cm) wide

£30-50   **TGM**

A 1970s Murano glass cylinder vase, the graduated blue to colourless body overlaid with multicoloured star murrines, unmarked.

9.25in (23.5cm) high

£300-500   **QU**

A Murano glass cylinder vase, the colourless body with graduated violet, yellow and purple bands.

c1965   9.5in (24cm) high

£300-500   **QU**

A Murano glass footed vase, the conical form with cylindrical neck and flared rim overlaid with multicoloured millefiori murrines.

c1910   5.5in (14cm) high

£300-400   **QU**

A small Murano glass teardrop shaped vase, the colourless glass overlaid with columns of zanfirico canes and multicoloured ribbon twist canes, unmarked.

5.5in (14cm) high

£100-150   **QU**

GLASS

A 1950s-60s Murano glass sommerso bird, the red core cased with uranium glass, unsigned.

Although unsigned, the way the tail and beak are handled is indicative of Seguso.

6in (15cm) long

£20-30   TGM

A Cenedese sommerso glass vase in the form of a bird, the tail forming the vase, designed by Antonia da Ros, the blue core covered with a layer of colourless glass and an outer layer of green glass.

c1961   10.75in (27cm) high

£80-120   VZ

A 1960s Murano glass bird with applied and hot-worked features, on a spiralling base containing aventurine inclusions.

17.25in (44cm) high

£40-60   RET

QUICK REFERENCE - MURANO GLASS ANIMALS

An entire zoo of glass animals has been produced on Murano since the 1950s. Although leading designers and factories produced examples, the many smaller factories produced their own versions copied from, or inspired by, the works of the masters. There is an enormous gap in values, with most copies or pieces by smaller factories being worth under £150, and usually under £80. The work of a master can fetch many thousands. The key is to study original factory catalogues and books, and identify items by their shape and colour. The work of leading factories is also very well executed, sometimes using complex techniques that require skill, experience and time. Size can also indicate a finer quality piece. This fish is a good example. Antonio da Ros joined Cenedese in 1958, where he was encouraged to experiment by Gino Cenedese. His early works were thickly blown, with simple forms. He explored colour by using one or two colours in different tones, usually in different internal layers.

A Seguso Vetri d'Arte yellow glass cockerel, designed by Flavio Poli.

7in (18cm) wide

£1,000-1,500   DOR

A Cenedese sommerso glass fish, designed by by Antonio Da Ros, with cobalt blue core overlaid with dark violet and light blue layers.

1962   6in (15cm) wide

£600-800   DOR

A Cenedese sommerso glass fish, designed by Antonio Da Ros, the multi-layered deep rose pink core overlaid with light blue glass, with a rose pink tail and a matching light blue cube pedestal.

1965-66   10.5in (27cm) high

£1,800-2,200   DOR

QUICK REFERENCE

- Post WWII Scandinavian glass has increased in popularity and value, as glass collectors re-evaluate its importance to 20thC glass design, due to a widening knowledge base.
- 1950s pieces were predominantly asymmetric, with curving forms and cool colours. Designers took their inspiration from natural forms. By the 1960s, this became a clean-lined, geometric, brightly coloured Modern style. Textured forms became popular and continued to be so into the 1970s.
- Both the factory and the designer are important in determining value and desirability. Factories include Orrefors, Kosta Boda and Iittala, with stylish pieces by Riihimäen Lasi Oy and Orrefors currently proving popular. Look for the work of leading designers, who influenced others and helped define the movement, such as Vicke Lindstrand, Simon Gate, Tapio Wirkkala, Sven Palmqvist, Tamara Aladin and Nanny Still. This can seem confusing,

because some designers, such as Lindstrand, moved between factories, or the factories merged. Examination of the engraved marks on its base may identify the designer or, if unmarked, the designer and maker may be identified from the style, colour and way it was made.
- Investigate the secondary factories, designers or ranges that are still being researched. These include John Orwar Lake for Ekenas, Strömbergshyttan, and Erik Höglund for Boda. Now may be the time to buy, as these designers may become more collectable and valuable later.
- Consider how a piece was made and its colour, as some techniques and colours are rare. Unique vases are usually worth more than mould-blown pieces. Condition and 'eye appeal' are a major factors in determining desirability. Examine pieces for damage which detracts from the purity of colour and form that is typical of Scandinavian glass.

A mid-late 1970s Finnish Riihimäen Lasi Oy green footed waisted cylindrical vase, by an unknown designer and produced from 1976 as part of the 'Export Collection'.

10in (25cm) high

£20-30   M20C

A mid 1960s-70s Finnish Riihimäen Lasi Oy green footed vase, with trumpet neck, by an unknown designer.

10in (25cm) high

£20-30   M20C

A 1960s-70s Finnish Riihimaki Lasi Oy mould blown cased green tapered 'Stromboli' vase, designed by Aimo Okkolin in 1963.

7in (18cm) high

£20-30   NPC

A 1960s Finnish Riihimäen Lasi Oy green 'Chimney' vase, designed by Aimo Okkolin in 1960.

10in (25cm) high

£20-30   M20C

A Finnish Riihimäen Lasi Oy cased green vase, with solid, heavy foot, by an unknown designer.

4.5in (11.5cm) high

£20-30   M20C

GLASS

A 1960s-70s Finnish Riihimäen Lasi Oy mould blown cased green vase, designed by Helena Tynell.

7in (18cm) high

£80-120　　　　**GC**

A Finnish Riihimäen Lasi Oy cased blue large vase, with disc centre and waisted neck and base, by an unidentified designer.

10.5in (26.5cm) high

£30-50　　　　**M20C**

A Finnish Riihimäen Lasi Oy green mould blown vase from the 'Fossil' range, designed by Helena Tynell.

8.75in (22.5cm) high

£100-150　　　　**GC**

A Finnish Riihimäen Lasi Oy blue mould blown vase from the 'Fossil' range, designed by Helena Tynell.

In taking its inspiration from natural history rather than the drawing board and geometry set, the Fossil range is very rare.

6.25in (16cm) high

£100-150　　　　**GC**

A Finnish Riihimäen Lasi Oy blue 'Safari' textured vase, no.1495, designed by Tamara Aladin in 1970.

Unusually for Riihimaki, this was machine blown into a mould, rather than being spun to create the textured finish. As such, a mould line appears down each side of the vase. It was produced in three sizes, of which this is the medium. Colours include green, dark blue, this blue and colourless.

10in (25cm) high

£40-50　　　　**M20C**

A Riihimäen Lasi Oy mould blown blue decanter, the front and back with a moulded stylised flower design, designed by Helena Tynell.

6.75in (17cm) high

£60-90　　　　**UCT**

A Riihimäen Lasi Oy, blue mould blown 'Pala' vase, with textured surface, designed by Helena Tynell in 1964.

1964-76　　*2.75in (7cm) high*

£15-18　　　　**UCT**

A CLOSER LOOK AT A RIIHIMAKI VASE

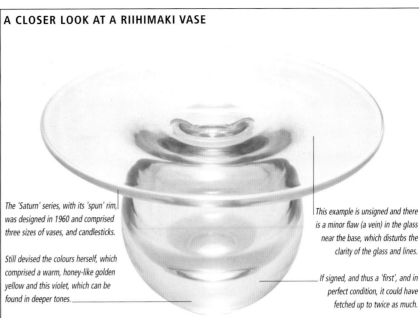

The 'Saturn' series, with its 'spun' rim, was designed in 1960 and comprised three sizes of vases, and candlesticks.

Still devised the colours herself, which comprised a warm, honey-like golden yellow and this violet, which can be found in deeper tones.

This example is unsigned and there is a minor flaw (a vein) in the glass near the base, which disturbs the clarity of the glass and lines.

If signed, and thus a 'first', and in perfect condition, it could have fetched up to twice as much.

A Finnish Riihimäen Lasi Oy 'Saturn' light violet vase, designed by Nanny Still in 1960.

3.25in (8cm) high

£50-80   **UCT**

A 1960s Finnish Riihimäen Lasi Oy cased yellow vase, no.1379, the design attributed to Tamara Aladin, the base with acid etched mark and engraved '1379'.

The presence of the mark indicates this was produced for the mainland European market: examples intended for the UK market are generally unmarked.

8in (20cm) high

£30-40   **M20C**

A Finnish Riihimäen Lasi Oy yellow vase, the design attributed to Tamara Aladin.

1965-1971   *11in (28cm) high*

£40-50   **M20C**

A 1980s Finnish Riihimäen Lasi Oy red waisted and tapered vase, shape no.6012, designed by Aimo Okkolin in 1982.

10in (25cm) high

£20-30   **M20C**

A Finnish Riihimäen Lasi Oy 'Tuulikki' range red vase, designed by Tamara Aladin in 1972.

1972-76   *8in (20cm) high*

£20-25   **M20C**

GLASS

A Swedish Orrefors cut and fire-polished vase, by an unknown designer, the base inscribed 'Orrefors'.

After being cut, the body was reheated and the edges of the facets were smoothed off and rounded using a fire torch, or by inserting the piece back into the glory hole for a short time.

9in (23cm high

£80-120   GC

An Orrefors '1000 Windows' series glass vase, cut with semi-circular lenses, by Simon Gate, the base inscribed 'Orrefors 90895/211'.

Gate designed this Regency style pattern in 1934. Sales remained strong and this vase, modified from earlier vase shapes, was still sold by Orrefors in 2003.

7.75in (19.5cm) high

£20-30   AEM

A Swedish Orrefors 'Selina' opalescent bowl, designed by Sven Palmqvist from 1954, the base engraved 'Orrefors Pu XXXX'.

8in (20.5cm) diam

£80-120   PC

A 1930s Orrefors Art Deco decanter, designed by Simon Gate, the base slice-cut with facets and acid-etched to give a frosted finish, the base inscribed 'Orrefors GE75 Sweden'.

This mark is useful – the 'G' indicates Simon Gate, the 'E' shows it is frosted cut glass, and the '75' allows it to be dated to 1928.

1928   10.25in (26cm) high

£80-120   GC

A CLOSER LOOK AT AN ORREFORS GOBLET

Designed in 1957, the Tulpan series won a gold medal at the important Milan Triennale exhibition in 1957, the year this piece was made. It has become an icon of Scandinavian glass design.

Tulpan is Swedish for 'tulip', the form of the flower being echoed in the gently curving bowl.

At 17in (27cm) high, the size is important – larger examples do exist, but are very rare.

This required great skill to create, particularly the regularity of the form and the hollow conical foot. Landberg is known for his elegant, classical shapes at this time.

An Orrefors ruby red 'Tulpanglass' vase, designed by Nils Landberg in 1954, the base engraved 'Orrefors Expo Nu 312-57'.

1957   17in (43cm) high

£1,200-1,800   DRA

An Orrefors colourless glass seated polar bear, the base inscribed 'Orrefors CB4354 - 1/1'.

3.75in (9cm) high

£35-40   TGM

A Kosta Boda 'October' bowl with applied enamelled trees and birds and multicoloured chips to form the flowery meadow, designed by Kjell Engmann in 1983, the base signed 'Bow 68628 K. Engmann'.

6.25in (15.5cm) high

£50-70   **TGM**

A 1930s Kosta colourless optic tapering cylindrical vase, designed by Elis Bergh, with an applied black foot.

10in (25.5cm) high

£120-180   **UCT**

A 1990s Kosta Boda vase, designed by Göran Wärff, with cut panel to front, and low-relief, moulded star shape surrounded by applied powdered enamels to the reverse, the base engraved 'KOSTA 47317 WARFF', and with cellophane label.

4.5in (11.5cm) high

£70-90   **TGM**

A Swedish Kosta bottle vase, with randomly applied coloured trails and chips, designed by Bertil Vallien, the base with broken pontil mark, unsigned.

9in (23cm) high

£80-100   **GC**

A 1970s-80s Kosta Boda bowl, designed by Göran Wärff in 1973, the exterior with applied purple and black enamels over a colourless base, with star and irregular shaped exclusions, the rim signed 'KOSTA 56773 WARFF'.

Five digit numbers have been used for designs from the 1970s onwards, with the last two numbers indicating the year of design rather than production of that piece. Wärff joined Orrefors from Pukeberg in 1964, before leaving to travel and teach in 1974. He returned in 1984 and still produces organic, earthy inspired designs, that accentuate the qualities of glass.

6in (15cm) diam

£70-100   **TGM**

A Kosta solifleur vase, designed by Vicke Lindstrand, of tapered cylindrical form, cased in clear over a graduated colour ground, with a single tear-shaped bubble to the base, the base with full engraved signature.

11in (28cm) high

£100-150   **FLD**

A Swedish Kosta carafe or decanter, with applied spout, designed by Vicke Lindstrand in 1959, the base inscribed 'Kosta LH1463'.

11.5in (29cm) high

£60-80   **GC**

A Swedish Flygsfors cased vase, with angled cut rim, designed by Paul Kedelv, the base inscribed 'Flygsfors 63'.

11in (28cm) high

£50-70   RET

A 1960s Boda orange goblet, designed by Eric Hoglund, with random internal bubbles.

6.75in (17cm) high

£30-50   GC

A 1960s Swedish Gullaskruf mould blown teal blue bottle vase, designed by Arthur Percy.

Percy (1886-1976) worked for Gullaskruf from 1951-70.

9.75in (24.5cm) high

£8-12   M20C

A Norwegian Hadeland cased olive green tapering vase, possibly designed by Willy Johansson.

6.5in (15cm) high

£20-30   M20C

A 1970s Hadeland ovoid vase with acid etched and sandblasted design of a little girl seated and hugging a doll, with factory foil labels, unsigned.

7.5in (19cm) high

£60-80   GC

A 1970s Norwegian Hadeland troll, with applied ears, nose and eyes, the base acid stamped 'Hadeland'.

3in (7.5cm) high

£22-28   RET

A Finnish Iittala blue 'Bird' bottle vase, shape no. i-401, from the i-line range, designed by Timo Sarpaneva in 1956.

1957-68   *6.75in (17cm) high*

£80-120   QU

A Finnish Nuutajarvi Nostjo cased blue footed vase, with heavy colourless foot and machine-cut rim, designed by Kaj Franck in 1962, the base inscribed 'KF Nuutajarvi Nostjo-62'.

The restrained, sombre colour and austere form with its clean lines are typical of Franck's Modernist designs.

6.25in (16cm) high

£280-320   UCT

A 1970s Swedish Reijmyre colourless cased purple vase, with tapering neck, machine-cut rim and base moulded with concentric circles.

10in (25.5cm) high

£40-50   UCT

A 1960s Swedish Ruda Glasbruk mould blown textured blue 'Kobalt' bottle vase, designed by Göte Augustssen, the base with polished concave pontil mark.

8.75in (22cm) high

£30-50   M20C

A CLOSER LOOK AT A RUDA VASE

Ruda Glasbruk was based near other Swedish glass factories Orrefors and Kosta from 1910-72 - their decorative glass was always secondary to their industrial glass.

Augustsson was designer from 1947-72 and most of his designs are textured, having been blown into a mould, before being finished by hand.

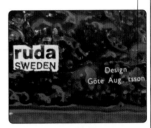

This was from a range that also included tankards, jugs and other vase shapes.

'Kobolt' Blue is the most common colour found, with green (known as 'Turkos') and an amber-brown (known as 'Orient') being harder to find.

A 1960s Swedish Ruda Glasbruk mould-blown textured blue 'Kobalt' vase, designed by Göte Augustsson, with factory label, the base with polished concave pontil mark.

6.5in (16.5cm) high

£30-50   M20C

A Swedish Skruf tapering cylindrical glass vase, by Bengt Edenfalk, cased in colourless glass with applied ribbon trail decoration, the base etched 'Edenfalk Skruf'.

This range can be found in a number of shapes and colours, including grey, brown and sage green. A vase from this range was included in an exhibition of modern glass at the Corning Glass Museum in 1959. Edenfalk (b.1924) worked for Skruf from 1953-78, leaving to produce designs for Kosta.

13in (33cm) high

£120-180   WW

A 1930s Strömbergshyttan brown vase with scalloped rim, the base with polished pontil mark.

These were imported into the UK by Elfverson & Co., run by H.J. Dunne Cooke. This shape, available in 6in, 8in, 10in and 12in sizes, was numbered 3055A.

8.25in (21cm) high

£60-90   GC

QUICK REFERENCE

- Peter Layton was born in Prague in 1937, and brought up in England. He studied ceramics at the Central School of Art and Design in London, before discovering glassblowing while teaching at the University of Iowa in the 1970s.
- Largely self-taught, he established his own glass studio at his pottery at Morar in the Highlands of Scotland, before moving to Rotherhithe in London. He went on to establish a glass department at Hornsey College of Art (Middlesex University), and founded the influential London Glassblowing Workshop in 1976.
- Layton has since played a major role in the development of studio glass in Britain. As well as mentoring many new glassmakers and designers, helping them mould their style, identity and confidence, he has offered facilities enabling them to work.
- His designs are inspired by the fluidity of molten glass, vivid colour and controlled yet asymmetric form. Nature and landscape are also influences. Pieces are typically built up using a number of layers of glass, with patterns being created with applied coloured swirls, speckles and trails.
- Smooth, rounded forms inspired by pebbles are typical, and the 'dropper bottle', with its thin, elongated neck, is a hallmark form that can be found in many of his ranges. As each piece is handmade and freeblown, each one is unique in terms of its precise form and patterning. Values depend on the size, range, colour and complexity of the design, and range from as little as £150 to over £5,000.
- Layton has also produced a number of unique, individual works for exhibitions that explore themes such as the human body, life and death. These usually incorporate other materials such a metal piping and even medical equipment. He is also known for his architectural commissions in association with Simon Moss. Layton's designs can be found in many private and public collections across the world.

A Peter Layton 'Turquoise Paradiso' stone form vase, the graduated sky blue, yellow, green and cream core with a diagonal black striped orange zig-zag, the base signed 'Peter Layton'.

2007   6.75in (17cm) high

£800-1,200   GC

A Peter Layton 'Aeriel' stone form vase, the blue core overlaid with ochre and cream swirls, and cased in colourless glass, the base signed 'Peter Layton'.

2006   7in (18cm) high

£300-400   GC

A Peter Layton 'Spirale' stone form, the spiralling burgundy and blue and yellow striped core overlaid with a colourless layer, the base signed 'Peter Layton'.

8in (20.5cm) high

£700-1,000   GC

A unique Peter Layton stone form vase, the buff-grey core with a yellow grid-like pattern and applied large yellow stylised floral murrines with orange stripes, the base signed 'Peter Layton'.

The murrines have been applied to a colourless layer over the core, giving depth to the design, which is further highlighted by the yellow and grey grid pattern of the core.

c2004   7.5in (19cm) high

£1,000-1,500   GC

A Peter Layton 'Forest Floor' stone form vase, the core with applied multi-coloured chips, and cased in colourless glass, the base signed 'Peter Layton'.

2006   7in (18cm) high

£300-400   GC

A Peter Layton 'Yellow Paradiso' large flattened bottle, the base signed 'Peter Layton'.

2006   11.25in (28.5cm) high

£1,000-1,500   GC

A Peter Layton 'Turquoise Paradiso' ovoid vase, the base signed 'Peter Layton'.

c2007 6.5in (17.5cm) high

£800-1,000 GC

A Peter Layton 'Aurora' ovoid vase, the base signed 'Peter Layton'.

c2005 9.5in (24cm) high

£300-500 GC

A Peter Layton 'Kimono' ovoid vase, with matte finish, the base signed 'Peter Layton'.

1989 8in (20.5cm) high

£400-600 GC

A Peter Layton 'Landscape' dropper bottle, the base signed 'Peter Layton'.

1995 9in (23cm) high

£250-350 GC

A CLOSER LOOK AT A PETER LAYTON BLOWN BASKET

This unique bowl is related to the 'Ice Basket' range, like the vase shown on the left, but colours were not used in the 'Ice Basket' range.

The random rim and trails on the body give a sense of great movement, and suggests water, or glass in a molten state.

This bowl was created by blowing a purple bubble of molten glass into a colourless 'Ice Basket' form, causing it to open up in a random manner.

Although the 'Ice Basket' range was put into production, these 'blown out' pieces were not – to date only three pieces are known.

A Peter Layton 'Ice Basket', the colourless glass cage form with acid-etched surface, the base signed 'Peter Layton'.

2003 9in (23cm) high

£600-800 GC

A Peter Layton 'Blown Basket', the purple core overlaid with colourless random trails, the base signed 'Peter Layton'.

2006 7in (17.5cm) high

£800-1,200 GC

GLASS

QUICK REFERENCE

- Studio glass is glass produced by individual glass artists working outside a factory environment. This became possible after Americans, Harvey Littleton and Dominick Labino developed a process in the early 1960s by which individuals could melt, form and blow glass. Artists could work alone, although many still chose to work in teams. The movement spread to Europe in the late 1960s-70s.
- As artists developed and shared skills, pieces became more complex and appealing. Glass began to be considered an art form and has developed into a vibrant movement, with major museums exhibiting studio glass by the 1980s.
- Be aware that with studio glass, date is not always a good indicator of value. Some early examples of styles are crude, although they do represent notable developments. Learning about key makers and styles helps with identification.

- Pieces by major names, such as Dale Chihuly and Marvin Lipofsky, already make high sums. However, works by those they taught, or those by lesser-known makers, are usually more affordable and may appreciate in value, as more people become aware of these artists and start collecting their work. Learn about your chosen artist's background, whom they studied with, and their style, to help you identify their work. Many pieces are signed but are often hard to read; others may be unsigned.
- Study how glass is made, so you can spot complex pieces, that would have been time-consuming to make and therefore expensive at the time. Such pieces may be rare today as fewer were made. Large pieces, and pieces by well-known makers may make good investments as more collectors are drawn to the area and demand rises.

A 1980s Iestyn Davies cased cylindrical vase, cut with windows containing Japanese symbols and with mottled black and white surface, applied gold and silver leaf and red trailed band, the base signed.

This heavy vase was complex to produce, and incorporates a number of hot and cold working steps including cutting and The application of gold and silver foil and hot red trails. The Japanese symbols are typical of 1980s and early 1990s fashions.

13.5in (34cm) high

£600-800   GC

A Glasform bowl, designed by John Ditchfield, no.1917, of compressed spherical form with a swirled tonal green to blue body, engraved to the base and with foil label.

5in (13cm) high

£150-250   FLD

A Julia Donnelly flattened oval vase, with mottled surface of coloured chips, signed 'Julia Donnelly 1990'.

Julia Donnelly worked for Siddy Langley from 1987-2002 - pieces produced during this period are signed with her initials only.

1990   *6in (15cm) high*

£30-40   TGM

A Glasform 'Lily pad' pebble shaped vase, designed by John Ditchfield, with applied trails and waterlily leaves and iridescent surface, the base signed 'Glasform1=8/L'.

4.25in (11cm) high

£70-100   GAZE

A Carin von Druhle tall ovoid vase, the exterior with applied random trails and strong iridescence, the base signed 'Carin von Druhle 1990'.

1990   *7in (17.5cm) high*

£80-120   TGM

A Robert Eickholdt studio glass vase, the cobalt blue body overlaid with fragmented silver foil, cased in clear glass and then with a layer of fragmented gold foil and a final layer of colourless glass, the base signed 'Eickholdt 1996'.

1996   *10.25in (26cm) high*

£120-180   **TGM**

An Island Glass vase, with mottled blue and violet decoration, green trail and lobed rim, the base with impressed three lion pontil mark.

Island Glass was co-founded by Michael Harris in the early 1980s on the island of Guernsey in the Channel Islands. The mottled effects, and particularly the lobed rim, are style hallmarks.

6.75in (17cm) high

£25-30   **GC**

A CLOSER LOOK AT A SAM HERMAN VASE

Sam Herman (b.1936) is considered by many to be the father of the British studio glass movement, introducing studio glass techniques to the UK in 1966.

This is a very early piece and was made at either the Royal College of Art in London, where Herman was tutor in glass, or at the newly founded Glasshouse.

This style of applied trailing is very similar to designs produced for Herman's exhibition at the Victoria & Albert Museum, London in 1971.

One side appears cracked, but this contains silver chloride and is completely fused, leaving just a line – it is likely that the piece cooled slightly when being made.

A Sam Herman studio glass vase, with applied purple trail and silver chloride decoration on a translucent white base, trapped air bubbles and colourless outer casing, the base inscribed 'Samuel J. Herman 1970'.

1970   *9.75in (24.5cm) high*

£300-400   **PC**

A Sam Herman for Val St. Lambert studio glass sculpture, with heavily cased wings, the base inscribed 'Val 212 Samuel Herman 1979'.

Herman worked at Val St Lambert over a number of years, becoming a consultant in 1990. Although he produced the designs, not all the pieces were produced by him.

1979   *15.75in (40cm) high*

£1,500-2,000   **GC**

A Sam Herman for Val St Lambert glass vase, of swollen cylindrical form with tapering shoulder, signed in script 'Samuel Herman 1979 VAL 88'.

1979   *12.25in (31cm) high*

£650-850   **L&T**

A 1970s Scottish Kirkhill Glass blue vase with random applied trails, designed and made by John Airlie, the base with broken pontil mark, unsigned.

5.5in (14cm) high

£40-60   **GC**

GLASS

QUICK REFERENCE - FAKES

Over the past few years, as prices for Whitefriars' Textured range have risen, a number of fakes, produced in the Far East or Eastern Europe, have appeared. The iconic 'Drunken Bricklayer' was the first, but others from the range are now being made. These fakes can be identified from a number of features that differ from those on authentic examples. These features comprise colour, texture, the pontil mark, and the general feel and appearance. The glass used for most fakes has an almost waxy feel, and the colourless casing is different, not being as well balanced or executed as on authentic examples. The next page features authentic examples of the 'Drunken Bricklayer' and 'Hoop' vases.

The colours are wrong – colours of fakes currently comprise red, green, cobalt blue and a strong amber. In cases where Whitefriars used these colours, the fakes are the wrong tone.

There is a moulded long, shallow trench on the top of the bottom brick – this does not appear on originals.

The middle brick has more dimples (28) than authentic examples, and they are also in a different formation.

The concave pontil mark is a part of the moulded design, rather than being polished out by a machine as with authentic examples.

A modern fake Whitefriars cased Ruby red 'Drunken Bricklayer' vase, copied from pattern no.9673 designed by Geoffrey Baxter in 1966.
c2008   8.25in (21cm) high
£15-20   GC

A fake Whitefriars cased red 'Onion' vase, copied from pattern no.9758 designed by Geoffrey Baxter in 1972.

This vase was not originally produced in this colour, the polished pontil mark is a part of the moulded design, and the textured design is smoother and less detailed than on originals.
c2008   5.5in (14cm) high
£8-12
                                                             GC

A fake Whitefriars cased Ruby red 'Hoop' vase, copied from pattern no.9680, designed by Geoffrey Baxter in 1966.

Of all the identified Whitefriars fakes, this is the perhaps the easiest to spot as the textured pattern is completely different to the original. The red tone is also wrong, and this shape was never made in red.
12in (30.5cm) high
£20-30   GC

A Whitefriars Willow 'Totem' vase, no.9671 from the 'Textured' range designed by Geoffrey Baxter in 1966.

1967-72   *10.25in (26cm) high*

£120-180   **FLD**

A Whitefriars Willow 'Cucumber' vase, no.9679 from the 'Textured' range designed by Geoffrey Baxter in 1967.

1967-73   *12in (30.5cm) high*

£120-180   **RET**

A Whitefriars Tangerine 'Hoop' vase, no.9680 from the 'Textured' range designed by Geoffrey Baxter in 1966.

1967-73 11.5in (29.5cm) high

£200-250   **WW**

A Whitefriars Tangerine 'Drunken Bricklayer' vase, no.9672 from the 'Textured' range designed by Geoffrey Baxter in 1966.

1967-74   *8.25in (21cm) high*

£200-300   **WW**

A Whitefriars cased Cinnamon brown 'Bark' vase, pattern no.9691 from the 'Textured' range designed by Geoffrey Baxter in 1966.

1966-69   *7.75in (18.5cm) high*

£60-80   **M20C**

A Whitefriars cased Kingfisher blue 'Bottle' vase, pattern no. 9730 from the 'Textured' range, designed by Geoffrey Baxter in 1969.

1969-72   *8in (20.5cm) high*

£50-70   **M20C**

A Whitefriars Aubergine 'Stitched Square' vase, no.9811, from the 'Late Textured' range, designed by Geoffrey Baxter in 1972.

6in (15cm) high

£120-160   **GC**

GLASS

A Whitefriars Sea Green vase with applied band of swags, pattern no.9004, designed by William Wilson in 1938, the base with broken pontil mark.

7.25in (18.5cm) high

£60-80   GC

A late 1920s-30s Whitefriars green and blue 'Cloudy' glass vase, no.8608, with white and air bubble inclusions, cased in clear glass.

9in (23cm) high

£280-320   WW

A 1930s Whitefriars vase, the Sea Green body overlaid with blue applied threads, no.8894, designed by Barnaby Powell in 1938.

9in (23cm) high

£200-300   GC

A Whitefriars Ruby red three-cornered bowl, no.9588 designed by Geoffrey Baxter.

1964-70   *9.5in (24cm) widest*

£35-50   RET

An extremely rare Whitefriars Ruby red eight-lobed 'Tricorn' vase, no.9570 designed by Geoffrey Baxter in 1961.

As its name suggests, these vases usually have three lobes. Only one or two examples with more than three lobes have been found, and were probably prototypes.

1962-78   *8in (20.5cm) high*

£80-100   GC

A Whitefriars flared vase, with a Tangerine swirl applied on a Pewter grey body, no.9708 designed by Geoffrey Baxter in 1969.

1969-71   *8in (20.5cm) high*

£50-70   MHC

A Whitefriars 'Antique' baluster vase, with blue, brown and purple random streaks, no.9784, designed by Geoffrey Baxter.

c1972   *7in (18cm) high*

£80-120   GC

FIND OUT MORE...

Lesley Jackson, Whitefriars Glass: Art of James Powell & Sons *Richard Dennis, 1996*
Wendy Evan, Catherine Ross and Alex Werner, Whitefriars Glass: *James Powell & Sons of London, Art Books International, 1996*

An Anchor Hocking Forest Green 'Shell' Depression glass dish.

7in (17.5cm) wide

£3-5   AEM

An Imperial 'Heavy Grape' pattern purple or amethyst Carnival glass bowl.

4.5in (11.5cm) diam

£12-18   AEM

A Dugan-Diamond 'Grapevine Lattice' purple Carnival glass dish.

7in (17.5cm) diam

£60-100   BH

A Northwood 'Singing Birds' pattern marigold Carnival glass mug.

3.75in (9.5cm) high

£20-40   AEM

A set of six amorphous glass bottles, screen-printed with Surrealist designs after Salvador Dali, each with facsimile 'Dali' signature.

Tallest 13.5in (34cm) high

£100-150   WW

A rare Davidson orange cloud glass powder jar.

Red is even rarer and more valuable.

1933-35   *5.5in (14cm) high*

£80-120   BAD

An unusual Davidson brown cloud glass ovoid vase, pattern no.34 SVG.

This shape is comparatively hard to find.

1934-41   *7.5in (19cm) h*

£70-100   BAD

A Duncan Miller 'Sandwich' pattern Crystal Depression glass 9oz (255g) goblet.

Note the difference in the design to Anchor Hocking's version. Coloured examples by Duncan Miller are harder to find than colourless 'Crystal'.

1924-55   6in (15cm) high

£7-12   **AEM**

A CLOSER LOOK AT A HARTLEY WOOD VASE

Hartley Wood was founded in 1837 in Sunderland, and produced 'crown' window and other similar types of glass. It produced limited quantities of decorative wares from the 1930s onwards.

The bright colours that had been used for the company's stained glass windows were emulated. The larger or more colours a piece has, the more desirable it will be.

Known as 'Antique Glass', each piece is unique as it was handmade, charming, slightly off-centre and uneven forms are typical.

Earlier pieces from the 1930s have an oily feel to the thickly blown glass, later pieces are thinner and lighter in weight, and were often blown into moulds so are more regular in form.

A 1930s Hartley Wood hollow-footed 'Antique Glass' vase with flared rim, and random green, yellow, blue, purple and red swirling pattern, the base with broken pontil mark.

8in (20cm) high

£80-120   **GC**

A Fenton hand painted pink graduated vase, the base with a square Fenton label and signed 'handpainted by A Findlay' and 'W.C. Fenton'.

5.75in (14.5cm) high

£50-80   **TSIS**

A Fenton Topaz 'Coin Dot' ruffled vase, shape no.1441.

Made for only a short period of time, Topaz Coin Dot is hotly sought after.

1959-61   7in (17.5cm) high

£50-80   **TSIS**

A 1990s Gozo Glass 'Sea Collection' perfume bottle, with deep internal pulled swirls, inscribed "Gozo Glass" on the base.

5.25in (13cm) high

£28-32   **TGM**

A 1930s Hartley Wood 'Antique Glass' vase, with random green, yellow and orange swirling pattern, the base with broken pontil mark.

9.5in (24cm) high

£100-150   **GC**

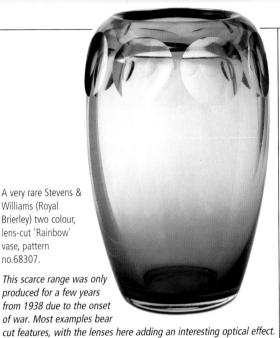

A very rare Stevens & Williams (Royal Brierley) two colour, lens-cut 'Rainbow' vase, pattern no.68307.

This scarce range was only produced for a few years from 1938 due to the onset of war. Most examples bear cut features, with the lenses here adding an interesting optical effect.

c1939   10in (25.5cm) high

£800-1,200   **GC**

A 1930s Stevens & Williams (Royal Brierley) pink glass vase with random internal bubbles, designed by Keith Murray, on an applied colourless pad foot.

Known as 'Cased Bubbly', pink and blue were the first colours to be produced in this scarce range, and were followed by amethyst and green. Some pieces bear acid etched marks with Murray's name.

c1938-39   8.5in (22cm) high

£300-400   **GC**

A CLOSER LOOK AT A STEVENS & WILLIAMS VASE

The bubbly, mottled design follows the 1930s fashion for bubbly glass, such as that produced by Monart, Graystan and Walsh Walsh.

The surface is rough to the touch, and may have been treated with chemicals or coloured enamels to further the 'ancient' feel.

The surface is also treated with metal oxides to give it an iridescent finish, which was inspired by ancient Roman glass.

This is a pleasing classic form, more valuable forms have applied prunts or handles with impressed patterns inspired by Ancient designs.

A 1930s Stevens & Williams 'Caerleon' range baluster vase, with random internal air bubbles, blue and yellow powdered enamel mottled design and iridescent surface, the base with broken pontil mark.

8in (20.5cm) high

£200-250   **GC**

A Strathearn cylindrical vase sandblasted and vibropen etched with a fisherman and net, the base signed in vibropen 'STRATHEARN 1978'.

1978   7.75in (19.5cm) high

£70-100   **GC**

A 1980s Stuart 'Dark Crystal' rectangular vase, designed by Iestyn Davis, with mottled red textured surface and machine-cut rim.

3.75in (9.5cm) high

£20-30   **MHC**

A 1980s Stuart 'Dark Crystal' baluster vase, designed by Iestyn Davis, with mottled red textured surface and machine-cut rim.

Introduced in 1982 along with 'Ebony & Gold', Dark Crystal is much harder to find today. Both ranges were only produced for a few years, and Dark Crystal appears to have sold in much lower quantities at the time.

5.25in (13.5cm) high

£40-60   **GC**

A green beeer bottle, Brown & Plummer, Swindon.

8in (20.5cm) high.

£2-5   BS

A green half pint beer bottle, Marchants, Reading.

8in (20.5cm) high.

£2-5   BS

A late Georgian blue spirit bottle, Bristol, with wheel engraving 'Speed of the Plough', dedicated to M. Dickson Aug 1832.

11in (28cm) high

£200-250   AG

A Ye Olde Fulham Pottery stoneware bottle, with original top.

9in (23cm) high.

£50-60   BS

QUICK REFERENCE

- Though the Inuit art heritage goes back to the Athabascan and Thule cultures of 10thC Alaska and Northern Canada, most collectable Inuit art dates from the 1950s onwards. It first came to prominence in 1949 after James Houston, a young Canadian artist, visited the Canadian Arctic with the intention of finding out whether the native art was appealing and could be sold. Creation and trade became increasingly organised in the 1950s and 1960s. Interest has subsequently grown across the world, with the market seeing rapid development in the last 25 years.
- Most works are sculptural and created from the native soft yet durable soapstone. Soapstone ranges in colour from deep grey through to green and can be polished to a high shine, earning it a reputation as 'Canadian jade'. Drawings, textiles and prints are also collected. Subjects include scenes from Inuit daily life as well as myths, Shamanism and abstract ideas. Well-executed, stylised or even abstract designs, particularly those displaying wit or humour, find the most

favour with collectors. Polar bears, real and mythical creatures and 'transformation' sculptures are also desirable.
- Influential artists such as John Pangnark, Osuitok Ipeelee, Pauta Saila, Jessie Oonark and Judas Ullulaq are the most collectable. A large proportion of the most valuable pieces were made by these artists, many of whom are now dead. The growing popularity of Inuit art has resulted in many pieces of average or poor quality coming onto the market. Of the many contemporary artists working today, only a few will come to be considered masters of the form. Research artists and market trends in reference books, or visit dealers and auction to inspect desirable examples yourself.
- Many pieces are signed on the bottom with syllabics (the Inuit form of verbal lettering), or with a disc number beginning with an E or W, which can be used to identify the artist by consulting an online reference guide. Look out for the Canadian government sticker on more contemporary Inuit pieces.

A stone 'Embracing Mother, Child and Bird' figure, by Kenojuak Ashevak, E7-1035, from Cape Dorset.

9.75in (25cm) high

£4,500-5,500   **WAD**

A stone 'Mother Holding Children' group, by Miaiji Uitangi Usaitaijuk (1911-1965), E9-1174, from Salluit, signed in syllabics with disc number.

c1950   6in (15cm) wide

£2,200-2,800   **WAD**

A stone 'Mother and Child' figure, by an unidentified artist, from Cape Dorset.

This early sculpture was acquired by Sir Norman Hartnell, the Queen's dressmaker, during one of his visits to Canada in the 1950s.

c1955   9.5in (24cm) high

£5,000-7,000   **WAD**

A stone 'Mother and Child' figure, by Mannumi Shaqu, E7-824, from Cape Dorset.

Shaqu (1917-2000) is considered an early master of Cape Dorset sculpture. An example of his work is owned by HM The Queen, and has appeared on a postage stamp. His work has also been included in a large number of exhibitions in Canada, the UK and the US.

c1970   12in (30.5cm) high

£5,000-7,000   **WAD**

INUIT ART

A stone figure of a drummer, by Adamie Alariaq, (1930-1990), E7-1090, from Cape Dorset, signed in Roman.

16in (40.5cm) high

£450-550   WAD

QUICK REFERENCE – WHALEBONE

As well as various forms of soapstone, Inuit artists used materials found in the environment, such as this section of whale vertebra which has been cleverly used to form a body and arms. Bone is usually found in distressed condition, having been exposed to the weather and elements. It has been used for centuries by Inuit and pre-Inuit communities such as the Thule. Apart from considering the style and subject matter, dating a piece such as this is usually impossible. Also most are not signed by the sculptor. Collectors should find out about the import and export regulations that apply to this material before buying or selling.

A carved weathered bone 'Drum Dancer', the front and back with inset ivory discs carved with faces, and holding a carved bone drum and beater, by Hank Napuwatuk from Alaska.

3.5in (9cm) high

£300-400   THG

A carved whalebone bone 'Drum Dancer' figure, by an unidentified artist.

c1970   20in (51cm) high

£3,000-4,000   WAD

A stone and ivory 'Articulated Fisherman' figure, by Charlie Ugyuk, E4-341, from Spence Bay, signed in Roman.

Charlie Ugyuk (1931-1998) was the uncle of top-rated Inuit sculptor Karoo Ashevak. Typical of the Taloyoak (Spence Bay) style, this particular work is detailed and highly expressive, particularly the face. Ugyuk's work can be found in many private and public collections across the world.

18in (45.5cm) high

£15,000-25,000   WAD

A dark soapstone figure, by Annie Okalik (b.1927), E1350, from Arviat, with a multicoloured beaded coat.

4in (11cm) high

£400-500   WAD

A stone, sinew, antler and ivory figure of a shaman, by Judas Ullulaq, (1937-1998), E4-342, from Gjoa Haven.

The depiction of a mystical figure, the grotesque appearance and the use of inset bone or ivory teeth and eyes are all typical of Ullulaq, whose work is highly sought after.

c1980   7in (18cm) high
£3,000-5,000   **WAD**

A stone and antler 'Shaman' figure, by Josiah Nuilaalik (1928-2005), E2-385, from Baker Lake, signed in syllabics.

15in (38cm) high
£4,500-5,500   **WAD**

A stone 'Shaman Posing' figure, by Davie Atchealak (1947-2006), E7-1182, from Iqaluit, signed in Roman.

12.5in (32cm) high
£4,000-5,000   **WAD**

A soapstone 'Shaman/Bird' figure, by Elizabeth Tunnuq (b.1928), E-2133, from Baker Lake.

c1968   7in (18cm) high
£1,500-2,500   **WAD**

A stone figure of Tupilak, from Cape Dan, unsigned and by an unknown artist.

A Tupilak is a mystical and gruesome 'doll' made from materials such as human hair, animal parts, and even parts of a dead child's body. Once carved, magic spells were chanted and the figure was imbued with power from its creator's sexual organs. The Tupilak was then cast into the sea to seek and destroy an enemy. However, if the enemy had greater powers than those of the person who created it, the Tupilak was reversed and could destroy its creator. As original Tupilaks were destroyed or lost, reproductions made for sale were carved in bone, horn or stone.

c1971   6.5in (16.5cm) high
£1,500-2,000   **WAD**

A CLOSER LOOK AT A JOHN PANGNARK FIGURE

Pangnark is known for his highly abstract forms that resemble hills or rocky outcrops, and have a monumental feel despite their small size.

Most are inscribed or carved with simple lines to form basic facial features.

The subject matter of a shaman transformation figure is very unusual for Pangnark, which adds value to this piece.

The Inuit believed that shamen gained many of their mystical powers from an animal 'familiar' (here it is a seal), which they could transform into at will.

A stone seal/shaman transformation figure, by John Pangnark, (1920-1980), E1-104, from Arviat.

7.5in (19cm) high
£12,000-15,000   **WAD**

An untitled coloured pencil drawing, by Luke Anguhadluq (1895-1982), signed in syllabics.

30in (75cm) wide

£400-500　　　　　　　　　　**WAD**

A 'Sentient Owl' stonecut by Kenojuak Ashevak, (b.1927), E7-1035, from Cape Dorset.

1970　　　　　　　　*33.5in (85cm) wide*

£1,000-1,500　　　　　　　　　　**WAD**

A 'Loon Protects The Owl', limited edition stonecut, by Kenoujak Ashevak (b.1927), E7-1035, numbered 6 from an edition of 100, from Cape Dorset.

2002　　　*31in (78.5cm) wide*

£1,000-1,500　　　**WAD**

An untitled coloured pencil drawing by Luke Anguhadluq (1895-1982), signed in syllabics.

26in (66cm) high

£1,000-1,500　　　**WAD**

A limited edition 'Eskimo Boat in Ice' woodcut print, by James Houston (1921-2005), from Baffin Island, from an edition of 30, framed.

Artist James Houston 'discovered' Inuit art, and brought it to the world's attention during the 1950s.

14.5in (37cm) wide

£700-1,000　　　　　　　　　　**WAD**

An 'Angagok Conjuring Birds' stencil print, by Jessie Oonark (1906-1985), E2-384, from Baker Lake, from a limited edition of 45.

30in (76cm) high

£1,500-2,000　　　**WAD**

A graphite drawing, by Parr (1893-1969), E7-1022, from Cape Dorset, marked 'June 1961'.

1961　　　　　　　　*24in (61cm) high*

£5,000-7,000　　　　　　　　　　**WAD**

QUICK REFERENCE

- 'Casino Royale', the first novel to feature Ian Fleming's super spy James Bond, was first published in 1953. Fewer than 5,000 'true first editions' (first print run of the first edition) of the novel were printed and many went to libraries, leaving them in poor condition. This means good condition copies of this book are rare and sought after.

- In general, true firsts are most desirable, however, the first batch of Fleming's fifth Bond novel, 'From Russia, With Love' was sent to a book club due to their poor quality. The effective second printing (marked Cape) is therefore considered the true first edition. 'From Russia, With Love' is widely considered not only Fleming's best book but also the best film adaptation, and good condition copies are extremely sought after and valuable. A copy signed by Fleming, especially one dedicated to a close friend or colleague, will be particularly desirable. Other Bond authors, such as John Gardner who revived the Bond series in 1981, are also collectable.

- EON Productions were granted the film adaptation rights for all the Bond novels in the 1950s (except 'Casino Royale', which was only granted in the 1990s). The first adaptation, 'Dr. No', was released in 1962 and featured Sean Connery as Bond. The film launched Bond as a global phenomenon. Connery was followed in the role by George Lazenby (1969), Roger Moore (1973-1985), Timothy Dalton (1987-1989), Pierce Brosnan (1995-2000) and Daniel Craig (2006-). In general, merchandise from the immensely popular Sean Connery era is most desirable.

- James Bond's many cars and gadgets have been made into toys by a wide variety of manufacturers. Iconic cars, such as the Aston Martin, are likely to be most desirable. Condition is important, with mint condition examples usually commanding the highest prices. Models should also ideally be accompanied by their original boxes, which should also be in good condition. Always look for licensed products by known makers, although some unlicensed toys can be rare.

Ian Fleming, 'Live and Let Die', first edition of 7,500 copies, first impression, with original boards, first state dust jacket, price-clipped and slightly rubbed at corners.
1954

£5,000-7,000 BLO

Ian Fleming, 'From Russia, With Love', first edition of 15,000 copies, with original boards, dust jacket with small tear to head of spine, otherwise a very good copy.
1957

£1,200-1,800 BLO

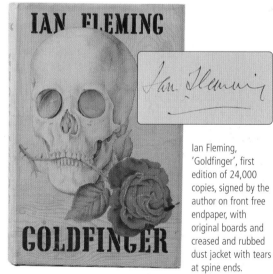

Ian Fleming, 'Goldfinger', first edition of 24,000 copies, signed by the author on front free endpaper, with original boards and creased and rubbed dust jacket with tears at spine ends.

1959

£3,500-4,500 BLO

Ian Fleming, 'Moonraker', first edition, first impression, with original boards and price-clipped dust jacket, with some browning, rubbed at edges, and spine slightly dulled.

The first print run comprised 9,900 copies. The word 'shoot' on p.10 is sometimes misspelt 'shoo' in the first edition. In general, the correct spelling (in this example) is preferred.
1955

£1,500-2,000 BLO

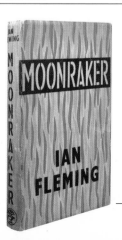

Ian Fleming, 'Dr No', first edition of 20,000 copies, first impression, with small contemporary ink name on front free endpaper, original plain first state boards, dust jacket, rubbed at corner tips and spine ends.

1958

£800-1,200 BLO

JAMES BOND

Ian Fleming, 'Goldfinger' paperback, published by Pan Books Ltd., a reprint with the same cover as the first paperback edition.
1962

£7-10   **PC**

Ian Fleming, 'On Her Majesty's Secret Service', first edition, numbered 151 from a limited edition of 250 copies signed by the author, with colour portrait by Amherst Villiers, original vellum-backed black buckram boards and original glassine plastic jacket.
1963

£3,800-4,800   **BLO**

A CLOSER LOOK AT A JAMES BOND FIRST EDITION

Thunderball was the ninth Bond book, and was written with the intention of being turned into a film, making it the first novelisation of a Bond screenplay.

The cover design was by illustrator and artist Richard Chopping (1917-2008) who produced a number of cover designs for Bond books, typically in a trompe l'oeil style.

Fleming's signature automatically adds value, but the witty and Secret Intelligence Service (MI6) related inscription adds even more interest and value.

More importantly, 'Jack' may be Jack Whittingham, who worked with Fleming on the initial screenplay for the film, before a legal case erupted, making this an important dedication.

Ian Fleming, 'Thunderball', first edition of 50,398 copies, near full-page inscription from the author on front free endpaper that reads 'To Jack, By appointment, M.O. to the SIS!, Ian', original boards, dust jacket, slightly rubbed at tips of corners.
1961

£8,000-12,000   **BLO**

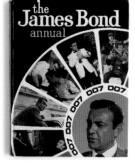

Ian Fleming, 'You Only Live Twice', first edition, signed and dedicated 'To Julie...' on the front free endpaper, minor spotting to extreme edges, with original boards and dust jacket, in excellent condition.

Julie was the lady who hand-rolled Fleming's cigarettes – dedications connected with Fleming's life or work are sought after. Although Bond smokes rarely on screen, the character in the novels was a heavy smoker, puffing his way through some 60 cigarettes a day.
1964

£3,500-4,500   **BLO**

A 'The James Bond Annual', including pictures from 'Goldfinger' and 'You Only Live Twice', and with Sean Connery cover.
1968   *10.75in (27cm) high*

£20-30   **PC**

Peter Haining, 'James Bond: A Celebration', published by Planet, page 187 with a dedication and Desmond Llewelyn (Q) signature.
1987   *10.75in (27cm) high*

£70-100   **SAS**

An American 'Dr. No' one sheet poster, linen-backed.
1962 *41in (102cm) high*
£1,200-1,800 **ATM**

An American 'From Russia with Love', one sheet poster, linen-backed.

This was chosen as the second 007 film after President John F. Kennedy listed the book among his top ten favourite novels.
1964 *40in (101.5cm) high*
£600-900 **ATM**

An Italian 'Dalla Russia Con Amore' ('From Russia With Love') locandino poster, linen-backed.
1964 *26.75in (68cm) wide*
£200-300 **ON**

An American 'Goldfinger' one sheet poster, linen-backed.
1965 *41in (104cm) high*
£1,200-1,500 **P**

An American 'Diamonds Are Forever' three sheet poster produced for the foreign market, with blue ink Dutch stamp, with folds and minor holes, dated.
1971 *74.75in (190cm) high*
£120-180 **SAS**

A CLOSER LOOK AT A JAMES BOND POSTER

It was designed by notable poster artists Robert McGinnis (b.1926) and Frank McCarthy (1924-2002), who designed a number of Bond posters, with McGinnis also designing the famous 'Breakfast At Tiffany's' poster.

This scene, with Bond taking a bath with exotic women, is the desirable style C version of the poster.

Style A shows Blofeld's volcano lair from the film, and Style B featured Bond's 'Little Nellie' mini-helicopter in a mid-air fight.

International versions of this poster usually used the Little Nellie image, with only a few exceptions.

A British 'You Only Live Twice', style 'C' one sheet poster, linen-backed.
1967 *40in (101.5cm) high*
£1,000-1,500 **ATM**

A Corgi James Bond silver Aston Martin, no.270, with gold bumpers, revolving number plates and tyre slashers, in excellent condition, with unopened packet, in good condition original window box.

This type of box is particularly scarce, and the envelope of accessories is unopened – both contribute to the price.
1968-73

£300-500   SAS

A Corgi James Bond silver Aston Martin, no.270, with lapel badge, unused number plate labels, instructions and spare assassin, in excellent condition, in excellent condition original striped window box.
1973-76

£250-300   SAS

A Corgi James Bond Lotus Esprit, no.269, with nine rockets on sprue, in excellent condition, in very good condition original box.
1977-83

£40-60   SAS

A CLOSER LOOK AT A CORGI ASTON MARTIN

This model is complete with all its accessories, including the spare assassin and the sticky lapel badge, which was usually used and lost.

It is important that the model, box, and accessories are all in the best condition possible.

This was released to coincide with the release of 'Goldfinger' in 1964 and dominated Christmas sales in December 1965.

It also includes the catalogue, which indicates an early example from the four year production run.

A Corgi James Bond gold Aston Martin DB5, no.261, with two assassins, lapel badge, instructions, packets, with 'Car Makers To James Bond' catalogue, in very good condition with original box in very good condition.
1965-69

£180-220   SAS

A Corgi James Bond CC07505 'Die Another Day' Aston Martin Vanquish, in original box, signed by Barbara Broccoli and Michael G. Wilson.

c2003

£1,000-1,500   SAS

A Corgi Rockets D928 James Bond 'On Her Majesty's Secret Service' Spectre Mercedes-Benz 280 SL, in unopened vacuform packaging.

1970-72

£250-300   SAS

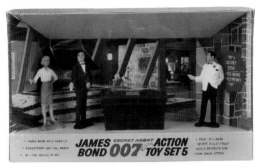

An A.C. Gilbert James Bond 'Action Toy Set 5', no.16565, in excellent condition, in original box.

£70-100   SAS

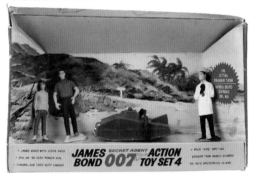

An A.C. Gilbert James Bond 'Action Toy Set 4', no.16564, in original box, lacking cellophane, one ankle fractured.

£35-45   SAS

QUICK REFERENCE - A.C. GILBERT & JAMES BOND

The A.C. Gilbert Co. was founded in 1909 and grew to be one of the largest American toys companies. It is best known for its Erector Set, similar to Britain's Meccano, and also produced model trains. After the death of founder Alfred Gilbert in 1961, the company struggled financially but won the license to produce James Bond toys in 1965. A large number of figures and toys were produced, and are hotly sought after by collectors today. In 1966, the company's fortunes took a turn for the worst when large numbers of their hastily produced 'James Bond Road Race Set' were returned to retailer Sears due to poor quality. In 1967, they went out of business, and lost the license, with companies such as Mego stepping in to create licensed Bond toys. This desirable set contains all ten small figurines produced by Gilbert and is complete with the speargun, rifle and breathing tank accessories, which are often lost.

An A.C. Gilbert James Bond 'Ten Movie Characters' set, no.16525, in excellent condition, in original box.

£120-180   SAS

An A.C. Gilbert James Bond figurine.

This figurine is from the boxed sets also shown on this page. When the Gilbert company went bankrupt, all remaining stocks were sold off by Sears individually or in sets, usually without the original boxes.

3.5in (9cm) high

£7-11   KNK

A late 1960s A.C. Gilbert James Bond Auric Goldfinger figurine.

3.25in (8.5cm) high

£6-9   KNK

A Triang TG4 James Bond 'Thunderball' '007 Underwater Battle Game', with frogmen figures, strip catalogue, in excellent condition in fair condition original box.

£350-450   SAS

JAMES BOND

An American MB Games 'James Bond 007 Secret Agent' game, with original box in very good condition.

c1964   19in (48cm) wide

£70-100   **NOR**

An Australian Milton Bradley 'James Bond 007 Thunderball' game.

c1966   19in (48cm) wide

£40-60   **GAZE**

A Spears 'James Bond 007 Secret Service Game' board game, in excellent condition, in very good condition box.

1966   19in (48cm) wide

£15-25   **SAS**

A late 1960s Jumbo Games 'James Bond 007' game, with instructions in Dutch, in original 'snakeskin' look attaché case box, some graffiti.

£25-35   **SAS**

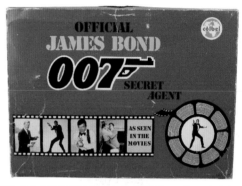

A 1980s Coibel 186 'Official James Bond 007 Secret Agent Set', in original box.

£180-220   **SAS**

An Arrows 'James Bond Thunderball' jigsaw, in near mint to mint complete condition, in good condition picture boxes.

c1966

£70-100   **VEC**

A Multiple Toymakers James Bond 'Bond-X Automatic Shooting Camera', no.3021, in worn original box.

Multiple Toymakers made a number of James Bond toys and were a major producer of toys in the 1970s.

A Lone Star James Bond 'Super Action Set', no.1210, in excellent condition in original window box.

1973

£300-500   **SAS**

1966

£350-450   **SAS**

QUICK REFERENCE

- Interest in marbles is increasing as yesterday's children become today's collectors. Collectable marbles can be divided into three groups: handmade, machine-made and artist marbles.
- The earliest marbles were handmade, primarily in Germany from the 1860s to the 1920s. M. F. Christensen developed a marble-making machine in 1905, and companies in the USA began to produce machine-made marbles. Production of this sort of marble peaked in the 1920s and 1930s.
- Handmade marbles can be identified by the presence of rough pontil marks, where they were broken away from the glass rod to form a sphere. Rarer marbles such as the opaque Indians and 'sulphides' (which have internal white porcelain-like forms) are the most sought after, as are large marbles and those in truly mint condition. Handmade marbles are typically the most desirable, but they have become so hard to find and valuable that many collectors' interest has shifted to the best machine-made marbles.
- By the 1950s and 1960s, poorer quality machine-made marbles, such as 'cat's eyes', were being produced in large numbers. These are generally of little interest to collectors.

- Machine-made marbles have no pontil mark. Makers to look out for are Christensen Agate (1905-1917) and the largest USA producer, Akro Agate, which produced marbles from 1910 until 1951, when the factory closed.
- Several artists, including Mark Matthews, still produce contemporary pieces, which are often collectable. Many are made from dichroic glass, which contains micro-layers of metal oxide, creating an iridescent effect. When viewed from different angles and under different lighting conditions, the marble's colours appear to shift and change.
- The type of marble affects value: pattern, colour and size are important, with symmetry in design, and unusual or very bright colours typically popular with collectors. 'Eye appeal' will also determine value, as what may appeal to one collector may not appeal to another. Mint condition marbles can often be worth twice as much as a damaged version. Chips, scuffs, marks and wear will reduce value, particularly of machine-made marbles. Chips are less important on handmade-marbles, unless the pattern is affected. Packaging can also be desirable, as so much was thrown away.

A German handmade solid core 'lobed swirl' marble.

c1860-c1920   0.75in (2cm) diam

£30-40   AB

An American Akro Agate Company 'Popeye Corkscrew' machine-made marble.

c1927-35   0.5in (1.5cm) diam

£15-25   AB

A German handmade 'Mist' marble, with translucent and transparent blue and yellow strands over a transparent core.

Note the rough top area of the marble, which shows where it was broken off the rod before being formed and finished.

c1860-c1920   0.5in (1.5cm) diam

£30-40   AB

An American Peltier Glass Company National Line Rainbo 'Burnt Christmas Tree' machine-made marble.

c1925-32   0.5in (1.5cm) diam

£60-100   AB

An American Champion Agate Company Furnace 'Scraping Swirl' machine-made marble.

c1980-1990   0.5in (1.5cm) diam

£15-25   AB

An American Christensen Agate Company 'Bloodie' machine-made marble.

c1927-28   0.5in (1.5cm) diam

£25-35   AB

An Eddie Seese six-panel swirl marble, with alternating bands of dichroic glass and multicoloured swirling bands over a cobalt blue ground, signed.

1.5in (4cm) diam

£40-60   **BGL**

A Shane Caswell dichroic blue and green 'vortex' marble, the back with torchwork 'rake pull' decoration, signed.

1.75in (4.5cm) diam

£30-40   **BGL**

A Francis Coupal limited edition floral marble, with stretched and pulled murrine canes, signed.

2in (5cm) diam

£200-300   **BGL**

A Bobbie Seese multicoloured Onionskin marble, with pulled multicoloured caned and dichroic glass over an opaque white base, signed.

1.75in (4.5cm) diam

£40-60   **BGL**

A CLOSER LOOK AT A JOSH SIMPSON MARBLE

Simpson's immensely popular 'Planet' range began in 1976 when he was demonstrating glassmaking to school children, who reacted better to stories about imaginary planets than to goblets and vases.

Traditional techniques associated with Murano glass, such as ' millefiori' and sections of twisted 'filigrana' canes, are combined with more modern innovations such as dichroic glass.

Each element is hand-applied, making every planet unique and creating complex patterns mimicking land masses, deep seas and even cities that draw the eye in.

The presence of an 'orbiting spaceship', here a section of ' filigrana' cane, show that this planet is 'inhabited'.

A Josh Simpson 'Inhabited Planet' marble, containing canes, murrines, dichroic 'gold glass' and a 'spaceship' on a blue ground, signed.

1.75in (4.5cm)

£120-180   **BGL**

A Julie Powell translucent purple marble, with a hand-painted overlay of a hummingbird, flowers and leaves, signed.

Powell designed Fenton glass before she began producing these unique works.

1.5in (4cm) diam

£60-80   **BGL**

A Milon Townsend studio glass sphere or marble, with lampworked three-dimensional horse and paddock enclosed within colourless glass.

Townsend is a key American studio glass artist, who specialises in lampworked designs. This piece crosses the boundary between studio glass and contemporary marble making. His marbles containing human figural forms are particularly sought after.

1.5in (4cm) diam

£100-120   **BGL**

QUICK REFERENCE – CONRAH

The Conrah range was designed by Ronald Hughes in 1967, and produced in south Wales during the 1970s. The range of vases, bowls and candlesticks was made from anodised aluminium in bright colours, which were cut through by machine, leaving reflective sparkling geometric patterns arranged in wide bands around the bodies. Fine lines may also be found in addition to the main pattern. Often misread as 'Conran', marks were tooled or printed on to a plastic disc set into the base. The range was also known as 'Cristillium'. Currently, prices and understanding of the area are low, but this may change as the vases are both visually appealing and typical of the time they were produced. Avoid scratched, and especially dented, examples as damage is impossible to restore.

A Conrah green anodised aluminium large cylinder vase, cut with faceted lozenge motifs, the base with inset black plastic Conrah mark.

10in (25.5cm) high

£60-80   GC

A Conrah pink anodised aluminium large cylinder vase, cut with a faceted lattice design, the base with inscribed Conrah mark.

10in (25.5cm) high

£60-80   GC

A Conrah gold-finish anodised aluminium small cylinder vase, cut with a faceted lattice design, the base with inset black plastic Conrah mark.

8in (20.5cm) high

£30-40   GC

A 1970s Conrah anodised aluminium medium cylinder vase, finely cut with horizontal lines and cut with faceted lozenge shapes, the base with inset plastic disc.

9in (23cm) high

£60-80   GC

A Conrah black anodised aluminium candlestick, cut with a faceted lattice design, the base with inset black plastic Cristillium mark.

6.75in (17cm) high

£20-25   GC

A Conrah blue anodised aluminium flower pot, cut with a faceted lattice design, the base with inset black plastic Conrah mark.

3.75in (9.5cm) high

£15-20   GC

A Conrah black anodised aluminium bowl, cut with a faceted lattice design, the base with inset black plastic Conrah mark.

5.25in (13cm) diam

£20-25   GC

QUICK REFERENCE – VINERS & STUART DEVLIN

Stuart Devlin (b.1931) is one of the most innovative British silversmiths and metalworkers of the late 20thC, and was awarded a Royal Warrant in 1982. He is best known for his silver and gold designs, which contrast shiny silver with textured gold areas. Viners commissioned Devlin to produce a range of stainless steel tableware in the early 1970s, following the success of, among others, Robert Welch's stainless steel designs for Old Hall. Nine shapes were produced, including the iconic spherical 'rose bowl' below, which was said to have been inspired by the 1969 moon landing. A limited number of pieces were produced in solid silver, but are very rare today. The range was phased out in 1979, and prices are much more affordable than for his solid silver and gold designs, allowing collectors to buy into the classic Devlin look at a much lower price.

A 1970s Viners 'Devlin Collection' stainless steel and gold plated metal tall wine goblet, designed by Stuart Devlin, the base with inset plastic disc.

7in (18cm) high

£25-35   **GC**

A 1970s Viners 'Devlin Collection' stainless steel and gold plated metal champagne goblet, designed by Stuart Devlin, the base with inset plastic disc.

4.5in (11.5cm) high

£15-20   **GC**

A 1970s Viners stainless steel and gold-plated metal candleholder, designed by Stuart Devlin, the base with inset plastic disc.

£20-30   **GC**

A 1970s Viners 'Devlin Collection' stainless steel and gold-plated metal nut dishes or candleholders, designed by Stuart Devlin.

5in (13cm) diam

£20-30   **GC**

A 1970s Viners 'Devlin Collection' stainless steel and gold-plated metal small wine or water goblet, designed by Stuart Devlin, the base with inset plastic disc.

5.25in (13.5cm) high

£25-35   **GC**

A 1970s Viners 'Devlin Collection' stainless steel and gold-plated metal 'Violet Bowl', designed by Stuart Devlin, with pull-off, friction fit textured, domed top.

3.25in (8cm) high

£40-50   **GC**

QUICK REFERENCE – OLD HALL

Old Hall stainless steel tablewares were produced by J. & J. Wiggin Ltd from 1934-84, and have become highly collectable. The mark can help to date a piece: 'Staybrite' marks date from before WWII, 'Olde Hall' was used from 1928-59, 'Ye Olde Hall' in 1934-35 only, with 'Old Hall' being used from 1959-84. Pieces designed by Robert Welch after 1955 are perhaps the most desirable today due to their fashionable modern styling, but look out for pre-war designs such as those by Dr Harold Stabler. Quality was very high and ranges to look out for include 'Cottage', 'Avon', 'Alveston' and 'Campden'.

An Olde Hall 'Cottage' range stainless steel one-pint teapot, with 'Staycool' handle, designed by Nellie Wiggin, the base with registered design no.828398 for 1938.

1938-59   *6in (15cm) high*

£25-30   **GC**

A 1950s Olde Hall honey or conserve pot, with lid attached to the geometric handle, the base with registered design no.627169 for 1949.

3.5in (9cm) high

£15-20   **GC**

An Old Hall 'Avon' range stainless steel teapot, designed by Robert Welch in 1966, the base with registered no.928252 for 1966.

5.75in (14.5cm) high

£45-50   **GC**

An Old Hall 'Avon' range stainless steel milk jug, designed by Robert Welch in 1966, the base with registered no.928252 for 1966.

4in (10cm) high

£10-15   **GC**

An Old Hall 'Oriana' range stainless steel milk jug, with angled handle, designed by Robert Welch in 1958.

3.5in (9cm) high

£8-12   **GC**

An Old Hall 'Avon' range stainless steel coffee pot, designed by Robert Welch in 1966, the base with registered no.928252 for 1966.

7in (17.5cm) high

£45-50   **GC**

An Old Hall 'Oriana' range stainless steel teapot, with angled handle and 180 degree flip lid, designed by Robert Welch in 1958.

This range was designed for the P&O cruise liner 'Oriana', although examples were also sold commercially. Those produced for use on the ship were marked 'P&O Line' or 'ShipCo' on the base.

5.75in (14.5cm) high

£35-40   **GC**

ORIENTAL

QUICK REFERENCE – OKIMONO

An okimono is the Japanese term given to small or medium sized ornamental objects placed near altars or in the traditional 'tokonoma' display alcove. The name means 'object for placement on display', and okimono are larger than netsuke, which saw their origins as functional toggles in traditional Japanese dress. They are carved in ivory, but may also be found in wood, bronze or stone. The late 19thC until the 1920s saw a boom in the production of okimono, with many being exported to the West. Human figures or animals are the most commonly found subjects, and they may show scenes from Japanese life or mythology. Value is determined by the carver, the skill of the carver, and the subject, size, date and complexity of the piece itself. Those that are well-detailed, with realistic, expressive features are usually the most desirable and valuable.

A Japanese Meiji period ivory okimono of a basket maker, carrying various baskets in both hands and on his back, his clothing decorated with red, green and mother-of-pearl inset roundels, with red seal mark.

5.75in (14.5cm) high

£800-1,200   L&T

A Japanese Meiji period carved ivory figure of a father, feeding grapes to his two small boys, cracks and chips.

10in (25.5cm) high

£280-320   WW

A Japanese late Meiji period one piece carved ivory figure of a hunter, standing with one foot on a cut tree stump, holding a matchlock gun, wearing straw hood and outer jacket and stockings, game birds hanging from his belt, with three character engraved mark on the base.

8in (20.5cm) high

£550-750   TEN

A Japanese one piece carved ivory figure of a poultryman, standing full length and smiling, holding a chick in his upheld right hand, a hen beneath his left arm, a cockerel at his feet, incised two character mark on inset red kakihan.

c1900   *6.75in (17.5cm) high*

£500-700   TEN

A Japanese one piece carved ivory figure group, with bijin standing wearing a kimono and elaborate chignon, the base with inset rectangular kakihan with incised two character mark, and with rustically carved shaped oval wood base.

c1920   *7.25in (18.5cm) high*

£300-500   TEN

A Japanese Meiji period one piece carved ivory mythological scroll painter figurine, a figure of Hotei on horseback appears magically from mist issuing from the scroll, the base with inset red kakihan with incised two character mask.

A kakihan is an artist's mark.

9.25in (23.5cm) high

£250-350   TEN

A Chinese jade carving of an elephant, with three boys scrambling on its back, two holding onto a string of cash, one pouring water out of a cornucopia, a figure to the reverse holding up a tall lingzhi fungus.

3in (7.5cm) high

£120-180   WW

A Chinese pale celadon jade carving of a recumbent hound, its neck twisted and looking back, raised on a wood stand.

In 2009, an 18thC spinach green jade water buffalo made for a Qing dynasty Japanese emperor, and with an all-important impeccable noble provenance, sold for £3.4 million at the same salerooms as this later piece. The quality and expressive nature of a piece of carved jade, together with a cast-iron provenance allowing it to be dated and identified, are key factors for value.

5.5in (14cm) wide

£180-220   WW

A Chinese pale celadon jade carving of a boy, dancing and wearing flowing robes.

2.5in (6.5cm) high

£120-180   WW

A 19thC/20thC Chinese jade Buddhistic lion, with areas of rust coloured stone.

4.25in (11cm) wide

£120-180   WW

A 19thC Chinese bronze censer, cast in relief with scaly dragons highlighted in gold, the base with a Qianlong mark.

6.75in (17cm) wide

£150-250   WW

A 19thC Japanese Meiji period bronze figure of a rat, the crouching animal holding a nut between its front feet, signed to base.

2.75in (6.75cm) high

£400-600   JA

A 17th or 18thC Chinese bronze model of a crouching horned lion dog, baring its teeth.

5.5in (14cm) high

£450-550   WW

PAPERWEIGHTS

A Baccarat pansy paperweight, with a millefiori garland and a star cut base.

c1850   2.5in (6.5cm) diam

£1,000-1,500   **DCP**

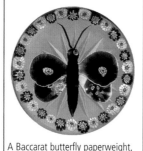

A Baccarat butterfly paperweight, with millefiori wings, surrounded by a millefiori garland, and with a star cut base.

c1850   3in (7.5cm) diam

£1,300-1,600   **DCP**

A Baccarat flat bouquet paperweight, with a pansy, red double clematis and three forget-me-nots.

This contains a larger number of different flowers, hence the higher value. Each element of the flowers was made when the glass was hot, using a 'lampworking' technique. The bunch was encased in colourless glass when finished. The glassmaker had to be skilled enough to ensure no air bubbles are trapped under this layer.

c1850   2.5in (6.5cm) diam

£4,000-5,000   **DCP**

A Baccarat red 'thousand petalled; rose paperweight, with a star cut base.

c1850   3in (7.5cm) diam

£2,500-3,000   **DCP**

A Clichy concentric millefiori paperweight, the petalled design set on an opaque turquoise ground.

c1850   3in (7.5cm) diam

£1,000-1,500   **DCP**

A Clichy swirl paperweight, with an opaque light blue and white swirl emanating from a single large millefioricentral cane.

c1850   3in (7.5cm) diam

£1,300-1,600   **DCP**

A CLOSER LOOK AT A CLICHY PAPERWEIGHT

This is known as a 'barber pole' design due to the blue and white spiral pattern canes, which resemble barber's poles – some collectors call them 'candy cane'.

The design, with its sectioned-off millefiori, is also known as a 'chequer' pattern, and is time-consuming to make.

Clichy is famous for its trademark rose millefiori, of which there are three different examples in this weight.

This example is regular, colourful and well organised, and would have been made by a skilled glassmaker.

A Clichy 'barber pole' chequer paperweight, with three different roses.

c1850   2.75in (7cm) diam

£2,000-3,000   **DCP**

A mid-19thC Clichy 'scramble' paperweight, the jumble of canes including pink, yellow and white roses, some scratching.

'Scramble' designs include many different types and colours of millefiori and canes, arranged and melted together in a random pattern. They tend not to be as valuable as complex set-ups.

2.25in (6cm) diam

£250-350   **WW**

A St. Louis mixed fruit paperweight, with two pears and two cherries, on an opaque white double swirl ground.

c1850   2.75in (7cm) diam

£600-800   **DCP**

A Pantin paperweight with a bunch of grapes and vine leaves on a plain white ground.

c1878   3in (7.5cm) diam

£4,000-5,000   **DCP**

QUICK REFERENCE – ST LOUIS

St Louis was founded in French Alsace-Lorraine in 1767 and, like other French makers, produced paperweights from the mid 19thC. Single flower or fruit designs are typical of its weights, which also often have higher domes than those of its competitors. Swirling white or pink grounds are another hallmark feature. Some weights have been found with date canes, these usually read 1848, with dates of 1845 and 1849 being much rarer.

A 1930s Scottish paper weight, in the style of Paul Ysart for Monart, with a radial star formation of ruffle and cog millefiori canes on a turquoise powder ground, the base with rough pontil.

3in (7.5cm) diam

£180-220   **FLD**

A St. Louis purple dahlia paperweight, with striped petals, a millefiori centre, and green leaves.

c1850   2.25in (6cm) diam

£1,300-1,600   **DCP**

A Liskeard Glass paperweight, with blue internal swirls over a trapped air bubble, designed by John Randle, the base with impressed stamp and dated 1976.

3.25in (8cm) diam

£20-25   **GC**

A Caithness Glass paperweight with opaque multi-coloured internal swirl core under a curtain of trapped air bubbles, the base with acid mark.

The mark on the base is 'CIIG', with the 'II' mark indicating this is a second. Looking closely, there is a piece of grit or other material from the manufacturing process trapped inside.

3.25in (8cm) diam.

£10-15   **GC**

An English Parker 61 'Presidential' 9ct solid gold trio set, comprising capillary-filling pen, twist-action pencil and push action ball-pen, with fine barley pattern, with London hallmark for 1974, in original presentation box, with instructions and two pouches, with original clip labels in place.

Introduced in 1956, the 61 used a special spongey material in a tube to absorb and hold the ink. If clogged with dry ink, they are almost impossible to repair. The solid gold 'Presidential' was the most expensive model in the line.

£1,000-1,500   HSR

An American Parker red Super 21 aerometric-filler, with Lustraloy cap, fine octanium nib, and original nib grade label.
1956

£35-45   HSR

A 1950s-1970s English Parker Teal blue 51 Classic aerometric-filler, with medium nib and Lustraloy cap.

£30-50   PC

A Parker 61 'Heirloom' green pencil, with two-colour 'Heirloom' cap.

This is a very rare cap finish, as it tended to wear away with use and polishing.

£60-80   BPH

A 1950s American Parker 51 'Signet' aerometric-filler and Clutch pencil, with gold-plated barrels and caps.

c1952

£150-200   BPH

A CLOSER LOOK AT A PARKER 51 DEMONSTRATOR

Introduced in 1941, Parker's modern, rocket-shaped 51 was revolutionary – its hooded nib allowed the use of a special, quick drying ink known as 'Quink'.

This example shows Parker's 'Vacumatic' system, which was introduced in 1932 and uses a plunger and diaphragm to create a vacuum in the body, sucking in the ink.

The plastic plunger on this example dates it to after 1941. Examples made from 1948 onwards used Parker's 'Aerometric' squeezable tube system.

Transparent 'Demonstrator' pens were used by pen salesmen to show retailers how the mechanism worked, with shop owners also often using them to show customers.

A Parker 51 Vacumatic Lucite 'Demonstrator' pen, with medium nib and Lustraloy cap.
1945

£150-200   PC

A Parker Lucky Curve 'True Blue' ring-top button-filler, with Canadian Lucky Curve nib.

This example has a very good colour, the white often goes yellow due to the internal rubber ink sac degrading.
1928

A Parker Lucky Curve Pastel Green Moiré ring-top button-filler, with a Lucky Curve nib and engraved barrel.
c1927

£40-60 AMER

A Parker Gold Pearl Vacumatic Standard, with later English Parker nib.
c1942

£120-180 AMER

£150-200 BPH

A Parker Silver Pearl Vacumatic Maxima, with matching cap and barrel end 'jewels', and two-colour Parker Arrow fine nib.

The Maxima was the largest and most expensive model in the Vacumatic series. The partly transparent hallmark ' Vacumatic' striped plastic barrel allowed the ink level to be seen.
c1936

£220-280 HSR

A 1980s French Parker 75 gold plated 'Cisele' convertor/cartridge-filler, in mint condition.

£70-100 BPH

A 1980s Parker 45 'Grey Shield' Harlequin convertor/cartridge-filler, with medium nib.

£30-40 PC

A Parker limited edition 'RMS Queen Elizabeth' convertor/cartridge-filler, numbered 1558 from an edition of 5,000, with fine nib, wooden presentation box, card outer, certificate, instructions, guarantee card, nib adjuster, two cartridges and convertor.

These pens were made from brass taken from the propeller of this luxury liner, which sank in Hong Kong harbour in 1972. Each pen is numbered. Ensure that the accessories are complete and the packaging and certificate bear matching numbers.
1977

£650-750 HSR

A Parker 180 'Bark-finish' silver-plate convertor/cartridge-filler, with two sided gold medium nib, with shop tag, boxed.

£50-80 HSR

A rare early Waterman's chased black hard rubber No.22 'Taper Cap' eyedropper pen, with glass and rubber eyedropper.

c1904

£60-80 PC

A 1910s-20s Waterman's chased black hard rubber no.12 eyedropper, with crisp barrel imprint and Waterman's Ideal no.2 nib, and box, in near mint condition.

£30-50 PC

A Waterman's chased black hard rubber no.12P pump-filler, with Waterman's Ideal Reg US Pat Off 2 nib and added accommodation clip.

Introduced in 1903, this used a piston mechanism to fill the pen. It was not very successful, so was discontinued soon after.

c1904

£100-150 AMER

A 1920s Waterman's chased black hard rubber 42 1/2 V safety pen, with two 9ct gold bands with London hallmarks for 1929 and marked 'F.D.W.', with Watermans Ideal no.2 nib, in excellent condition.

£40-60 PC

A Waterman's red and black 'Woodgrain' mottled hard rubber No. 16 eydropper, with Waterman's Ideal New York no.6 nib.

The final number in a Waterman's model number indicates the size of the nib, and so the size of the pen. A 6 is larger than a 2.

c1915

£180-220 AMER

A CLOSER LOOK AT THE SMALLEST PEN IN THE WORLD

This very rare fully functional miniature pen was made as a display of Waterman's skill, and as a marketing tool in shops, or for travelling salesmen.

It was also made in 'Cardinal' red hard rubber – only five are thought to exist and an example could be worth up to twice this price.

It was also made as a safety pen, with a telescopic nib mechanism – these are extremely rare, and can fetch over 50 per cent more.

It is sometimes called the 'Doll Pen' as an example can be seen in Queen Mary's dolls house, in Windsor Castle, which was made in 1924.

A Waterman's 'Smallest Pen in the World' black hard rubber eyedropper pen, with plain gold nib with circular vent, slit and iridium point, in an original plush and satin lined case, with metal clasp.

c1914

Pen 1.5in (4cm) long

£2,000-2,500 AMER

A 1920s American Waterman's red and black Ripple no.42 safety pen, with Italian scrolling hexagonal gold-plated overlay, and Waterman's no.2 nib.

£200-300   PC

A 1920s Italian Waterman's rolled gold overlaid no.42 safety pen, with alternating engine turned, wavy line and plain panels, ivy motif barrel and cap band, marked 'Waterman's Ideal 18KR' with a Waterman's No.2 nib, initialled and dated by turning screw.

Most Waterman safety pens with fancy rolled gold overlays marked as this example were made in Italy.

£300-400   AMER

An American Waterman's no.0552 lever-filler, with gold filled 'Pansy Panel' overlay and Waterman's Canada no.2 Ideal nib.

c1925

£200-250   HSR

A Waterman's black hard rubber 552 lever-filler, with 9ct gold 'Gothic' overlay with London hallmarks for 1923 and marked F.D.W., with Waterman's no.2 Ideal nib, the barrel with engraved name.

Engraved names and initials usually reduce desirability, unless the name is famous, or the initials are exceptionally beautiful.

1923

£120-180   AMER

A 1920s Waterman's red and black 'Ripple' hard rubber no.52V lever-filler, with ring-top cap, and fine Waterman's Ideal no.2 nib.

£200-250   PENF

A Waterman's 'Turquoise' Lady Patricia lever-filler, with gold plated trim, initialled and dated, with Canadian Waterman's no.2 nib.

This is a scarce colour in excellent condition.

c1932

£100-150   AMER

QUICK REFERENCE – WATERMAN'S RIPPLE SERIES

With its bright orange colour, the 1921 Parker Duofold revolutionised pen design at a time when most pens were black. In answer to this, Waterman's released its 'Ripple' range in 1923. The pattern on each pen is unique due to the way the plastics were mixed. Resistant to staining, colours comprised orangey red and black, green and blue, and red and tan. Produced until the 1930s, they are popular with collectors today. Look out for the scarce no.5 and no.7 series, which were fitted with special nibs for specific tasks such as 'stiff fine' for accountants. The different nib grades were indicated by coloured cap bands.

A Canadian Waterman's no.56 red and black Ripple hard rubber lever-filler, with matching Ripple feed and Waterman's New York no.6 nib, with replaced lever.

c1923

£220-280   HSR

A 1920s Conway Stewart red and black mottled hard rubber Lady-sized lever-filler, with Conway Stewart 14ct nib.

£60-80   BPH

A Conway Stewart no.388 light and dark pink pearl and black marbled lever-filler, with a medium 14ct Conway Stewart nib.
c1939

£50-80   HSR

A 1920s Conway Stewart black hard rubber 'The Duro' lever-filler, with early lever and clip, and medium Conway Stewart 14ct nib.

The large size of this pen adds to its desirability.

£220-280   BPH

QUICK REFERENCE – THE 'CRACKED ICE' SERIES

The 1930s and the 1950s saw Conway Stewart using a wide variety of different types of coloured plastic for their pens. Marbled plastics are the most common, and alternatives sometimes very scarce. Perhaps the most desirable is this black plastic shot through with silver veins, which has been dubbed the 'Cracked Ice' by collectors. Larger-sized examples with evenly distributed, bright silver veins will be more desirable than those with duller, uneven veins. Version from the 1950s, recognised by their tapered ends, are often brighter and more visually appealing. Also look out for the rare 'Reverse Cracked Ice' plastic, with silver marbling shot through with black veins, as these can fetch around 25 per cent more.

A Conway Stewart No. 22 'Floral' lever-filler, with Conway Stewart no.5 nib.

The pattern is printed on paper, sandwiched between two layers of celluloid. Over time, the paper discolours from cream to yellow, reducing the value. It was generally believed that this pen had a limited production run of 200 examples, but this is not true, although it is hard to find.

A Conway Stewart no.15 black veined light and dark green pearl lever-filler, with a medium 14ct Conway Stewart nib.
c1953

£40-60   HSR

£120-180   PC

A 1930s Conway Stewart No.475 'Cracked Ice' celluloid lever-filler, with a medium Conway Stewart 14ct nib.

£120-180   BPH

A De La Rue 'Onoto' chased black hard rubber Self-Filling Pen, with four wide gold bands, one with initials, with Onoto medium nib.
c1912

£50-80 AMER

A De La Rue 'Onoto The Pen' Regina blue plunger-filler, with wide oblique Onoto no.3 nib.
c1935

£80-120 AMER

An De La Rue 'Onoto The Pen' No.3234 burgundy pearl and black marbled plunger-filler, with Onoto medium no.5 two tone nib.

These handsome and elegant marbled pens, dating from the 1940s and early 1950s, are of high quality and have become very desirable over the past few years.
c1948

£120-180 HSR

A De La Rue Onoto 'Magna' No.1873 piston-filler, with engine-turned wavy line decoration and Onoto two-tone no.7 nib, in excellent condition.

As its name suggests, the 'Magna' was De La Rue's largest standard production pen, and is sought after today. The hallmark plunger mechanism and 'Onoto' brand name were developed in 1905. The name Onoto was chosen because it had no meaning and the pronunciation was similar in all languages.
c1947

£250-350 PC

A De La Rue 'Onoto' green pearl and black marble lever-filler, with Onoto fine no.3ST nib.
c1950

£60-90 HSR

A 1920s Sheaffer 'Secretary' bright red flat top lever-filler, stamped 'C' on the barrel end, with a Sheaffer Secretary nib.

£80-120   AMER

A 1950s Sheaffer green Sentinel snorkel-filler, with silver tone cap, and Sheaffer two-colour 14k nib.

£40-60   BPH

c1930

£80-120

A Sheaffer Balance pearl and black lever-filler, with ring-top cap, and Sheaffer two-tone 15k nib.

     BPH

QUICK REFERENCE – SHEAFFER'S PFM

PFM stands for 'Pen For Men', and is often said to have been the last great design of the golden age of the fountain pen. Introduced in 1959, it came in five different models, ranging from the PFM I, with a plastic barrel, stainless steel clip and palladium silver nib, upwards. All were set with Sheaffer's new 'inlaid' nib that has since become a hallmark of the company. Despite being popular with collectors today, it was not successful at the time. By 1963, the range was cut down to the III and V, and the model was phased out in 1968. This PFM V fountain pen retailed at £15 in 1959, and was marketed as having a 'man-sized barrel' with 'the only inlaid point in the world...built to take man-sized pressure'.

An American Sheaffer PFM V snorkel-filler, with gold-filled cap and burgundy barrel, and medium Sheaffer 14K inlaid nib.

1955

£60-90   HSR

A 1980s Sheaffer Targa convertor/cartridge-filler, with 18k Sheaffer inset nib.

£100-150   BPH

An American Sheaffer PFM V blue snorkel-filler and ballpen set, with gold-filled caps, and with Sheaffer fine 14ct inlaid nib.

1959-68

£200-250   HSR

A Sheaffer limited edition Lifetime Balance lever-filler, from an edition of 6,000.

This is a faithful copy of Sheaffer's 1929 Balance pen.

1997

£500-700   PC

An English Mabie Todd & Co. Swan chased black hard rubber eyedropper 'Chatelaine' pen, with scroll embossed gold-plated cap and barrel ends and chain.

c1905

£80-120 PC

A Mabie, Todd & Co. Swan black hard rubber eyedropper pen, with gold-filled scrolling filigree overlay, metal overfeed and a medium flexible Mabie, Todd & Co. nib, the barrel engraved 'H.H.S'.

It is rare to find Swan pens with gold-plated filigree overlays from this period in such excellent condition.

c1910

£320-380 HSR

A late 1920s Mabie, Todd & Co. Swan Eternal no.644B/61 red and black mottled hard rubber lever-filling pen, with Swan no.8 nib.

This is a scarce large no.8 size pen, and is highly desirable.

£200-300 PC

Two Mabie Todd & Co 'Blackbird' lever-filling pens one in green, the other in blue, in mint condition, with original price bands.

c1948

£50-80 BPH

A Mabie Todd & Co 'Blackbird' red lever-filler, with Blackbird nib and period box.

The Blackbird range was the company's mid-range brand, and was sold at more affordable prices. This bright, pillar box red is the rarest colour in the series.

c1948

£50-70 BPH

A CLOSER LOOK AT A SWAN PEN SET

Swan's Leverless pens were introduced in 1932 and were filled by twisting the bottom part of the barrel, which moved an internal metal bar to compress the ink sack and draw in ink when released.

This model is rare, and it is even harder to find a pen and pencil set in such excellent condition.

The Art Deco styling with its flat-top, which is typical of the period, and repeated gold plated band design, is appealing.

The pen became even more desirable after it was featured on the cover of the landmark book 'Fountain Pens Vintage & Modern' by Andreas Lambrou.

A Mabie Todd Swan no.275/60 Leverless pen and Fyne Poynt pencil set, with rolled gold overlay and bands to cap and barrel, with broad Swan no.2 nib.

c1934

£400-500 HSR

A 1920s Montblanc smooth black hard rubber 4B safety pen, with Montblanc 14ct no.4 nib.

The barrel is marked Simplo, which was the original brand name used by the company founded in Hamburg, Germany in 1908 that became Montblanc. Many early Montblanc, and all Simplo 'Rouge et Noir' pens were safety pens.

£300-400   AMER

A 1930s Montblanc 333 1/2 EF black celluloid piston-filler, with plain ink window and Montblanc 3 1/2 14ct nib, in excellent condition.

£200-300   AMER

A 1950s Montblanc Meisterstück 144G-F black celluloid piston-filler, with striped ink window and two-colour Montblanc 14ct fine nib.

£150-200   AMER

A Montblanc 254 black celluloid piston-filling pen, with gold plated trim, clear ink window and Montblanc medium 14ct nib. *c1955*

£70-100   PC

A Montblanc 'Peter I The Great' fountain pen, numbered 412 from a limited edition of 888, in dark green resin with white gold overlay, the cap top set with emeralds, with a Montblanc 18k medium nib, in presentation box, with paperwork and card outer box.

Montblanc has become known for its limited-edition pens, which must be in unused, mint condition and complete with their boxes and paperwork to fetch high values. This was the sixth pen in the 'Patrons of Art' series. A version with a gold-plated overlay was made in an edition size of 4810, which corresponds with the height of Mont Blanc in metres.
1997

£2,000-2,500   AMER

A CLOSER LOOK AT A MONTBLANC PEN

This rare and unusual model is not recorded in any Montblanc reference book. The steel nib and brass trim indicate that this was a budget 3-series pen.

Montblanc often sold branded components, such as nibs, to factories in countries such as Spain, Denmark and Italy, where they would be assembled.

Spanish and Italian examples are often marked with the country of manufacture, but this simply bears the Montblanc cap star and the Montblanc name and mountain logo.

It is likely that this was made in France, as the size, clip style, and torpedo shape bear similarities to pens made in France at the time.

A 1940s probably French Montblanc black celluloid button-filler, with brass trim and a medium-oblique Montblanc no.3 steel nib.

£100-150   PC

A rare 18thC rootwood inkhorn, with screw-off cover over the inkwell, and screw-off base with pierced wooden plate for pounce, in excellent condition.

Pounce was a powder sprinkled over a newly written document to dry the ink. Once it was dry, the pounce was poured back into its container.

3.5in (9cm) high

£100-150   **BLO**

An unusual late 19thC spelter inkwell, probably Scandinavian, the hinged cover with mask of a Green Man, the body decorated with female heads at each corner, lion maks and floral garlands, the legs decorated with lion masks and pad feet, with ceramic liner.

4in (10cm) wide

£70-90   **BLO**

A German Soennecken black hard rubber füllflacshe (inkflask) Nr 902, in original card box, together with a Montblanc-style black hard rubber inkbottle with cracked cap and oxidation.

c1920

£70-100   **BLO**

A rare English travelling writing compendium, the rectangular red morocco leather case in two parts to hold quill pens, with a Sheffield Plate inkwell with screw-off cover, and a similar pounce pot, in excellent condition.

c1810-20   *7.25in (18.5cm) long closed*

£350-450   **BLO**

A 1920-1930s Stephens' travelling ink bottle case, the top embossed 'Stephens', with an empty bottle of Stephens red ink.

£20-30   **PC**

A 1980s English Parker Duofold-style ceramic oversized display pen, with lift-off lid.

These were also used as counter top displays in shop.

£20-30   **PC**

A 'Parker Quink Ink' ceramic jar, designed by Hobbs Welch, with printed mark and Design Centre paper label.

Modelled on the famous Quink bottle, these were typically used as countertop displays and storage jars in shops. This is a particularly strong price for one of these, as they often fetch around half this price or under. Always look out for cracks, as they were easily damaged.

c1982   *7.75in (20cm) high*

£70-100   **WW**

PLASTICS AND BAKELITE

QUICK REFERENCE – BAKELITE

- In 1907 Belgian chemist Dr Leo Baekeland developed the first entirely synthetic plastic, known as Bakelite. Cheap to produce and extremely versatile, it became known as 'the material of 1,000 uses' and was used both in industry and for decorative and functional purposes in the home.
- Bakelite was produced in a range of different colours with black and brown being the most common. Rarer colours were red, green and blue.
- The development of Bakelite prompted a boom in the plastics industry that led to many variants being produced. Although these are slightly different materials, the name 'bakelite' is commonly used to refer to many early plastics.

A 1920s Linsden multicoloured mottled Bakelite box, with revolving compartmentalised tray, the base moulded 'Linsden'.

These can also be found in mottled brown Bakelite, which is less desirable. This example is unfaded, with even the outside retaining its variety of strong colours. The Bakelite around the metal pins that allows the panel to revolve, and between the top and sides, is also not damaged. Although it is often mistaken for a stationery box, this was actually a smoker's companion.

3.75in (9.5cm) high

£30-50 P&I

A 1930s brown Bakelite inkwell and pen box, marked 'INSURE WITH THE BRITISH GENERAL INSURANCE COMPANY'.

The well proportioned, rounded form is particularly well made.

6in (15.5cm) long

£50-60 P&I

A rare 1930s Bonbons Martougin mottled brown Bakelite box, the top with moulded head of Minerva.

6.25in (15.5cm) diam

£70-100 P&I

A 1960s-70s German Helit '11 Sinus' orange Melamine stacking ashtray, designed by Walter Zeischegg in 1966, the base moulded 'HELIT 84005 MADE IN GERMANY'.

This famous ashtray can be found in a range of colours, and the form was also produced in Bakelite by Kartro in Brazil. Walter Zeischegg (1917-1983) studied sculpture in Vienna, and was one of the founders and lecturers of the Ulm School of Design. Devoting himself to design from 1950 onwards, he followed the work of Max Bill and worked with Carl Aubock, before designing primarily for Helit.

5.25in (13cm) diam

£10-15 M20C

Four 1970s Pentagram stacking and interlocking plastic dishes or ashtrays, the bases moulded 'DO REG.NO.954,589 PENTAGRAM'.

The design registration number dates from late 1971.

4.25in (10.5cm) diam

£20-25 EACH M20C

A rare brown Bakelite miniature quaitch, marked 'MADE IN SCOTLAND'.

Scottish-made Bakelite is scarce.

4.25in (11cm) long

£8-12 P&I

A French Art Nouveau glamour postcard, by Raphael Kirchner.

£40-60 MCS

A comic postcard, by Donald McGill.

£4-5 MCS

A 'The Bully' cat postcard, by Louis Wain.

Louis Wain (1860-1939) was an English artist, known for his illustrations of cats with personality. In 1917, he began to suffer from schizophrenia and was admitted to a mental hospital in 1924.

5in (12.5cm) high.

£25-35 M&C

A hand embroidered silk postcard, of the kind made by Second World War troops.

£5-7 MCS

A black and white photographic postcard, depicting the Cairngorm Mountains, from The Best of All Series, published by J. B. White, Dundee.

50P-£1 SOR

QUICK REFERENCE

- Promotional film posters come in many shapes and sizes, ranging from small glossy stills for display inside cinemas to 24-sheet billposters. The most popular of these are the more easily displayed US one-sheet 27in (68.5cm) by 41in (104cm) size and the UK quad 30in (76cm) by 40in (84cm) size.

- Posters for popular films, classic and cult favourites are usually desirable, particularly those with an appealing image or style. Little-known films are generally less sought after, unless the poster was created by a famous artist, such as Robert Peal, Giuliano Nistri or Saul Bass.

- Different promotional posters are produced for each country the film is released in. Apart from being in a foreign language, they can also have different artwork and vary from the original in other ways. For example, Belgian posters tend to be smaller but often have visually stunning artwork, while Australian posters are larger but sometimes have weaker artwork. In general, you should look out for original posters

produced for the film's country of origin, as these are usually most popular.

- Posters may be re-issued if a film is re-released or has won an award, or following its release on video or DVD. These re-releases should not be confused with the originals, which are usually more valuable. Reproductions (photographic images of the original, printed on shiny poster paper) are also common, as are fakes. In forged or reproduced posters, the image may be pixelated or in different tones of colour. The best way to avoid buying a fake is to gain familiarity with originals from reputable dealers or auction houses.

- Condition is important, with folding, tears and stains reducing value, particularly if the surface of the image is affected. However, mint condition examples can be hard to find, and some damage can be restored. Posters can also be professionally backed onto linen or other materials. This does not reduce value and can enhance desirability.

'A Bigger Splash', by David Hockney (b.1937), printed by Nonsdale & Bartholomew, Nottingham, original UK quad, in near mint condition, linen-backed.

1974   40in (102cm) wide

£200-300   BLNY

'Batman', American one sheet, framed and glazed, in very good condition.

1966   40in (101.5cm) high

£500-750   MAS

'A Clockwork Orange', designed by Philip Castle, printed by W.E. Barry, Ltd., Bradford, original UK quad, linen-backed.

1971   40in (102cm)

£300-450   BLNY

'Blow-Up', printed by Rotolito, original Italian due-foglio (two-sheet), linen-backed.

1967   55in (140cm) high

£550-750   BLNY

'Charlie Chan I London', Swedish film poster by Rohman, lithograph in colours printed by J. Olsens, linen-backed.

1934   39in (99cm) high

£300-500   BLNY

'Andy Warhol's Flesh', American one sheet, in near mint condition, linen-backed.

Directed by Joe Morrissey, the controversial 'Flesh' was one of the first general release films to objectify the naked male body, in this case that of the New York hustler, Joe Dallesandro.

1948   47in (119cm) high

1970   *41in (104cm)*

£300-450   **BLNY**

'Jour de Fête', by Rene Péron, French issue for the 16mm release, lithograph in colours, linen-backed.

1948   *47in (119cm) high*

£450-550   **BLNY**

'The Godfather', American one sheet, offset lithograph in black and white, in near mint condition, linen-backed.

1972   *41in (104cm)*

£150-250   **BLNY**

POSTERS

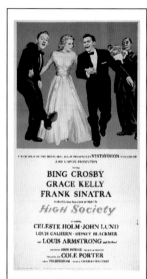

'High Society', by an unknown designer, American one sheet, linen-backed.

1956   *81in (206cm)*

£500-750   **BLNY**

'The Lord of the Rings', British one sheet artists' poster, printed by Berry Ltd, folded.

The first film produced from Tolkien's famous series is best known for its use of 'Rotoscope' animation, where live-action film images are traced over into animation. Although a financial success, it was panned by many critics and the second half was never made.

1978   *40in (101.5cm) wide*

£80-120   **GORL**

'Manhattan', American one sheet, Style B, in near mint condition, linen-backed.

This Style B version is considered scarcer and more desirable than others.

1979   *41in (104cm) high*

£150-200   **BLNY**

'Evanjelium Sv. Matusa' Czech one sheet, by Josef Vyletal, lithograph in colours, linen-backed.

Vyletal is considered a leading and innovative designer, working from the 1960s onwards.

1967   33in (84cm) high
£200-300   BLNY

'Wakacje Pana Hulot' (Mr Hulot's Holiday), by Zbigniew Lengren (1919-2003), original Polish issue, offset lithograph in colours, linen-backed.

1953   33in (84cm)
£350-450   BLNY

QUICK REFERENCE – EASTERN EUROPEAN POSTERS

Poster design from the former Eastern Block, particularly the Czech Republic and Poland, has become highly desirable over the past decade. Innovative artists produced startling designs that often incorporated unusual visual elements, such as photomontage, collage and a dynamic use of composition, colour, perspective and typography. This Russian poster, by the noted Stenberg brothers, is typical. The Stenbergs, who created most of their work in Moscow from 1924-33 following the principles of Russian avant garde art, are considered forerunners of this diverse and increasingly popular style.

'Mabul', by Vladimir & Georgii Stenberg, Russian lithograph in colours, linen backed.
1927   28in (71.5cm) high
£2,000-3,000   BLNY

'Moulin Rouge', by Rosie, East German lithograph poster in colours, linen-backed.

This design clearly uses Toulouse Lautrec as inspiration, a theme that marries up with the title of the film perfectly.

1952   33in (84cm) high
£1,000-1,500   BLNY

'Vecírek' (The Party), Czechoslovakian poster, by an unknown designer, linen-backed.

1970   33in (84cm) high
£150-200   BLNY

'Takoví Jsme Byli' (The Way We Were), by an unknown designer, Czechoslovakian poster, in near mint condition, linen-backed.

1973   33in (84cm)
£150-200   BLNY

QUICK REFERENCE

- By the mid20thC, travel was available and cheap enough to be a viable option for more people than ever before. As more people took holidays, travel posters began to rapidly increase in popularity. The earliest and most prolific of these were ocean-liner and railway company posters, and these continue to be the most popular with collectors. Airlines began to compete commercially with cruise liners from the 1950s onwards and, despite the arrival of television advertising, many appealing and collectable posters were produced during this period.

- Many railway posters did not feature images of trains or railways. Instead, most aimed at luring people away from their everyday lives by displaying brightly-coloured, exotic scenes, unlike any to be seen in the busting city. These included ships, golfing scenes or hotels, and town, seaside an countryside views. Images of green, rolling hills in England tend to be particularly popular with collectors.

- Artwork by popular designers, such as Cassandre (Adolphe Mouron), Frank Brangwyn and Tom Purvis, will usually be desirable, as will major names in travel, such as White Star, BOAC, Air France and Canadian Pacific. However, the 'eye appeal' of the image is often the primary indicator to value, because many buyers will wish to display these posters in their homes. Striking, brightly coloured designs that display the excitement and glamour of travel are desirable, particularly those in popular styles, such as Art Deco or 1950s.

- As aesthetic appeal is paramount, condition is important. Many posters were folded in storage before they became popular collectables, so folds are acceptable and can often easily be removed by a professional restorer. However, tears that extend into the image and any damage that seriously mars the surface of the image will reduce a poster's value and desirability considerably.

'Helensburgh', by Frank H Mason, railway poster printed for LNER by McCorquodale & Co Ltd.

1941   40in (102cm)

£350-450   ON

'North East England Warksworth Castle', railway poster printed for the North Eastern Railways by Albery & Co., with small losses to margins.

40in (102cm) high

£150-200   ON

'Dorset' by Eric Lander, railway poster printed for the Southern Railway (British Rail) by Leonard Ripley & Co Ltd.

40in (102cm) high

£120-180   ON

'Great Western Railway, Sunny South Wales', by an anonymous designer, with vignettes showing golf, tennis, yachting and a map of the system, printed by Felix J Pole.

40in (102cm) high

£250-350   ON

A Longman Facts and Figures 1 Passenger Services poster, printed for BR(WR) by Stafford & Co Ltd.

40in (102cm) high

£150-200   ON

'Brides les Bains', by Leon Benigni, for PLM railways, lithograph in colours, linen-backed.

1929   *39in (99cm) high*

£1,200-1,500   **BLNY**

'Val D'Esquières', by Michel Bouchaud, printed by Lucien Serre & Cie for PLM railways, linen-backed.

c1930   *39in (99cm)*

£1,000-1,500   **BLNY**

A CLOSER LOOK AT A FRENCH RAILWAY POSTER

The flat planes of colour and limited palette recall the work of the famous French Art Deco poster designer Adolphe Mouron, known as 'Cassandre', whose work can fetch thousands of pounds.

The use of the railway, and the sharp angle and sense of perspective it gives, are also hallmarks of Cassandre, and many of the best Art Deco travel posters.

PLM was the Paris to Lyon and the Mediterranean railway. Its appealing posters for desirable holiday spots along its routes are highly sought after.

This poster can be found in three different colourways, this purple, green, and white and light blue – there is little difference in the price.

'Vers le Mont Blanc', by George Dorival, printed by Lucien Serre & Cie for PLM railways, linen-backed.

1928   *41in (104cm) high*

£1,500-2,000   **BLNY**

'Saint Raphaël', by J. Munier, lithograph in colours printed by Moullot for SNCF, linen backed.

As well as railway collectors, this colourful and attractive French poster would also appeal to tennis memorabilia collectors, and posters with this theme are hard to find.

c1925   *39in (100cm) high*

£600-950   **BLNY**

'Paris Tanger Casablanca Par Marseille, Cie de Navigation Paquet', by Hardy, lithograph in colours printed by M. Dechaux for PLM railways, linen-backed.

1933   *39.5in (100cm) high*

£600-950   **BLNY**

'The Ancient Theatre at Arles' by Leopold Lelée, printed by Lucien Serre & cie for PLM railways, with folds.

39.5in (100cm) high

£40-60   **ON**

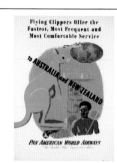

'Pan American World Airways to Australia and New Zealand', by an anonymous designer, lithograph in colours, linen-backed.

c1950   *39.5in (101cm) high*

£450-550   **BLNY**

'Fly BEA to Spain for Silver Wing Holidays', colour photographic poster by an anonymous designer.

c1965   *40in (102cm) high*

£30-40   **ON**

A CLOSER LOOK AT AN AIRLINE POSTER

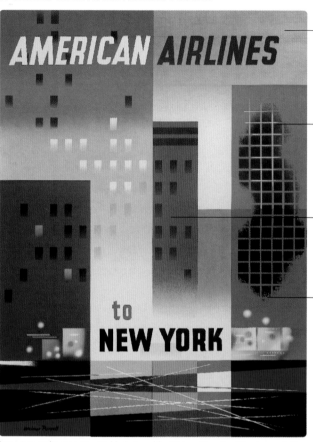

Award-winning artist Weimer Pursell (1906-1974) produced poster designs for major companies including Coca Cola, Standard Oil and American Airlines.

The use of geometric forms and lines in bright colours contrasted against black is typical of Pursell's work, and reflect his interest in modern abstract art.

The abstract forms are buildings in Manhattan, with the lines on the 'pavement' hinting at people going places, or even the subway system.

He is also known for his Art Deco poster designs for the 1933 Chicago World's Fair. His work is sought after and can be hard to find.

'American Airlines to New York', designed by Weimer Pursell, with minor wrinkles.

c1956   *39.75in (101cm) high*

£3,000-5,000   **SWA**

'Pan Am's Supersonic Clipper' photographic poster featuring Concorde, printed in America.

c1965   *111.5in (283cm) wide*

£120-180   **VSA**

'Blue Star Line to South America', by Norman Wilson, lithograph in colours, printed by McCorquodale & Co., London, linen-backed.

c1930   *40in (102cm) high*

£600-950   **BLNY**

'Blue Star Line A Europa', by an anonymous designer, lithograph in colours printed by John Waddington, London, linen-backed.

c1925   *40in (102cm) high*

£1,500-2,000   **BLNY**

'This Is Alaska', by an anonymous designer, lithograph in colours printed for the Alaska Steamship Line, backed on linen.

c1950   *34in (86cm) high*

£300-400   **BLNY**

'Spiez', by Otto Baumberger, lithograph in colours, printed by Fretz & Frères, Zurich, backed on Japan paper.

1938   *40in (102cm) high*

£400-500   **BLNY**

'Route des Pyrènnées, Services d'autocar de la Cie du Midi', by Roger Soubie, printed by Baudelot, with tears, folds and losses.

40.5in (103cm)

£300-400   **ON**

'Roman & Mediaeval France', coaching poster by Lajos Marton, printed by McCorquodale for PLM Autocars.

1935   *39.5in (100cm) high*

£40-60   **ON**

'Avranches Baie de Mont St Michel', by Albert Bergevin for the Avranches Syndicat D'Initiative, lithograph in colours, linen-backed.

Bergevin (1887-1974) lived in Avranches, a hillside town that overlooks the bay of Mont St Michel. The colourful Art Nouveau style, very much inspired by Henri de Toulouse Lautrec, is appealing.

c1920   *42in (107cm) high*

£1,200-1,500   **BLNY**

'Play Golf in Germany', by Osswald, lithograph in colours, printed by Oscar Consee, Munich, linen-backed.

As with the tennis-themed poster on a previous page, the golfing theme adds value to this poster.

1930   *39in (99cm) high*

£800-1,000   **BLNY**

'Coq Sur Mer', tourism poster by Martin Melsen, printed by Henri Melsen, Brussels, linen-backed.

1923   *39in (99cm) high*

£500-700   **BLNY**

QUICK REFERENCE

- Pictorial posters advertising products enjoyed a golden age that began in the late 19thC and lasted for almost a century. The 1920s and 1930s saw particularly innovative posters, as influential and prolific designers pushed boundaries to see what they could create. Although the advent of television largely took over the advertising market, product posters are still sought after today due to their visual appeal and their importance to the 20thC poster and graphic design.

- Always consider the brand and the item depicted. Certain long-lived brands have become 'household names' and these are usually desirable and often valuable as they have a large following of collectors. Meanwhile, posters advertising smoking are becoming more sought-after, partly as a document of social history as the habit becomes less popular. Smoking posters also have cross-market interest (as they appeal to collectors of smoking memorabilia as well as poster collectors), and other products with cross-market interest, such as cars or cycling, may also prove to be desirable. It is also worth considering 1970s posters advertising brands that are now popular. Posters from this era onwards are usually not as highly priced as earlier posters, and may be worth investing in, particularly if nostalgia for the brand grows in the future.

- In general, look for striking images with bold, bright colours, and designs that are typical of the period – Art Nouveau and Art Deco posters are sought after, as are those from the 1950s. A strong design by a notable designer, such as Jean Carlu, Paul Colin or Bernard Villemot, will also be desirable. However, visual appeal is paramount – an attractive poster for an unknown brand will usually prove popular.

- Condition is very important, so avoid those examples with tears and damage. This is particularly true of posters from the 1970s onwards, which you should buy in as close to mint condition as possible.

'Lefèvre-Utile Gaufrettes Vanille', biscuit poster by Alphonse Mucha, lithograph in colours, framed and glazed.

c1890   *8in (20cm) high*

£350-450   **BLNY**

A CLOSER LOOK AT A LEFEVRE-UTILE POSTER

French biscuit maker Lefèvre Utile is a collectable name, particularly designs by notable Art Nouveau designer Alphonse Mucha like the one on the left.

This is a complex and highly detailed image, printed with many different colours and tones, that gives a superb period feel.

Bocchino produced a number of designs for Lefevre-Utile, all with a wholesome feel that has led to him being dubbed the 'Norman Rockwell of the biscuit world'.

'Lefèvre-Utile', by Vincent Bocchino, printed by F. Champenois, Paris, lithograph in colours, in near mint condition, backed on card.

1911   *27in (68cm) wide*

£1,000-1,500   **BLNY**

'Caramel Klaus' by Giovanni Bonfatti, printed by Raimondi & Zaccardi, Milan, in very good condition, linen-backed.

c1920   *55in (140cm) high*

£800-1,200   **BLNY**

'Souriez Madame! C'est du Cleret' by Jean d'Ylen, printed by Vercasson, mounted on linen with restoration.

15.75in (40cm) high

£150-250   **ON**

'Mazawatte Tea', by an unknown designer, printed by Stafford & Co., two sheet poster, lithograph in colours, mint condition, linen-backed.

c1920   *40in (102cm)*

£600-900   **BLNY**

'Monet Goyon', by P.D., printed by Affiches Gaillard, Paris, lithograph in colours, linen-backed.

c1930   *43.5in (110cm) high*

£1,000-1,500   **BLNY**

'Monet Goyon', by P.D., printed by Affiches Gaillard, Paris, lithograph in colours, in near mint condition, linen-backed.

Art Deco and later posters that hint at the speed of cars or motorcycles, as here, are usually highly sought after.

c1930   *44in (112cm)*

£1,200-1,600   **BLNY**

A CLOSER LOOK AT A SHELL POSTER

This is executed in the typical muted colour palette found on many Shell posters of the 1930s-50s, and is titled in the same way as much of the rest of the series.

Mann is not considered one of the most sought after designers in the series, but the angular, abstract and modern style is appealing.

The campaign, aimed at making people drive more, included designs by leading and innovative modern artists including Edward McKnight Kauffer and Hans Schleger.

Cathleen Mann (1896-1959) studied at the notable Slade School of Fine Art and produced a number of designs for Shell, British Petroleum and the London Underground.

'Film Stars use Shell', by Cathleen Mann, printed by The Baynard Press, lithograph in colours, in near mint condition, linen-backed.

1938   *45in (114cm) wide*

£800-1,200   **BLNY**

'Roval Voiture Pratique & Economique' by an anonymous designer, printed by Wall, Paris,, mounted on linen.

40in (102cm) wide

£500-700   **ON**

'Eco-Pneus', by an anonymous designer, lithograph in colours printed by Havas, Caen, linen-backed.

c1930   *46in (117cm) high*

£300-400   **BLNY**

'Pneu-Velo Continental', by an anonymous designer, printed by Editions & Publicité, Paris, linen-backed.

c1910   *30.5in (77cm) high*

£800-1,200   **BLNY**

'Starlight Savon', by Henri Meunier, lithograph in colours, printed by O. de Rycker, Brussels, linen-backed.

1899   34in (87cm) high

£1,000-1,500   **BLNY**

'Ripolin' paint advertising poster, by Jean d'Ylen, printed by Vercasson, mounted on linen with restoration.

29.5in (75cm) high

£400-600   **ON**

'Lord' hat advertising poster, by Paolo Federico Garretto, Alfieri & Lacroix S.A.-Milano, in excellent condition, linen-backed.

1930   36in (91.5cm) high

£150-250   **SAS**

'Splendid' cigar advertising poster, by Fred Neukomm (1905-1988), printed by Kummerly & Frey, Berne, lithograph in colours, linen-backed.

c1930   50in (127cm) high

£800-1,200   **BLNY**

QUICK REFERENCE - BERNARD VILLEMOT

French artist, illustrator and poster designer Bernard Villemot (1911-89) is considered one of the most important French post-war poster designers. He created his first poster for Bally in 1967 and worked with them for 22 years until his death. His first poster, known as 'Legs', won the Martini Prize Gold Medal, and subsequent designs went on to win the Grand Prix for poster design more than five times. This design, released during the peak of his skills, is known as 'Bally Kick'. He also worked for Air France, Orangina, and other companies. Influenced by the Bauhaus, his hallmark style uses flat planes of bold, contrasted colours, thin outlines and stylised abstracted forms. The result is a simple, yet highly feminine image that promotes Bally shoes as being glamourous and modern, and having great flair.

'Bally' shoe advertising poster, by Bernard Villemot, offset lithograph in colours, printed by A. Kacher, Paris, linen-backed.

1972   65in (166cm) high

£300-400   **BLNY**

'Vichy', by Bernard Villemot, lithograph in colours, printed by S.A. Courbet, Paris, linen-backed.

1953   39.5in (100cm) high

£500-600   **BLNY**

QUICK REFERENCE

- One of the first kinds of attractive packaging, these ceramic lids were used to cover pots containing products such as food, bear's grease (a hair product), or toothpaste. They were manufactured in Staffordshire, by companies including F. & R. Pratt, who were granted a related patent in 1848, T. J. & J. Mayer and J. Ridgway.
- The first pot lids were produced in the 1820s, and were transfer printed in blue and white, or black and white. By the 1830s they were being produced in bulk. Coloured lids appeared in the early 1840s. Over 350 images are known, some of which featured bears, which indicated bear's grease in the pot below. Some collectors choose to collect by image type, with bears and scenes of Pegwell Bay most popular.
- Before 1860, lids were flat and lightweight, and had a screw thread. The quality of these early pieces was high, and so they are usually the most desirable. The lids became heavier and convex between 1860 and 1875, and heavier still with flat tops after 1875. It is a good idea to handle as many lids

as you can to get a feel for these weights.
- It is not possible to narrow down the date of most pot lids beyond these periods, as most are not dated and many images were produced for long periods. Examples that commemorate specific event, such as the Great Exhibition in 1851, can be dated c1851 as it is unlikely they were produced for long afterwards. Changes to design and some maker's marks can also help with dating.
- Collectors look for examples in excellent condition or those with unusual variations in design or borders. Always examine a scene carefully to identify any variations. Chips to flange and rim do not seriously affect value, but chips to design can cause a drop of 50-75 per cent. Be aware of reproductions – run your finger over a lid. If you feel the transfer, the piece is likely to be a later reproduction.
- The numbers given are used in K. V. Mortimer's 'Pot Lids Reference & Price Guide', the current standard reference guide for pot lids.

A Staffordshire 'The Volunteers' pot lid, no.217, probably produced by the Bates, Brown-Westhead, Moore & Co. factory from 1859.

£120-180   SAS

A Staffordshire 'The Wolf And The Lamb' pot lid, no.343, produced by the Pratt factory.

4.25in (10.5cm) diam

£25-35   SAS

A Staffordshire 'Our Pets' pot lid, no.330, with glaze flaking, produced by the Pratt factory, with registration diamond for March 1852 near the horse's tail.

4in (10cm) diam

£120-180   SAS

A Staffordshire 'On Guard' pot lid, no.334, with dog under the bench, produced by the Pratt factory.

On some lids, the dog is replaced by a bucket, but this does not usually affect the value.

4.25in (10.5cm) diam

£40-60   SAS

A Staffordshire 'The Snow-drift' pot lid, no.267, with a line and dot border.

The scene was based on Sir Edwin Landseer's oil painting 'Highland Shepherd's Dog In The Snow'.

4.25in (10.5cm) diam

£30-40   SAS

A Staffordshire 'New Houses of Parliament, Westminster' later issue pot lid, no.232, produced by the Pratt factory.

5.25in (13cm) diam

£100-150　　　　SAS

A Staffordshire 'Albert Memorial' pot lid, no.241, produced by the Pratt factory.

This variation with the carriage is slightly less valuable than the one without. Earlier examples have green, rather than brown, trees.

4.25in (10.5cm) diam

£70-90　　　　SAS

A large Staffordshire 'Drayton Manor' pot lid, no.102, with gilt-lined border, produced by the Mayer factory.

Showing the residence of politician and Prime Minister Sir Robert Peel, this lid was reproduced up to the 1960s by Mayer and Kirkhams, explaining its low value.

£50-70　　　SAS

A Staffordshire 'Great Exhibition 1851' pot lid, no.142, produced by the Mayer factory, restored.

4.25in (10.5cm) diam

£40-60　　　　SAS

A Staffordshire 'Windsor Castle and St. George's Chapel' pot lid, no.175, without wording, damaged.

A variation with advertising wording for Royal Windsor Toilet Cream can fetch over five times the price of this damaged example.

3.5in (9.5cm) diam

£60-80　　　SAS

A very rare Staffordshire 'Holy Trinity Church' pot lid, no. 229, with leaf and scroll border, produced by the William Pratt factory, restored.

This is the rarest of the series of lids showing buildings associated with Shakespeare.

5in (13cm) diam

£650-750　　　　SAS

A Staffordshire 'Paris Exhibition 1878' pot lid, no.153, produced by the Pratt factory, with a dotted border and hairline crack.

4.5in (11cm) diam

£40-60　　　　SAS

A Staffordshire 'The Administration Building World's Fair, Chicago 1893' pot lid, no.156, with a grey print.

Look out for other colours such as buff or a yellowy brown as these are extremely rare and may fetch over five times this sum.

4.25in (10.5cm) diam

£350-450　　　　SAS

A Staffordshire 'The Ins' pot lid, no.15.

Produced as a pair with 'The Outs' shown below, examples with fancy borders fetch more. For an example, see 'Miller's Collectables Price Guide 2009', p.371.

3.5in (8cm) diam

£250-300　　　SAS

A Staffordshire 'The Village Wakes' pot lid, no.321, with fancy border, produced by the Pratt factory.

A very rare variation lacking the title, two children and the monkey can fetch over four times the value of this standard scene.

4in (10cm) diam

£450-550　　　SAS

A Staffordshire 'Bears on Rock' pot lid, no.10, with brown bears and gold banded border and flange, produced by the Mayer factory.

Brown bears on this early and small lid are very rare – black is more common.

3.25in (8cm) diam

£700-1,000　　　SAS

A Staffordshire 'The Outs' pot lid, no.16, by the Pratt or Ridgway factory.

3.5in (9cm) diam

£150-250　　　SAS

A Staffordshire 'The Bear Pit' pot lid, no.6, with wavy line border and without the dome on the left, produced by the Pratt factory.

3in (7.5cm) diam

£120-180　　　SAS

A CLOSER LOOK AT A POT LID

This is part of a popular trio of lids which includes 'The Village Wakes'.

Bear subjects are sought after, and this has a green printed base, as well as an unusual and fancy border which adds value.

'The Village Wakes' was taken from a watercolour by Jesse Austin. This was taken from a painting by the notable painter David Wilkie RA (1785-1845).

This lid bears a diamond registration mark near the roof of the house, showing it was registered in July 1852.

A Staffordshire 'The Parish Beadle' pot lid, no.322, complete with green printed Punch base.

4in (10cm) diam

£1,000-1,500　　　SAS

QUICK REFERENCE

- Surprisingly, the most important factor to consider is the case, as to most collectors the style and colour matter more than the internal radio mechanism. The golden age of radio design lasted from the 1930s until the late 1950s, with pre-war radios generally the most valuable.
- Most examples from the 1930s are in the Art Deco style. Look for strong geometric or stepped forms and designs influenced by architecture such as skyscrapers. Grilles were the first feature to change in the early 1930s, and examples with decorative grilles are worth looking out for. During the 1950s, shapes generally became more streamlined and curved.
- As well as the form consider the material. The first radios were housed in simple wooden cases, but during the late 1920s inlays and other materials were used, with plastics such as Bakelite and Catalin beginning to appear in the

1930s. Although most Bakelite examples are found in brown, plastics freed radios from the dull monotony of woods.
- Bright colours such as red, green and blue are therefore highly desirable, but the classic Art Deco combination of black and chrome is also sought after. Coloured British radios are particularly scarce. Brand names are another important factor, with desirable names including FADA, EKCO, Philco and Emerson.
- The highest prices paid today are for classic Art Deco radios in brightly coloured Catalin by American makers. In 2007, a very rare baby blue 'Air King' fetched $51,000 at auction.
- However, as few can afford to buy at this level, and examples in good condition are limited, many collectors look elsewhere. Appealing radios in wooden cases that represent the style of the 1930s represent the largest part of the market, and prices look set to remain strong.

A Philips model 2531 radio and separate hexagonal speaker, with brown Bakelite cases and stylised floral grille.

c1930   19in (48cm) high

£150-250   OTA

A German Mende radio, with black Bakelite case and original grille cloth.

German sets from this period are not common.

c1933

£400-600   OTA

An E.K. Cole Ltd Ekco SH25 radio, designed by J.K. White, with brown Bakelite case, anodised copper grille, and original grille cloth.

This classic design incorporates some of the Egyptian references found in the Art Deco style of the period.

1932   18in (45.5cm) high

£450-650   OTA

A Co-operative Wholesale Society 'Defiant' radio, model M900, with brown bakelite case and printed factory label.

A rare Zetavox model ST radio, with stepped and geometric brown Bakelite case and geometric speaker panel.

1933

£400-600   OTA

This is the most desirable Co-operative Society Defiant radio, due to the shaped case, as well as the rarest model. The 'Defiant' name was used as the company was defying industry rules concerning the minimum cost of a radio at the time.

1935   13.25in (34cm) high

£1,000-1,500   WW

A CLOSER LOOK AT AN EKCO RADIO

A Philco 'People's Set' radio, model no. 444, with mottled dark brown Bakelite case, applied factory labels.

This was designed purely for the UK market and was sold at a very low price, hence the 'People's Set'.
1936   16.5in (42cm) high

£320-380   **WW**

A German model VE301 DYN radio, from the 'Volksempfänger' (People's Radios) range commissioned by the National Socialist government, with brown Bakelite case.
1936

£100-200   **OTA**

Originally released as an economy radio, this was available in black and chrome or brown Bakelite versions.

Although the black and chrome version was only slightly more expensive, it is usually worth up to double the value of the brown today!

Wells Coates (1895-1958) was an important Modernist designer, best known for his architecture, which included London's Isokon Building.

There were five models of round EKCO radio, each with different front designs – this is one of the most popular.

An E.K. Cole Ltd Ekco AD36 black Bakelite radio, designed by Wells Coates, with chrome detailing.
1935   14.5in (37cm) high

£450-650   **OTA**

An E.K. Cole Ltd Ekco AC97 black Bakelite radio, with chrome and ivory Bakelite detailing and original grille cloth.

The striking Modernist design of this radio was also available in brown, which is less desirable to collectors today.
1937   21in (53cm) high

£700-1,000   **OTA**

A Murphy Radio Ltd model AD94 radio, with black Bakelite cabinet.

This was Murphy's first bakelite cabinet, and was produced to meet wartime conditions.
1940   13.5in (34cm) high

£80-150   **OTA**

A Fada Streamliner Model 1000 'Bullet' radio, with Butterscotch Catalin case and knobs.
1940   10.25in (26cm) wide

£300-400   **OTA**

RADIOS

A Raymond 'Minit' radio, with red bakelite case and grille.

1949   *10in (25cm) long*

£70-150   **OTA**

A scarce 1950s French Marquett type 63 radio receiver, with brown and cream bakelite case, and applied factory label to base.

8.25in (21cm) wide

£120-180   **WW**

A Murphy Model A3A radio, with walnut veneered wooden case designed by R.D. Russell, and original stand and grille cloth.

The stand is rare and worth £50-80 alone. At the time, detractors called the radio the 'Pentonville Special', as the grille bars resemble those of a prison cell.

1932   *18.5in (47cm) high*

£150-250   **OTA**

A CLOSER LOOK AT A PYE RADIO

A newer type of valve developed during the war enabled small battery powered radios to be made for 'personal' portable use.

Also available in black and cream Perspex, this model was unsuccessful, largely due to poor construction.

The Pye 'Sunrise' trademark (used since 1929) was similar to the Japanese flag – as news came in of prisoners of war being ill-treated in Japanese camps it fell in popularity.

This model is made of flimsy Perspex, and examples in perfect condition are rare, particularly with an original instruction booklet.

A Pye model M78F battery powered portable radio, with light green and pinky-cream Perspex case, and original instruction leaflet.

7.25in (18.5cm) high

1948

£300-850   **OTA**

A late 1950s Czechoslovakian Tesla Talisman, no.308U, with streamlined brown bakelite case, designed in 1956.

This stylish design was made under licence in Czechoslovakia. Once considered vary rare, after the fall of the Berlin wall many examples were suddenly found on street markets, severely reducing the value.

12.5in (32cm) long

£50-150   **OTA**

A rare Pye Model K radio, with a solid walnut case and 'Sunrise' design speaker grille.

1932   *15.5in (39cm) high*

£100-200   **OTA**

A Western Electric Co. Model 44001 crystal radio set with built-in 2-valve amplifier.

Most crystal sets were intended for headphone use and did not use any power source. This set had an optional amplifier to enable more headphones or a horn speaker to be used for family listening. This was an expensive extra for a cheap set, and few have survived.

1924   *5in (12.5cm) high*

£200-400   **OTA**

A Kenmac 'The Listener' crystal set, contained in a tortoiseshell effect celluloid case in the form of a book.

c1924   4.75in (12cm) high

£400-600   **OTA**

A Japanese Matsushita Electrical Industries Panasonic red plastic model R-70 Panapet transistor radio.

Examine the case as damage reduces the value considerably. The rarest colour is purple, which often fetches up to twice the value of more common colours such as red. The Panapet radio was made only for the Western market.

4in (10cm) high

£30-40   **M20C**

An S.G. Brown Ltd model H2 black metal horn-shaped radio speaker.

As early radios had no built in speakers, many types of speaker were made, often using a horn to amplification. Value depends mainly on the appearance.

c1924

£60-80   **OTA**

FIND OUT MORE...

Jonathan Hill ' Radio! Radio!' . Exeter: Sunrise Press, 1996

Tony Thompson ' Collecting Vintage Radios' . Marlborough: The Crowood Press Ltd, 2007

RAILWAYANA

A C/I 'Chelford No. 2' rectangular plate, face restored.

12in (30.5cm) wide

£50-60   **GWRA**

A Henschel & Sohn worksplate, kassel number "28977", dated.

Ex Malawi Railways G Class 2-8-2 Locomotive number 64.
1954

£400-500   **GWRA**

A Beyer Peacock & Co. 'Manchester' brass worksplate, dated.

Ex Bengal & Assam Railway 4-6-0 'RS' class in the range 31863 - 31870.
1914   *9.75in (25cm) wide*

£150-200   **GWRA**

A Hudswell Clark & Co Ltd Railway Foundry Leeds brass worksplate, number "D1254", in ex loco condition, "D10" stencilled onto reverse, dated.

Ex Manchester Ship Canal 204hp 0-6-0DM which was sold to Hunslet January 1976 where it was rebuilt under order HE 8522.
1962

£60-80   **GWRA**

A 'The Thames-Clyde Express' cast aluminium locomotive name plate, with letters in relief on red background.

40in (101.5cm) wide

£2,500-3,000   **HT**

A 'Melton Mowbray' enamelled totem station sign.

36.5in (92.5cm) wide

£500-700   **HT**

A British Railways E. R. 'Fairlop' enamelled station name board, in good condition, with two chips and some fading to background.

58in (147.5cm) wide

£80-100   **W&W**

A 'Road Narrows' alloy sign, fitted with reflective beads, all beads intact, stress cracks at the top of sign, one fixing bracket remains.

£50-70   **GWRA**

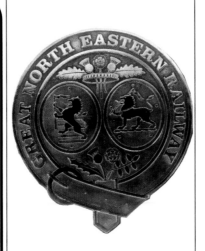

A brass plaque, with belt-shaped rim and raised lettering 'Great North Eastern Railway', two lion crests and Scottish Thistle and English Rose decoration.

23in (58.5cm) diam

£450-550   A&G

A Letterkenny railway gate crossing lamp, the interior stamped with the company initials 'L.R.', with brass plate marked 'SAXBY FARMER LTD SIGNALLING ENGINEERS LONDON'.

£80-120   GWRA

A Beatles metal lunchbox, by Aladdin Industries, with embossed 3-D portraits and signatures, with thermos flask.

This was the first metal box to feature pop music performers

Lunchbox 8in (20.5cm) wide

£200-250 HER

A Beatles unused diary, by Beat Productions, Glasgow, Scotland, the pages printed with 'fun Fab four facts'.

1965

£60-80 KA

The Beatles 'New Beat Guitar', by Selcol Ltd., of orange and burgundy plastic with four strings, in original box with applied sticker of the band and facsimile signatures, with instructions and song chart.

£250-300 GORL

An American Beatles 1964 scrap book, published by Whitman (linked with NEMS Enterprises).

Originally sold for 29cents, filled with American newspaper clippings from August 1964 when "A Hard Day's Night" premiered at the Salem Paramount movie theatre (13 August 1964).

£70-80 KA

A Washington Pottery 'Beatles' plate, transfer printed with an image of the Beatles and their script signatures.

£40-50 KA

A set of four coloured plastic figures of The Beatles, made by Emirober.

£45-50 KA

A CLOSER LOOK AT A PICTURE DISC

The value of picture discs is dependant on the recording artist, with popular artists, such as Madonna and Queen, commanding higher values.

Look for examples with high quality and appealing artwork that is typical of the artist or album. Some images are rare and, if desirable, may be valuable.

The sound quality produced by picture discs is typically poor, so visual appeal is perhaps the most important factor to value.

Picture discs were produced from the early 1930s, when they were made from a sheet of thin vinyl film placed over a thick paper print and pressed with grooves. Coloured vinyl picture discs were introduced in the 1970s by Metronome Records.

Queen, I'm Going Slightly Mad, EMI, shaped single picture disc.

SINGLE £25-30   PC

Queen, Innuendo, 12" single picture disc, EMI.

SINGLE £25-30   PC

A Bob Dylan 'The Freewheelin' Bob Dylan' US stereo LP, by CBS label, serial no BPG-62193.

£25-30   PC

A Manic Street Preachers 'You Love Us' UK stereo LP, by Heavenly, serial no. HVN 10.

£20-25   PC

An Oi Polloi 'Unite and Win!' UK LP, by Oi! records, serial no OIR-011.

£20-25   PC

A Pink Floyd 'The Best of Pink Floyd' stereo LP record, by Colombia.

£100-120   PC

A Michael Jackson vinyl doll,
by Ljn, NY under licence from
MJJ Productions Inc, in the
'Beat It' outfit .

*This is one of a series of four
dolls, originally retailed for
$14.99.*

14in (35.56cm)

£70-90   MTB

An 'Improved Patent Magneto-Electric Machine for Nervous Diseases', with a brass and steel frame and ebonised handled grips, with a printed label to the interior of the mahogany case, with winding handle.

10.25in (26cm) wide

£100-150   WW

A pair of 19thC apothecary's balance, by S. Mawson & Sons, with brass beam and pans, standing on stained wood base with two underlying drawers, with various weights.

Balances are a very specialised market, with few dedicated collectors. Value depends on the maker and the use: coin or cabinet scales can be more desirable.

A Fuller calculator, by Stanley, London, with bakelite mounts, in a fitted bow with brass mounting arm, with copies of instructions.

£250-300   WW

£100-150   A&G

An 18thC brass gunner's sector, divided in eight horizontal scales, including 'Paces Pynt Blanck, Bredth of the Ladell Waight of the Shot'.

8in (20.5cm) long

£350-400   WW

A silver pincushion shaped as a swimming duck, by Crisford & Norris of Birmingham, with textured plumage.

1908   *2in (5.5cm) long*

£150-200   **WW**

A silver plated pincushion, modelled as a pig, unmarked.

                    2in (5cm) long

£30-40   **SAS**

A pair of silver novelty pincushions, by Adie & Lovekin of Birmingham, in the form of a swimming swans.

Pairs of novelty pincushions by the same maker are rare, as most people only needed one pincushion.

1907   *Larger 2.75in (7cm) wide*

£300-400   **WW**

A silver pincushion shaped as a seated chick emerging from an egg, by S. Mordan & Co., with Chester hallmarks.

Sampson Mordan & Co. was a well known maker of fine silver and gold objects, as well as propelling pencils, whose work is sought after. The Chester assay office closed in 1962.

1906   *1.75in (4.5cm) high*

£120-180   **WW**

A CLOSER LOOK AT A NOVELTY PIN CUSHION

Rollerskating themed items are scarce, particularly of this early date.

The first recorded use of roller skates was in 1743, with the four wheeled version we know today being invented in the US in 1863 by James Leonard Plimpton.

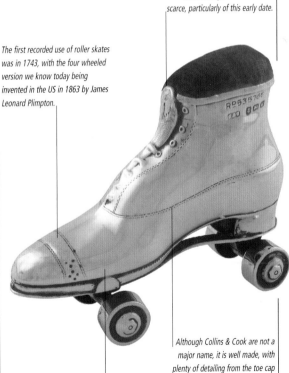

Although Collins & Cook are not a major name, it is well made, with plenty of detailing from the toe cap to the serrated sole welt and wheel axles.

The shape and style of the boot is consistent with Edwardian fashions

A silver pincushion in the shape of a small standing pig, by Henry Matthews of Birmingham.

1906   *2in (5cm) long*

£120-180   **WW**

An Edwardian silver novelty pin cushion, Saunders & Shepherd, Birmingham, in the form of a standing elephant.

1905   *2in (5cm) wide*

£100-150   **WW**

An Edwardian silver novelty roller skate pin cushion, by Collins & Cook of Birmingham, with registered design number '535766' for 1909.

1909   *2.75in (7cm) long*

£180-220   **WW**

SILVER

A pair of Russian silver multi-coloured, cloisonné enamel sugar tongs, by Mari Serrenova, with shaded floral designs.

1908-1917

£220-280   WW

A pair of late 19thC to early 20thC Russian silver gilt and cloisonné enamelled sugar tongs, initialled, with Russian state marks.

1896-1908

£250-350   WW

A late Victorian silver cigar cutter, by H. Matthews of Birmingham, in the form of a pair of scissor snuffers.

1894   4.5in (11.5cm) long

£150-200   WW

A set of four late Victorian silver menu holders, by S. Clifford of London, on a fox hunting theme.

Despite the recent ban in the UK, pieces related to fox hunting and country pursuits are sought after. Even though their use is now outdated, menu holders are strongly collectable.

1899

£250-350   WW

A Victorian silver heraldic menu holder, by Henry William Dee of London, in the form of a squirrel eating a nut, on a curved base.

Certain animals are more collectable than others, especially dogs and cats. Squirrels are comparatively rare, however, hence the higher price. This is also well made, with plenty of detail.

1877   2in (5cm) high

£320-380   WW

A silver commemorative model of a pile driving engine, by Sunard & Co., inscribed 'Rowden Barter & Co. presented to Sir George LE Hunt, as a memento of the ceremony of driving the first pile – outer Harbour S.A. 20/7/04'.

c1904   8.75in (22cm) high

£380-420   WW

A pair of Edwardian silver mounted boar tusk pepperettes, by Atkin Brothers of Sheffield, mounted on oval bases.

1902   2.5in (6.5cm) high

£400-600   WW

QUICK REFERENCE – DUNHILL LIGHTERS

Dunhill are often called the 'Rolls Royce' of cigarette lighters, having produced some of the most luxurious models ever made. The 'Unique' lighter was developed by scientific instrument makers Wise & Greenwood in 1919. With its snuffer arm and a mechanism that allowed it to be operated with one hand, it became a bestseller. Look out for examples in precious metals, those with lacquered designs by Japanese company Namiki, or ones that contain hidden features, such as watches or compacts. Prices range from under £100 for a plated 'Unique', to over £10,000 for a rare watch lighter in a precious metal.

A late 1930s Dunhill silver plated 'Unique' pipe lighter, with extending wick and slider, engine turned design.

The slider moves a tube containing the wick up and down, allowing tobacco in a pipe bowl to be lit.

2.25in (5.5cm) high

£100-150   SAS

A 1970s Dunhill 70 gold plated 'Rollagas' rolled gold cigarette lighter, with engine turned pattern, impressed 'DUNHILL 70' and numbered 'BR889', with some wear from use.

2.25in (6cm) high

£30-40   CARS

A Dunhill 9ct gold 'Unique' lighter, with engine turned design, and control marks.

2.25in (5.5cm) high

£350-450   SAS

A 1950s Dunhill 'Aquarium' table lighter, with reverse-cut and painted underwater scene of tropical fish, and metal fittings.

Look out for the half-size 'Miniature', as this is rarer. If birds or other animals or motifs replace the fish, the price will also rise, as these can be very rare.

4in (10cm) high

£600-900   SWO

An Elisorm Auto-Tank 9ct gold lighter, with engine turned decoration to the body, marked '9ct' and with 'JP' owner's initials.

£35-45   SAS

An Art Deco 9ct gold vesta case, with hinged lid, engine turned centre and Greek key border, and with London hallmarks for 1923.

1923

£200-300   SAS

A silver circular vesta case, decorated in low relief with figures playing bowls on the lawn, maker's mark worn, with Birmingham hallmarks for 1907.

As well as appealing to vesta case collectors, the bowls theme is very rare and would appeal to collectors of sporting memorabilia, which is why this example has a high price.

1907   1.5in (4cm) diam

£500-700   **WW**

A Victorian silver novelty vesta and slow match holder, in the form of a carriage lamp with clear convex lens, with London hallmarks for H.W. Dee, 1870.

Railwayana attracts a greater number of buyers than bowls, the subject of the vesta shown above. This is also an appealing shape and of an early date.

1870   1.75in (4.5cm) high

£800-1,200   **WW**

A CLOSER LOOK AT A NAMIKI CIGARETTE CASE

Maki-e lacquer is a historic technique that takes many years to learn and designs can take weeks of painstaking work to create, layer by layer.

The right hand column of the mark reads 'Namiki kan', showing this to have been made in the 1930s. The left hand column is the artist's name and red 'kao' symbol, revealing that it was decorated by Maizawa Shobi.

Cigarette cases are scarce, but the value of this example is reduced by more than half because it is worn, bears a presentation engraving and the design is comparatively simple.

The goldfish design is one of the most commonly found on Namiki products, with the fish representing good fortune and luck.

A 1930s Japanese Namiki maki-e lacquer metal cigarette case, decorated with a goldfish and pondweed design by Maizawa Shobi, the gold washed interior inscribed 'Jose Pablo Costa 8-12-41'.

Shobi was a pupil of Shiroyama in 1899, on the staff of the Iwate Prefecture Technical High School in 1905, and worked as an independent lacquer artist after 1907. He was also one of the six committee members at the time of the establishment of the school of lacquer artists known as the Kokkokai. The year of the inscription is interesting as this was the year Japan bombed Pearl Harbor.

4in (10cm) high

£150-200   **MHC**

An oak Zebrano effect smoker's cabinet, with doors backed with pipe racks, the fitted interior with square cut crystal decanter to the right, blue and white tobacco jar to the centre, with three drawers, the base moulded to edge.

15.75in (40cm) wide

£180-220   **DA&H**

An Art Deco silver cigarette box, with engine turned decoration, an ivory thumbpiece and an applied enamel plaque, with Birmingham hallmarks for Hassett & Harper Ltd, 1935.

1935   6.5in (17cm) long

£100-150   **WW**

An Art Deco bronze penguin floor smoker's ashtray, with circular top fitted with a well and verdigris finish.

23.5in (59.5cm) high

£400-500   **SK**

QUICK REFERENCE

- Football's continued popularity creates a strong demand for memorabilia, particularly for items connected to famous teams, popular players or important matches.
- Memorabilia relating to Manchester United is among the most widely collected. Other popular teams include Liverpool, Chelsea and Arsenal. Well-known Arsenal players of the past include Charlie George, Frank McLintock and Peter Storey; modern players include Thierry Henry, Ian Wright and Patrick Vieira. Memorabilia connected to Arsenal's 'Double' win (premier league and FA Cup) in 1970-71 is desirable, as is that connected to the "Invincibles", who won the Premiership (2003-04) unbeaten.
- Shirts, boots and other equipment are all sought-after and can be extremely valuable, particularly if they were used during an important match or signed by the player and their team mates. Items connected with footballing legends, such as Pelé, George Best, Bobby Charlton and Bobby Moore, are still in high demand, but today's football players and teams can attract equally significant sums.
- Medals, representing a team's success, are sought after with collectors, as are team caps.
- Programmes are another popular area of collecting. A large variety is available and values vary greatly. Programmes for FA and European Cup finals, international games and early, pre-WW1 games are typically the most desirable and valuable, but be aware that some matches (e.g. the 1966 World Cup) were are so obviously significant at the time that many programmes were stored in good condition keeping values low. Modern programmes are printed in large numbers and many fans keep them, meaning this is an affordable entry into collecting. Look for examples in clean condition.

A squad-signed red and white short-sleeved Tony Adams Arsenal no. 6 jersey, with Premier League flashes, 21 signatures in black marker pen, sold with a copy of Tony Adams' Testimonial programme.

£600-800   GBA

A long-sleeved yellow Arsenal no. 11 jersey from the 1969 League Cup final jersey worn by George Armstrong, embroidered club crest and inscribed 'WEMBLEY, 1969'.

Swindon Town defeated Arsenal 3-1 at Wembley. George Armstrong made 621 first-team appearances in a 15-year playing career.

c1969

£1,800-2,800   GBA

A signed short-sleeved white England no. 8 international jersey 1995 worn by Peter Beardsley, with a letter of authenticity signed by Peter Beardsley.

In his letter of authenticity Peter Beardsley states that he wore this jersey in a 1995 Umbro Cup match against Brazil.

£150-250   GBA

A white long-sleeved Real Madrid No.23 jersey worn by David Beckham in the Champions League match v Bayern Munich on the 10th March 2004, with UEFA Champions League flashes, dirt and blood stains; sold together with a certificate of authenticity issued by Star Chamber.

c2004

£800-1,200   GBA

An orange Holland no. 10 short-sleeved jersey worn by Dennis Bergkamp in the match v France at Euro 2000, embroidered with Dutch and French national flags and inscribed '21 JUNI 2000, Euro 2000 and Fair Play flashes.

In this group D match Holland beat France 3-2.

2000

£600-900   GBA

A short-sleeved red and white Arsenal no. 12 jersey worn by Martin Hayes in the 1988 Football League Cup final, inscribed '1988, WEMBLEY'.

Martin Hayes replaced Perry Groves and scored in the 74th minute. However, two late goals gave victory to Luton Town 3-2.

£1,000-1,500   GBA

A long-sleeved green Arsenal 1980 F.A. Cup final goalkeeping jersey worn by Pat Jennings, inscribed 'F.A. CUP FINAL, WEMBLEY 1980'.
1980

£1,500-2,000   GBA

A CLOSER LOOK AT AN ENGLAND FOOTBALL JERSEY

The Umbro diamond first appeared on England jerseys in the Greece match on 21st April 1971, with Banks wearing the yellow jersey in this and other 1971 matches.

Arguably the greatest goalkeeper England has ever produced, Banks is best remembered for saving Pele's header during the 1970 World Cup. He retired in 1973.

The jersey was purchased at a charity auction in 1971, an event which Gordon Banks attended.

As well as being worn by Banks, it is signed by him in a good, easily displayed position.

A signed long-sleeved yellow England international goalkeeping jersey worn by Gordon Banks, with Umbro diamond, three lions badge, the reverse with a red no. 1, signed by Gordon Banks in fine marker pen.
1971

£1,800-2,800   GBA

A white short-sleeved Chelsea No.8 jersey worn by Frank Lampard during the season 2006-07 season , with Premier League flashes, the reverse lettered LAMPARD.

This jersey was gained as a swap by a West Ham United player after the match at Upton Park on 18th April 2007.
c2006

£300-400   GBA

A short sleeved yellow and blue Arsenal no. 12 jersey worn by Paul Merson in the match v Manchester United 2nd April 1989.

In Arsenal's 1988-89 Championship winning season, this was the match when the famous Tony Adams ' donkey chant' was first heard.
c1989

£400-600   GBA

A short-sleeved white England no. 19 World Youth Championship jersey 1993, inscribed 'WORLD YOUTH CHAMPIONSHIPS, AUSTRALIA 1993'.

Although Brazil won the 1993 tournament. England attained their best finishing position in the competition's history.

£60-90   GBA

A Liverpool v Woolwich Arsenal 9th programme for February 1907, a combined-issue also covering Everton Reserves v Barrow, in very good condition.

1907

£700-1,000   **GBA**

A Woolwich Arsenal v Birmingham programme from the first season at Highbury 1913-14, played on the 22nd November.
1913
£1,000-1,500   **GBA**

An Arsenal v Tufnell Park programme for 19th September 1914, first-team fixture in the London F.A. Challenge Cup, a combined issue also featuring the reserves fixtures v Swindon Town.

£600-800   **GBA**

An Arsenal v Bolton Wanderers four-page programme for 9th October 1920.

1920

£250-350   **GBA**

An F.A. Cup final programme for Arsenal v Huddersfield Town, on 26th April 1930.

The 1930 F.A. Cup Final was won by Arsenal who beat Huddersfield Town 2-0. This was the first cup final in which both teams entered the pitch side-by-side, and was in honour of Arsenal manager Herbert Chapman who had managed Huddersfield very successfully in the 1920s. The 1930 F.A. Cup Final is also remembered for the sinister image of the Graf Zeppelin looming over Wembley Stadium during the first half.

1930

£800-1,200   **GBA**

An Arsenal v Burnley four-page programme for 28th August 1922.

£250-350   **GBA**

A copy of the official programme for Arsenal v Tottenham Hotspur played at Highbury 29th August 1925, including an article titled 'Permit me to introduce Mr Herbert Chapman'.

£550-650   **GBA**

=ٗٗ

ٗٗٗٗٗ

ٗ

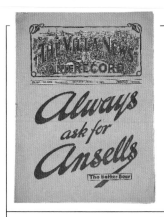

An F.A. Cup semi-final programme Arsenal v Manchester City played at Villa Park 12th March 1932, with Sellotaped repairs to centre pages.

1932
£300-500   GBA

An F.A. Cup final programme for Huddersfield Town v Preston North End on 30th April 1938.

1938
£300-400   GBA

An F.A. Cup final programme for Arsenal v Sheffield United, on 25th April 1936.

Although there is some staining through age, the blue and red are comparatively unfaded, and the inclusion of one of Wembley's famous 'twin towers' in an Art Deco-style design is appealing.
1936
£400-600   GBA

A European Cup final programme for Real Madrid v Stade Reims, played in Stuttgart on 3rd June 1959.
1959
£250-350   GBA

A Belgium v England international programme, played at the Heysel Stadium on 21st September 1947.

1947
£300-500   GBA

A souvenir tournament programme from the Campeonato Mundial de Futball in 1962 in Chile, the Spanish text by Bernard Joy and David Bravo, printed in Chile.
1962
£220-280   GBA

A 15ct gold London Football Combination winner's medal presented to Arsenal's R. Robinson, for the 1927-28 season, inscribed 'LONDON FOOTBALL COMBINATION, ARSENAL F.C., WINNERS, R. ROBINSON, 1927-28', in original fitted case.

£450-550   **GBA**

A CLOSER LOOK AT A MEDAL

Herbert 'Herbie' Roberts (1905-1944) was a serving police officer and played amateur football for his local side Oswestry Town.

In 1926, he was signed to Arsenal by Herbert Chapman for £200, and turned professional.

He was the team's first choice centre-half from 1930-37, and went on to win F.A. Cup runners-up and winner's medals in 1932 and 1936.

He retired after breaking his leg in 1938. He then trained the reserves team until war broke out. He died in 1944 while serving with the Royal Fusiliers.

A 9ct gold F.A. Cup runners-up medal for the 1931-32 season, awarded to Arsenal's Herbie Roberts, inscribed 'THE FOOTBALL ASSOCIATION CHALLENGE CUP, RUNNERS-UP', in original fitted case inscribed 'THE FOOTBALL ASSOCIATION CHALLENGE CUP, 1931-32'.

£2,000-3,000   **GBA**

A silver and enamel medal for the 1930 World Cup finals, by Stefano Johnson of Milan, with enamelled obverse, the reverse inscribed '1ER CAMPEONATO MUNDIAL DE FOOTBALL, URUGUAY, MONTEVIDEO, 15 JULIO AGOSTO 15'.

The enamelled design is after Guillermo Laborde's official poster design for the 1930 World Cup.

£550-750   **GBA**

A 15ct gold F.A. Charity Shield medal presented to Arsenal's George Male in 1931, inscribed 'FOOTBALL ASSOCIATION CHARITY SHIELD', in replacement case.

Arsenal beat West Bromwich Albion 1-0.

£1,000-1,500   **GBA**

A 14ct gold F.A. Cup winner's medal presented to Arsenal's goalkeeper Alex Wilson in 1936, inscribed 'THE FOOTBALL ASSOCIATION, WINNERS, ARSENAL F.C. 1935-36, A. WILSON', in fitted case.

Alexander Wilson (1908-1971) was signed by Arsenal in 1933.

£7,000-10,000   **GBA**

A 9ct gold and enamel Football League Division Three Championship medal awarded to Neil Webb, the obverse inscribed 'FOOTBALL LEAGUE CHAMPIONSHIP, DIVISION 3, WINNERS', the reverse inscribed 'SEASON 1982-83, N WEBB', in original fitted case.

Neil Web won this medal during his first season at Portsmouth. They finished the season with 91 points, five clear of their nearest rivals Cardiff City.

£1,000-1,500   **GBA**

SPORTING

A pair of Ashley Cole football boots, white, black and red Adidas Predators, the right tongue inscribed 'COLEY 3'.

£150-250   GBA

A pair of Saloman Kalou football boots, white and blue Adidas F50 boots, the tongue bearing the national flag of the Ivory Coast and inscribed 'KALOU' and 'JUNIOR'.

£150-250   GBA

A pair of Adidas football boots worn by Steven Gerrard in an England training session prior to the World Cup qualifier vs. Greece. Embroidered 'SG', signed by Gerrard, Nick Barmby and Sammy Lee, together with a letter of authenticity signed by Gerrard and a colour photograph of Gerrard wearing the boots and with Barmby and Lee.

2001

£350-450   GBA

A panelled leather football signed by the Celtic 1967 European Cup final team, with printed inscription, and eleven faded autographs in ink.

£150-200   GBA

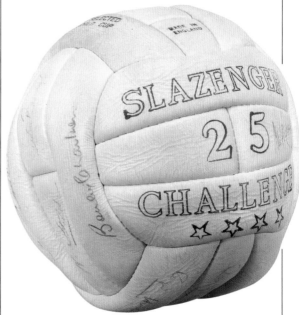

A white Slazenger 25 Challenge leather football signed by the England 1966 World Cup winners, signed in pen by Sir Alf Ramsey, the 11 England finalists and additionally by squad members Greaves and Bonetti, with a programme for the final and a souvenir magazine.

£1,200-1,800   GBA

Jack Kelsey's last Wales international cap for season 1961-62, the red cap inscribed '1961-62, E, S, I, B, B'.

Kelsey is regarded as one of Wales' greatest goalkeepers. In the 1961-62 season, he played in the internationals v England, Scotland and Northern Ireland, and in the two friendlies against Brazil. He injured his back while trying to save at the feet of the Brazilian Vavà and, despite extensive attempts to rectify the problem, he was forced to retire a year later.

£1,500-2,000   GBA

An old Highbury red and white corner flag, lettered 'A.F.C.'

£650-750   GBA

A German stoneware half-litre stein with football decoration, inscribed "Hipp Hipp Hurrah".

7.25in (18.5cm) high

£80-120   **GBA**

A full-size silver plated replica of the Football Association Challenge Cup Trophy, the two-handled cup and cover realistically modelled and inscribed, fitted to ebonised plinths, with F. A. Cup ribbons, with a custom-built portable and lockable wooden cabinet.

27.25in (69cm) high

£5,000-7,000   **GBA**

Jimmy Dugdale's electroplated winner's tankard from the first Football League Cup final in 1961, engraved with the crest of the Football League and inscribed 'THE FOOTBALL LEAGUE CUP, 1960-61, WINNERS'.

5in (13cm) high

£1,000-1,500   **GBA**

A large Bohemian porcelain figure, decorated as a Uruguayan Olympic footballer in sky blue and white, in commemoration of their gold medal winning team at Amsterdam, the base inscribed 'OLYMPICOS', factory marks to underside of base, restored.
c1928

£450-650   **GBA**

An extremely rare Marx "World Cup Willie' Rollakin miniature figure, the base with ball-bearing to allow him to roll along.

With its original box, the value can rise to over £100.

1.5in (4cm) high

£60-70   **MTB**

A 1966 World Cup first day cover signed by Bobby Moore, postmarked Wembley 1st June 1966, signed in black biro.

1966

£300-500   **GBA**

An official poster for the England 1966 World Cup July 1966, after Carvosso, published by McCorquodale & Co. Ltd, framed and glazed.

26in (66cm) high

£600-800   **GBA**

QUICK REFERENCE

- Baseball cards were introduced in 1933 by the Goudey Gum Company to encourage children to buy more gum. This idea was copied from cigarette cards, which had been produced from the 19thC.
- By 1951 other companies, including Bowman Gum and Topps Chewing Gum, began producing collectable baseball cards. When Topps acquired Bowman in 1956, they became the world's largest sports card manufacturer.
- Collecting cards was largely a pastime for children until the early 1970s. Once adults began collecting too, prices for rare and desirable cards leapt in value. Only a few hundred

examples of the legendary 1909-1911 T206 Honus Wagner card were produced and only 57 examples are known today, one of which sold for £1.5 million in 2007. Backs and colours of backgrounds can differ.
- Aside from rarity, one of the most important indicators to value is 'centring'. The printed image should ideally be surrounded by an even amount of white space.
- Condition is also important. Creases, abrasions, folds, tears and other damage will lessen value.
- Fakes are common, but these can often be identified by a blurred or pixellated image and the thickness of the card.

An American Tobacco Co. Piedmont Cigarettes Albert (Chief) Bender baseball card, with trees in the background.

1909   *2.75in (6.8cm) high*

£100-150   **AEM**

A Crofts Candy 'Dots Miller Fielding' baseball card, E92, with rare red-printed back.

1909

£1,200-1,500   **MAS**

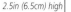

A Bowman Richie Ashburn rookie baseball card.

This very rare card is not in the best condition and is not well centred, hence its lower value. If in better condition, it could fetch well over twice this value.

1949   *2.5in (6.5cm) high*

£150-250   **BH**

A Topps 'Connie Mack's All-Stars Eddie Collins' baseball card, sealed in box with SGC rating of 40 (VG3).

1951

£100-150   **MAS**

A Topps 'Connie Mack's All-Stars, Jimmy Collins' baseball card, sealed in box with SGC rating of 60 (Ex5).

1951

£150-250   **MAS**

A Topps Rocco Colavito rookie baseball card.
1957 *3.5in (9cm) high*
£30-50 BH

A Sport Magazine Willie Mays baseball card.
1959 *3.5in (9cm) high*
£20-30 AEM

A CLOSER LOOK AT A BASEBALL CARD

Mickey Mantle and Hank Aaron are two of baseball's greatest names. They are both depicted on this card.

The card is also signed by them. Had it not been signed, its value would have been around $200-400, depending on condition.

Showing switch-hitting Mantle, who was pitted against right-handed slugger Aaron in front of the Yankee stadium, this style was used again in 2006 with opponents Pujols and Ordonez.

The signatures have been certified as authentic by the official PSA/DNA authentication service, and the card has been sealed in a protective wallet.

A Topps 'World Series Batting Foes Mickey Mantle and Hank Aaron' baseball card, number 418, dual signed, PSA/DNA authenticated.
1958
£1,000-1,500 MAS

A Topps Jim Palmer rookie card, priced according to condition.
1966 *3.5in (9cm) high*
£25-35 BH

A Topps Bob Clemente baseball card.
1964
3.5in (9cm) high
£50-70 BH

A Topps Hank Aaron baseball card.
1968 *3.5in (9cm) high*
£25-35 AEM

A Topps Willie Mays baseball card.

1968   3.5in (9cm) high

£25-35   AEM

A 1968 Rookie Stars baseball card featuring Jerry Koosman and Nolan Ryan.

This card, featuring Hall of Famer Nolan Ryan, is one of the iconic cards of the period. Koosman's appearance is considered less important by many and, although Ryan was not the greatest pitcher in baseball, he was considered dominant in his prime. Nevertheless, Koosman also made a number of high achievements, making this a superb example of a dual rookie card. Prices have fallen over the past few years, with this card once fetching around £1,000 in the 1990s.

1968   3.5in (9cm) wide

£250-350   AEM

A Topps Cal Ripken, Bob Bonner and Jeff Schneider baseball card.

This was Ripken's rookie card, with Ripken entering the Hall of Fame in 2007.

1982   3.5in (9cm) high

£20-40   BH

A Score Joe DiMaggio signed baseball card, numbered 'JD18' from 56 examples from a limited edition of 2,500, with certificate of authenticity, from the DiMaggio estate.

1992 was the first year that baseball card companies began inserting signed cards into their packs. This was from a series of five, which is considered highly desirable as it features the legendary DiMaggio, has his signature on a card, and was one of the first signed series sold in this way.

1992   3.5in (9cm) wide

£200-300   BH

A Nabisco All Star Autographs Ernie Banks baseball card, signed by Banks, together with a certificate of authenticity.

1993   3.5in (9cm) high

£20-30   BH

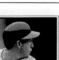

An Upper Deck Brooks Robinson baseball card, signed in blue marker by Robinson.

1998   3.5in (9cm) high

£15-25   BH

A Hillerich & Bradsby & Co. 'The Famous Slugger Year Book', with Mize and Di Maggio '1939 Batting Champions' cover.

1940 6.5in (16.5cm) high

£40-60 **BH**

'Major League Baseball Facts & Figures', featuring Ted Williams on the cover, published by Whitman Publishing Company.

Williams was Player of the Year in 1941.

1942 6.75in (17cm) high

£10-15 **BH**

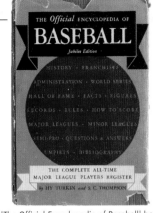

A 'The Official Encyclopedia of Baseball' book, first edition, published by A.S Barnes & Company.

1951 10in (25.5cm) high

£30-50 **BH**

A very rare early 1950s Babe Ruth photographic miniature Flip Book, with pictorial cover, with wear and damage.

4in (10cm) high

£100-150 **BH**

Baseball magazine, January 1937, with wear and damage.

1937 11.5in (29cm) high

£7-10 **BH**

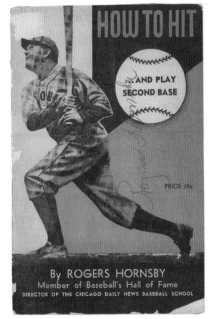

A Rogers Hornby 'How to Hit…And Play Second Base' signed booklet.

1945

£600-800 **MAS**

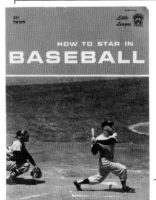

A Little League 'How To Star in Baseball' book, with Mickey Mantle photographic cover.

1961 8in (20.5cm) high

£5-7 **BH**

SPORTING

A very rare Babe Ruth Memorial Mission tract (and 1927 Yankee), published by Faith, Prayer & Tract League of Grand Rapids, Mich.

1948   5.75in (14cm) high
£20-30   BH

A 1924 World Series Washington Base Ball Club Pennant Winners program and score card.
1924
£200-300   MAS

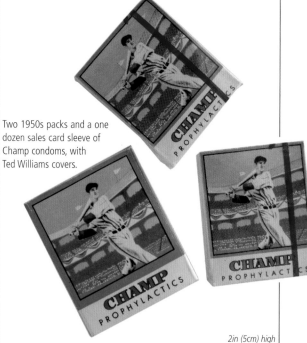

Two 1950s packs and a one dozen sales card sleeve of Champ condoms, with Ted Williams covers.

A 1950 World Series Yankees vs Phillies multi-signed program, with ten signatures including Joe DiMaggio.

1950
£600-800   MAS

£200-300 FOR THREE

2in (5cm) high
BH

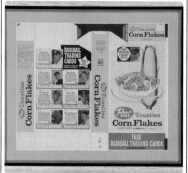

A Post Toasties corn flakes cereal box, complete and in mint condition with baseball cards back, framed and glazed.

1962
£450-550   MAS

A 1950s Dizzy Dean endorsed 'Falstaff Beer' advertising sign.

£250-350   MAS

A Ty Cobb Detriot American League printed felt B18 baseball blanket, issued as a cigarette premium.

This is in slightly poor condition, and has its top left margin cut off. In better and brighter condition, it can fetch up to £300 due to Cobb's popularity.
1914   5.25in (13cm) wide
£100-150   BH

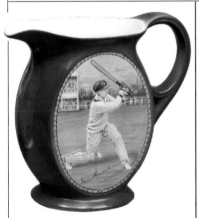

Two New Hall Pottery Staffordshire water jugs, both featuring an oval portrait of Don Bradman with printed oval signature, one white glazed, the other blue glazed, the reverse with a vignette of crossed bats, balls and stumps, chips and staining.

6.75in (17cm) high

£350-450   **GBA**

A sterling silver mounted cricket ball, with presentation inscription,

£300-400   **GORL**

A Bussey cricketers' tape measure.

4.5in (11.5cm) diam.

£80-120   **MSA**

SPORTING

A Victorian silver and enamel 'Cricket' fob, Robinson Brothers, Birmingham.

1889

£250-300 BEX

A silver snuff box, Edward Smith, with engine-turned decoration, the cover with cartouche engraved with the inscription 'Presented to John Sherman by Members of the Manchester Cricket Club, 1848'.

It was noted in Lillywhite's Cricketing Almanack of 1850, that John Sherman's 'slow bowling proved very effective against the Eleven of England in 1848', this at the age of 60.

7.75in (19.5cm) wide 3.31oz

£550-650 BEA

A silver 'S.B.S.' (Special Boat Service) inter-port cricket game medal, Phillips, Aldershot.

£50-80 FOF

QUICK REFERENCE – CRICKET

Apart from a move to straight bats from curved in the mid-18thC, cricket equipment has changed very little since the invention of the game in the 17thC. Collectors' interest is therefore largely focused on memorabilia connected to famous matches, events or players. Items connected or signed by players such as Dr. W. G. Grace (1848-1915), Gary Sobers (b1936), and Don Bradman (1908-2001) are usually extremely desirable, although firm provenance must be established. Items associated with popular modern players, such as Andrew Flintoff, also attract interest. A great deal of other memorabilia has been produced from the mid-19thC, including ceramics, programmes, tickets, photographs and accessories and, in good condition, these are all popular with collectors.

A Boy's Own Paper 'Famous English Cricketers' supplement print, mounted.

1880 *15in (38cm) wide*

£150-250 GBA

Grace, W. G., 'W G, Cricketing Reminiscences & Personal Recollections', published by James Bowden.

1899

£25-35 GBA

A Jack Hobs Press Club dinner menu profusely signed by guests, signatures in ink to the reverse.

£250-300 GBA

An autographed display for the 1957 West Indians to England, including the signatures of the touring squad on Surrey CCC headed paper, a tour brochure, dinner menu and squad photograph, mounted, framed and glazed.

34in (86.5cm) high

£300-400 GBA

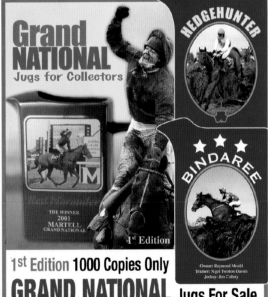

A set of Stavros Niarchos racing colours signed by Cash Asmussen in 1993, Gibson (Saddlers) of Newmarket, the white cap signed in blue biro.

The most successful horse to carry Mr Niarchos's familiar colours was the filly Miesque who won the English and French 1,000 Guineas, the Breeders' Cup Mile and many other important races. Mr Niarchos (1909-1996) was the leading owner in France on two occasions, and topped the breeders' list three times.

£450-550 **GBA**

An antique dark green satinised cotton jockey's jacket and cap, Merry & Co. of St James's, cap and sleeves light green sleeves, in good condition.
c1900

£150-200 **GBA**

A silver picture frame containing locks of mane hair from the 1989 Derby winner Nashwan and his half-brother Unfuwain, the hair mounted alongside colour portrait photographs of the two stallions.

The photos and mane hair were obtained at a Shadwell Stud open day in 2001.

8.5in (19cm) high

£150-200 **GBA**

An enamel stickpin, picturing the racehorse 'Spearmint'.

'Spearmint' won the 1906 Grand Prix de Paris - one of the most important horse races in France outside the Classics. 'Spearmint' also won the prestigious Derby in 1906. He was owned by Major Edmund Loder and trained by Peter Gilpin.

0.75in (2cm) diam.

£15-20 **WORA**

Walter Hagen, "The Walter Hagen Story" as told to Margaret Seaton Heck, published by Simon and Schuster, first edition, with dustwrapper, and a presentation inscription from Hagen.
1956
£300-400   L&T

A 1950s Walter Hagen black and white photograph, showing Hagen seated on a golf course with a club.

£80-120   MAS

After Michael Brown, 'Life Association of Scotland Calendar 1903', 'First International Golf Match – England v Scotland – Hoylake, 1902, framed.
21.75in (55cm) wide
£700-1,000   L&T

A silver-plated three-piece mesh pattern ball bachelor's tea set, comprising teapot, cream jug and sugar basin.

Had the golfing shape and theme not been here, a standard silver plated teaset would usually be worth under £100.

c1900
£2,000-2,500   L&T

A late Victorian electroplated inkstand, decorated with foliage engraving, crossed clubs and a mesh pattern ball, with hinged cover enclosing a glass liner, on four volute supports, bearing trade label for John Macfarlane, Alloa.
6.75in (17cm) long
£200-300   L&T

A silver golfing medal, one side with a scene of a golfer and inscribed Amateur Golf Championship, the other with a ribbon tied laurel wreath in relief, with ring suspension, no inscription, with Birmingham hallmarks for 1954.
1954   *1.75in (4.5cm)*
£800-1,200   L&T

An American Amateur Championship gilt metal and enamel contestant's badge, reading "September 1-6. 1913", centrally with the initials of "USGA", by The Whitehead & Hoag Company, lacks pin .
1.25in (3cm) wide
£800-1,200   L&T

A Michael Jordan North Carolina signed replica basketball jersey.

£300-400   MAS

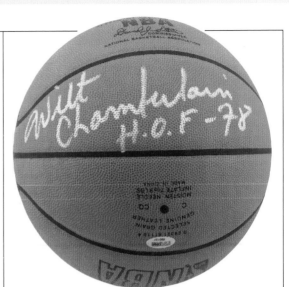

An official Spalding basketball, signed by Wilt Chamberlain.

Wilton Norman Chamberlain, also known as 'Wilt The Stilt', was inducted into the Basketball Hall of Fame in 1978. Considered one of, if not the, best player in basketball to date, he had a good rapport with this fans. The fact that this is on a baseball is a nice touch.

£1,200-1,800   MAS

A Hawthorne Milk 'Jerry Sloan, Chicago Bulls' basketball card.

1970-1

£400-500   MAS

A bronze figure of an American footballer, with pale brown patina, mounted on a wooden plinth.

10.5in (27cm) high

£80-120   GBA

A rare Moyer football player ceramic money bank, with orange, black and white uniform, marked '© Moyer' on side of base, with some wear to the painting.

Mr. Moyer reportedly used his own face to model this player.

7.5in (19cm) high

£70-100   BEL

A 1970s Wilson OJ Simpson signature series plastic football and original box.

11.5in (29cm) high

£50-70   BH

A Mitre '5' white rugby ball signed by the England squad from the inaugural Rugby World Cup in 1987, stamped 'OFFICIAL MATCH BALL, RUGBY WORLD CUP 1987', signed by the team manager Geoff Cooke, the coach, and a total of 21 players including Rendall, Moore, Probyn, Dooley, Skinner, and others, mounted in a wooden display case.

c1987

£500-600   GBA

An limited edition 1997 New Zealand 'All Blacks' rugby shirt display, numbered 59 from an edition of 300, the shirt with two columns of signatures, framed with certificate of authenticity taped to the backboard.

The signatures are of all the All Blacks who played in the undefeated run of eight test matches during 1997 season.

1997 | 42.5in (108cm) wide
£450-650 | GBA

A Pennsylvania Resident Citizen's Fishing License pin, numbered 57318.

1941 | 1.75in diam
£20-25 | BH

A Victorian brass paper holder, with spring-loaded crossed racquets and balls clip, on a shaped wooden base.

5in (13cm) wide
£120-180 | GBA

A bronze figure of a boxer, with rich brown patina, mounted on a marble base.

8.5in (21.5cm) high
£120-180 | GBA

Two Kinsella ceramic figures of boy cricketers, one titled 'The Hope of his Side', the other based on the Kinsella print 'Out First Ball', with the two Kinsella cricket prints that the figures were based on.

Largest 5in (13cm) high
£400-500 | GBA

A silvered metal figurine of a stylised fencer, mounted on a black striated marble base.

13in (33cm) wide
£120-180 | WW

A 1939 World Student Games poster, designed by Franz Kralicek, the colour lithograph printed by Christoph Reisser Sohne, Vienna.

Note the strong Fascist version of the Art Deco style.

1936 | 38.5in (98cm) high
£100-150 | GBA

QUICK REFERENCE

- Teddy bears are named after American president, Theodore (Teddy) Roosevelt, who refused to shoot a bear-cub on a hunting trip in 1902. Morris Michtom (who later founded the Ideal Novelty and Toy Company) produced a soft toy 'teddy bear' to sell at his Brooklyn store. The bear was so popular that it started a craze, which is still with us today.
- Despite the teddy's American origin, German company, Steiff (founded 1886) are considered the best maker. Other collectable German makers include Gebrüder Hermann, Bing and Schreyer & Co. (Schuco). British companies to look out for include Farnell, Merrythought and Chad Valley. The American companies Ideal, Gund and Knickerbocker have also produced collectable bears.
- Bears can be identified and dated from labels, if they are still attached, or from their materials, colour and form. Before WWII, bears tended to have long limbs with large, upturned paw pads, pronounced snouts and humped backs. They were usually made from mohair and feel solid, as they were stuffed with wood shavings or kapok. Post-war bears usually have shorter limbs and plumper bodies, less pronounced snouts, and rounder heads. Synthetic materials were used from the 1960s. Try to handle as many bears as possible to get a feel for the different styles
- Large bears in unusual colours are often more desirable to collectors, as are those with 'eye appeal' – an appealing expression will always capture a collector's heart. A lot of damage can be restored, but tears, stains, replaced pads and worn fur will often reduce value.
- Bears by contemporary bear artists and modern limited edition bears, from notable makers such as Steiff, are beginning to fetch good prices on the secondary market. Always keep limited edition bears in mint condition, and retain the box and paperwork. Some limited editions, particularly those of Steiff, are replicas of older bears, and these should not be confused with the originals, which are usually worth more. If in doubt, smell a bear, as the scent of an old bear cannot be faked.

A Steiff blonde mohair bear, with boot button eyes, original pads and ear button.

This bear displays all of the features associated with pre-war bears, particularly those by Steiff, such as a hump and long limbs.

c1908   9.5in (24cm) high

£700-900   PC

A 1930s Steiff small blond 'Teddy Baby', with velvet fur, internal wire frame and large feet allowing him to stand, and ear button.

3in (7.5cm)

£300-400   PC

A 1930s-40s Steiff golden mohair small bear, with glass eyes and ear button, in very good condition.

5.25in (13.5cm) high

£350-400   PC

A late 1940s Steiff blond mohair bear, with glass eyes, original pads and stitching and ear button, lacking tag.

13.5in (34cm) high

£300-400   PC

A 1950s Steiff white mohair miniature bear, with original features, in excellent condition.

3.5in (9cm)

£60-80   PC

A 1950s Steiff bear, from the 'Original Teddy' range, bright golden mohair and original red ribbon, no button.

5.25in

£80-100   PC

A Steiff red and blue mohair 'Harlequin' teddy bear, from a limited edition of 6,850, with ceramic medallion, certificate, and white ear tag numbered '420214', in mint condition with box.

2000-2001   *14in (35.5cm) high*

£100-150   VEC

A Steiff 'Schwarzbar' black mohair bear, from a limited edition of 1,500 exclusive to the UK market, with certificate, in mint condition with box.

2001   *13.75in (35cm) high*

£100-150   VEC

A CLOSER LOOK AT A STEIFF ZOTTY BEAR

'Zotty' bears were introduced by Steiff in 1951, and are named after 'zottig', the German word for shaggy, due to their fur. They are currently less popular meaning prices have fallen – it is therefore a good time to buy,

As well as the distinctive fur, they typically have open felt-lined mouths, and they were copied by many makers including Hermann.

Steiff was the only company to use plain 'bibs' on their bears' chests, which helps with identification.

The fur is often tipped with a different tone – do not confuse these with the similar but rarer Steiff 'Petsy' bears from c1929, which have reddy-brown tipped blond mohair and closed mouths.

A 1950s-60s Steiff 'Zotty' bear, with tipped fur, original felt pads and mouth and original eyes and stitching, in excellent condition.

£100-150   PC

A Steiff '1908 Rosé Replica' bear, from a limited edition of 3,000, with felt paws, black glass eyes and growler, in presentation box with certificate.

In 1908 Steiff produced samples in black, pink, green or yellow mohair for the English market. No more were then produced. This is a replica of the pink sample bear.

2008   *13.75in (35cm)*

£120-160   TBW

A Steiff 'Henderson' bear, from a limited edition of 2,000, with long curled mohair and growler, together with a presentation box and certificate.

This bear was named after pioneer teddy bear collector and researcher Lt Col Bob Henderson, whose collection was sold at aution in 1994. The highest price was £110,000, paid for his life-long companion, a 1904 cinnamon mohair Steiff known as 'Teddy Girl'.

1997   *21.5in (55cm)*

£220-280   TBW

A late 1920s Schuco brown mohair 'Piccolo' bear, with original foot pads, boot button eyes and stitching, with worn fur.

At a tiny 2.5in (6.5cm) high, this was the smallest bear produced by Schuco.

2.5in (6.5cm) high

£200-250   PC

A 1930s Schuco gold mohair miniature bear, with a metal internal body and original eyes and stitching.

3.5in (9cm) high

£180-220   BEJ

A 1920s-30s Schuco orange mohair miniature bear, with original stitching, the head removing to reveal a glass perfume bottle, in excellent condition.

3.5in (9cm) high

£200-250   PC

QUICK REFERENCE – SCHUCO MINIATURES

Along with Steiff, Schuco are well-known for their miniature bears, which were produced in large numbers during the 1920-70s. The most commonly found are in gold mohair, but look out for a number of unusual variations, as these can fetch higher values. The rarest colour is purple, but examples were also produced in other colours including red, orange, peach, green, grey and pink. Some also hide a secret, having removable heads, or opening to reveal accessories such as perfume bottles, or compacts. These are particularly sought after, and can fetch over £500 in complete and excellent condition.

A 1920s-30s Schuco gold mohair miniature bear, with removeable head, which conceals a glass perfume bottle, in excellent condition.

5in (12.5cm) high

£500-700   PC

Three miniature Schuco bears, in red, green and pink mohair, each wearing knitted tunics, possibly given them by their original owner.

3.5in (9cm) high

£450-550 EACH   PC

A Schuco brown mohair miniature bear, with metal crown, and a green and yellow cord with 'BP' embossed tinplate button.

This bear was given away as a promotional present at BP petrol station from 1958-60. Complete examples are rare today.

1958-1960   5in (12.5cm) high

£100-150   **PC**

A CLOSER LOOK AT A SCHUCO YES/NO BEAR

This bear is known as a 'Yes/No' bear as he has an internal mechanism that makes him nod or shake his head, depending on how his tail is moved.

Many collectors prefer post-war examples as they have appealing and charming round faces – but look out for rare pre-war bears, especially in different colours, as they are valuable.

Schuco were better known for producing a large range of clockwork metal toys, enabling them to make such mechanisms. This type of bear was introduced in 1921.

Post-war bears also have downturned paws on longer limbs, and flat feet, allowing them to stand.

A 1950s Schuco gold mohair 'Yes/No' bear, with original stitching, pads and glass eyes, and later neckerchief, with internal mechanical.

9in (29cm) high

£400-600   **TED**

A 1920s-30s Schuco gold mohair tumbling miniature bear, with working clockwork mechanism that moves his long arms.

5in (12.5cm) high

£650-750   **PC**

A 1950s Schuco gold mohair small 'Yes/No' bear, with working tail mechanism to nod and shake head.

5in (13cm)

£250-350   **PC**

A 1960s-70s Schuco 'footballer' bear, with golden mohair head and 'pipe cleaner' body and limbs, in original woven football kit with plastic boots.

3.75in (9.5cm)

£150-200   **PC**

An early Schuco gold mohair plush bear, with a home-knitted dress, with re-covered felt pads and wear to fur.

10in (25.5cm) high

£250-300   **BEJ**

A 1930s Merrythought bear, with long golden mohair and kapok and excelsior stuffing, felt paw pads, stitched nose, amber and black glass eyes, celluloid button in the ear and fabric label to foot.

This bear can be identified from the the foot label and ear button. Had these not been present, the characteristic paw stitching combined with the shape of the body and his head would have helped indicate the maker. Only Farnell and Merrythought used this style of stitching, but their bears are different in form.

19in (45.5cm) high

£600-800 PC

A CLOSER LOOK AT A MERRYTHOUGHT BEAR

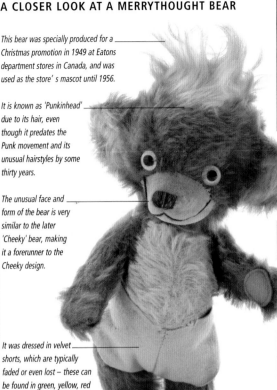

This bear was specially produced for a Christmas promotion in 1949 at Eatons department stores in Canada, and was used as the store' s mascot until 1956.

It is known as 'Punkinhead' due to its hair, even though it predates the Punk movement and its unusual hairstyles by some thirty years.

The unusual face and form of the bear is very similar to the later 'Cheeky' bear, making it a forerunner to the Cheeky design.

It was dressed in velvet shorts, which are typically faded or even lost – these can be found in green, yellow, red or blue.

A Merrythought 'Punkinhead' bear, with brown mohair body and pale chest and ear linings, sewn-on velvet shorts, fully jointed, in good condition.

c1950 16in (40.5cm) high

£800-1,000 TBW

A Merrythought 'Cheeky' gold mohair bear, the large ears with bells sewn inside them, one foot with 'Regd. Design' Merrythought fabric label.

1960

£300-400 PC

A rare Merrythought gold mohair and fabric 'Mr Twisty Cheeky' bear, with internal wire frame.

Look out for rare Mrs Cheeky.

1966-68 11in (28cm)

£200-250 TBW

A 1960s Merrythought gold mohair 'Cheeky' bear, with bells in his ears, and original pads and stitching in excellent condition, with 'Reg'd Design' Merrythought label to foot.

The instantly recognisable 'Cheeky' bear with bells in its ears was released in 1957. Labels typically carry 'registered design' wording as this popular design was distinctive enough to be registered, and therefore protected.

10in (25.5cm) high

£150-200 PC

A late 1960s-70s Merrythought 'Cheeky' rare blue plush bear, in very good condition, with original stitching, eyes and label to foot pad.

18.25in (46cm) high seated

£380-420 LHT

TEDDY BEARS

A 1970s Merrythought gold mohair bear, with original stitching and plastic eyes, and label on the right foot.

10in (25.5cm) high

£30-40　　　　　　PC

A Merrythought 'Little Patchwork Punkie' limited edition pellet-filled mohair bear, from a limited edition of 150, with 23 patches in different colours, felt paws, glass eyes, and certificate.

8in (20cm) high

£65-85　　　　TBW

A Merrythought brown tipped cream mohair 'Happy Cheeky' bear, from a limited edition of 50.

2009　　　*25.25in (38cm)*

£150-180　　　TBW

QUICK REFERENCE - DATING MERRYTHOUGHT

Before 1945, Merrythought usually marked its bears with a metal button. Often missing, other hallmarks such as claw style can help with identification. Also look out for remains of labels or stitching or a lack of fading or wear in a label-sized area, as the position and size of this are also useful. After WWII, Merrythought bears were labelled, and the style of the label will help with dating.

A 1990s Merrythought golden mohair bear, with leather paw pads and original labels, in mint condition.

£200-300　　　BEJ

From 1945-56, an embroidered fabric label with the company name and 'Hygenic Toys' wording was used.

From 1957 until 1991, a printed fabric label was used, including the wording 'Ironbridge Shropshire'.

From 1991 onwards, the label included a 'wishbone' motif as well as wording.

A limited edition Merrythought 'Cheeky Toggles' bear, in felt duffel coat.

2009　　　*11.5in (29cm) high*

£100-150　　　TBW

A limited edition Merrythought bear, 'Sleepy Cheeky', in matching nightshirt and cap.

2009　　　*25.25in (38cm)*

£80-120　　　TBW

A scarce Farnell white or blond mohair 'Alpha' bear, with pale brown rectangular vertically stitched nose, webbed paw stitching and flat foot pads.
c1925

£1,000-1,500   TBW

A 1930s Farnell rare blue mohair bear, with original glass eyes, pale brown facial stitching and pads, with some wear to his fur.

9.25in (23.5cm) high

£1,800-2,200   PC

A 1930s Farnell bear, with wool plush fur and replaced pads, wearing a later leather collar, with patches of wear to his fur.

20in (50.5cm) high

£200-300   PC

A 1930s Farnell bear, with blond mohair head and paws and blue and red plush integral clothing, with original blue eyes and stitching.

10in (25.5cm) high

£100-120   PC

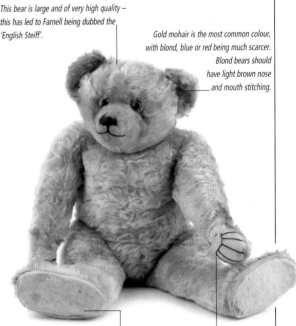

A Farnell red mohair 'soldier' miniature bear, with original eyes.

These were often sold as gifts for sweethearts to take with them during WWI, their upturned faces allowing them to peek out of the breast pocket of a soldier' s uniform. They were made in patriotic colours of red, white and blue, as well as the traditional gold colour.
1915

3.75in (9.5cm)

£300-400   TBW

A CLOSER LOOK AT A FARNELL BEAR

This bear is large and of very high quality – this has led to Farnell being dubbed the 'English Steiff'.

Gold mohair is the most common colour, with blond, blue or red being much scarcer. Blond bears should have light brown nose and mouth stitching.

The long limbs, shaved protruding snout, large flat foot pads, rounded face and humped back are typical features of pre-war Farnell bears.

The paw stitching is a characteristic feature of Farnell bears made before 1930 – it was also used by Merrythought, which hired one of Farnell's directors in 1920.

A late 1920s Farnell gold mohair large bear, with original stitching and eyes and webbed claws, with broken growler.

25in (63.5cm) high

£1,500-2,000   PC

TEDDY BEARS

A late 1940s/50s Chiltern gold mohair bear, with original paw pads, stitching, woven nose and glass eyes, in excellent condition.

The thick-thighed 'drumstick' legs are characteristic of Chiltern bears from the 1930s onwards.

£200-250   TBW

A Chiltern gold mohair 'Hugmee' teddy bear, with original foot pads, woven nose, glass eyes and original tag.

1930s-40s   *13in (33cm) high*

£400-500   LHT

A 1930s-40s Chiltern pale gold mohair 'Hugmee' bear, with original velvet paw pads, stitching and amber and black glass eyes.

Chiltern released the 'Hugmee' bear in 1923, and it became extremely popular. Note the shape of the head, and the size and length of the arms and legs –these are all typical of features of Hugmee bears from the 1930s onwards.

15in (38cm) high

£350-450   BEJ

A late 1940s-early 1950s Chiltern small gold mohair 'Hugmee' bear, with card-lined paws, velvet pads and original stitching and eyes.

8in (20cm) high

£200-300   PC

A late 1950s Chiltern large blond mohair 'Hugmee' bear, with original stitching, eyes and paw pads, lacking label.

This was the largest standard production size in the Hugmee range.

26in (66cm) high

£400-600   PC

A 1950s Chiltern golden moahir 'Ting-a-Ling Bruin' musical bear, with Rexine pads and original pads, stitching and eyes.

The Ting-a-Ling Bruin bear was introduced by Chiltern after WWII, and contained a mechanism that produced a musical tinkling sound when moved.

12in (30.5cm) high

£250-350   PC

A 1960s Chiltern 'Ting-a-Ling' musical bear, with gold, light blue and pink plush, and original stitching, plastic label and card label, in mint condition.

7in (17.5cm) high

£200-250   PC

QUICK REFERENCE – AMERICAN TEDDY BEARS

Many US bears were not labelled and so identification is difficult for today's collectors. A great many factories sprang up during the teddy bear 'fever' of the 1910s and 20s, including Ideal, Knickerbocker, Bruin, Aetna and Gund. However, many were short-lived and most did not mark or label their bears. Typical features of pre-war American bears include a wide, triangular head, large ears at the corners, arms slung lower down on the body and the bodily shape of German bears. This example, by market leader Ideal, is typical.

An early American gold mohair bear, with replaced foot pads, original stitching and boot button eyes, with some wear to the fur.

1905-06   *18in*

£300-400   **PC**

An early American pale gold plush bear, with original nose stitching, boot button eyes, and 'pinched' ears, paw pads re-covered in chamois.

c1910   *20in (51cm) high*

£700-800   **BEJ**

An American gold mohair 'sleepy eye' bear, with original stitching and celluloid spherical eyes, one paw pad recovered, with wear to his fur.

Rather than the standard boot button or two-colour glass eyes, these eyes are made from celluloid balls fixed in a metal mounting. The balls are weighted so that when the bear is laid down on its back, they roll down showing a plain side, thus appearing 'closed'.

1910-12

£800-1,000   **PC**

A 1920s American Ideal cinnamon mohair bear, with large flat feet, felt paw pads, small amber coloured glass eyes and a long snout.

15in (38cm) high

£700-800   **BEJ**

A 1950s American gold mohair 'mascot' bear, made for the University of California, with matching blue felt paw pads, sewn-on 'C' and 'California' badge, with original light blue eyes and stitching.

£40-50   **TBW**

An American bear-on-wheels, with fixed head position, original tail and metal frame and wheels.

American bears-on-wheels are more unusual than German.

1900-10

£300-500   **PC**

TEDDY BEARS

A Chad Valley blond alpaca fur 'Cubby' bear, with original stitching, eyes and original label to foot pad.

c1954   9.5in (24cm) high

£150-250   **PC**

A 1950s Chad Valley golden mohair 'Bear Brand' shop display large bear, with original paw pads, stitching and glass eyes, with panel where a label was once sewn on.

This enormous bear was originally part of a display selling women's stockings.

45in (114cm) high

£450-550   **PC**

A CLOSER LOOK AT A CHAD VALLEY BEAR

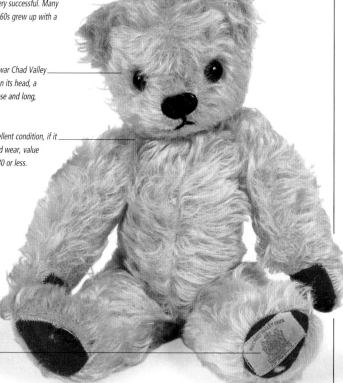

Chad Valley, founded in 1820, produced its first bears in 1915 and became very successful. Many British children of the 1940s-60s grew up with a Chad Valley bear.

This is characteristic of post-war Chad Valley bears, with ears placed flat on its head, a vertically stitched bulbous nose and long, curving arms.

Its fur and stitching is in excellent condition, if it had enjoyed years of love and wear, value would plummet to around £30 or less.

It still bears the company label on its foot pad. The label wording can help to date the bear, as it refers to Elizabeth Queen Consort of King George VI as 'Her Majesty the Queen', and can therefore be dated to before the 1953 Coronation of Queen Elizabeth II, when wording changed to 'Queen Mother'.

A late 1940s-early 1950s Chad Valley golden mohair small bear, with original paw pads, stitching and eyes, with label to right-hand paw pad.

£500-700   **TED**

A 1930s Chad Valley white mohair polar bear, with down-turned paws, original stitching and eyes, and Chad Valley label on left foot pad.

Polar bears were popular from the 1930s onwards, but grew again in popularity in the 1950s after the birth of a polar bear cub named Brumas in London Zoo in 1949.

£600-800   **PC**

A rare German Eduard Crämer musical bear, with internal mechanism operated by moving the neck up and down, with original stitched woollen nose and claws.

c1930   18in (45.5cm) high

£2,200-2,800   **TCT**

A 1930s Dean's Rag Book Co. rare blue mohair bear, with original paw pads, shaved snout and original stitching and eyes, and cupped ears.

c1926

£400-500   **TBW**

A 1950s German Diem yellow mohair bear, with short plush mohair on snout and paws, with internal growler.

£200-250   PC

A 1930s French Faye gold silk plush teddy, with original eyes and stitching, in excellent condition.

6.5in (16.5cm) high

£120-180   BEJ

A rare Einco white mohair bear, with side-glancing 'googly' type eyes, and original paw pads, in good condition.

Einco was the trade name used by Eisenmann & Co., a toy import company based in London. Founded in the late 19thC by brothers Josef and Gabriel Eisenmann, the company had an office in Germany and distributed bisque dolls, teddies and other toys. In 1908, Josef and Leon Rees founded the Chiltern Toy Works in Buckinghamshire, producing their first bear (Master Teddy) in 1915. This 'mousey' look is unusual, and is even more rodent-like than Deans' bears.

1915-20

£400-600   TBW

A 1960s German Grisly Spielwaren blond bear, with synthetic plush fur, open mouth, original eyes, and manufacturer's button to chest.

Grisly Spielwaren was founded In Germany in 1954, and saw a peak in sales during the 1960s and 70s. The company is still active today.

£80-120   PC

A 1930s German Hermann pin-jointed blond mohair bear, in period South German style woven wool outfit, with original stitching, eyes and paw pads.

6.75in (17cm) high

£200-300   PC

A 1930s German Hermann 'Helvetic' pale gold plush bear, with Rexine pads and original eyes, stitching and paw pads.

The term 'Helvetic' is used to describe a mechanical music box, usually Swiss, inside the bear.

18in (46cm) high

£700-900   BEJ

A 1950s Australian Joy Toys bright gold mohair plush bear, with original paw pads and eyes.

£200-300   TBW

A British Gabrielle Designs 'Paddington' bear, designed by Shirley Clarkson in 1972, with hat, duffel coat, Wellingtons and luggage tag.

The earliest versions from around 1973 have no hint of a foot inside their child's Dunlop wellington boots.

£40-60 PC

A Gabrielle Designs 'Aunt Lucy' bear, complete with clothing and accessories, including Peruvian coins in a pocket in her petticoat.

As she was not as popular as Paddington, Aunt Lucy is much harder to find today.

£150-200 PC

An American R. John Wright alpaca plush Paddington Bear, with 'Please look after this bear' label to neck, leather suitcase complete with marmalade, from a limited edition 2,500, in mint condition and with box in excellent condition.

R. John Wright is a noted American bear and doll artist whose work, often produced under license from Disney and others, is highly sought after by collectors.

2001 13.5in (34cm) high

£380-420 VEC

A Steiff 'Rupert Bear', with white alpaca fur, wearing traditional outfit, with stitch-sculpted fingers and thumb, from a limited edition.

2008 11in (28cm) high

£100-150 TBW

An unusual cotton plush 'Rupert Bear' style bear, with pale gold mohair head and paws, with wooden mechanism that opens the mouth when the tummy is squeezed.

c1930

£300-400 BEJ

A 1960s Chad Valley plush 'Sooty' teddy bear, wearing red dungarees, with original paw pads.

£15-20 PC

A Steiff 'Karl Lagerfeld' white alpaca fur bear, designed by Karl Lagerfeld, with Italian wool jacket over striped denims, a black silk cravat set with a Swarovski crystal, miniature Lagerfeld Eyewear Collection glasses, and exclusive white gold ear button, from a limited edition of 2,500, with box and certificate.

2008 15.5cm (40cm)

£600-800 TBW

T E D D Y B E A R S

of Witney

A British 'Brennus' (King) artist bear, by Jean and Bill Ashburner, jointed at the wrists and with two joints to the neck, with a needle sculpted nose and realistic three-dimensional polymer pads on unltrasuede paws, numbered five from a limited edition of eight.

18in (46cm)

£320-370

A German Freche Früchte Bären 'pumpkin' bear, by Kerstin Jeske, with label at the back in seam.

4in (10cm) high seated

£90-110   PC

A German 'Freche Früchte Bären' 'cake' bear, by Kerstin Jeske, with label at the back in seam.

5in (12cm) high seated

£80-90   PC

TEDDY BEARS

A British 'Miranda' artist bear, by Elizabeth Leggat, made from antique short pile plush mohair, and wearing a 1920s-style silk dress trimmed with vintage ribbon, with silver purse made from vintage material, weighted with steel shot, from a limited edition of six.

The purse is made from pieces of an original Edwardian purse.

2008	4in (10cm)
£450-500	**TBW**

An American 'Stella' artist bear, by Sue Lain, made with dusky pink mohair, and wearing a vintage broderie anglaise dress, numbered four from a limited edition of eight.

2008	12in (30cm)
£120-180	**TBW**

A British 'Gabriel Oak' artist bear, by June Kendall, with gold mohair and ultrasuede paws, glass eyes, and green-checked scarf, part filled with steel shot for weight, numbered six from a limited edition of twelve.

June Kendall is based in Hampshire, England, and was inspired to make bears at a time when she was involved in events in Dorset celebrating the 150th anniversary of Thomas Hardy. As a result she named her creations ' Hardy Bears' . This bear is themed on a character from ' Far From the Madding Crowd' .

2008	4.25in (11cm) high
£40-60	**TBW**

An English miniature 'Mikey' artist bear, by Elisabeth Marsden, with knitted wool golly doll and yellow cardigan, and split pin joints and glass eyes.

	2.75in (7cm) high
£45-50	**PC**

An American 'Algernon' artist bear, by Jeanette Warner, made of sparse cinnamon mohair with black glass bead eyes and aged felt paws.

2008/09	13in (33cm) high
£100-140	**TBW**

A Japanese 'Puu' artist bear, by Yuki Yamanaka, made of aged viscose, with a gingham patch and 'replaced' footpad, numbered four from a limited edition of ten.

Yuki Yamanaka, from Chiba, Japan, designed clothes after leaving university. She was inspired to start making bears in 1997 by an antique teddy that she particularly loved. The large head and tiny eyes are typical of contemporary Japanese animated and cartoon characters.

2007	8in (20cm)
£80-120	**TBW**

A Dany-Bären Riualdo artist bear, by Danielo-Rebecca Melse, in red aged mohair, with tags, black glass eyes, black vertically stitched nose, felt pads, and black claw stitching, numbered one from a limited edition of two, in near mint condition.

	16in (41cm) high
£300-500	**VEC**

A Swedish L. M. Ericsson telephone, the black tinplate body with gilt transfer decoration, nickel-plated cradle, and original cable.

c1910   *13.25in (33cm) high*

£100-150   **WDL**

A 1960s replica of the famous 'candlestick' telephone, originally manufactured by GEFA A.G. of Vienna in the 1920s.

c1965

£250-350   **ATK**

A 1930s black bakelite 200 series telephone.

8in (20cm) wide

£180-220   **L**

A 1950s black bakelite 300 series telephone, with original lead.

6in (15cm) wide

£100-150   **L**

A 1960s red plastic telephone, by the Reliance Telephone Co.

5in (12.5cm) wide

£40-60   **L**

A 1970s cream plastic Ericofon telephone, by Ericsson.

8.25in (21cm) high

£70-100   **L**

TELEPHONES

A Northern Telecom moulded plastic airplane telephone, in two tones of orange, with rotary dial and large Lucite 'propeller', embossed mark and foil label.

9in (23cm) wide

£50-80   **CRA**

A blue plastic 'Ola' T1000GD telephone, by Thomson, designed by Phillipe Starck.

11in (28cm) long

£50-60   **L**

An American candlestick telephone, with 'Stars & Stripes' decoration.

c1974   *11in (28.5cm) high*

£70-100   **NOR**

A Swatch Twinphone transparent green plastic telephone, Deluxe model.

9.5in (24cm) long

£30-50   **MHT**

A wooden Trub telephone, by gfeller, designed in the 1970s.

c1994   *8.25in (21cm) wide*

£70-90   **L**

A 1980s red plastic 'Hot Lips' telephone.

8.5in (21.5cm) wide

£35-45   **L**

QUICK REFERENCE

- Corgi toys were first produced in 1956 by Welsh toy company Mettoy, founded in 1933 by Phillip Ullman of the German toymaker Tipp & Co. Corgi toys were released to compete with Dinky's successful range of diecast toys, including the new Supertoys range. However, Corgi's vehicles featured exciting additions, such as plastic windows, and doors and boots that opened.

- Suspension, marketed as 'Glidamatic' was introduced in 1959. Clockwork, self-propelled versions were also introduced and are generally worth more than 'free-wheeling' models today. Innovations continued during the 1960s, including steering and jewelled head lights. Faceted ruby rear lights were introduced on a Bentley Continental released in 1961. 'Trans-o-lite' headlamps that transmitted daylight to give the appearance of illumination

were introduced in 1963.

- The 1960s and 70s also saw a range of models tied in with popular TV programmes and films. These included Batman's Batmobile, James Bond's Aston Martin and Chitty Chitty Bang Bang. These models were enormously popular at the time, and remain so with collectors today. Other popular ranges include Chipperfields Circus, and boxed gift sets which have seen an enormous rise in popularity over the past few years.

- As with other diecast toys, look out for variations by considering the colour, decals or stickers and other features such as the interior or wheels. To fetch the best prices, models should be accompanied by their boxes and any accessories they were sold with. The inclusion of the inner packaging is also a desirable feature. Always look for models in mint condition, and avoid pieces with repainting.

A Corgi No.351 Land Rover 'RAF' Vehicle, greyish blue, spun hubs, tow hook, in near mint condition, with good condition carded box.

The version of this model with suspension is worth roughly 25 per cent more.

1958-62

£100-150   VEC

A Corgi No.472 Land Rover public address vehicle 'Vote for Corgi', with spun hubs and two figures, in near mint condition, with good condition carded box.

1964-66

£100-150   VEC

A Corgi No.438 Land Rover 'Lepra', metallic green, cream plastic canopy, lemon interior, cast hubs, silver plastic tow hook, in mint condition, with mint condition window box.

This is a scarce variation with different coloured canopy. It is usually found with a green canopy and no decal, which would usually be worth under £100 in excellent, boxed condition.

1963-77

£650-850   VEC

A Corgi No.417 Land Rover 'Breakdown Service', red, yellow tin canopy, spun hubs, in mint condition, with mint condition, inner carded packing Collectors Club leaflet, in good condition box.

1960-62

£120-180   VEC

A Corgi No.487 Land Rover 'Chipperfield Circus' parade vehicle, red, blue, lemon interior, spun hubs, clown and monkey figures, in excellent condition, with good condition carded box.

1965-69

£80-120   VEC

A Corgi No.348 Ford Mustang Fastback, in lilac with a pale green interior, cast hubs, psychedelic 'flower power' decals with racing number 20 to doors, in near mint condition, with near mint carded box, with Collectors Club leaflet.

Produced for only a short period of time, this a very rare model in mint condition. The 'Pop Art' decoration is also obviously of its time and, along with that on a Mini Cooper, has become sought after in recent years.
1968-69

£1,000-1,500 VEC

A Corgi No.233 Heinkel Trojan Economy Car, red body, lemon interior, flat spun hubs, in mint condition, with mint condition carded box complete with Collectors Club folded leaflet.
1962-72

£70-100 VEC

A Corgi No.341 Mini Marcos GT850, maroon body, grey chassis, cream interior, golden jack take-off wheels, in mint condition, with near mint condition box, with Collectors Club folded leaflet.
1968-70

£50-70 VEC

A Corgi No.437 Cadillac Superior 'Ambulance', with battery operated red roof-light and cast hubs, in mint condition, with inner packing card and Collectors Club leaflet, with excellent condition carded box.
1965-68

£120-180 VEC

A Corgi No.474 Ford Thames 'Walls Ice-cream' Van, with musical chimes and spun hubs, in excellent condition, with good condition carded box.
1965-68

£150-200 VEC

A Corgi No.431 VW Pick-up, with plastic canopy and spun hubs, in mint condition, with mint condition Collectors Club leaflet and carded box.

The variation with a metallic gold body and red VW emblem can be worth around 50 per cent more.
1964-66

£100-150 VEC

A Corgi No.490 VW Breakdown Truck, with tan body, spun hubs, in mint condition, with good condition carded box with Collectors Club leaflet.
1967-69

£100-150 VEC

A Corgi No.1121 'Chipperfield Circus' six-wheel Crane Truck, with chrome jib, lacking hook and string but otherwise in excellent condition, with good condition carded picture box.

1963-69

£70-100   **VEC**

A Corgi No.1142 Ford Holmes Wrecker Truck, with unpainted booms, in excellent condition with two figures and instruction sheet, with excellent condition inner tray, and good condition outer window box.

1967-74

£150-200   **VEC**

A Corgi No.1120 Midland Red Motorway Express Coach, with yellow interior and flat spun hubs, in mint condition, with near mint condition box with Collectors Club leaflet.

£120-180   **VEC**

A Corgi No.50 Massey Ferguson 65 Tractor, with excellent condition carded box with inner packing card.

1959-66

£100-150   **VEC**

A Corgi Major Toys gift set no. 28, 'Car Transporter with four cars', comprising a Bedford TK cab transporter in red with mid and light blue trailer, Fiat 2100 (232), Renault Floride (222), Ford Consul Classic (234) and a Mercedes Benz 220 SE couple (230), vehicles in mint condition, with Corgi dog dummy boxes, box complete with internal packaging and instructions, minor wear to lid.

This is a very rare and desirable set and is in superb condition. Corgi gift sets in similar condition have been rising rapidly in value over the past few years.

1963-65

£600-800   **W&W**

A CLOSER LOOK AT A CORGI TANKER

The dark blue colour and decals on this model were produced as a special promotion for Shell Chemicallen of Holland c1963-64 only.

The variation of the lighter blue 1129 'Milk' Bedford tanker with an S-Type cab produced from 1962-65 is more common and worth around £150-200.

They were sold in special boxes with leaflets promoting Shell's various products – a mint and boxed example may sell for over £1,000 if found.

Reputedly only around 500 examples were ever made, making them very rare today and explaining the high price for this example in poor condition.

A Corgi 1129 blue and white Bedford S-Type 'Shell Petrol' Tanker, in poor condition.

c1963-64

£250-350   **SAS**

A Corgi 'Batman' 107 Batboat, in excellent condition, in excellent condition original striped window box.

1974-81

£70-100 SAS

A Corgi 259 Penguinmobile, in excellent condition, in excellent condition original striped window box.

1979-80

£50-70 SAS

A CLOSER LOOK AT A BATMOBILE

Corgi released the Batmobile for Christmas 1966, having dominated the Christmas market in 1965 with James Bond's Aston Martin – the Batmobile proved just as popular.

It was produced in different variations until 1979, but the rarest examples are the first issues from 1966-67, of which this is one.

This example is rarer still as it has a matte, not gloss, black body and is in excellent condition.

Although it retains its appealing pictorial box, it is not in great condition, and some of the many accessories are missing, which reduces the value by as much as a third.

A Corgi matte black 267 Batmobile, with three rockets and Club Slip, in excellent condition, in fair condition original box, inner plinth slightly torn.

1966-67

£600-800 SAS

A Corgi 647 'Buck Rogers' Starfighter, with Wilma and Tweaky plastic figurines, in excellent condition, in very good condition original striped window box.

1980-83

£50-70 SAS

A Corgi 434 'Charlie's Angels' Van, in excellent condition, in very good condition original pictorial window box.

1978-80

£30-40 SAS

A Corgi 342 'The Professionals' Ford Capri, in excellent condition, in very good condition original box.

1980-82

£80-120 SAS

A Corgi 320 'The Saint' Jaguar XJS, in excellent condition, in excellent condition original striped pictorial window box.
1978-81

£20-30   SAS

A Corgi 436 Spidervan, in excellent condition, in excellent condition original striped pictorial window box.
1979-80

£25-35   SAS

A CLOSER LOOK AT NODDY'S CAR

This model is hard to find, particularly in such excellent condition, as it was produced for only one year.

Always look closely at the Golly's face – the value can nearly double if Golly has a tan face, and can triple if he has a black face.

At the time, Noddy's popularity was waning, meaning fewer were sold and the model was discontinued relatively quickly.

If Golly has been replaced by a brown Master Tubby, the value falls to around half this price.

A Corgi 801 Noddy's Car, with Noddy, Big Ears, and a grey-faced Golly, in excellent condition, in excellent condition original box.
1969

£300-400   SAS

A Corgi 292 'Starsky & Hutch' Ford Torino, in excellent condition, in very good condition original box.

Unusually, an export model (produced in 1986) is worth around a tenth of this value – mainly as it was made in a run of 20,000 and was generally kept in mint condition by many collectors.
1977-82

£80-120   SAS

A Corgi 348 Vegas Ford Thunderbird, with Dan Tanner as driver, in excellent condition, in excellent condition original striped pictorial box.

1980-81

£30-40   SAS

A Corgi 497 'The Man From U.N.C.L.E.' Thrush-Buster, with purplish-blue body, Waverly Ring, Club Slip, packing disc, packing ring and corrugated packing piece, in excellent condition, in very good condition original box.

To fetch this price, the model must have the ring and both internal card packing components. Look out for the white finished body, which was produced in the first year only (1966) and can fetch over twice this price.
1966-69

£300-400   SAS

QUICK REFERENCE

- Dinky toys were first produced in 1933 by Meccano Ltd as accessories to their popular range of Hornby model railways. They originated in a range known as 'Model Miniatures' introduced in 1931, which comprised 22 sets including one of model vehicles. In 1934, this set became the first set of 'Meccano Dinky Toys', intended to compete with America's Tootsie Toys, which were being imported into the UK and proving very popular with children.
- Dinky toys were made in Liverpool until 1979, and also at Bobigny in France from 1937–72. Following the closure of the Liverpool factory in 1979 the name was acquired by Matchbox in 1987, and then Mattel, who have not used it since 2001.
- Collectors consider the 'golden age' of Dinky to be the 1930s. By 1935, over 200 models were made, and examples are usually highly sought after. Survivors are rare as many pre-war models were made from a metallic alloy that tends to crumble over time.
- In 1947 the smaller scale 'Supertoys' range was released, followed by the 'Speedwheels' range in 1969. These are easier to find, and often less expensive to collect. Supertoys are particularly sought after by collectors.
- When buying, look for models in good condition, and beware of any repainting, even in small areas, as this reduces desirability considerably. If the original box is present and in good condition it can add over 40 per cent to the value.
- Look out for variations in paint colour, details such as cab stripes and hubs, and even plastic interiors. Some variations may indicate special models that were exported to certain countries in limited numbers, and can fetch high prices today.

A Dinky No.110 Aston Martin DB3S, mid-green, red seats, ridged hubs, white driver, racing number 22, in excellent condition, with good condition correct colour spot card picture box.
1956-59

£180-220 VEC

A Dinky No.176 Austin A105 Saloon, grey body, red side flash and ridged hubs, in near mint condition, with near mint condition correct colour spot card picture box.
1958-59

£100-150 VEC

A Dinky No.167 A.C. Aceca Coupé, grey body, red roof, shaped spun hubs, in excellent condition, with excellent condition incorrect colour spot card picture box.

The colour of the car on the box does not match the colour of the model. For some collectors, this makes this example less desirable. This is more valuable than the example with matching red hubs.
1958-63

£100-150 VEC

A Dinky No.112 Austin Healey Sprite MkII, red body, cream interior, spun hubs, in near mint condition, with good condition card picture box.

Look out for the South African export variation with a turquoise, pink, light blue or dark blue body, as this can fetch around four times as much as this.

1961-66

£80-120 VEC

A Dinky No.38A Frazer Nash BMW Car, grey, red seats and ridged hubs, in excellent condition, needs cleaning.

Frazer Nash were a British car manufacturer who were active from 1922-c1957. From 1934-39, they were the offical importer and assembler for BMW in the UK.
1947-50

£220-280 VEC

A French Dinky No.500 Citroen 2CV, orange body, plastic open-top, cream interior, shaped spun hubs, near mint condition, with near mint condition colour card picture box.

£100-150 VEC

A Dinky No.515 Ferrari 250GT 2 + 2, red body, white interior, concave spun hubs, in near mint condition, with near mint condition full colour card picture box.

£100-150 VEC

A Dinky No.1408 Honda S800, yellow body, red interior, concave spun hubs, in excellent condition, with near mint condition card picture box.

£80-120 C

A Dinky No.57/005 Ford Thunderbird, mid blue body, white roof, shaped cast wheels, plated bumpers, red interior, in near mint condition, with excellent condition card picture box.

This number indicates this model was made in Hong Kong, and is one of the more desirable and valuable of the small range made there from 1965-80. Yellow 'see-through' window boxes for Hong Kong models are scarce.
1965-67

£150-200 VEC

A Dinky No.165 Humber Hawk, maroon roof, lower body, cream middle, shaped spun hubs, slight spotting to roof, otherwise excellent condition, with excellent condition correct colour spot card picture box.
1959-60

£100-150 VEC

A CLOSER LOOK AT A DINKY CAR

This model was also produced from 1950-54 numbered 139b.

Many colour variations of this model number are sought after. Cream bodies with dark maroon roofs are more affordable at around half this value.

This colour variation with a 'lowline' long-slung configuration and blue hubs was only available from 1958-59, making it rarer than other variations.

As this is an American car, it has appeal to diecast collectors on both sides of the Atlantic, widening demand.

A Dinky No.171 Hudson Commodore Sedan, lowline, light grey body, mid blue upper and ridged hubs, factory paint touch-in to bonnet, in excellent condition, with near mint condition correct colour spot card picture box.
1958-59

£200-300 VEC

A Dinky no.157 Jaguar XK120, turquoise lower body, cerise upper body, red ridged hubs, in excellent condition.
1957-59

£100-150 VEC

A Dinky No.22A Maserati Sport 2000, dark red, plated convex hubs, white driver, in excellent condition, with good condition yellow card picture box.

£70-100 VEC

A Dinky No.108 MG Midget Sports Car, red body and ridged hubs, tan interior, racing number 24, white driver, in excellent condition, with excellent condition white colour spot card picture box.

This is a desirable car and is in red, rather than the plainer white.
1955-59

£200-300 VEC

A French Dinky Simca 8 Sport, pale duck egg green, red interior, chromed convex hubs, white tyres, in near mint condition.

£300-500 VEC

A Dinky pre-war No.22G Streamlined Tourer, dark blue body and smooth hubs, white tyres, upper windscreen missing, steering wheel complete, some light play wear but in overall good condition.
1935-41

£120-180 VEC

A rare Dinky no.105 Triumph TR2 touring with spun hubs, in light grey, with red interior, spun hubs with black knobbly tyres, includes driver, in excellent condition.

This variation, with its spun hubs, is usually worth up to twice the amount of the more common version with red cast hubs.
1957-60

£180-220 VEC

A Dinky No.254 Austin Taxi, green lower body, yellow upper and ridged hubs, black interior and baseplate, in near mint condition, with excellent condition correct colour spot card picture box.

Look out for the rarer blue variation, with matching blue hubs, as this can be worth over three times the value of this two-tone variation.
1956-59

£100-150   VEC

A Dinky No.273 Mini Van 'RAC Road Service', blue, white roof, red interior, in near mint condition, with good condition carded box.
1965-70

£100-150   VEC

A Dinky No.987 Mobile Control Room 'ABC Television', blue, grey, red, plastic hubs, in excellent condition, complete with cameraman and camera, with good condition lift-off-lid box.

1962-69

£150-200   VEC

A Dinky No.491 'Jobs Dairy' Van, cream, red chassis and ridged hubs, black knobbly tyres, in excellent condition, with excellent condition correct colour spot yellow card box.

This model was made for promotional purposes, and is rare today. Always check the transfers, as wear reduces value. Job's Dairy was founded in 1819 in Middlesex, London and is still selling milk today.

£150-200   VEC

A Dinky No.923 Big Bedford Van 'Heinz', red cab, chassis, yellow back, hubs, replacement decals.

The Heinz transfers on this rare model have been replaced. Had they been original and the model in mint condition and complete with its box in similar condition, the value could have been £2,000.

1958-59

£80-120   VEC

A CLOSER LOOK AT A DINKY VAN

Dinky's ranges of delivery vans are one of the most collectable Dinky areas, with the '28' series being highly popular.

Pre-war models are harder to find, particularly in excellent or mint condition, and most were only produced for short time periods of a few years or less.

Values depend on the 'decal' transfers. Other desirable examples include 'Pickfords', 'Wakefield's Castrol' and 'Hornby Trains'.

Learn the differences between the three different shapes, or 'types', as this affects value. Early 'type one' shapes are usually the most valuable.

A Dinky No.28L 'Crawfords' Delivery Van, type one, red body, metal wheels, solid casting, some traces of original green lacquer, slightly distorted, some restoration to paint and decals on rear section, otherwise in good condition.

1934-35

£300-500   VEC

A Dinky No.25B Covered Wagon, type four, black chassis, cream cab, back, red tin tilt, ridged hubs, chrome loss to grille assembly, otherwise in excellent condition.

1947-50

£180-220   VEC

A Dinky No.575 Panhard SNCF Semi Trailer, dark blue cab, trailer, concave metal hubs, tin tilt with printing to both sides, in near mint condition, with fair condition complete card picture box.

£150-200   VEC

A Dinky No.502 Foden Flat Truck, green cab, flatbed, ridged hubs, black chassis, silver flash, black herringbone tyres, overall in good condition.

Foden flatbed trucks are popular with collectors, with rare export models in mint condition sometimes fetching over £10,000.

1947-48

£80-120   VEC

A Dinky No.434 Bedford TK Crash Truck 'Auto Services', metallic red cab, deep red interior and plastic hubs, grey back, in excellent condition, with good condition carded picture box.

The 'Auto Services' transfer is rarer than the 'Top Rank Motorway Services', although values do not differ too much.

1966-70

£80-120   VEC

A Dinky No.430 Breakdown Lorry, dark tan cab and chassis, green back, red ridged hubs, 'Dinky Service' in black to sides, in excellent condition, with excellent condition blue and white striped lidded box.

The most valuable variation has a red, glazed cab and a pale grey back, and can fetch over double the value of this colourway.

1954-64

£180-220   VEC

QUICK REFERENCE

- A nostalgic name from many childhoods, Matchbox toys were produced by Lesney Products. Founded in London in 1947, the company produced its first toys in 1949. Aiming to produce pocket-sized toys for pocket money prices, its first major success was a coronation coach, produced from 1952 for the coronation of Queen Elizabeth II. The 'Matchbox' name was registered in 1954, and was used on base plates from 1955.

- Although no consistent scale was used, the most common was the 1-75 range, launched in 1953. This forms the core of most collections, along with the 'Models of Yesteryear' range launched in 1967. From 1953–69, Lesney's toys were distributed by Moko, whose name appeared on packaging, with Lesney acquiring the company in 1959. Metal wheels were discontinued in 1958 and were replaced with plastic.

- The 1960s were a 'golden age' for Matchbox, and by 1966 the company was producing 100 million models per year. In 1969, the 'Superfast' range, with suspension, was launched to compete with 'faster' cars such as those made by Corgi, or Mattel's 'Hot Wheels'. 'Superfast' cars were made until 1983.

- Later ranges, from c1971 onwards, include 'Super-Kings' and 'Speed Kings', although these are not currently as popular with collectors, they may prove to be an area to watch for the future. Lesney closed in 1982, with the brand being acquired by Tyco in 1992. Modern limited editions 'collectors' models may turn out to be a very long term investment, as so many have been kept mint and boxed.

- The majority of examples to be found cost under £30 and allow a collection to be built up affordably. However, look out for rare variations, considering features such as colours, decals, wheels, base plates and the interior, which can fetch hundreds of pounds. Always aim to buy in mint condition, as this is most likely to ensure an item holds or increases its value.

A Matchbox 'Regular Wheels' No.65b Jaguar 3.8 Saloon, in red, with a silver base and black plastic wheels, in near mint condition, with box in excellent condition.

Check the wheels, as the same model and colour with silver plastic wheels can be worth over twice the value of this version.
Introduced in 1962

£120-180   VEC

A Matchbox 8e Ford Mustang, in orange with red interior and solid chrome hubs, in very good condition, with good condition original box.

The orange body is the most valuable variation, white bodies are usually worth roughly a tenth of this value if they are in similar condition.

Introduced in 1966

£280-320   SAS

A Matchbox 31b Ford Station Wagon, in yellow with maroon baseplate, with windows and silver plastic wheels, in excellent condition, in good condition original box.
Introduced in 1960

£150-200   SAS

A Matchbox 'Models of Yesteryear' No.Y5-2 1929 Bentley 4.5 litre, metallic apple green, red seats and tonneau, racing number 5, Union Jack decals to both side doors, in excellent condition, unboxed.
1963

£70-100   VEC

A Matchbox Superfast No.57f Range Rover Carmichael Rescue Vehicle, finished in yellow with black base and trim.

The yellow body and lack of decals indicate that this is a very rare pre-production model – production models were in red or white and had 'Police Rescue' or 'Fire' decals.
c1982

£200-300   VEC

A Matchbox 'Models of Yesteryear' No.Y11 Aveling and Porter Road Roller, green, red, gold trim and maker's plate, in near mint condition, unboxed.

The gold maker's plate on this example makes it around twice as valuable as those without.

1958

£100-150   VEC

A Matchbox 'Models of Yesteryear' No.Y9 Fowler Showman's Engine in bright red with 'Lesney Modern Amusements' decal, with white roof, yellow wheels, in excellent condition, with box in near mint condition.

1965

£40-60   VEC

A Matchbox 'Regular Wheels' No.G3 'Farm' gift set, containing No.4 Dodge Stake Truck, No.12 Land Rover Safari, No.37 Dodge Cattle Truck, No.39 Ford Tractor, No.40 Hay Trailer, No.43 Pony Trailer, No.65 Claas Combine Harvester and No.72 Standard Jeep, all in mint condition, with near mint blue and yellow window box with detailed picture, still shrink-wrapped.

1968

£200-300   VEC

A Matchbox No.G1 'Auto Transporter' gift set, comprising five cars and car transporter, overall conditions are generally near mint, with good condition presentation window box, inner plastic tray is in near mint condition.

£25-35   VEC

A Matchbox 'Kingsize' No.G8 gift set, containing No.K1 Foden 'Hoveringham' Tipper, No.K11 Fordson Super Major Tractor with Farm Tipping Trailer, No.K12 Foden Wreck Truck and No.K15 Merryweather Turntable Fire Engine, in mint condition, with inner plastic tray, near mint condition outer blue and yellow window box, still shrink-wrapped, with original Sellotape marks to window.

The addition of the K1 Foden tipper is unusual.

c1965

£280-320   VEC

A Matchbox 'Kingsize' No.G8 'Construction' gift set, containing No.K1 Foden 'Hoveringham' Tipper, No.K7 'Curtiss' Rear Dumper, No.K10 'Aveling Barford' Tractor Shovel, No.K13 ERF Concrete Mixer and No.K14 'Taylor' Jumbo Crane, in mint condition, with excellent condition box.

The inner plastic tray is both rare and in excellent condition. The pictorial sleeve is also in unusually excellent condition. This example shows how the combination of models and a box in mint condition can push up the price for desirable gift sets.

£750-850   VEC

A Matchbox 'Leslie Smith OBE' poseable figure, no.186 of only up to 500 produced, dressed in grey suit and holding Matchbox book, in mint condition, with carded box.

Smith (1918-2005) was the co-founder of Lesney in 1947. This model was produced in 1990 to commemorate the Matchbox MICA UK Convention on the 24th March 1990.

1990

£70-100   VEC

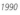

QUICK REFERENCE

- Tinplate toys are made from sheets of steel plated with tin. These sheets were painted by hand, or decorated with lithographic transfers, and cut into shapes, bent, embossed and fixed together to form toys. Tinplate became popular in the mid-19thC and replaced wood and cast iron as it was more economical and provided wider scope for manufacture.
- Germany was the 'home' of the tin toy, with factories exporting toys around the world. Notable makers include Märklin (founded 1856), Gebrüder Bing (1863-1933), and Schreyer & Co (1912-78), whose Schuco name is still used for toys today. Toys by these companies are particularly popular. The US became a secondary centre from the 1880s onwards, with names such as Marx (1896-c1982) and Ferdinand Strauss (c1914-42) being sought after.
- From the late 19thC-1930s, production focused on cars, trucks, zeppelin airships and aircraft. The earliest examples from the mid-late19thC were hand-painted. Look closely to see brush marks, especially on details.
- After WWII, the centre of production moved to Japan and names such as Horikawa (SH), Nomura (TN Toys) and Yonizawa are sought after. The development of the battery allowed for novelty features such as flashing lights and sounds; the more numerous and bizarre the 'actions' the more a toy is likely to be worth. Robots and spacecraft also became popular reflecting the excitement of the 'Space Race' to the moon in the 1950s and 60s.
- Value is dependent on the type of toy, the maker, the size, the date and the condition. Scratched transfers are almost impossible to restore, although shallow dents can sometimes be fixed. Early hand-painted pieces are highly sought after, but the desirability of humorous features in later toys should not be underestimated. Large, early ships or zeppelins by Märklin can fetch over £20,000, while a simple 1960s Japanese spacecraft can be found for under £50.

A 1920s-30s Bing black lithographed tinplate clockwork 19872 Model T Ford, with driver.

6.25in (16cm) long

£300-500   SAS

A late 20thC reproduction JB Carette-style navy blue non-powered painted tinplate Limousine, with bisque driver and passenger, in excellent condition.

If this were an original Carette limousine, it could have fetched over £3,000.

12.5in (32cm) long

£30-50   SAS

A 1920s German Gebrüder Bing red lithographed tinplate clockwork tourer, with driver, in good condition, but lacking rear seat.

5.5in (14cm) long

£120-180   SAS

A US Zone German Schuco Kommando Anno 2000, red, plated radiator, opening bonnet to reveal engine, paint finish crazed overall, otherwise in excellent condition, with good condition box and instructions.

c1946-c1949   6in (15cm) long

£80-120   VEC

A US Zone German Schuco Varianto-Limo 3041, red tinplate clockwork car, complete with control wire, very minor wear to edges, otherwise in excellent condition, with fair condition box and instructions.

The 'US Zone' wording refers to the period from 1945-49, when Western Germany was divided into administrative zones by the Allies, following WWII.

c1946-c1949

£100-150   VEC

A US Zone German Schuco Fex 1111, green bodywork with plated radiator and windscreen, red wheel hubs, very minor chips, wear to edges, otherwise in good condition, boxed.

c1946-c1949

6in (15cm) long

£80-120   VEC

A rare French CIJ clockwork tinplate Renault Fregate, finished in greyish-green, with electric head lights, opening driver's door, steerable front wheels, plated bumpers and grille, lacking rear seat assembly, otherwise in good condition.

CIJ is a sought-after name, and this is very good quality car.

12.5in (32cm) long

£350-450   VEC

A 1950s German Tipp & Co. US Navy Staff Car, tinplate friction drive car in dark green, with US Navy 63 transfers, plastic hubs and tyres, plated parts, in near mint condition.

7.5in (19cm) long

£60-90   VEC

A Japanese TN Toys tinplate 'Sonic Dodge Charger', battery operated, with passenger detail to interior, rubber tyres, whistle and aerial accessory, in generally excellent condition, with good condition card box.

16in (41cm) long

£80-120   VEC

A rare French CIJ two tone friction drive Renault Dauphine, with detailed printing, rubber wheels, and registration number '5-56', light scratching on roof, otherwise in excellent condition.

8.75in (22cm) long

£250-350   VEC

A rare Japanese Modern Toys large tinplate American Car, finished in red, battery-operated, with steerable front wheels, rubber tyres, some discolouration to plated parts, lacks aerial, in good condition, with some wear.

14in (36cm) long

£70-100   VEC

A late 1960s Japanese Ichiko friction-powered lithographed tinplate pop-art Jaguar Saloon, in good condition, headlamps replaced.

It's the fabulous graphics that make this car so desirable and valuable, as well as the fact that it is a Jaguar.

7.75in (20cm) long

£150-200   SAS

A German Gama large tinplate Tipper, with orange tipping body and lower cab, hub caps, beige cab roof, black trim, opening rear tailgate and steerable front wheels, in good condition but some wear to edges.

14in (36cm) long

£120-180   **VEC**

A German Gama Articulated Transport Truck, with detailed interior, steerable front wheels, silver trailer with 'International Transport' to sides, detailed tin-printing, drop-down rear door, rubber tyres, in overall good condition, but lacking spare wheel.

19in (48cm) long

£150-250   **VEC**

A CLOSER LOOK AT A RICH TOYS VAN

The Rich Manufacturing Company was founded in Illinois in 1915 and produced toys until 1962, being known as 'Rich Toys Inc' from 1935 when the company moved to Clinton, Iowa.

This example retains many of its original accessories, including wooden and glass milk bottles and carriers, and has a driver and opening doors – all are desirable features.

Their pre-war toys are prized and comparatively scarce. Most were pull-along and made of wood, or where tinplate was used, they were usually horse-drawn.

Advertising toys can be scarce and also appeal to collectors of advertising memorabilia, a factor which often drives prices up.

A rare Rich Toys lithographed tin 'Bordens' delivery van, with yellow wooden roof and wooden bonnet, stencilled 'Bordens', with seated driver and two cases of milk bottles, one with four glass bottles, the other two wooden bottles, rear doors open, in good condition.

13.5in (34cm) long

£4,500-6,000   **BER**

A German Arnold large tinplate Tipper Truck, with friction drive, orange chassis and hub caps, detailed tin-printed interior and steering wheel, yellow tipping body with opening tailgate, in good condition but lacking driver.

11in (28cm) long

£250-350   **VEC**

A rare German Gama No.291/1 'International Express' Van, with opening rear door, friction drive, detailed cab interior, lacking one rear door handle, head light lenses and front hub caps, otherwise in good condition.

13.75in (35cm) long

£100-150   **VEC**

A rare German Goso miniature clockwork Breakdown Truck, with blue cab, silver chassis, brick red jib and rubber wheels, in excellent condition.

5.25in (13cm) long

£40-60   **VEC**

A 1950s German Tipp & Co. transfer-printed tinplate motorcycle and rider, the rider wearing a red jacket and plus fours, marked 'MADE IN U.S. ZONE GERMANY' and with 'TCO' maker's monogram.

Known for their motorbikes, Tipp & Co. (1912-71) are a sought-after name. The Ullman Brothers, who owned Tipp & Co., fled Germany during WWII after the government seized their company, and founded Mettoy in Britain. After the war, both companies ran concurrently.

7.5in (19cm) long

£250-350   QU

A Spanish Rico clockwork Touring Motorcyclist, with brown and red rider with white helmet on blue bike, plain brown tinplate wheels and stabilisers, clockwork inoperable, otherwise in good condition.

£120-180   VEC

A US Zone German Huki clockwork red and white motorbike with sidecar, with brown and grey rider, registration 'K-1021', sidecar with number '21', in excellent condition.

c1946-c1949   6.25in (16cm) long

£250-350   VEC

A German Günthermann tinplate Crawler Tractor, with driver, orange wheels, working motor, lacking tracks, otherwise in excellent condition.

7in (18cm) long

£60-£80   VEC

A 1960s Japanese Marusan friction-powered lithographed 'Silver Pigeon' Motorcycle, in good condition, part of base-plate overpainted.

5.25in (13.5cm) long

£200-300   SAS

A CLOSER LOOK AT A FISCHER MOTORCYCLE

This toy's small size indicates that it is a penny toy, an inexpensive toy sold for a penny in stores and by street vendors.

Despite so many having been made and sold, few have survived the ravages of a child's attention as they are so small and fragile, making them scarce today.

Fischer is a notable German maker and their unusual, amusing toys, such as this example, are sought after.

Value also depends on the level of detail and the condition. Although this piece is well-detailed, it is worn; had it been in mint condition it may have fetched up to twice as much.

A Fischer penny toy red and gold motorcycle, with rider and passenger in front chair, in fair condition, slight varnishing to wheels.

3.5in (8.5cm) long

£400-600   SAS

A Gama lithographed tinplate clockwork tractor and trailer, with plastic driver, lacks clockwork motor.

1937   *12in (30.5cm) long*

£50-80   VEC

A Marx clockwork crawler tractor, finished in orange with yellow detailing, with silver metal wheels and black rubber tracks, lacking seat and chimney stack, otherwise in good condition.

£25-35   VEC

A 1920s German Lehmann 651 EPL 1 Zeppelin, lacking celluloid blades and in poor condition, bent at back, scratched surface and rusting.

This very worn example is worth as much as this due to the notable maker and the subject matter. Zeppelins are highly sought after.

£120-180   SAS

A clockwork painted tinplate airship, finished in grey and red.

By an unknown maker, the form of this example is not as realistic or detailed as the one above.

7.75in (20cm) long

£60-80   SAS

A tinplate clockwork submarine, possibly by Bing, finished in grey, with black hand-rails, brass screw on cap, propeller and rudder, in good condition.

10in (25cm)

£150-200   VEC

A 1920s German Fischer yellow and blue speedboat penny toy, numbered '5', lacking rear flag, wheels overpainted, otherwise in good condition.

The overpainting and missing part reduce the value of this whimsical wheeled boat.

6.25in (16cm) long

£180-220   SAS

A rare 1930s German Günthermann acrobatic aircraft, in dark blue and grey, with clockwork motor and flip-over acrobatic action, lacks tailfin and rear jockey wheel but includes pilot, permanent key, in fair condition.

7.75in (20cm) wingspan

£80-120   VEC

A French JRD novelty character driving a clockwork eccentric action tinplate car, with logo to bonnet and boot '1949 RF', the driver with moustache and bowler hat, blue jacket, yellow waistocat and red bow tie, in good condition with some wear to finish.

7in (18cm) long

£80-£120   **VEC**

A Greppert & Kelch 552 clockwork lithographed tinplate red, white and blue three-wheel trolley car, with lady driver, dog and boy.

6in (15cm) high

£100-150   **SAS**

A CLOSER LOOK AT A LEHMANN TOY

Lehmann were founded in Nuremberg in 1881 and produced often complexly constructed lightweight tinplate toys that were exported across the world.

Along with Günthermann, their toys are loved for their fun and inventive forms, often with a bizarre sense of humour – the Balky Mule is typical.

The clown is well dressed and the mule has a textured finish. When wound the clown rocks back and forth as the mule bucks.

The theme and unusual action were popular with children and this toy was made for decades from the early 1900s, making it one of the more common and affordable of Lehmann's toys.

A Lehmann transfer-printed tinplate EPL 245 Balky Mule, in good condition.

7.5in (19cm) long

£280-320   **SAS**

A 1950s American Marx 'Milton Berle' lithographed tinplate 'Crazy Car', with vivid and colourful illustrations and catchphrases, revolving head and 'eccentric' movements, in fair condition with some wear and damage.

Milton Berle (1908-2002) was a famous 1950s US radio and television star known to millions as 'Uncle Miltie'. The damage and lack of a box has reduced the value, although he does retain his plastic hat, which is often missing.

7in (18cm) long

£60-90   **VEC**

A 1960s Japanese Masutoku Toy Factory M-T Co Hand Car, no.3296, battery operated, three actions, in near mint condition, with good condition illustrated box.

£70-£100   **VEC**

A Lehmann transfer-printed tinplate Sea Lion, with key, in very good condition.

Lehmann's animal toys are highly collectable. Including a climbing monkey and a walking crocodile, they were often inspired by German colonial activities in Africa.

7.25in (18.5cm) long

£250-350   **SAS**

A Schuco clockwork pig violinist, complete with sailor's uniform, cap, violin and bow, in good condition.

5.5in (14cm) high

£80-120   **SAS**

QUICK REFERENCE - SCHUCO FIGURES

Schuco was the tradename used by Schreyer & Co., founded in Nuremberg, Germany in 1912, until 1921 when the company was renamed Schuco. Their mechanical toys were loved before and after the war, and included bears (such as the famous Yes-No teddy bear) and cars. These small clockwork figures form a collecting area of their own – many are animals that play instruments or perform acrobatics. Look out for unusual figures that may not have appealed at the time so would have sold in fewer numbers making them rarer today. One example is a monk with a beer tankard, or 'Mr Atom' who can fetch over £500. Unless very rare, to be of interest the clockwork mechanism must work, accessories should be complete and the clothes must not be faded.

A Schuco clockwork Pig drummer, complete with drum, sticks, hat and clothes, in good condition.

5.5in (14cm) high

£80-120   **SAS**

A Schuco 882 clockwork acrobatic 'Turn Clown', in fair condition with original clothes by wear to his face, in poor condition original box.

£60-80   **SAS**

A Schuco 986 'Solisto' clockwork monkey drummer, complete with drum, sticks, hat and clothes, in good condition.

5.5in (14cm) high

£60-80   **SAS**

A Japanese 1950s-60s Nomura 'TN Toys' transfer-printed tinplate, fabric and soft vinyl bartender clockwork toy in mint condition.

11.5in (29cm) high

£50-80   **MA**

A British lithographed tinplate lever-action red, blue and yellow minstrel dancer, in good condition.

£40-60   **SAS**

A 1950s Japanese grey transfer-printed tinplate clockwork robot.

5in (12cm) high

£150-180   QU

A 1960s Japanese Yonezawa transfer-printed tinplate and plastic robot, marked 'MADE IN JAPAN'.

8in (20cm) high

£500-700   QU

A Mainland battery operated 99/30 dark metallic grey painted and lithographed tinplate 'Moon Explorer', in good condition, in good original box.

£70-100   SAS

A 1950s-60s Japanese TM Modern Toys tinplate and plastic 'Mischief Monkey' clockwork toy, in mint condition.

The scarce box refers to this toy as 'Mischievous Monkey' and can add more than 50 per cent to the value.

8in (20cm) long

£20-30   MA

A Zeppelin tinplate carousel, probably German, crank handle operates musical roundabout, in generally excellent condition, with original plain card box.

8in (20cm) high

£120-180   VEC

A 1950s Czechoslovakian transfer-printed tinplate clockwork train scene, unmarked, in mint condition with original card box.

9.5in (24cm) long

£18-22   MTB

A 1950s Louis Marx 'G Man Automatic' tinplate child's pistol, with rare original box and decals.

This is in excellent condition and retains its box, hence the high value. However, look for signs of age and wear as the box is being reproduced today for a collectors' market.

3.25in (8cm) high

£100-150   BB

QUICK REFERENCE

- The first model trains, produced in the 1850s, were stylised, bulky and unrealistic. By the 1890s, more realistic tinplate models, with clockwork- or steam mechanisms, were being produced by German manufacturers such as Märklin (est 1759) and Gebrüder Bing (1863-1933). Many of these were exported to the US and Europe, although production and exports ceased during the two World Wars.
- Gauge sizes were introduced by Märklin in 1891. Their larger gauges (II and III) were quickly replaced by smaller gauges (I and 0) in 1910 as demand for smaller trains sets grew. By 1938, gauge I had also been discontinued, and in 1935 even gauge 0 had been replaced by the smaller 00-gauge. Märklin's HO gauge, which was even smaller, was used from 1948.

- The well-known British company Hornby began making trains in 1920 and their pre-WWII gauge 0 trains are now widely collected. Post War examples were of comparatively poor quality, and the range was discontinued in 1969. Hornby's Dublo range, designed to compete with small gauge sets by Märklin and Trix, was introduced in 1938 and is also highly collectable today. Nationalised livery trains (produced 1953-1957) are less desirable. Hornby was taken over by Tri-ang in 1964, with the name Tri-ang Hornby being used from 1965.
- As many trains were played with and have become worn or damaged, good condition examples will command the highest prices. The precise model, date and livery also affects value, with rare models being more desirable.

An early Hornby O gauge No. 2 4-4-4 clockwork Tank locomotive, LMS maroon No. 4-4-4, with nickel couplings and brass buffers, in excellent condition.

This was the only 4-4-4 gauge model made by Hornby, with the earliest models being in LMS and LNER liveries.
1923-29

£420-480 VEC

A Hornby O gauge EM120 0-4-0 tank loco, LNER green No.2900 20v electric, in very good condition, with reproduction box.

£150-200 VEC

A Hornby O gauge No. 2 Special 4-4-0 Loco and Tender 'COUNTY OF BEDFORD' GWR green No. 3821, 20v electric, repainted, lined and transferred.

With the crest on the tender and a black running plate used from 1930-36, this scarce 20v electric version is usually worth up to twice the value of the clockwork version.
1936-41

£700-1,000 VEC

A Hornby Dublo three-rail pre-war EDL1 4-6-2 LNER blue A4 Class Loco No. 4498 'Sir Nigel Gresley', in good condition with some wear to paint, in fair condition box, dated '9/38'.

Made from 1938-41, prewar models have full wheel valances and a push rod gear, instead of valve gear.
1938

£600-800 VEC

A Hornby Dublo three-rail EDG7 0-6-2 GWR green Tank Loco No. 6699, with gold decal to bunker rear, with horseshoe-type motor and instruction booklet dated '8/49', in excellent condition, and good condition pale blue box with 'GW' sticker to one end and dated '6/48'.
c1948

£700-1,000 VEC

A CLOSER LOOK AT A HORNBY DUBLO TRAIN

This is a rare version of this model with smoke deflectors on each side of the front of the boiler.

The deflectors indicate models that were repaired at the Binns Road factory using new 'Duchess of Montrose' bodies painted in 'Duchess of Atholl' livery.

A standard 'Duchess of Atholl' model, made from 1947-53, is usually worth under £200.

Also look out for the version with a cream nameplate, as this can fetch up to twice the price of the standard model.

A Hornby Dublo three-rail EDL2/D2 4-6-2 LMS maroon Princess Coronation class locomotive and tender No.6231 'Duchess of Atholl', in excellent condition, with repair box with end packing pieces and repair No.34064 to both ends, with tender box in good condition and dated "2/50".
1950

£700-1,000   VEC

A Hornby Dublo three-rail EDL7 0-6-2 LNER green N2 Class Tank No. 9596, with horseshoe type motor and gold decal to bumper rear, in excellent condition with faded pale blue box, the lid dated '5/49'.
1949

£220-280   VEC

A Hornby Dublo three-rail 3232 Co-Co green Diesel Loco, complete with instruction booklet dated '8/60', in excellent condition, in excellent condition box.
1960

£180-220   VEC

A rare Hornby Dublo three-rail EDL7 LNER Tank Goods set, containing 0-6-2 black N2 Class Tank No. 9596, with gold decal to bunker rear and horseshoe type motor, with three NE Goods Vehicles in green/grey Open, brown Vent Van and Brake Van, and with track, controller with wires, instruction flyer, oil bottle, instruction booklet dated '9/47', purple guarantee slip, pre-war printed and tested/guarantee slip dated 30th January 1947, in excellent condition, in complete excellent condition box.

This first post-war set is very rare as most were exported when it was issued in Autumn 1947.
c1947

£1,200-1,800   VEC

A Hornby Dublo two-rail 2220 4-6-0 BR green Castle class locomotive No.7032 'Denbigh Castle', with instructions dated "8/59", in excellent condition with excellent condition plain red box.
1959

£200-300   VEC

A Hornby Dublo Suburban Electric train set, comprising SR Electric Motor Coach RN 265326, SR Electric unpowered Driving Trailer RN S77511, both in BR SR green livery, with track, in very good condition with box and instructions.

£280-320   W&W

TOYS AND GAMES

QUICK REFERENCE - BASSETT-LOWKE

Founded in Northampton in 1901, Bassett-Lowke was primarily a sales organisation that marketed and distributed model trains, ships and other toys made by other manufacturers. These included Wintringham of Northampton, and German companies Gebrüder Bing (from 1902), Carette, and Trix (from 1935). However, it also produced its own models, the first locomotive being made in 1903. As can be expected from such notable German makers quality was high. Many trains were designed by the company's designer Henry Greenly. It began to decline in the 1950s as children moved away from mechanical trains, and less expensive models were produced by competitors. In 1964, it sold its shops and closed a year later. The brand was acquired by a number of different people, and is owned today by Hornby, which produces new ranges under this historic name.

A Bing for Bassett-Lowke gauge I locomotive and tender 'SINGLE', GNR green No. 266, three-rail Electric, finished in green and black, with running number '266', with a modern mechanism with a Skate Pick-up, tender with 'GNR' lettering and 'Bassett-Lowke' transfer to back, in very good condition.

£800-1,200   VEC

A Bing for Bassett-Lowke gauge 1 4-4-0 clockwork locomotive and tender, LNWR black 'PRECURSOR' No. 513, finished in black, lined in red and white with 'Precursor' over front splasher and running number '513', in good condition.

£800-1,200   VEC

A Basset-Lowke Gauge 1 4-4-0 live steam locomotive and tender, Midland maroon 'COMPOUND' No. 1000, with 'LOWKE' transfer to tender, and running number '1000' sides, in fair condition.

Despite its poor condition, this is a mechanically and structurally sound model train. Some restoration will improve its visual appeal and increase its value.

£800-1,200   VEC

A Carette for Basset-Lowke gauge 1 4-4-2 three rail electric locomotive and tender, 'ATLANTIC' GNR green No. 1442, finished in green and black, lined in yellow and orange, with running number '1442', and tender with 'GNR' lettering, in good condition.

£800-1,200   VEC

A modern Hornby for Basset-Lowke Princess class 4-6-2 three-rail electric locomotive and tender, 'Princess Victoria' No.46205, in British Railways black, numbered 85 from a limited production range, in mint condition, with guarantee slip, instructions and Basset-Lowke cloth, with box in excellent condition and with outer mailer.

£550-750   VEC

A Carette for Bassett-Lowke Gauge 1 LNWR 12-wheel Dining Saloon No. 13210, the sides in good condition, roof in fair condition.

£250-350   VEC

A Tri-ang R56 4-6-4 maroon Baltic Tank locomotive No. 4830, with Tri-ang Railway decals, fitted with closed couplings but missing rear lamp, in excellent condition, in good condition box.

£80-120   VEC

A unique Australian Tri-ang R52 0-6-0 maroon plastic Jinty Tank locomotive, with head-lamp and no buffers, in excellent condition.

£250-350   VEC

A Tri-ang R155 Bo-Bo yellow Diesel switcher No. 5007, the early style body moulding with 'Tri-ang Railways' to sides and maroon stripe to running board, with open couplings, in excellent condition, in good condition box.

£60-90   VEC

A Tri-ang R155 Bo-Bo green Diesel switcher No. 5007, with Tri-ang Railways to sides, open couplings, fading to numbers and Tri-ang Railways transfer, in good condition with some rusting, in good condition box with lower insert.

£60-90   VEC

A rare Tri-ang TT unboxed gold-plated 4-6-2 Streamlined Merchant Navy Class Loco 'Clan Line' and three Mk. 1 Coaches, slide bar detached from connecting rod to loco left side, tender right side has glue repair to rear, in good condition, the coaches in excellent condition, but Brake Coach has rear coupling missing.

This very rare set is one of only 500 made in the mid-1960s for the Kays Mail Order Catalogue Co.

£400-600   VEC

A rare Australian Tri-ang R450A plastic New South Wales (NSWR) Suburban Overhead Electric Motor Car, in dark brown, rusting and slight damage to pantograph, in production box.

£250-350   VEC

A Tri-ang Hornby R644A Inter City passenger train set, comprising Bo-Bo BR blue class AL1 overhead electric loco No.E3001 single pantograph, two blue/grey Mk.2 second class coaches with lights and one blue/grey Mk.2 brake/first class, with instruction booklet dated "15/9/69" and instruction flyer for overhead power supply system, in excellent condition with good condition complete box with fair condition lid.

Models marked with the Tri-ang Hornby brand date from after 1964, as Tri-ang acquired the troubled Meccano Group, which owned Hornby, in that year.
1969

£80-120   VEC

A Marklin Gauge 1 clockwork tinplate 4-4-0 locomotive and tender 'Precursor' LNWR black No. 513, finished in black red and white with 'Precursor' to front splasher and running number '513' to cab side, with a modern 3-rail four coupled mechanism fitted, the tender with the Marklin stamp under the tender, both couplings refixed, in excellent condition.

£800-1,200   **VEC**

A Wrenn W2213 4-6-2 NE Wartime black A4 Class locomotive No. 4903 'Peregrine', with larger driving wheels fitted to Mk 1 chassis, in near mint condition, in mint condition box with base stamped '91 729'.

£800-1,200   **VEC**

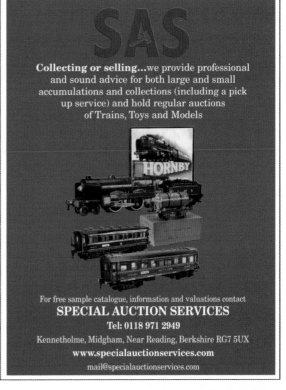

TOYS & GAMES

QUICK REFERENCE

- Lead figures became the favourite toys of young boys in the late 18thC and early 19thC, and are now collected by grown-ups for their nostalgic value.
- Made as early as the 18th century, the first mass-produced lead figures were flat. As their popularity increased, solid figures ('rounde-bosse') were introduced. However, lead figures did not become ubiquitous until 1893, when William Britain Jr., founder of Britains (established in 1845), introduced the 'hollow-casting' method, which released the molten lead from the centre of a figure: halving the cost of a box of soldiers. This began the 'golden age' of the lead soldier, which ran until to the late 1950s, when lead was replaced by cheaper, safer plastics.
- William Britain became the largest maker of lead soldiers in the world, producing more than 100 different British Army regiments sets, and setting the standard size (2in/5.5cm) for toy soldiers. Other well-known and

collectable makers include Charbens, C.B.G. Mignot, Taylor & Barrett, and John Hill Co.
- Though soldiers were the most popular form of figure, domestic and pastoral scenes, such as farms and zoos, were also produced. These were most popular after World War I, when interest in military subjects waned after the horrors of the war.
- Look for fine detailing and original paint. Completely opaque, overly bright paint or unusual colour tones may indicate a repainted figure. These should be avoided, as should figures that have had parts replaced, re-attached or customised. If you are buying a set, ensure that it is complete, and that the figures match: paintwork can vary subtly from batch to batch. Original boxes will typically add value, particularly if they are in excellent condition, as these were often thrown away or damaged, and examples are therefore scarce.

A Britains Regiments Of All Nations series Indian Army Services Corps set no. 1893, comprising officer, mule, handler and four soldiers with rifles at the trail, in mint condition, tied into box.

£100-150   W&W

A rare Britains Regiments of All Nations Australian Army Infantry set no. 2030, comprising officer and seven soldiers, all unusually in black ceremonial dress.

£150-200   W&W

A rare Britains Zoological series set no. 4Z, including rhinoceros, hippopotamus, elephant, giraffe, crocodile, camel, lion, tiger llama, penguins, three palm trees, all in good condition, in original box with good reproduction inserts, orange box with applied label, some wear.

£700-1,000   WW

A Britains Regiments Of All Nations Danish Army soldiers set no. 2018, comprising eight mounted Gardehusarregimete, a trumpeter and six Hussars and officer, in very good condition, in original box with insert, pieces not tied in, minor wear to lid.

£150-250   WW

A rare mid-1950s Britains Mammoth circus set no. 1539, comprising circus ring, ring master, four horses, lion tamer and two lions, boxing clown and kangaroo, four elephants, three additional clowns, one with long stilted legs, equestrienne and clown with hoop, both with horses, red painted wooden ring with central raised dias, two small black painted, leaf shaped metal bases, in very good condition, orange paper covered box with applied label, contents tied in.

£800-1,200   WW

An early 1950s Britains Rodeo set no. 2043, including stockade bars, posts and feet, three mounted cowboys (two with lassoos), a cowboy with lasso, a cowboy with rifle, four sitting cowboys, one additional horse, one steer and one bench, in very good condition, in original box with applied paper label andinstruction sheet to inside of lid, tied into original insert, some age wear to box.

£380-480   WW

A Britains set 178 Austro Hungarian Foot Guards, comprising eight figures, in overall good condition.

£400-600   SAS

A Britains set 225 The Kings African Rifles, with matt black face paint, in fair condition.

£15-25   SAS

A Britains Spanish Cavalry Review Order, comprising four mounted soldiers, in fair condition, two swords missing.

£150-250   SAS

A Johillco Union Confederates Set no.359, in good condition, figures lack two swords and one head, incomplete, in fair condition box with end-label.

£80-120   SAS

TOYS & GAMES

A Schoenhut reduced size jointed wood buffalo, painted in deep brown, with leather horns and rope tail.

Introduced in 1906, around six versions are known. The earliest versions had fabric manes.

6in (15cm) long

£120-180   BER

A Schoenhut Bactrian hand-painted, jointed wood camel, two hump moulded and textured head and body, rope tail, painted eyes.

Introduced in 1908, this is the later version with a moulded, rather than carved, body and head.

£120-180   BER

A Schoenhut reduced size hippo jointed wood figure, with painted eyes, leather ears, red painted mouth and white teeth, brown painted overall.

The reduced size hippo did not have tusks.

6.5in (16.5cm) long

£150-250   BER

A Schoenhut jointed wood elephant, with glass eyes, leather ears, tusks, original trunk, brightly coloured woven original blanket and headdress.

Of the three versions of this popular and long-lived figure, those with howdah blankets are the most sought after.

1903-1930s   9.75in (25cm) long

£250-350   BER

QUICK REFERENCE – SCHOENHUT FIGURES

German immigrant Albert Schoenhut founded his toy company in Philadelphia, Pennsylvania in 1872. His clown toy, introduced in 1903, became a bestseller in its day and was soon followed by the 'Humpty Dumpty' circus. Over the next few years, the range was expanded to include all manner of animals and characters and it became immensely successful. There are many variations in terms of size, shape and materials used – values vary accordingly. A smaller-sized range was introduced in the 1920s, with a very rare miniature series being sold in 1929 only. Unusually, this kangaroo was produced in one size only. Another notable variation is the type of eye. Glass eyes were used until c1918, when Schoenhut lost its supply of German-produced glass eyes due to WWI. Eyes were then painted, and many animals were also redesigned at this point. During the 1930s, handpainting proved to be too expensive and variable in terms of quality, so transfer printed (decal) eyes with black borders were used instead. Today these unique and often amusing toys are popular with folk art and toy collectors.

A Schoenhut white horse with circus platform jointed wood figure, with glass eyes, bride and platform saddle.

Introduced 1905   10.25in (26cm) long

£150-250   BER

A Schoenhut kangaroo jointed wood figure, with painted eyes, wooden tail, leather ears, open carved mouth.

Introduced 1907   7.25in (18.5cm) highest

£450-550   BER

A 1920s Schoenhut reduced size lion jointed wood figure, with carved mane and rope tail.

There are over seven different types of lion. The first was produced for the circus range in 1906 and has a fabric mane. This all-wood, smaller size was sold separately in a box during the 1920s and came with either an open or closed mouth.

5.5in (14cm) long

£100-150   BER

A Schoenhut jointed wood monkey figure, with white face, two-part head, red felt outfit with yellow fringe, rope tail.

Produced from 1906-1930s, this two tone faced monkey is the earliest version. Values are reduced by over a third if the clothing is missing or damaged.

8in (20.5cm) high

£300-400   BER

A Schoenhut reduced size painted eye ostrich wood jointed figure, with closed mouth.

9.5in (24cm) long

£250-350   BER

A Schoenhut reindeer jointed wood figure in greenish-tan with white undercoat and white spots, with glass eyes, closed mouth, with leather ears, antler and tail.

This was part of the Teddy Roosvelt series – few were sold and examples are scarce today.

Introduced 1909   7in (18cm) long

£300-400   BER

A rare Schoenhut wolf wooden jointed figure, with painted eyes, brown hues, long wood tail, open mouth.

Introduced in 1908 as a farm animal as well as a circus animal, early versions of this scarce figure have fabric tails and felt tongues.

8.5in (21.5cm) long

£400-500   BER

A Schoenhut hand-painted, wooden jointed African Chief (Dude) figure, with two part face, leather ears, purple jacket, checked trousers, yellow waistcoat and tall white top hat.

The leather ears indicate that this figure was made after the Teddy Roosevelt safari sets had been discontinued. When a number of African Chief heads were discovered, leather ears were added to turn them into a different 'African Dude' character. The Arab Chief is the rarest character from the set.

c1915

£600-800   BER

QUICK REFERENCE – THE MAN FROM U.N.C.L.E.

The Man From U.N.C.L.E. was a popular American spy series comprising 105 episodes in four series originally broadcast on NBC from September 1964 to January 1968. Ian Fleming contributed to the series, which originally featured a girl teamed with Napoleon Solo: Russian agent Illya Kuryakin replaced her after a popular walk-on role in the pilot. The United Network Command for Law and Enforcement agents battled agents from Technological Hierarchy for the Removal of Undesirables and the Subjugation of Humanity (T.H.R.U.S.H.) and captured the minds of a generation. Nostalgia drives most collectors, who were young at the time the series was aired. Memorabilia is harder to find than than for most other cult TV series, particularly in good and complete condition like this action doll.

An A.C. Gilbert The Man From U.N.C.L.E. 'Napoleon Solo' doll, no.16120, with raising arm, pistol with clip, agent card, folding badge and instructions, in very good condition, in very good condition original box.
c1965   12.5in (31.5cm) high
£200-300   **SAS**

An A.C. Gilbert The Man from U.N.C.L.E. 'Illya Kuryakin' doll, no.16125, with raising arm, pistol with clip, agent card, folding badge and instructions, in excellent condition, in very good condition box.
c1965   12.5in (31.5cm) high
£180-220   **SAS**

A rare 'Made in Hong Kong' The Man From U.N.C.L.E. HC1/1718 'Illya Kuryakin' doll, in very good condition, in fair condition original box.

£280-320   **SAS**

An A.C. Gilbert The Man from U.N.C.L.E. 'Spy Magic Secret Agent Tricks' set, no.15330, comprising Mystery Gun, Magic Money Converter, Jewel Trick, X-Ray Scope, Lie Detector, Spy Tag, Double Agent Card Trick and Vanishing Key, in very good condition, in good condition box.

c1965
£150-250   **SAS**

A The Man From Uncle 'The Getaway' jigsaw puzzle, complete with box in fair condition.
c1967
£12-18   **SAS**

A Lone Star 'The Girl From U.N.C.L.E. Spy Kit', no.1337, complete and in original box in excellent condition.

The Girl from U.N.C.L.E. was a spin-off TV series that aired on NBC for one season from September 1966 to April 1967. Although the 'girl' was first played by Mary Ann Mobley in 'The Moonglow Affair' episode of The Man from U.N.C.L.E. in February 1966, Stefanie Powers played 'April Dancer' in the spin-off series. Merchandise is unsurprisingly scarce, particularly in good condition, although it tends to be less popular than that produced for the main series.

£300-500   **SAS**

A 1960s base metal ring, with 'winking' image of Illya Kuryakin and Napoleon Solo.

0.75in (2cm) high
£9-12   **GCHI**

A Denys Fisher 'Muhammad Ali' action figure, with punching action, complete, mint and boxed.

The yellow and white attachment fits around his waist and gives him the punch action. The clips that hold it on his body were frequently broken – if this piece is broken or missing, the value plummets to under 50% of a complete example.

1976   Box 12in (30.5cm) high

£120-180   **MTB**

A Marx black battery-operated black plastic Dalek, with flashing light, in excellent condition, in good condition original box.

This first toy Dalek, with its 'bump 'n go' movement is complete and in excellent condition. Look out for the examples made in the UK as they are more desirable than the majority of toys that were made in Hong Kong. The Daleks were created by famed Dr Who writer Terry Nation, designed by BBC designer Raymond Cusick, and first shown on screen in December 1963 in the second Dr Who serial.

c1964

£100-150   **SAS**

A very rare Pedigree "Candy" soft vinyl doll, with original clothes.

This example lacks a couple of the fingers, but a truly mint condition example could fetch over £100.

c1967   6.5in (16.5cm) high

£60-80   **MTB**

A PPC Mork & Mindy 'Mork' poseable action figure, with original space suit and silver plastic boots.

c1979   9.5in (24.5cm) high

£15-20   **NOR**

A CLOSER LOOK AT STAR TREK FIGURE

A Thermos 'Knight Rider' metal lunchbox, with K.I.T.T., Michael Knight, Devon Miles and Bonnie Barstow artwork, lacks Thermos flask, but in excellent condition.

c1983   8.5in (21.5cm) wide

£10-15   **BH**

This second series of Star Trek action figures was released to coincide with the first movie in 1979 and was an attempt to cash in on the success of the Star Wars figures released in 1977.

They were produced by Mego Corp. and distributed in the UK by Pedigree – sales were not as high as expected, perhaps due to the film being slow and disappointing compared to Star Wars.

They are in mint, unopened condition which helps their value – but the discovery of a cache of mint and carded Star Trek figures in a Canadian warehouse in the late 1980s held values down.

The Kirk figure was produced for sale in Germany and bears Mego affialites Lion Rock and Airfix branding.

The Decker character only appeared in the film.

Three American Mego Corp. Star Trek action figures, comprising Captain Kirk, Spock and Willard Decker, in unopened, carded condition.

c1979   Card 9in (23cm) high

£80-120   **W&W**

WATCHES

QUICK REFERENCE

- The wristwatch is a 20thC phenomenon, although examples were produced for the German navy in the late 19thC, and in 1904 Brazilian aviator Alberto Santos-Dumont ordered a wristwatch from Cartier. They became popular with the general public after WWI.
- In the last five years, vintage wristwatches have become popular as a smarter look returns to fashion. Men's magazines have promoted this look, and vintage wristwatches are now widely sought after by those wishing to own an unusual yet elegant watch. Rolex and Longines watches from the mid-20thC are sometimes more affordable than modern examples.
- Value depends on the maker, complexity of movement, style, and materials used. High-end, high quality brands such as Patek Philippe and Rolex are sought-after, with iconic models,

such as Rolex's Submariner, being the most desirable. The more complex a watch is the more valuable it is likely to be. Chronographs and watches with extra features, such as moon phases, alarms or perpetual calendars are highly desirable.
- The style of a watch can help date it. Small round faces (almost like pocket watches) date from the early 20thC, with rectangular watches taking over in the 1930s. Watch cases became more stylised and innovative from the late 1940s, as well as taking on period jewellery styles. Simple, circular faces and rectangular watches were again popular during the 1950s, though this had changed by the late 1960s and 70s when many watches were made with large sculptural cases in futuristic styles. The simple, classic styles of the 1930s and 1950s are particularly popular today.

An Audemars Piguet 'Royal Oak' gentleman's brushed grey stainless steel and gilt wristwatch, no.056D34567, with a 33 jewel automatic movement adjusted to heat/cold and five positions, and original bracelet, dial and movement signed.

c1990

£2,500-3,000   DN

A 1950s Swiss Audemars Piguet gentleman's wristwatch, with 18ct solid gold case with two tone white and yellow gold bezel, ultra-thin 17 jewel movement with four adjustments, and signed on the dial, case and movement.

£1,500-2,000   ML

A 1950s-60s Ernest Borel gentleman's 'Cocktail' watch, with display skeleton back, and 17 jewel movement.

The dial on this sought-after watch is made up of moving discs with arrowheads to indicate the time. As the discs revolve, the printed 'starburst' pattern changes, creating an interesting optical effect.

£150-200   ML

A 1920s-30s Bulova doctor's watch, with gold-filled rectangular case, three dials, and 12-jewel movement.

This watch, used for timing in medical examinations, is rare with three dials.

£500-800   ML

A 1940s LeCoultre gentleman's wristwatch, triple signed on the case, dial and movement, with stainless steel case, two tone military-style 24 hour dial with luminous hands and numbers, and LeCoultre 17-jewel movement.

£250-300   ML

A Longines 'Flagship' automatic gentleman's wristwatch, with 18ct gold case, silvered dial, and date aperture.

c1970   1.5in (3.5cm) diam

£300-500   **GHOU**

An Omega Seamaster De Ville gold-plated gentleman's wristwatch, with matching bracelet, with baton numerals and date.

£150-200   **SAS**

A CLOSER LOOK AT A WRISTWATCH

Designed in the late 1960s by André Le Marquand as a tribute to man landing on the moon, the watch was inspired by the astronauts' space helmets and visors.

It was released at the Basel Watch fair in 1972 and was followed by the rectangular and more valuable Spaceman 'Audacieuse' a few years later.

It was produced until 1977 in a range of colours, with the brighter ones being more popular. It was also produced under a variety of brands, including Fortis and Jules Jürgensen.

If the strap has been replaced with a different type, the value falls by over a third. Correct replacement straps can be found for around £20-30.

A 1970s Tressa Lux 'Spaceman' automatic wristwatch, designed by André Le Marquand, with shiny stainless steel case, copper and black face, and Corfam strap.

£80-120   **RSS**

An Omega 'Constellation' Chronometer automatic gold plated and steel gentlemen's wristwatch, the brown dial with baton markers, with a calibrated 751 jewel movement.

1.5in (3.5cm) diam

£200-300   **GHOU**

A 1930s Rolex Art Deco wristwatch, the square dial with Roman numerals and silver square case, marked 'Rolex' to movement.

£150-200   **SAS**

An Edwardian Goldsmiths and Silversmiths ladies silver wristwatch, with white enamel face with Roman numerals, and plain silver case with Birmingham hallmarks.

1905

£40-60   **SAS**

QUICK REFERENCE - SWATCH

The first Swatches were released in 1983, and were plain by comparison to the colourful, design or designer led, models the brand is known for today. With only 51 components, and plastic cases and straps, the watches could be easily mass-produced. By 1984, over one million had been made. A number of designers have produced designs for the company including Keith Haring, Vivienne Westwood and Christian Lacroix, and these are among the most valuable today. Also look out for the famed 'Jellyfish' transparent watches, commemorative Olympic watches, and limited editions. To be of interest to a collector, the watch must be in excellent condition with its original strap. Being in mint condition, with its box and paperwork makes a watch even more desirable. Although Swatch collecting has declined since the glory days of the 1990s, there is still a healthy trade over the internet, with most fetching under £200. The watch below was the first special edition produced. It is a US Special, and commemorates the First Breakdance World Championship held at the Roxy in New York City. Designed by the artists Marlyse Schmid and Bernard Muller, variations of the hands, dial and colour of the case are known and are worth roughly the same.

A Swatch 'Stormy Weather' wristwatch, GV 100, from the Dream Waves series, with multi-coloured strap.

Look for rare variation without the Swatch logo at '12 o'clock', which is worth about twice the normal version.
1989
£30-40   ML

A Swatch 'Needles' wristwatch, GB 408, from the Signal Corps series, with original perforated red strap.
1988
£30-50   ML

A Swatch 'World Record' wristwatch, GB 721, from the Sprint series, with original ribbed yellow and green straps.

1990
£30-40   ML

A limited edition Swatch 'Breakdance' wristwatch, GO 0001, from an edition of 9,999.
£500-600   ML

A Swatch 'Cappuccino' wristwatch, GG 121, from the Sunday Brunch series, designed by Jennifer Morla.
1992
£30-40   ML

A Swatch 'Silver Patch' wristwatch, GN 132, from the Nespolo series, with original multicoloured strap.
1993
£30-40   ML

A Hamilton gold-filled pocket watch, the dial and movement signed "Motor Barrel 952", with 19-jewel movement, adjusted to five positions.

2in (5cm) diam

£250-350   **GHOU**

A Tiffany & Co 18ct gold hunter pocket watch, the engraved scroll body with sprung cover, white enamel face with painted centre, Roman numerals and subsidiary seconds dial, the case marked 'Tiffany & Co New York No. 38676', cover marked 'T&Co 0.750'.

£450-650   **SAS**

A CLOSER LOOK AT A POCKET WATCH

The psychedelic design and 'Flower Power' wording are typical of the late 1960s when this watch was designed and made.

Loftus designed a range of watches for The Beatles' 'Apple' boutique store which opened on London's King's Road in 1967 and closed 8 months later due to financial problems. It is possible that this watch was designed for sale there.

The 'Old England' brand was used by Accurist, which made this watch. Its designer, Richard Loftus, was one of three sons of Accurist founders Asher and Rebecca Loftus.

Accurist watches were highly successful, and were worn and endorsed by celebrities including The Beatles, Twiggy and The Princess Royal.

An Old England 'Flower Power' medallion watch, probably designed for the Beatles' Apple store, by Richard Loftus, the square pendant on a gilt metal chain.

Chain 27.5in (70cm) long

£150-200   **DN**

A Waltham 10ct gold pocket watch, with Roman numerals, the engraved case marked '10ct'.

£60-90   **SAS**

A 1920s-30s Continental silver pocket watch, the gold circular face with Arabic numerals, and second subsidiary seconds dial, European control marks to interior.

£20-30   **SAS**

An unmarked silver pocket watch, with white enamel dial, Roman numerals and seconds subsidiary dial, engraved monogram to reverse.

£30-40   **SAS**

The following list is organized by the type of collectible. If you would like your club, society or organization to appear in our next edition, or would like to update details, please contact us at email info@millers.uk.com.

ADVERTISING

Antique Advertising Signs
The Street Jewellery Society, 11 Bowsden Ter, South Gosford, Newcastle-Upon-Tyne NE3 1RX

AUTOGRAPHS

A.C.O.G.B. (Autograph Club of Great Britain)
info@autographcouncil.co.uk
www.acogb.co.uk

AUTOMOBILIA

Brooklands Automobilia & Regalia Collectors' Club,
P.O. Box No 4,
Chapel Terrace Mews,
Kemp Town, Brighton,
East Sussex BN2 1HU
Tel: 01273 622 722
www.barcc.co.uk

BAXTER PRINTS

The New Baxter Society
c/o Reading Museum & Art Gallery, Blagrave Street, Reading, Berkshire RG1 1QH
www.rpsfamily.demon.co.uk

BANK NOTES

International Bank Note Society
43 Templars Crescent,
London N3 3QR
www.theibns.org

BOOKS

The Enid Blyton Society
93 Milford Hill, Salisbury,
Wiltshire SP1 2QL
Tel: 01722 331937
www.enidblytonsociety.co.uk

The Followers of Rupert
www.rupertthebear.org.uk

BOTTLES

Old Bottle Club of Great Britain
2 Strafford Avenue,
Elsecar, Nr Barnsley,
South Yorkshire S74 18AA
Tel: 01226 745 156
www.onlinebbr.com/home/

BREWERIANA

The British Beermats Collectors' Society
69 Dunnington Avenue,
Kidderminster DY10 2YT
www.britishbeermats.org.uk

CERAMICS

Beswick Collectors Club,
PO Box 310, Richmond,
Surrey TW10 7FU
www.collectingdoulton.com

Carlton Ware Collectors' International
The Carlton Factory Shop,
Copeland St, Stoke-upon-Trent,
Staffordshire ST4 1PU
Tel: 01782 410 504
www.lattimore.co.uk/deco/
carlton.htm

Clarice Cliff Collectors Club
PO Box 2706,Eccleshall,
Stafford ST21 6WY
www.claricecliff.com

Fieldings Crown Devon Collectors Club
P.O. Box 462, Manvers,
Rotherham S63 7WT
Tel: 01709 874 433
www.fieldingscrowndevclub
.com

Friends of Blue Ceramics Society
PO Box 122, Didcot D.O.,
Oxford OX11 0YN
www.fob.org.uk

Goss Collectors' Club
Tel: 01159 300 441
www.gosschina.com

Hornsea Pottery Collectors' & Research Society
128 Devonshire St, Keighley,
West Yorkshire BD21 2QJ
www.easyontheeye.net/hornsea
/society.htm

M.I. Hummel Club (Goebel)
Porzellanfabrik, GmbH & Co.
KG, Coburger Str.7, D-96472
Rodental, Germany
Tel: +49 (0) 95 63 72 18 03
www.mihummel.com

Keith Murray Collectors' Club
Fantasque House, Tennis Drive,
The Park, Nottingham NG7 1AE

Lorna Bailey Collectors' Club
The Old Post Office, 12
Wedwood, Burslem,
Stoke-on-Trent ST6 4JH
Tel: 01782 837 341
www.lorna-bailey.co.uk

Mabel Lucie Attwell
Abbey Antiques,
63 Great Whyte, Ramsey,
Huntingdon PE26 1HL
Tel: 01487 814753
www.mabellucieattwellclub.com

Moorcroft Collectors' Club
Sandbach Rd, Burslem,
Stoke-on-Trent, ST6 2DQ
Tel: 01782 820500
www.moorcroft.com

Myott Collectors Club
P.O. Box 110,Sutton SM3 9YQ
www.myottcollectorsclub.com

Pendelfin Family Circle
Cameron Mill,
Howsin St, Burnley,
Lancashire BB10 1PP
Tel: 01282 432 301
www.pendelfin.co.uk

Poole Pottery Collectors' Club
The Quay, Poole,
Dorset BH15 1RF
Tel: 01202 666200
www.poolepottery.collectorsclu
b.co.uk

Potteries of Rye Collectors' Society
22 Redyear Cottages,
Kennington Rd, Ashford,
Kent TN24 0TF
www.potteries-of-rye-socie-
ty.co.uk

Royal Doulton International Collectors' Club
Minton House, London Road,
Stoke-on-Trent, ST4 7QD
Tel: 01782 292292
www.royaldoulton.com/
collectables

Royal Winton International Collectors' Club
Dancers End, Northall,
Bedfordshire LU6 2EU
Tel: 01525 220 272

The Shelley Group
7 Raglan Close, Frimley,
Surrey GU16 8YL
Tel: 01483 764097
www.shelley.co.uk

Susie Cooper Collectors' Group
Panorama House,
18 Oaklea Mews,
Aycliffe Village,
County Durham DL5 6JP
www.susiecooper.net

The Sylvac Collectors' Circle
174 Portsmouth Rd, Horndean,
Waterlooville, Hampshire
www.sylvacclub.com

Novelty Teapot Collectors' Club
Tel: 01257 450 366
vince@totallyteapots.com

Official International Wade Collectors' Club
Royal Works, Westport Rd,
Stoke-on-Trent, Staffs ST6 4AP
Tel: 01782 255255
www.wade.co.uk

Wade Collectors Club
PO Box 3012
Stoke-on-Trent ST3 9DD
Tel: 0845 246 2525
www.wadecollectorsclub.co.uk

Royal Worcester Collectors' Society
Severn Street,
Worcester, WR1 2NE
Tel: 01905 746 000
www.royal-worcester.co.uk

CIGARETTE CARDS

Cartopulic Society of GB
7 Alderham Avenue, Radlett,
Herts WD7 8HL

COINS, BANKNOTES & PAPER MONEY

British Numismatic Society
c/o The Warburg Institute,
Woburn Square,
London WC1H 0AB
www.fitzmuseum.cam.ac.uk/coi
ns/britnumsoc/

Royal Numismatic Society
c/o The British Museum,
Great Russell Street,
London WC1B 3DG
Tel: 020 7636 1555
www.numismatics.org.uk

International Bank Note Society
www.theibns.or

International Bond and Share Society
www.scripophily.org

COMMEMORATIVE WARE

Commemorative Collectors Society & Commemoratives Museum
Lumless House, 77 Gainsborough Road, Winthorpe, Newark, Nottinghamshire NG24 2NR
http://commemoratives collecting.co.uk

COMICS

Association of Comic Enthusiasts
L'Hopiteau, St Martin du Fouilloux 79420, France
Tel: 00 33 549 702 114

Comic Enthusiasts Society
80 Silverdale, Sydenham, London SE26 4SJ

The Beano & Dandy Collectors' Club,
PO Box 3433, Brighton BN50 9JA
www.phil-comics.com/ collectors_club.html

COSTUME & ACCESSORIES

The British Compact Collectors' Society
P.O. BOX 64, Langford, Biggleswade SG18 9BF
www.compactcollectors.co.uk

The Costume Society
28 Eburne Road, London N7 6AU
www.costumesociety.org.uk

Hat Pin Society of GB
PO Box 089, Maidstone, ME14 9BA
www.hatpinsociety.org.uk

DISNEYANA

Walt Disney Collectors' Society
c/o Enesco, Brunthill Road, Kingstown Industrial Estate, Carlisle CA3 0EN
Tel: 01228 404 062
www.wdccduckman.com

DOLLS

Barbie Collectors' Club of GB
117 Rosemount Avenue, Acton, London W3 9LU
wdl@nipcus.co.uk'

British Doll Collectors Club
'The Anchorage', Wrotham Rd, Culverstone Green, Meopham, Kent DA13 0QW

Doll Club of Great Britain
PO Box 154, Cobham, Surrey KT11 2YE

The Fashion Doll Collectors' Club of GB
PO Box 133, Lowestoft, Suffolk NR32 1WA
Tel: 07940 248127
voden@supanet.com

EPHEMERA

The Ephemera Society
PO Box 112, Northwood, Middlesex HA6 2WT
Tel: 01923 829079
www.ephemera-society.org.uk

FILM & TV

James Bond 007 Fan Club
PO Box 007, Surrey KT15 1DY
Tel: 01483 756007

Fanderson – The Official Gerry Anderson Appreciation Society
www.fanderson.org.uk

GLASS

The Carnival Glass Society
P.O. Box 14, Hayes, Middlesex UB3 5NU
www.carnivalglasssociety.co.uk

The Glass Association
150 Braemar Road, Sutton Coldfield B73 6LZ
www.glassassociation.org.uk

Isle of Wight Studio Glass Collectors' Club
Old Park, St Lawrence, Isle of Wight, PO38 1XR
www.isleofwightstudioglass .co.uk

Jonathan Harris Studio Glass Collectors Club
Woodland House, 24 Peregrine Way, Apley Castle, Telford TF1 6TH
www.jhstudioglass.com
Pressed Glass Collectors' Club
4 Bowshot Close, Castle Bromwich B36 9UH
Tel: 0121 681 4872
www.webspawner.com/users/ pressedglass

KITCHENALIA

National Horse Brass Society
2 Blue Barn Cottage, Blue Barn Lane, Weybridge, Surrey KT13 0NH
Tel: 01932 354 193

The Old Hall Stainless Steel Tableware Collectors Club,
Sandford House, Levedale, Stafford ST18 9AH
www.oldhallclub.co.uk

The British Novelty Salt & Pepper Collectors Club
Coleshill, Clayton Road, Mold, Flintshire CH7 15X

MARBLES

Marble Collectors Unlimited
P.O. Box 206 Northborough, MA 01532-0206 USA
marblesbev@aol.com

MECHANICAL MUSIC

Musical Box Society of Great Britain
www.onbsgb.org.uk

The City of London Phonograph & Gramophone Society
www.clpgs.org.uk

METALWARE

Antique Metalware Society
PO Box 63, Honiton, Devon EX14 1HP
amsmemsec@yahoo.co.uk

MILITARIA

Military – Crown Imperial
37 Wolsey Close, Southall, Middlesex UB2 4NQ

Military Historical Society
National Army Museum, Royal Hospital Rd, London SW3 4HT
Orders & Medals Research Society
123 Turnpike Link, Croydon CR0 5NU

PAPERWEIGHTS

Paperweight Collectors Circle
P.O. Box 941, Comberton, Cambridgeshire CB3 7GQ
Tel: 02476 386 172

Caithness Glass Paperweight Collectors' Society
Caithness Glass Perth PH1 3TZ Scotland
www.caithnessglass.co.uk/ collectors

PENS & WRITING

The Writing Equipment Society
www.wesonline.org.uk

PERFUME BOTTLES

International Perfume Bottle Association
www.ipba-uk.co.uk

PLASTICS

Plastics Historical Society
31a Maylands Drive, Sidcup, Kent DA14 4SB
www.plastiquarian.com

POSTCARDS

Postcard Club of Great Britain
Drene Brennan, 34 Harper House, St.James Crescent, London SW9 7LW
Tel: 0207 771 9404
www.postcards.co.uk

POTLIDS

The Pot Lid Circle
Collins House, 32/38 Station Road, Gerrards Cross, Buckinghamshire SL9 8EL
Tel: 01753 279 001
www.thepotlidcircle.co.uk

QUILTS

The Quilters' Guild of the British Isles
St Anthony's Hall, York YO1 7PW
Tel: 01422 347 669
www.quiltersguild.org.uk

RADIOS

The British Vintage Wireless Society
59 Dunsford Close, Swindon, Wiltshire SN1 4PW
Tel: 01793 541 634
www.bvws.org.uk

RAILWAYANA

Railwayana Collectors Journal
7 Ascot Rd, Moseley, Birmingham B13 9EN

INDEX